Four Decades On

., the United States, and the Legacies of the Second Indochina War

SCOTT LADERMAN AND EDWIN A. MARTINI, EDITORS

Duke University Press *Durham and London* 2013

© 2013 Duke University Press

All rights reserved

Printed in the United States of America on acid-free paper ♾

Typeset in Minion by Tseng Information Systems, Inc.

Library of Congress Cataloging-in-Publication Data

Four decades on : Vietnam, the United States, and the legacies of the
Second Indochina War / Scott Laderman and Edwin A. Martini, eds.

pages cm

Includes bibliographical references and index.

ISBN 978-0-8223-5462-8 (cloth : alk. paper)

ISBN 978-0-8223-5474-1 (pbk. : alk. paper)

1. Vietnam—History—1975- 2. United States—History—1969-
3. Vietnam War, 1961–1975—Influence. 4. Vietnam War, 1961–1975—
Vietnam. 5. Vietnam War, 1961–1975—United States.

I. Laderman, Scott. II. Martini, Edwin A.

DS559.912.F678 2013

959.704′4—dc23

2012048669

FOR OUR PARENTS

CONTENTS

ACKNOWLEDGMENTS

This collection originated with a series of conversations about what seemed to us the surprising lack of scholarship on the United States and Vietnam since 1975. It has been quite some time since those initial discussions, and some impressive work has been published in the interim, but we are confident that this book still represents something significant: a broad, interdisciplinary analysis of a number of the war's most important legacies. We are grateful to its outstanding contributors, whose perseverance was instrumental in completing the volume, and to the anonymous referees for their excellent suggestions. We thank Susan Maher of the College of Liberal Arts at the University of Minnesota, Duluth, for providing funds for the index and the Burnham-Macmillan endowment in the Department of History at Western Michigan University for funds enabling us to reprint, in an updated version, H. Bruce Franklin's essay from *Vietnam and Other American Fantasies* (University of Massachusetts Press, 2000). We thank Binh Danh for so generously allowing us to use his work on the book's cover. And we thank Valerie Millholland, Miriam Angress, Susan Albury, and Amy Buchanan at Duke University Press for their wonderful advice, guidance, and assistance—and their patience. Most of all, we thank our wonderful families, whose love and support continue to fuel us.

National Amnesia,

Transnational Memory,

Scott Laderman and and the Legacies of the

Edwin A. Martini Second Indochina War

What's in a Name?

The Vietnam War. The American War. The Vietnamese-American War. The American War in Viet Nam. The Second Indochina War. All wars have multiple names, but the Second Indochina War seems to have more than most.[1] Embedded in the words and phrases used to describe the long war, fought by multiple entities on multiple fronts from at least 1961 to at least 1975, are assumptions and biases about who was to blame, who did the fighting, and how this war fits into larger historical narratives. As with most names, however, these obscure much more than they reveal.

The Vietnam War—the name of choice in the United States, Australia, New Zealand, and much of the West—indicates how this war fits into the larger thrust of American history, describing the choice of the United States and its allies to fight a war in Viet Nam, as opposed to Laos, Korea, or Iraq. This name carries with it connotations of a global war against communism, a deeply divided home front, and the oft-repeated but rarely answered question, "Why Vietnam?" Conversely, the American War, as many Vietnamese call it, places the war against the United States during the 1950s, 1960s, and 1970s in a longer line of wars fought for Vietnamese independence against China, Japan, and France. It situates the United States as the latest in a long line of aggressors and would-be colonizers that attempted unsuccessfully to impose their will on the Vietnamese people.

Other names, such as the Vietnamese-American War or the American War in Viet Nam, carry similar meanings and similar questions, but what these names all have in common is their reliance on nation-states—the United States and Viet Nam—as the primary reference points for who fought in this war and why. They rely on the binary logic of subject and object, aggressor and victim, victor and vanquished, that serves as the foundation for many historical narratives, particularly America-centric narratives about the Cold War and, more recently, the "War on Terror," in which, according to proponents of these myths, the world can be divided easily into allies and enemies, good and evil. But names that rely on the unified subjects supposedly signified by "America" and "Vietnam" obscure not only the local but the international and transnational nature of this particular war that is critical to understanding its history and its legacies.

"The Second Indochina War," while far from perfect, provides the discursive space for scholars and citizens to write and speak back against history, to fill in the transnational gaps in the narratives that have defined this conflict, and to provide a more complete understanding of a lengthy and complex struggle that will long serve as a defining moment in the histories of many nations and, indeed, the world. This is a war that directly involved, among others, the United States, the Democratic Republic of Viet Nam, the Republic of Viet Nam, Cambodia, Laos, Australia, New Zealand, the Republic of Korea, China, the Soviet Union, Canada, and Thailand and indirectly involved numerous others. This is a war in which national borders were drawn, redrawn, contested, violated, transgressed, ignored, defended, occupied, defoliated, and bombed. The effects of that war have been similarly transnational, most immediately for Viet Nam, Cambodia, and Laos, but also for its millions of veterans around the world and for the diasporic populations from Southeast Asia who have spread out globally since the early 1970s. These transnational subjects— their bodies, their experiences, and their histories—belie any narratives that rely on stable national subjects and stable national borders. If we think about transnationalism as social fields, identities, and relationships constructed across geographic, cultural, and political borders, it becomes clear that transnational narratives and interventions are required to address the history and legacies of the Second Indochina War.[2]

Nations and Narrations

Acts of war, Jill Lepore reminds us, inevitably generate acts of narration, and the Second Indochina War has generated as much narration as any war in history. "Waging, writing, and remembering a war," Lepore writes, "all shape its legacy, all draw boundaries."[3] Year after year more histories, memoirs, novels, films, war stories, ghost stories, and other acts of narration intervene in the field of cultural memory, fighting and refighting the "Vietnam War," the "American War," and the battle over the contested memory and meaning of this long and bloody conflict, however it is labeled, drawing, tracing, reinscribing, and reinforcing geographic and temporal boundaries. For the thousands of scholarly works published on the war, the overwhelming majority have remained locked in frameworks that place the nation-state at the center of analysis and focus on the years of "official conflict" between the United States, its clients in southern Viet Nam, and the revolutionary forces throughout the Vietnamese nation. The result has been the persistence of a framework that has rendered largely invisible the Vietnamese in general and the divisions within Vietnamese society in particular.[4]

Over the past decade or so, these boundaries have become much more fluid and porous. Since the end of the Cold War, scholars from around the world have sought to internationalize the history of the Indochinese conflict.[5] More recently, a new generation of Western scholars has explored the early period of U.S. involvement in Viet Nam, often reclaiming a greater sense of Vietnamese agency in the process.[6] Other studies have decentered not only the United States but the nation-state in general by focusing more on the ways in which the Vietnamese revolution shaped and was shaped by everyday life in southern Viet Nam.[7] A recent special edition of the *Journal of Vietnamese Studies* took this trend even further, focusing on the admittedly ironic topic of the "Vietnamization of Vietnam War Studies."[8]

Only very recently, however, have we seen the emergence of work from either U.S.-centric or Vietnamese-centric perspectives that takes as its focal point the period after 1975. This growing body of literature addresses the political, environmental, and cultural legacies of the war, postwar relations between the United States and the Socialist Republic of Viet Nam, tourism and global economic transformations, and the mythologies the war engendered, particularly in the United States.[9] As these studies have shown, the period after 1975 provides a rich source of topics and developments for study.

When the United States finally left in 1975, two years after the withdrawal of its combat troops, Viet Nam faced the challenge of reconstructing its devastated nation and society while at the same time fighting wars against China and the Khmer Rouge. Washington, having failed to fully achieve its political and military objectives in Southeast Asia, turned to economic and cultural warfare against its Vietnamese foes. At the grassroots in both nations, the suffering persisted. For Vietnamese, the physical legacies of Agent Orange, landmines, and unexploded ordnance did not dissipate with the American withdrawal; rather, these menaces claimed tens of thousands of new victims. American veterans, too, dealt with the physical and psychological hardships the war unleashed, dying from allegedly war-induced diseases and experiencing the sometimes painful challenges of "coming home." Thousands of Vietnamese chose to flee their homeland for new homes in the United States, France, Australia, and elsewhere in the West. Others, too young to guide their own destinies, unwittingly entered the ranks of the adopted. Scholars, writers, and artists in both countries set before themselves the tasks of introspection—or denial—and renewal. Veterans from a variety of nations sought to initiate transnational healing. At the broader level of the economy, the United States remained belligerent, seeking to punish Viet Nam for its stubborn resistance to the American intervention. Viet Nam, having fought for a socialist revolution, succumbed to the forces of international capitalism that, with the collapse of the Soviet Union, rendered the hegemony of "the market" inevitable.

With few exceptions, most of the recent works on the post-1975 period remain limited in part by the state-based frameworks they adopt. We anticipate that the next generation of scholarship on the legacies of the Second Indochina War will come from interdisciplinary scholars employing transnational perspectives. Thus, the essays gathered here, representing scholars working in a variety of fields, from a variety of backgrounds, and at various stages of their careers, seek collectively to transcend and transgress the chronological and national boundaries that have characterized much of the earlier scholarship. While the United States and Viet Nam remain the focal point of this collection, the legacies of the Second Indochina War for those nations and for a variety of actors within and beyond their borders are situated by the scholars here in global and transnational frameworks through a variety of disciplinary and interdisciplinary lenses.

The Essays

When the Second Indochina War abruptly ended in 1975, its Vietnamese victors were left with little time for reflection. They faced a nation to rebuild and reunite, a socialist revolution to consolidate, and renewed threats to regional and national security on their borders. Of immediate significance, the Communist Party was forced to reconcile memories of the short-lived Republic of Viet Nam ("South Vietnam") with post-1975 policies and historical narratives that legitimized the Vietnamese revolution. How the revolutionaries arrived at this particular moment is a story with which most Americans remain unfamiliar. In "Legacies Foretold: Excavating the Roots of Postwar Viet Nam," Ngo Vinh Long provides a historical foundation for our understandings of postwar Vietnamese society, examining the still largely unexplored topic of South Vietnamese politics between 1970 and 1975. His essay seeks to move beyond existing treatments of the challenges facing a reunified Viet Nam, most of which focus on simplistic formulations that pit the demands of a centralized communist state against the challenges of markets, privatization, and democracy. Instead, Long locates many of the challenges facing the Socialist Republic of Viet Nam in the political repression of the Thieu regime before and after the Paris Accords of 1973. By eliminating any possibilities of political pluralism in the south, Long argues, the Thieu regime made postwar reconciliation, political accommodation, social integration, and development that much more difficult. By recovering the role played by the regime in destroying the Provisional Revolutionary Government in particular, Long adds another dimension to recent work by Lien-Hang T. Nguyen and Sophie Quinn-Judge on this long-neglected topic and period.[10]

If the Vietnamese revolutionaries found themselves constructing and reinforcing a narrative of the past that would serve the postwar state, they have hardly been alone in this process of memory management. The memory of the Second Indochina War has taken on crucial national and transnational characteristics, affecting not only individual survivors but also the subsequent actions of the conflict's various belligerents. Demonstrating the importance of this memory to the exercise of postwar American power, Walter L. Hixson's essay "Viet Nam and 'Vietnam' in American History and Memory" centers on the cultural recasting in the United States of the history of the Second Indochina War and its implications for U.S. foreign policy. He argues that through a variety of means—including military revisionism, discourses targeting antiwar protesters and the "liberal media," and Hollywood's veteran-centered Vietnam War films—American culture recast the war in ways that allowed for the nation to "heal" and rebuild popular support for foreign intervention.[11] This process of healing, he demonstrates, marginalized narratives in which "Vietnam" could be viewed as a disastrous intervention illuminating—and thus inspiring a transformation of—the nation's militant national identity.

As Hixson shows, over the last quarter of the twentieth century and the first decade of the twenty-first, the shadow of the Vietnam experience hung over U.S. foreign policy, as well as over attitudes on the home front. This haunting aura of the Indochina war took on a name of its own, the "Vietnam syndrome," describing the cynical, frustrated, and pessimistic sense with which America approached the world. This troubled Americans deeply, as they feared that their vaunted sense of mission had given way to feelings of limitation and hesitancy. The success of every subsequent foreign intervention was hailed not only for its own sake but also as a demonstration that the nation had finally put "Vietnam" behind it. The basis for these feelings can be traced to those first moments that followed the end of the war. Indeed, some of the syndrome's elements began to coalesce even before American troops had come home for good. "Back in another America, people used to dance in the streets when a President declared the end of a war," *Newsweek* asserted in May 1975. Instead, almost immediately, there emerged a random, impressionistic, and frequently heartfelt array of observations about a nation trying to cope with a loss it once could not have envisioned but that now stared it squarely in the face. Those responses contained the first stirrings of what would often seem like the national mood for the next three decades. In "'The Mainspring in This Country Has Been Broken': America's Battered Sense of Self and the Emergence of the Vietnam Syndrome," Alexander Bloom focuses on these developments in the period that immediately followed the end of the war. Scholars have long noted how rapidly Americans went from a Second World War frame of mind into a Cold War mindset. Bloom shows that with equal or even greater rapidity, they went from the era of the Vietnam War to that of the Vietnam syndrome. His essay adds important new dimensions to the recent explosion of work on the cultural, intellectual, and political history of the 1970s, using the legacies of the Vietnam War as a way to connect to the decades that follow.[12]

Even more severely than the United States, Viet Nam emerged from the Second Indochina War a deeply divided society. The many challenges of reconciliation and integration in postwar Viet Nam were not easily overcome. Indeed, as Heonik Kwon shows in "Cold War in a Vietnamese Community," those challenges are still very much on display throughout the country, continuing to divide regions, villages, and, in some cases, families. Leaving aside the more familiar tales of economic reforms and the growing demands of global economic integration, Kwon demonstrates how the memory of the American war remains a powerful force in the everyday life of many Vietnamese. By combining the social history of the American war at the village level with the global, postcolonial history of the Cold War, Kwon highlights the challenges facing individual families and scholars of the war alike. Illuminating what he calls the "creative everyday practices" of Vietnamese families in overcoming the painful legacies of war, Kwon thus also offers a way forward for a more interdisciplinary, international history of the Second Indochina War.

Consistent with Kwon's desire to divert our gaze from states to citizens, including the fractious memories with which they often must contend, Christina Schwenkel, in "The Ambivalence of Reconciliation in Contemporary Vietnamese Memoryscapes," builds on extant studies that address American veterans' return to Viet Nam as postwar tourists seeking reconciliation with their onetime adversaries by exploring the often marginalized and largely absent role of veterans of the Army of the Republic of Viet Nam (that is, the "South Vietnamese Army") in transnational healing projects. Drawing on interviews and informal discussions with former Vietnamese soldiers, her analysis moves from the reconciliation of "former enemies" to irreconciliation among allies and the resulting unexpected solidarities that emerge. Schwenkel shows how two memoryscapes in particular—the Ho Chi Minh City Martyrs' Cemetery in Bien Hoa and the former "demilitarized zone" (DMZ) in central Viet Nam—"transgress the rigid boundaries that are often drawn between communities of memory, meaning, and practice." Her discussion of the DMZ in particular brings to light what she calls intersecting "topographies of memory," richly describing how the former Khe Sanh/Ta Con military base has been transformed into "a space of ritual care for the souls of the war dead, irrespective of side, ideology, or nationality." In light of these findings, she argues that the complex and internal tensions that have emerged under the postwar social and economic conditions of Viet Nam demand more complicated and multilayered understandings of the meanings and practices of healing and reconciliation that take place in the aftermath of war.

Continuing the exploration of postwar legacies beyond the realm of state actors and official discourses, Viet Thanh Nguyen draws on texts from American, South Korean, Japanese, and Vietnamese combatants, veterans, and novelists to show how writers from Asia and North America have drawn on the literary tools of compassion and cosmopolitanism to again fight the war, though this time in memory, with the purpose of illuminating a path to peace. His essay, "Remembering War, Dreaming Peace: On Cosmopolitanism, Compassion, and Literature," sweepingly covers these works to provide a more global focus than is found in most previous American studies of the literature of the Vietnam War. Placing these works in a transnational framework, Nguyen describes how a variety of narratives framed by compassion, cosmopolitanism, and empathy connect the terror of the war in Viet Nam to more contemporary preoccupations with the "war on terror" in the Middle East, North Africa, and Central Asia.

One of the most lasting transnational legacies of the war, of course, is the diaspora of millions of Vietnamese citizens and the complex cultural memory of the war and its legacies this diasporic process created. In "Việt Nam's Growing Pains: Postsocialist Cinema Development and Transnational Politics," Mariam B. Lam explores the contours of transnational Vietnamese cultural production, delineating how a rapidly growing global cultural tourism that requires the interdependence of the new transnational circulation of cultural forms, such as Vietnamese film, with a state's political-economic needs reveals ways in which academic approaches make manifest complex constructions of social and world cultural memory. Socialist realist cinema, cultural history and educational curricula, U.S. film festivals and tours, and anticommunist protest all infect the contemporary study of Vietnamese and diasporic film. Traveling filmmakers and artists, as well as postcolonial critics, she argues, must contend with such problems when invoking alternative forms of social and economic justice within the postwar socialist Vietnamese state and across international waters when the state itself is similarly working toward strengthening its global cultural value and authority within the international community. By exploring the intersection of these local and global forces through the work of filmmakers such as Đặng Nhật Minh, Buĩ Thạc Chuyên, Lu'u Huỹnh, and Mirabelle Ang, Lam also shows how the tools of academic disciplining create the conditions of possibility for the production of Vietnamese cultural studies.

It is not only at the level of culture that Viet Nam has sought to develop a broader international presence. Export-oriented trade has likewise driven the country's developing global profile, though often without the warm embrace its cultural strategies have engendered. In "A Fishy Affair: Vietnamese Seafood and the Confrontation with U.S. Neoliberalism," Scott Laderman examines the developing bilateral trade relationship of the United States and Viet Nam since the last decade of the twentieth century, focusing in particular on how U.S. politicians and trade officials attempted to undermine Vietnamese economic growth in the area of catfish exports. With Viet Nam's substantial entry into the American seafood market, U.S. producers, with the assistance of elected officials, fought back, attempting not only to argue that the Vietnamese were guilty of "dumping" their product at unfair prices but also drawing on racist arguments and the war's legacy—in particular, the American employment of Agent Orange in the 1960s and 1970s—as a rationale for denying the entry of Vietnamese seafood into the United States. "Never trust a catfish with a foreign accent," one anti-Vietnamese advertisement instructed, while American partisans in the trade dispute warned against dioxin-infested catfish that grew up "flapping around in Third World rivers" and dining on "whatever [they] could get [their] grubby little fins on." Laderman shows how all sides drew on the memory and legacies of the war, leading to situations in which American catfish farmers and their allies constructed narratives of victimization in the face of "unwarranted Vietnamese aggression." For the Vietnamese, this was a sobering and ironic lesson in what the country's turn to "market" reforms portended, as the United States, which for so many years attempted to remake the southern Vietnamese economy in its own capitalist image, was now using state-based protectionist measures to punish Vietnamese farmers who had embraced the principles of globalized "free trade."

Few war-related issues resonate more deeply among Vietnamese and Americans today than the legacy of those chemical defoliants employed by the United States in Southeast Asia. In "Agent Orange: Coming to

Terms with a Transnational Legacy," Diane Niblack Fox unpacks a number of the interdisciplinary threads tightly woven into the fabric of what we mean when we talk about "Agent Orange": medical science, public policy, law, humanitarian efforts, history, and lived experience. With Agent Orange, an enigmatic issue that has persisted for nearly half a century despite various attempts to define and resolve it through science and politics, Fox links local to global and individual lives to national policies across divides of time and space, across borders of nations, as well as those of class, wealth, gender, and ethnicity, with meanings that slip from person to person and from context to context and referents that range from the technical to the experiential and the metaphoric. Through her exploration of Agent Orange and its multivalent, location-specific meanings, Fox explores how individuals and institutions within and beyond the boundaries of the nation-state have constructed the meaning of the term "Agent Orange" and, in doing so, bridges the gap between discourses at the official, diplomatic, and state levels and the experiences of victims who are both the object and the subject of those discourses.

Bridging perspectives from the United States and Viet Nam, Charles Waugh investigates cultural attitudes toward the environment in contemporary Vietnamese and Vietnamese American literary writing. His essay, "Refuge to Refuse: Seeking Balance in the Vietnamese Environmental Imagination," begins with a discussion of the longstanding environmental theme in Vietnamese culture that is ubiquitous in its folk tales, folk wisdom, and folk poetry. During the American war—and in the literary representations of that war—this folk reliance on the environment was validated in another way: as a refuge or, sometimes, as a sacred place where the spirits of the dead still lingered. "The forests protect our soldiers but encircle our enemy," reportedly said Ho Chi Minh, who was photographed at Tet planting a tree in an act memorialized in several "public service" posters during the war. More recently, however, that time-honored and war-tested cultural basis in the environment has been challenged, if not supplanted, by a sense of expediency for economic growth and development. There is something startling, for instance, in the fact that the chemical companies Dow and Monsanto, which are widely despised for their wartime collusion with the U.S. military over the spraying of Agent Orange, today do a brisk business supplying Vietnamese farmers with agricultural chemicals and the general public with all sorts of household products. Waugh also explores a deviation between this older cultural basis in the environment and the exponentially increasing demand for supposed "virility enhancing" wildlife products, which is probably not a coincidence, since industrial pollutants are known to cause endocrine- and reproductive-system problems. As an enormous market has opened for Vietnamese men to consume bear bile, rice wine mixed with various snake parts, and all sorts of other, often critically endangered, wildlife species, the result is that in the present the Vietnamese environment has yet again fallen under a serious, multipronged attack, only this time it is the Vietnamese themselves who are responsible. Drawing on a range of literary sources, Waugh examines how economic expediency has managed to supplant this tradition.

Finally, H. Bruce Franklin, in "Missing in Action in the Twenty-First Century," explores what has been perhaps the most explosive and sustained political and cultural legacy in the United States of the American experience in Southeast Asia: the POW/MIA issue. For two decades following the war, the United States refused, in considerable part due to the potency of the belief that Viet Nam continued to hold live American prisoners, to normalize relations with its former enemy, choosing instead to squeeze Viet Nam both economically and diplomatically. Synthesizing his groundbreaking work on the issue in M.I.A., or, Mythmaking in America and, more recently, Vietnam and Other American Fantasies, Franklin brings this history up to date by addressing the resurrection of concerns about POW/MIAs in the first decade of the twenty-first century, such as in the Iraq war in 2003 and the presidential campaign of John McCain in 2008. While the important recent work of Michael Allen has deepened and complicated our understandings of the roots of the POW/MIA issue, the activists and everyday actors who carried the torch of the POW/MIA movement, and the role of both in recent American politics, Franklin's work continues to provide a broad framework for understanding the politics of memory in "post-Vietnam" America.[13]

Irony and Contradiction in Transnational Memory

Taken as a whole, these essays demonstrate a number of themes that emerge from interdisciplinary and transnational approaches to the legacies of the Second Indochina War. First, they show convincingly the links between nation and narration to which postcolonial literary critics and memory scholars have long implored historians and other social scientists to pay greater attention. At the level of state-based actors and official discourse, Walter Hixson, Alexander Bloom, and H. Bruce Franklin all demonstrate the problematic ways in which state-sanctioned narratives that denote the "meaning" of the war have been put to a variety of uses, from justifying punitive trade embargoes and market-based "reforms" to justifying a renewed and enhanced militarism. In each of these cases, we are reminded of Ernest Renan's axiom that forgetting, and even "historical error, is a crucial factor in the creation of a nation."[14] The United States and Viet Nam have been made and remade not only by wars and the narratives they engender, but also by what those narratives and the institutions and individuals who produce and disseminate them remember and forget.

As a host of other essays in the collection make clear, however, even official narratives must contend with the ways in which memory, conflict, and trauma are inscribed in and through artistic expression, cultural commodities, and everyday life. In this formulation, both Heonik Kwon's study of everyday practices of memory and reconciliation and Viet Thanh Nguyen's explorations of cosmopolitanism, empathy, and compassion serve as powerful counternarratives to the efforts described by Hixson and Franklin purposefully to forget the effects of war on the objects of its violence and to ignore the effects of war on those who fight it. Similarly, Mariam Lam situates various forms of cultural production by diasporic Vietnamese actors as transnational challenges and alternatives to state-based narratives, practices, and policies promoted by the Vietnamese government. The relatives of the millions of Vietnamese martyrs who populate the country's graves—marked and unmarked, official and improvised—across sites throughout the region also serve as a reminder of both the power and limits of state-sanctioned narratives. In Christina Schwenkel's telling, the complex transnational memoryscape of Khe Sanh both complements and complicates state-intended meanings and "reveal[s] the ways in which unreconciled pasts and the trauma that endures in landscapes, bodies, and memory are provisionally, though unevenly, resolved."

The global flows of people, capital, and ideas that form the heart of the transnational frameworks described in these essays in many cases have undermined official state practices, particularly in Viet Nam. Indeed, the essays lend weight to the argument made recently by Mark Bradley that, since the beginning of *doi moi*, the Vietnamese state "has increasingly lost the ability to control the memory of the war."[15] But other essays in the volume remind us of the stubborn persistence of state authority and state power in both the United States and Viet Nam. The same types of ironies and contradictions that arise from contests over cultural production and memorialization practices can be seen in the implementation of global political and economic frameworks at national and local levels. The same global flows that so easily transcend and transgress national boundaries are often negotiated, sanctioned, and supported by the very states they are supposedly undermining. Scott Laderman provides a powerful example of this, exploding the myth of global free markets so regularly championed by the United States by showing how bilateral "free trade" agreements— and the global capitalist infrastructure on which they rest—can be easily turned into tools of official protectionism, serving powerful interests and powerful nations at the expense of disenfranchised producers and developing states. Similarly, Charles Waugh shows how, in its rush to embrace that very development model, the Vietnamese government has jettisoned that nation's long tradition of balanced environmentalism and, along with it, has willingly exposed its citizens to the pernicious social and environmental effects of global capital. Diane Fox also shows us some of the ways in which nations still matter a great deal, given the refusal of the United States to come to terms with the legacy of the chemical war it waged in Viet Nam over many years. While a number of individual actors have shaped and been shaped by the multiple embodiments of Agent Orange—as science, law, history, and experience—the fight for environmental and social justice around these discourses remains thwarted by the state-based sovereignty of the U.S. government responsible for the spraying and by the increasingly elusive and disembodied power of the transnational chemical corporations who facilitated it.

All of the essays in this volume suggest that an interdisciplinary and transnational approach to the legacies of the Second Indochina War must be grounded in the spaces, ironies, and contradictions embodied in the narratives, policies, and practices that shape and are shaped by the intersections of nation-states and transnational flows, state and nonstate actors, the global and the local. They remind us that the legacies of the Vietnam War are significant not only for the ways in which they shaped geopolitics and international relations in the second half of the twentieth century but also for the ways in which they continue to shape everyday life for millions of citizens around the world. If Renan was right, finally—

if nations are defined largely by what they collectively forget about the past—then perhaps this collection also suggests a way forward: that by embracing a transnational approach to war and memory, we can offer at least a modest intervention against the seemingly inexorable march of historical amnesia.

A QUICK NOTE ON STYLE: Readers will notice that some authors have chosen to use the Vietnamese diacritics; others have not. We opted for consistency within chapters rather than the entire volume. Readers will also notice that "Vietnam" and "Viet Nam" both appear in the text. This is not an editorial oversight. We have used "Viet Nam" to refer to the place called Viet Nam, as we wish to reinforce that Viet Nam is not simply—as it is often treated in the United States—an American discursive construction. We have, however, retained the use of "Vietnam" when it appears in quoted material, titles, or names, or when referring to the Vietnam War, Vietnam veterans, the Vietnam syndrome, and other denotations of the American imagination. This would include, in our view, "North Vietnam" and "South Vietnam."

Notes

1. Lepore, *The Name of War*, xv. For more on the politics of language associated with the war, see Laderman, *Tours of Vietnam*, ix–xii.

2. This definition is based on the approach laid out in Basch et al., *Nations Unbound*, 7.

3. Lepore, *The Name of War*, x–xi.

4. For more on this trend in the historiography, see Bradley, *Vietnam at War*, 3.

5. For a sampling of these works, see Gaiduk, *The Soviet Union and the Vietnam War*; Zhai, *China and the Vietnam Wars*; Daum et al., *America, the Vietnam War, and the World*; Lawrence, *Assuming the Burden*; Rabel, *New Zealand and the Vietnam War*; Bradley and Young, *Making Sense of the Vietnam Wars*.

6. Among the many recent works in this area are Catton, *Diem's Final Failure*; Jacobs, *America's Miracle Man in Vietnam*; Miller, "Vision, Power, and Agency"; Chapman, "Staging Democracy"; Carter, *Inventing Vietnam*; Masur, "Exhibiting Signs of Resistance." Much of the trend in both internationalization and an earlier chronological focus followed the publication of Bradley, *Imagining Vietnam and America*.

7. Elliott, *The Vietnamese War*; Hunt, *Vietnam's Southern Revolution*.

8. Miller and Vu, "The Vietnam War as a Vietnamese War." Accompanying essays in that issue of the *Journal of Vietnamese Studies* by François Guillemot, Bussarawan Teerawichitchainan, Shawn McHale, David Biggs, and Peter Hansen explore a range of fascinating topics within this larger theme.

9. Among the landmark works on the post-1975 period in U.S.–Viet Nam relations and the cultural memory of the Second Indochina War are Duiker, *Vietnam since the Fall of Saigon*; Franklin, *M.I.A.*; Lembcke, *The Spitting Image*. More recent works that have sought to build on these studies include Schulzinger, *A Time for Peace*; Martini, *Invisible Enemies*; Laderman, *Tours of Vietnam*; Kuzmarov, *The Myth of the Addicted Army*; Allen, *Until the Last Man Comes Home*. From the perspective of Vietnamese, Tai, *In the Country of Memory*, paved the way for recent studies of war memory that have tended to come from more anthropological and transnational perspectives, including Kwon, *Ghosts of War in Vietnam*; Schwenkel, *The American War in Contemporary Vietnam*. See also the roundtable on the publication of *The Diary of Đặng Thùy Trâm* in the *Journal of Vietnamese Studies* 3, no. 2 (June 2008).

10. Nguyen's work on the "post-Tet" war and on Hanoi's role in undermining the possibility of greater reconciliation vis-à-vis the Provisional Revolutionary Government is in Nguyen, "Cold War Contradictions"; Nguyen, *Hanoi's War*. Quinn-Judge's informative essay "From the *Quiet American* to the Paris Peace Conference" offers yet another take on the possibilities, and ultimate demise, of the Provisional Revolutionary Government.

11. For more on the American need for postwar "healing," see Hagopian, *The Vietnam War in American Memory*.

12. Among the large number of fascinating recent works on the 1970s, see Borstelmann, *The 1970s*; Zaretsky, *No Direction Home*; Schulman and Zelizer, *Rightward Bound*; Kalman, *Right Star Rising*; Rodgers, *The Age of Fracture*; Cowie, *Stayin' Alive*.

13. Allen, *Until the Last Man Comes Home*.

14. Renan, "What Is a Nation?," 11.

15. Bradley, *Vietnam at War*, 185.

CHAPTER 1

Legacies Foretold

Excavating the Roots

Ngo Vinh Long | of Postwar Viet Nam

Wars usually create all kinds of dislocations—physical, economic, social, and moral, to name a few—and leave a legacy of polarization. The longer a war, the worse the dislocation and the deeper the polarization. Hence, efforts at reconciliation and accommodation, for example, have to be promoted in times of war to lay the foundations for the building of a pluralistic and democratic country in times of peace. Without such foundations, but with a military outcome in which one party becomes "victorious," then—as the case of Viet Nam illustrates—the tasks of "nation building" become painfully difficult.

Viet Nam experienced nearly half a century of incessant warfare, with direct and indirect U.S. involvement from 1945 to 1990. From the mid-1950s to the mid-1970s, the direct U.S. involvement in "South Vietnam" was justified in terms of nation building and promoting democracy. Yet the United States consistently supported efforts that destroyed every opportunity available for reaching these ends. Since it is not possible to cover such a long period in sufficient detail in this chapter, I will focus on a few aspects of the period since the United States, the Republic of Viet Nam (RVN; the South Vietnamese regime in Saigon), the Democratic Republic of Viet Nam (DRV; the government of North Vietnam), and the Provisional Revolutionary Government (PRG) of the Republic of South

Vietnam signed the Agreement on Ending the War and Restoring Peace in Vietnam in Paris on 27 January 1973.

Focusing on the last years of the war may seem odd in a book devoted to its legacies. But unless one understands how the policies of the RVN effectively destroyed the pluralistic potential of the south, one cannot understand the myriad developments that unfolded in Viet Nam in the years after the war came to an end. The repression that characterized South Vietnamese life from 1973 to 1975 mattered. It not only undermined hopes for a less violent end to the war—one that may have gone some distance in building a foundation for the reconciliation of the Vietnamese people—but it also indirectly empowered those elements of the revolutionary movement that pursued more hardline policies after 1975.

In signing the Paris Peace Agreement, the United States pledged that it would withdraw from Viet Nam both militarily and politically to allow the South Vietnamese people to "decide themselves the political future of South Vietnam through genuinely free and democratic general elections under international supervision" (Art. 9b). Article 4 stated that "the United States [would] not continue its military involvement or intervene in the internal affairs of South Vietnam." And Article 9c again stressed, "Foreign countries shall not impose any political tendency or personality on the South Vietnamese people." The agreement established two parallel and equal parties in South Vietnam: the RVN and the PRG. According to Article 11 of the agreement, immediately after the ceasefire went into effect on 27 January, these two parties had to "prohibit all acts of reprisal and discrimination against individuals or organizations that [had] collaborated with one side or the other" and ensure "personal freedom, freedom of speech, freedom of the press, freedom of meeting, freedom of organization, freedom of political activities, freedom of belief, freedom of movement, freedom of residence, freedom of work, right to property ownership, and right to free enterprise."

Article 12 further stipulated, "Immediately after the ceasefire, the two South Vietnamese parties shall hold consultations . . . to set up a National Council of National Reconciliation and Concord of three equal segments. The Council shall operate on the principle of unanimity. After the National Council of National Reconciliation and Concord . . . assumes its functions, the two South Vietnamese parties will consult about the formation of councils at lower levels." This National Council would have the task, among other things, of achieving "national reconciliation and concord and insurance of democratic liberties." The third "segment" identified in the agreement was generally understood as the "Third Force," composed of individuals and organizations that were not aligned with either the RVN regime under President Nguyen Van Thieu (the First Force) or the PRG (the Second Force).

The National Council, or Hội Đồng Quốc Gia (lit., Council of State), was thus supposed to represent the various political forces in South Vietnam and function with higher authority than both the Saigon regime and the PRG in certain areas of the south's political life. Three days before the signing of the Paris Peace Agreement, however, U.S. Secretary of State Henry Kissinger still insisted at a press conference that the policy of the United States was against "impos[ing] a coalition government or a disguised coalition government on the people of South Vietnam."[1] President Richard M. Nixon meanwhile ruled out any role for the PRG in the future government of South Vietnam. As Gareth Porter, an American specialist on Viet Nam, explained: "In his radio and television address on January 23, 1973, Nixon . . . announced that the United States would 'continue to recognize the government of the Republic of Vietnam as the sole legitimate government of South Vietnam.' . . . The statement that Nixon recognized the RVN as the 'sole legitimate government' in South Vietnam bore the seeds of a new war."[2] Emboldened, if not encouraged, by Kissinger and Nixon, President Thieu reiterated his "Four No's" policy as soon as the Paris Peace Agreement was signed: no recognition of the enemy, no coalition government under any disguise, no procommunist neutralization of the southern region of Viet Nam, and no concession of territory to the communists.

Later, in an interview published in the 15 July 1973 issue of *Vietnam Report*, the English-language publication of the Saigon Council on Foreign Relations that was distributed by the RVN regime's embassy in the United States, Thieu stated: "The Viet Cong are presently trying to turn areas under their control into a state endowed with a government, which they could claim to be the second such institution in the South. They probably also hope that when this government has achieved a degree of international recognition, international opinion will force the two administrations to merge into a coalition government. If that were to happen, they would only agree to a pinkish government of coalition, which then will try to enter negotiation with Hanoi easily." Thieu stated in the same interview: "In the first place, we have to do our best so that the [National Liberation Front] cannot build itself into a state, a second state within the South." In the second place, he continued, his government should use all means at its disposal to prevent the creation of a Third Force, branding all Third Force personalities procommunist.[3]

In late April 1973, Hoang Duc Nha, Thieu's cousin and most trusted adviser, had declared, "If you're not a Communist, then you're a Nationalist [i.e., pro-Thieu]; if you're not a Nationalist, then you're a Communist. There is no such thing as a third component or fourth component."[4] Again, in early October 1973, Thieu declared that all Third Force groups were "traitors," with their "strings pulled by the communists." Deputy Nguyen Ba Can, chairman of the National Assembly's Lower House in Saigon and one of Thieu's most effective supporters, said, "There is no such thing as national reconciliation and national concord" with other political forces.[5] These were the RVN's public answers to the proposal by Nguyen Van Hieu, head of the PRG delegation to the fourteenth session of the Consultative Conference for Implementation of the Paris Peace Agreement between the two South Vietnamese parties held on 28 June 1973 in La Celle-Saint-Cloud, France, that the National Council of National Reconciliation and Concord be set up as soon as possible. The proposal stated, among other things, that "the National Council [should] consist of three equal segments having the same footing. Each of the two South Vietnamese parties [should] nominate its delegates to its segments of the Council. The third segment [should] include those persons of different political and religious trends who belong to neither side but who approve the Paris Peace Agreement. It must be ensured that the above-mentioned political and religious trends be heard, that this segment be truly representative and that it must have an independent role and enjoy an equal status in the Council."[6]

To better understand the reasons and intentions behind the statements by Thieu and his officials, it is necessary to say a few words about the Third Force, or "third component," and why the Paris Peace Agreement stipulated that, "immediately after the ceasefire, the two South Vietnamese parties [should] hold consultations . . . to set up a National Council of National Reconciliation and Concord of three equal segments." The term *Third Force* or *Third Solution* had come into being with urban opposition to the various regimes in Saigon since the early 1960s.[7] According to Jacques Decornoy, a reporter for the French newspaper *Le Monde*, the term *troisième composante* (third component) came into existence during the fall of 1969 to indicate a group of people who opposed the Thieu regime and who supported the direction of "national reconciliation" for which former General Duong Van (Big) Minh was seen as the representative.[8] "Third component" or "third segment" was then used by the negotiating team of the DRV in Paris from 1968 until the agreement was signed to push for a coalition government of three equal segments. It was not until 1972 that foreign-language publications in Hanoi began to use the term *Third Force* to indicate, as a whole, all of the urban groups in the south that were opposed to Thieu's regime. For example, *Vietnam Courier*, a monthly publication of the DRV's Foreign Ministry, stated in December 1972 that "in Saigon, a third force was coming into being as a challenge to that tinhorn dictator [Thieu] who persisted in denying its existence."

From 1969 until the signing of the Paris Peace Agreement, about one hundred Third Force groups of varying sizes and political leanings had come into being in the urban areas in the south, and some of them had taken even more radical positions than those of the DRV and PRG in certain areas. This occurred partly because the Nixon administration escalated the war through the so-called Vietnamization program and the "Accelerated Pacification Program," which brought increased suffering to most strata of the rural and urban populations in South Vietnam.[9] The Vietnamization program involved the massive buildup of the Saigon forces in an attempt to get Vietnamese to kill Vietnamese or other Indochinese, or "to change the color of the corpses." This was being done not simply to save American lives but also to save American dollars. It cost the United States $38,000 to send an American to Viet Nam to fight for one year. But it cost only $400 a year to hire an Asian mercenary or to support a Saigon soldier. Saving American lives and dollars would serve to persuade the American public that the war was winding down and that it should be more patient with the administration's policy of "getting out." The press-ganging of Vietnamese youth into the army also served to deny the National Liberation Front (NLF) fresh supplies of troops. For these reasons, within a short time the Nixon administration increased the regular forces of the Army of the Republic of Viet Nam (ARVN) to more than 1.1 million men and the local forces to more than four million.[10] These local military forces, called by American military men "Oriental Minutemen," were the Regional Forces, the Popular Forces, and the Popular Self-Defense Forces (PSDF). The first two groups were full-time soldiers organized into companies and platoons under provincial and district control, respectively. The third group consisted of part-time militia, supposedly boys and men age fifteen to eighteen or older than forty-three, operating at the subdistrict or village level. In reality, anybody who could carry a gun was good enough for the PSDF.[11]

The Saigon troops were forced to go out on some three hundred mop-up operations in South Vietnam every day in 1969 to draw enemy fire so that American tactical air support and artillery strikes could destroy them. Such mop-up operations were also designed to "pacify" the countryside. As a result, increasingly large demonstrations that involved participation by groups with various social and political backgrounds broke out in most cities of South Vietnam, opposing the press-ganging of youths into the armed forces, calling for an end to all mop-up operations, and demanding an "immediate end to the war." One example is that when the strike by 124 labor unions with more than 100,000 members was declared on 25 June 1970, other labor unions, the Disabled Veterans Organization, the An Quang Buddhist Church, the Saigon Student Union, and other organizations promptly joined them. The Saigon Student Union and the various labor unions issued a joint declaration that included demands for an immediate end to the war, the immediate and total withdrawal of all U.S. and allied forces, and the immediate termination of all military training programs.[12] This made Thieu so nervous that on 15 July 1970 he ordered all-out repression of all movements calling for peace. He vowed to "beat to death" those calling for "immediate peace," saying, "I am ready to smash all movements calling for peace at any price because I'm still much of a soldier. . . . We will beat to death the people who are demanding immediate peace."[13] On the same day, Brigadier-General Tran Van Hai, the national police chief, told his police chiefs to use "strong measures, including bayonets and bullets," to smash all demonstrations "at any price."[14] Despite the threat, on 11 November 1970 more than one thousand representatives from many organizations met at the Minh Mang University campus in Saigon to form Mặt Trận Nhân Dân Tranh Thủ Hòa Bình (People's Front in the Struggle for Peace) with the aim of "rallying all strata of the population, irrespective of ethnic, social, political and religious backgrounds to bring about peace to the nation."[15]

Encouraged by the political atmosphere in the southern cities, on 10 December 1970 Foreign Minister Nguyen Thi Binh of the PRG proposed a ceasefire if the United States agreed to withdraw its troops by 30 June 1971 and the regime in Saigon agreed to the establishment of a provisional government composed of three equal segments: the RVN, the PRG, and representatives of groups that were not aligned with either government. But Nixon and Thieu did not want a ceasefire and a peaceful solution based on political competition in a coalition government for fear that eventually they would lose out. Instead, they wanted to escalate the war and increase the repression in the hope of wiping out the political opposition. On 8 February 1971, Saigon forces invaded Laos, with the United States supplying air support, including planes and helicopters to transport parachutists and commandos. Two thousand U.S. planes and helicopters, the best Saigon units (the paratroopers, rangers, armored units, and the First Infantry Division) and strong U.S. ground units — together totaling more than forty-five thousand men — were involved in the front along Route 9, which runs near the Seventeenth Parallel from the coastline of South Vietnam to the Mekong River. The aim of this gigantic invasion, as Nixon and Defense Secretary Melvin Laird phrased it, was "to protect the Vietnamization program." A U.S. State Department declaration the same day explained that the mission would "make the enemy less able to mount offensives, and strengthen South Vietnam's ability to defend itself as U.S. forces are withdrawn from South Vietnam. It will protect American lives. This ground operation by the South Vietnamese against the sanctuaries will thus aid in the Vietnamization program."[16]

But this grandiose mission, whose maximum aims were to cut Indochina in two at its "narrow waist" by occupying southern Laos right across to the borders of Thailand and then pushing east to occupy North Vietnam at a point just north of the Seventeenth Parallel, was strongly opposed by the Vietnamese population even before it started. Word of the campaign had leaked to the general population days before the actual invasion. According to most Saigon newspapers, on 5 February 1971 three major organizations in South Vietnam — the Women's Committee to Demand the Right to Life, the People's Movement for Self-Determination, and the People's Front in the Struggle for Peace — strongly denounced the expansion of the war into Laos in a joint declaration issued in Saigon. The declaration stated, "By sending South Vietnamese troops into Laos, the United States has taken another serious step along the line of the Nixon doctrine which seeks to use the Indochinese people to destroy one another."[17] To end the senseless massacre, the groups demanded that all U.S. and allied troops be withdrawn from Indochina immediately and totally.

In its issues of 9 February and 11 February 1971, *Tin Sang* (Morning News) reported that thousands of people had marched in Saigon on 8 February to protest the expansion of the war into Laos. Representatives of a multitude of groups (women's, students, workers, and religious) demanded that their husbands, sons, and brothers be returned to their families. Many of the marchers were arrested and beaten, which in turn prompted the Saigon Student Union to deliver a twenty-four-hour ultimatum to the RVN authorities for the release of their friends. The government responded by sending combat police and American military police (MPs) to charge Minh Mang University's Student Residence. The students retaliated by burning American vehicles and beating up American MPs they met in the streets. On 15 February 1971, *Tin Sang* reported that teams of students from the Saigon Student Union, protesting against the sending of Vietnamese soldiers to Laos, had burned fifteen U.S. Army vehicles in the city of Saigon the previous day. On the same day, the students also distributed 250,000 leaflets throughout the Saigon-Cholon area denouncing Nixon for this escalation of the war.

The invasion of Laos also met with strong opposition within South Vietnamese governmental circles. For example, Deputy Ho Ngoc Nhuan wrote in *Tin Sang* that most Vietnamese believed the invasion served no military purpose at all and that everybody knew the United States had been violating the territory of Laos in the air and on the ground for a long time:

> There is no need for a declaration to make known that American and South Vietnamese soldiers have been violating the territory of this neutralist kingdom. The real purpose is that President Nixon wants the other side to know that the United States will pay little attention to public opinion and that it can do what it did to Cambodia and now to Laos. Nothing is going to stop it from going further: the invasion by land and sea of North Vietnam. The Americans will have little to lose. The casualties will be on the ground, and they will not be Americans! Is this what President Thieu calls "an act to win the war and regain the peace," this invasion of Laos? It is exceedingly difficult to understand why, when the Saigon administration is not yet able to pacify and control the territory of South Vietnam and has to ask the Koreans, the Thais, the New Zealanders, and the Australians to stay here as long as possible, its own troops are sent outside of the country to stop infil-

tration. Such an expedition has turned the question of the presence of foreign troops in South Vietnam upside down: Has this presence become unnecessary? Are the foreign troops fighting to protect us, or are we fighting to protect them?[18]

On 15 February 1971, fourteen major organizations in Saigon issued a joint communiqué demanding the immediate withdrawal of all U.S. troops from Indochina and an end to all disguised activities aimed at expanding the war and preventing the restoration of peace. The slogans of these groups had changed from "Chống Mỹ Cứu Nước" (Oppose the Americans to Save the Country) and "Đuổi Mỹ Cứu Nước" (Expel the Americans to Save the Country) to "Diệt Mỹ Cứu Nước" (Kill the Americans to Save the Country). From then on, Saigon newspapers carried reports almost every day of U.S. military vehicles being burned in the streets of Saigon. This situation forced Nguyen Van Trung, dean of the Faculty of Letters at the University of Saigon and a Catholic, to write a long article explaining why many Vietnamese had come to hate the United States to such a degree that they resorted to setting fire to American vehicles and even beating up American soldiers whenever they saw them.[19] Of course, these activities only served to justify the increased repression by the RVN regime.

In the hope of destroying the urban movement in South Vietnam, President Thieu declared martial law on 19 May 1972. The repression escalated to such a degree that on 13 June 1972, the *New York Post* reported that in the few weeks since martial law had gone into effect, more than five thousand persons had been arrested. The *Post* volunteered that these people could not be called anything but political prisoners. The weekly *Far Eastern Economic Review* gave detailed descriptions of the arrests, which usually happened late at night, and the resulting torture in a long article published on 3 June 1972. Moreover, the Saigon regime had also declared that it would draft forty-two thousand students into the various armed forces in June of that year. On 10 July 1972, *Time* reported that "arrests [were] continuing at the rate of 14,000 per month." The *San Francisco Chronicle* reported on 5 August that fourteen thousand civilians had been arrested and imprisoned every month in South Vietnam since April of that year. Before the announcement in October 1972 of the draft of the Paris Peace Agreement that had been initialed by Kissinger and Le Duc Tho, the *New York Times* quoted Ngo Cong Duc, an authority on the prison system in Viet Nam, as saying that there were about 200,000 political prisoners in Thieu's jails.[20] After the draft of the agreement was made public, the number of arrests soared. On 10 November 1972, the *Washington Post* quoted Hoang Duc Nha, Thieu's cousin and most trusted adviser, as saying that forty thousand new political prisoners had been picked up in the two weeks after the agreement was announced. On 11 November, CBS *Evening News* reported that Hoang Duc Nha had boasted that the Thieu regime had arrested fifty-five thousand "communist sympathizers" since the announcement of the agreement and had killed five thousand others. The *San Francisco Chronicle* reported on 4 November 1972 that Thieu had stated on the same day that people who supported a coalition government were "pro-communist neutralists" and would not be allowed to live five minutes. And, according to one of the decrees that the regime promulgated after the agreement was announced, any individual who did not have a Saigon flag in his or her possession at all times to demonstrate allegiance to Thieu would be considered procommunist and subjected to five years' imprisonment. *Newsweek* reported on 13 November 1972 that hundreds of South Vietnamese had been arrested "for failure to produce on demand a South Vietnamese flag." *Newsweek* also quoted a highly placed U.S. official as saying that Thieu was "arresting anyone who has a third cousin on the other side." As reported by Viet Tan Xa (Viet News Agency), the Thieu regime's official press agency, during the week of 8–15 November 1972, Thieu's police carried out 7,200 raids in the urban areas alone in the effort to arrest "pro-communist neutralists."[21] However, in a statement designed to make the RVN regime accountable for fewer political prisoners than it actually held, Foreign Minister Tran Van Lam declared on 26 January 1973, the eve of the signing of the Paris Peace Agreement, that the number of political prisoners in South Vietnam's prisons was higher than 100,000.[22]

Article 8c of the Paris Peace Agreement specified that the issue of the return of Vietnamese civilian detainees, or political prisoners, should be resolved within ninety days of the ceasefire. In an attempt to sidestep the issue, the Thieu regime maintained that there were no political prisoners in Saigon's jails. For example, on 8 March 1973 Thieu was quoted by the *Washington Post* as saying, "There are no political prisoners in South Vietnam—only Communists and common criminals." Thieu repeated this assertion in a taped interview on the television news program *Face the Nation* on 8 April. He said it yet again in a meeting with Pope

Paul the same week: "There are no political prisoners in South Vietnam. There are only two kinds of prisoners—those of the common law, who number some 21,000—and communist criminals, who number close to 6,000."[23] Accusations of being a communist criminal or a communist terrorist were sometimes truly incredible. For example, on 6 May 1973, the Saigon authorities turned over a small number of civilians they had arrested to the PRG at Quang Tri City. Among the people who were released were Le Trung, who was six, and Le Ngoc Son, who was two. Three days later, at the consultative conference between the PRG and the RVN regime in La Celle-Saint-Cloud, Foreign Minister Nguyen Van Hieu of the PRG brought up the example of the two children to illustrate the prison system in South Vietnam. The RVN representatives at the conference retorted that the PRG had used Le Trung and Le Ngoc as "terrorists."[24]

In any case, to support its claim that there were no political prisoners in South Vietnam, the Thieu regime systematically changed the files of many political prisoners, shifting their category to "common criminal status." Senator Edward Kennedy, in a speech before the U.S. Senate on 4 June 1973, quoted the U.S. Embassy in Saigon as telling his subcommittee in a letter specifically that "before and since the ceasefire, the [Vietnamese government] has been converting detainees to common criminal status by the expedient of convicting them of ID card violations or draft dodging."[25] According to Kennedy, while the U.S. Embassy in Saigon and the U.S. State Department admitted that there were political prisoners and that there was torture in South Vietnam, they said that political prisoners were purely an internal matter for South Vietnam. This led Kennedy to exclaim in the same speech, "This American position is truly incredible." At that time, according to Kennedy, the U.S. government was still training police and torturers in Saigon and still paying for Saigon's prison system. According to the project budget submitted by the U.S. Agency for International Development (USAID) for fiscal year (FY) 1974, its goal was the establishment of a Jail Administration Program in 552 detention facilities by the end of FY 1973. The document also cited in its progress report the existence of the program in 329 detention facilities. Senator Kennedy said that the U.S. government had reported to his subcommittee that it was going to spend more than $15.2 million in FY 1974 (beginning 1 July 1973) on support for the South Vietnamese police and prison system. He noted, however, that the amount reported was far from the total that would go to the Thieu regime for repression of Vietnamese prisoners, since "presumably there is more buried elsewhere. . . . The administration's cover-up and deception on continuing support of the police and prison system in South Vietnam defies understanding."[26]

Given this situation, it is clear that one of the priorities of the individuals and groups in the urban movement was to fight the continuing political repression by the Saigon regime, supported by the United States, after the signing of the Paris Peace Agreement. Another priority was to use Article 3 and Article 11, which explicitly guaranteed the rights of "freedom of movement" and "freedom of residence" to all civilians in all parts of South Vietnam, to deal with the refugee situation. According to a U.S. Senate investigation, by 1972 South Vietnam had a cumulative total of more than ten million refugees in a country of about eighteen million.[27] The plight of the refugees was of special concern to the Vietnamese negotiators at the peace talks; hence, they fought long and hard for Article 3 and Article 11, as well as for Article 5, which further paved the way for such rights by calling for a total removal or deactivation of "all demolition objects, minefields, traps, obstacles or other dangerous objects placed previously, so as not to hamper the population's movement and work." Refugees therefore were supposed to be allowed to return to the countryside to rebuild their residences and begin the long and hard process of resurrecting their devastated paddy fields and farms.

Five days before the actual signing of the Paris Peace Agreement, however, the Saigon regime issued a series of edicts that were published in *Tin Song* (Living News), its semiofficial newspaper, on 22 January 1973 threatening arrest and on-the-spot executions of "persons who incite the people . . . to leave areas controlled by the government to go into the communist-controlled zones." As American journalists reported, Thieu's field commanders and local authorities did everything possible to carry out these edicts. According to a report by Daniel Southerland in the *Christian Science Monitor* on 29 January 1973, people were even "being prohibited from working in the outlying fields" of their own villages, apparently for fear that they might fall under communist control. Another report filed by Southerland in mid-March 1973 said that the Saigon regime was doing everything it could to stop refugees from returning to their former lands to farm and to rebuild their destroyed homes. Among other things, individuals and whole families were being forced to be photographed under anti-PRG banners to discourage them from going back. "The soldiers beat us up if we go to our fields. But if we don't work the fields, we won't have enough to eat," Southerland was told. Even if the refugees could make it back to their lands, their lives would be in constant danger from ARVN artillery practice. According to Southerland, Saigon forces made it a habit to shell the countryside surrounding their outposts regularly, although there was no evidence of any PRG activities.[28]

Frances FitzGerald reported similar conditions in the *New York Times*. "In many provinces officials have taken away these people's identity cards—forcing them to check in at the police station every few days—and threatened arrest or violence against those who moved from the wartime settlements," she wrote.

> Where refugees have disobeyed orders, the Government has carried out those threats. In many provinces it has made it a practice to bomb or shell all the newly-built houses in the PRG areas. In areas undefended by the PRG main forces, it has sent in ground troops to burn the new houses, strip the new fields, and, perhaps incidentally, to loot the farmers' belongings. The police and territorial forces that patrol the borders of Government zones have arrested farmers going to market and charged them with "supplying the VC [Viet Cong]." As was always the case during the war, these arrests are often followed by confiscation of the farmers' belongings and sessions of interrogation and torture.[29]

In November 1973, Thomas W. Lippman reported on the refugee camp on Thanh Thuy in Quang Nam Province, where more than 2,200 people had been forcibly relocated. They wanted to return to their homes, which were about a kilometer away, but, as the district chief frankly admitted to him, the Saigon regime prevented them from doing so.[30]

Of course, the RVN regime was not content with merely preventing the refugees from going home. The incessant attacks on rural areas described earlier were also meant to generate more refugees. Official USAID statistics given to the U.S. Senate Subcommittee on Refugees revealed that during the period from 28 January to the end of February 1973 alone, 213,400 additional refugees had been created. This statistic was said to have been scaled down by at least seventy thousand.[31] Villagers were often plucked out of their villages and literally dumped along the roads as the ARVN took over areas said to be under the control of the PRG. Lippman reported in late September 1973 that inhabitants of villages in a twenty square mile area near Bong Son in Binh Dinh Province had been removed when the

Saigon forces retook the area from the PRG. "Wrenched from their rice fields at harvest time," he wrote, "they are now camped in wretched huts along Highway 1, more bewildered than angry, watching the continuing war."[32] As the military attacks continued, the number of refugees kept climbing.

Besides generating new refugees, the Thieu regime forcibly relocated refugees from one province to another. On 22 March 1973, the *New York Times* reported a disclosure by the RVN regime that it had begun moving 100,000 of a planned 660,000 persons from the central provinces into areas directly north of Saigon. In July, the paper reported that more than 160,000 Vietnamese—or at least 30,000 more than the total number of people resettled during the first six months of 1972—were to be relocated in that month to areas that had been conceded to the PRG for years.[33] All of this was done under the guise of the Program to Improve the Life of Anti-communist Refugees and the Develop Virgin Land and Construct Hamlets Program, which were part of Saigon's four-year Community Defense and Local Development Plan (1972–75), developed in 1971 with the assistance of high-ranking American Civil Operations and Rural Development Support officials. The planned U.S. assistance to refugees for 1973 covered only 600,000 people and, even on paper, amounted to a meager $14 per refugee. Corruption and graft reduced refugee relief to almost nothing. According to the Saigon daily *Hoa Binh* (Peace), close to $500,000 in relief funds for a camp in Binh Dinh Province had been siphoned off in graft. The *New York Times* had also reported that corruption in the thirty-four refugee camps in the Da Nang area (where 300,000 refugees were kept) was so rampant that the camps' chiefs had to be replaced more than once within a period of five months.[34]

All of this graft and corruption at a time of critical rice shortages in the central and highland provinces meant increased suffering and hunger for the refugees.[35] Demanding their freedom, refugees demonstrated in September 1973 in the three central provinces of Quang Tri, Thua Thien, and Quang Nam. In the same month, hungry refugees rioted in Long Khanh Province, northwest of Saigon.[36] By the end of 1973 and the beginning of 1974, hunger had become so widespread in the central provinces, especially in the refugee resettlement areas, that there were almost daily reports in the Saigon press about the tragic situation. On 1 February 1974, for example, *Dai Dan Toc* reported:

In the areas of Ky Trong and Ky Phu in Quang Tin province where I travelled, many families have to eat leaves picked from the forest in order to survive. In the areas of Thu Lo and Can Cuong in Quang Nam province, in the resettlement areas of Dong Tac, in the villages of Hoa Thanh, Hoa Thinh, Hoa My, and so on, the inhabitants have to eat the bark and the tops of the manioc trees in order to survive. What is more heart-rending is the fact that many pregnant women have to eat roots of banana trees in order to save what little rice they have for their young children. This same situation confronts many families in the district of Duc Duc in Quang Nam province. Many families have had to go for three days with whatever greens that are still left on the ground.

On 19 February 1974, *Dien Tin* (Telegraph) reported that in the hamlet of Ma Voi in Phu Yen Province, two or three persons died every day because they had to eat snakes, centipedes, leaves, or banana roots. As a result, the paper stated, the majority of the village population had left for fear of more widespread starvation. On 24 February 1974, *Dai Dan Toc* reported on a statement by Deputy Nguyen Ngoc Nghia of the National Assembly's Lower House in Saigon that not a grain of rice was to be found anywhere in Thua Thien Province. In the capital city of Hue, however, each person could still buy 2.5 kilograms of rice a month. The same paper reported on 6 March 1974 that, according to Deputy Tran Ngoc Giao, the nine thousand inhabitants of the village of Phu Dien, in the Phu Vang District of Thua Thien Province, were going to the sea to find seaweed for their daily meals. The situation became so bad that 140 families had been forced to sign up to be relocated to Binh Tuy Province, near Saigon, and this was the first time any of these families had wanted to leave their native village. The deputy complained that the government had not done anything to help ease these harsh conditions.

Despite this reality, however, American officials in Viet Nam always pointed to the relocation of refugees as a showcase of the success of the American aid program in South Vietnam when they sought more aid for the Thieu regime. In February 1974, for example, they told a congressional fact-finding delegation that one of the major achievements of the RVN regime since the ceasefire had been the relocation of refugees, claiming that 500,000 persons had been relocated; that temporary shelter had been provided to the refugees; and that each refugee family had been given five hundred square meters of land for a house and garden plot, with up to three additional hectares of land to be given once it had been cleared. They assured the congressional leaders that the funds provided by USAID were administered by the capable, dynamic, and incorruptible Phan Quang Dan, director of the land-development and hamlet-building program.[37]

Newspapers and politicians in Saigon, however, frequently reported that most of the funds for refugees had been stolen by officials, that the refugees had never received what they were supposed to receive, and that most of them had not been resettled. A preliminary report released by Saigon's Office of Land and Paddy Fields in May 1974 indicated that in the first part of the year alone, at least 200,000 hectares (about 450,000 acres) of land had been fenced off by high officials.[38] A deputy in the Lower House of the National Assembly testified that, after traveling around to observe the living conditions of the refugees, he found that most of the land had been usurped by powerful people and that poor people had not been able to find any land at all to cultivate.[39] At least 550,000 refugees were still in camps as a result of the stealing of funds and land earmarked for them, the conservative Saigon daily *Chinh Luan* (Official Discussion), many of whose editors and staff members had been employed officially by the pacification program, reported in July 1974. *Chinh Luan* stated that, in 1974, Phan Quang Dan had received $65 million in "Food for Peace" funds in addition to regular refugee funds; the money, which was supposed to feed a million refugees, was not spent in any way that would really benefit the refugees however.[40]

In addition to repressing individuals and groups in the urban antiwar movement and causing untold misery to the refugees, the Thieu regime unleashed unprecedented attacks on areas of South Vietnam that were under the control of the PRG, partly because both the DRV and the PRG wanted to "give peace a chance," so to speak, and did not want the military war to resume. The DRV and the PRG continually stressed the importance of Third Force groups in bringing about reconciliation and in forming "a government of national concord," as stipulated in the Paris Peace Agreement. For example, Prime Minister Pham Van Dong had this to say in an interview with the French journalist Jean Lacouture in 1974: "The formation of a government of national concord in the South is key to peace, and the third force is an indispensable part of this solution. *As politics is the art of the possible*, we have concluded that this formula is the only one that can lead to peace. I would say that it is a providential solution. And there is no other apart from this, there is only war."[41]

Hence, Hanoi imposed the "Five Forbids" on all of the military forces from the north, as well as on PRG forces in the south. They were forbidden to attack the enemy, to attack enemy troops carrying out land-grab operations, to surround outposts, to shell outposts, and to build combat villages. Except in rare instances of local defiance, Hanoi's approach prevailed for almost a year after the Paris Peace Agreement was signed.[42] Le Duc Tho later admitted that a number of problems after the signing of the Paris Peace Agreement had influenced the cautious attitude of the Vietnamese policymakers, resulting in their defensive posture during the postagreement period. One was that both the Soviet Union and China cut off all military aid to Viet Nam and that China, for ulterior motives, also cut off all economic aid. Another was the fact that "some high [northern] cadres who went to the South to explain the situation had placed too much emphasis on maintaining a peaceful stance for the sake of reconstruction. . . . Therefore, at that time there were many cases in which our [southern] brothers simply withdrew from, or at best tried to maintain, the areas attacked by the enemies but did not fight back."[43] In fact, both Nixon and Kissinger informed Thieu during his visit to the United States in April 1973 that the Soviet Union and China would restrain the North Vietnamese by reducing military aid.[44]

The RVN government, however, was not subjected to any of the constraints faced by Hanoi and the PRG. Immediately before and after the signing of the Paris Peace Agreement, the United States supplied Thieu's government with so many arms that, as Major-General Peter Olenchuck testified before the U.S. Senate Armed Services Committee on 8 May 1973, "we shortchanged ourselves within our overall inventories. We also shortchanged the reserve units in terms of prime assets. In certain instances, we also diverted equipment that would have gone to Europe."[45] In FY 1974, Congress gave Saigon $1 billion more in military aid. Saigon expended as much ammunition as it could—$700 million worth. This left a stockpile worth at least $300 million, a violation of the Paris Peace Agreement, which stipulated that equipment could be replaced only on a one-to-one basis. For FY 1975, Congress again authorized $1 billion in military aid but appropriated $700 million—about what was actually spent in 1974.

In addition to military aid, the United States sent military technicians under civilian guise to operate and maintain the RVN regime's highly technological war machine. Gareth Porter had this to say after studying official U.S. sources: "Several thousands of these military technicians, many of them recruited directly from the military and officially 'retired' for the purpose, entered Vietnam just as the last American troops were being withdrawn. These military technicians may have successfully evaded the restrictions imposed on the United States by Article 5 of the agreement, but their employment also involved the United States so deeply in the Saigon army that it blatantly violated the more fundamental obligation of Article 4."[46] Thieu was certainly encouraged by the American military aid and immediately carried out the so-called military operations to saturate the national territory (*hành quân tràn ngập lãnh thổ*) through indiscriminate bombings and shelling, as well as ground assaults on areas controlled by the PRG. In its report of 11 June 1973, the U.S. Senate Subcommittee on U.S. Security Agreements and Commitments Abroad quoted the Defense Attaché's Office as saying that in the post-ceasefire period, Saigon's daily "firings of 105 mm. howitzers were continuing [in the northern provinces alone] at a rate which exceeded 31,000 rounds, the average daily production of this ammunition in the United States."[47] On 16 February 1974, the *Washington Post* quoted Pentagon officials as saying that the ARVN forces were "firing blindly into free zones [i.e., PRG-controlled areas] because they knew full well they would get all the replacement supplies they needed from the United States." According to the terms of the Paris Peace Agreement, there was no such thing as a "free zone" in South Vietnam into which one could fire blindly at any time. The agreement clearly specified only two zones of control in South Vietnam: one under the PRG, and the other under the RVN. Nevertheless, in mid-February 1974, James Markham, chief of the *New York Times*'s Saigon bureau, toured PRG areas and found random shelling of civilian areas by the ARVN everywhere he went.[48] A study by the U.S. Defense Attaché's Office in conjunction with the Saigon Joint General Staff and the U.S. Pacific Command revealed in May 1974 that "the countryside ratio of the number of rounds fired by South Vietnamese forces [since the signing of the Paris Peace Agreement] to that fired by Communist forces was about 16 to 1. In Military Regions II and III, where South Vietnamese commanders have consistently been the most aggressive and where some U.S. officials said that random 'harassment and interdiction' fire against Communist-controlled areas was still common, the ratio was on the order of 50 to 1."[49]

In addition to the shelling, about fifteen thousand bombs were dropped and ten thousand different military operations were conducted into the countryside each month. A classified study by the provincial authorities and revolutionaries of Long An Province documented that, in the post–Paris Peace Agreement period, every village under the control of the NLF was bombed four to five times and struck by an average of about one thousand artillery shells a day. Repeated assaults by large forces, sometimes consisting of several divisions, were conducted, and, as a result, in May–August 1973 the revolutionary forces in Long An Province had to battle the ARVN troops 3,300 times.[50] In a speech to the Self-Defense Forces on 6 August 1973, the anniversary of their creation, President Thieu ordered all of his forces and cadres to "be resolute in chopping up all the tricky communists," because "the Communists are demanding negotiations, democratic freedoms, freedom of the press, and freedom of speech to propagandize Communist ideology among the ranks [of the government] of the Republic of Vietnam."[51]

In addition to military attacks, Thieu's regime carried out an "economic blockade" that was designed to inflict hunger or starvation on the areas under PRG control.[52] But the U.S.-Thieu strategy of sabotaging the Paris Peace Agreement backfired. In carrying out such aggressive military attacks on the PRG's areas, Thieu's regime inflicted untold death and suffering on the civilian population and exposed its own armed forces to danger and death. As early as 30 August 1973, *Le Monde* was reporting that, according to the high command in Saigon, forty-one thousand of its troops had been killed and four thousand had gone missing since the Paris Peace Agreement was signed. Saigon was never known for inflating its own casualty statistics. The suffering and death caused by Thieu's sabotage of the Paris Peace Agreement made his regime increasingly unpopular with the general population.

The economic blockade, which in the rice-centered country included prohibitions on the transport of rice from one village to another, on the milling of rice by anyone except the government, the storage of rice in homes, and the sale of rice outside the village to anyone but government-authorized buyers, caused widespread hunger and starvation. According to reports by government officials and Catholic priests in Saigon, up to 60 percent of the population in the central provinces were reduced to eating bark, cacti, banana roots, and the bulbs of wild grass. Children and the elderly were the first victims; in some villages of central Viet Nam, death from starvation reached 1–2 percent of the total population each month. And in the once rice-rich south, acute rice shortages became commonplace in many provinces.[53]

Even when there was not outright famine or a serious food shortage, Thieu's blockade wreaked great hardship on the peasants. Under his program, hamlets under Saigon's control were classified as type A or type B. Inhabitants of type A hamlets were allowed to store only enough rice for a family's monthly consumption, while families in type B villages could keep only enough for a week. Any extra rice had to be given to the authorities for storage. When a family had consumed its quota, it had to file applications to take home another portion of its rice. The red tape was overwhelming, and the inhabitants usually lost a lot of time in the process. Moreover, much of their rice was usually "lost in storage."[54]

As for the economy, Thieu's policies precipitated a major depression. According to Deputy Prime Minister Nguyen Van Hao of the RVN government, one-and-a-half-million people (about one-fifth of the adult workforce) were out of work.[55] Throughout Thieu's territory, firms were firing workers in droves. The owners frequently mistreated and insulted their workers to force them to quit.[56] Even foreign companies, which enjoyed many special privileges (such as exemption from all income taxes), had to cut back their workforces by 30 percent.

Hunger and unemployment increased rates of crime and suicide, as well as the number of demonstrations, throughout the areas under the RVN's control. Demonstrations demanding jobs and food occurred almost daily. On 30 August 1974, for instance, Dien Tin reported that one thousand disabled veterans and other inhabitants of Do Hoa village in Thua Thien Province had blockaded the streets with barbed wire, demanding that the government provide food and jobs. On 19 September, 116 trade unions in Saigon and Cholon met to demand food and clothing and an end to mistreatment and unwarranted layoffs.[57] Two days later, on 21 September, the whole workforce of Saigon, Cholon, and Gia-Dinh demonstrated for food, clothes, and temporary relief.[58] While this was going on, huge numbers of workers in Danang, the second-largest city in South Vietnam, marched in the streets and then went on a mass hunger strike.[59] A month before these outbursts, on 6 August, Thieu was still exhorting his armed forces to implement the economic blockade to defeat the "communists" by starving them out.[60]

The death and suffering caused by Thieu's military attacks, his economic blockade, and his police-state tactics in the urban areas not only intensified the general population's hatred of his regime; they also forced the PRG to strike back, though in a limited way. "In the first year of the ceasefire," the *Manchester Guardian Weekly* reported, "the Communists pursued a policy of comparative restraint as they tried through diplomatic means to put pressure on Saigon to accept the political provisions of the Paris Agreement. Representations to the U.S. government and meetings with Kissinger leading nowhere, they seem to have decided, some time this spring, to go over to a limited offensive, which they announced on their radio and elsewhere, in a public way."[61] In the summer of 1974, the PRG's counterattack forced Thieu's armed forces to make one "tactical withdrawal" after another. Even in the heavily defended delta provinces, the ARVN was forced to abandon eight hundred firebases and forts to "increase mobility and defense."[62]

But instead of drawing lessons from the experience and responding to the demands of the PRG, as well as those of the country's general population, to return to the Paris Peace Agreement, both the Thieu regime and the administration of U.S. President Gerald Ford tried their own tricks to obtain more aid from Congress to shore up the already hopeless situation. For its part, the Ford administration tried to set in motion a plan it had long held in reserve: the replacement of Thieu by a right-wing coalition capable of winning more aid from Congress and of keeping some control of the country. High-level CIA agents were sent in droves to South Vietnam in September and October 1974.[63] The U.S. Embassy in Saigon publicly encouraged a coalition of conservative forces within the Catholic, Buddhist, Cao Dai, and Hoa Hao churches to give the appearance of widespread popular backing for Thieu's successor regime.[64] The opposition to Thieu by right-wing Catholics was based on the Anti-corruption Campaign, led by Father Tran Huu Thanh, who stated that "South Vietnam . . . needs a clean government so 'our allies will trust us' and will send foreign aid and investment."[65]

On 19 November 1974, Colonel Vo Dong Giang, the spokesman for the PRG at the two-party Military Commission in Saigon, held a press conference in which he criticized Father Thanh and his campaign for trying to maintain Thieu's regime, for following American policy, and for refusing to move toward peace as called for by the Paris Peace Agreement and the Vietnamese people. Vo warned the United States that unless it heeded the aspirations of the Vietnamese people and returned to the agreement, the Vietnamese people would soon rise up. The *New York Times* chided Vo for bragging and for being arrogant.[66]

Perhaps impressed by the show in Saigon and by the Ford administration's promise that Saigon would soon have a regime worth supporting, Congress authorized $450 million in economic aid to Saigon for FY 1975—$100 million more than the amount authorized for FY 1974. As noted earlier, 90 percent of U.S. economic aid to Saigon had been used to maintain the war. The PRG evidently interpreted Congress's action as a renewed commitment to the RVN regime. In answer, the PRG forces increased their counterattacks against Thieu's aggressive military stance, and by early January 1975, eight districts and a province (Phuoc Long) had fallen into the PRG's hands. This was clearly an attempt to show the United States and Thieu's regime that if the PRG was forced into military confrontation, Saigon's forces would not be able to stand up against it, as events in later days certainly proved true.

But the United States and Saigon refused to learn a lesson from all of this. As soon as the PRG began to relax its military pressure (around the second week of January 1975), waiting for an appropriate response, the RVN government and the right-wing Catholic opposition to Thieu said publicly that the PRG had been lucky in taking over a few isolated districts and towns, but it would not be able to take over more heavily defended areas.

Meanwhile, in mid-January 1975, CIA agents went to Capitol Hill to hold Senate briefings on the "heartland" policy. They maintained that the ARVN had high morale, was well trained, and was fully equipped but was overextended. They recommended abandoning some of the central highland provinces and withdrawing to coastal areas to preserve the strength of the Saigon troops.[67] This would also help provide tighter control of populated areas, making it possible to conduct and manage the upcoming elections to create the impression that a future regime in Saigon indeed had overwhelming popular support.

To convince congressional leaders that the ARVN's morale was high and that more aid was needed, the White House and various government agencies suggested that a congressional fact-finding delegation visit Saigon. A few days of conversations with various CIA agents and U.S. officials, as well as with influential politicians in Saigon, were enough to convince some congressional leaders. Even Representative Peter McCloskey, who had been a critic of the war, returned from the tour so impressed that he said he would recommend continued aid to Saigon for three more years. The DRV and the PRG, expecting another increase in congressional war appropriations (President Ford had requested $300 million in supplemental military aid), decided to mount an offensive in early March to try to get at the RVN regime and the United States by attacking the central highlands provinces of Ban Me Thuot, Kontum, and Pleiku. President Thieu was forced hastily to carry out an American "heartland" strategy by withdrawing troops to coastal areas, which caused a stampede, as one province after another fell with hardly a fight. But instead of returning to the Paris Peace Agreement, the United States decided to force a military solution. On 26 March, the U.S. Army's chief of staff, General Frederick C. Weyland, was sent to Saigon to assess the situation, as well as to help Saigon set up a defense anchor thirty-five miles north of the city. Frantic diplomatic and political maneuvers were employed with the hope of delaying the offensive, including getting China and the Soviet Union to put pressure on the DRV and finding a replacement for Thieu. On 21 April 1975, Thieu was forced to resign and was replaced by Vice President Tran Van Huong. In turn, Huong suggested that former General Duong Van Minh, who was leading a coalition of Third Force groups, be appointed by the two chambers of the Saigon National Assembly as the new president. Instead of doing so right away, the deputies and senators spent a whole week wrangling over which position should go to whom in the new government and acted on Huong's request only on 27 April. On 28 April, when fourteen divisions of the People's Army were moving into Saigon, Duong Van Minh was finally endorsed as the new president of the RVN. Instead of taking a last stand or giving in to the pressure of French Ambassador Jean-Marie Mérillion and making a last-minute demand to the PRG for the creation of a coalition government, Duong Van Minh decided to make an unconditional surrender. As he was sitting in wait for the representatives of the revolutionary side to accept his surrender, Minh told a correspondent for Agence France-Presse, "Human lives, Vietnamese lives, French lives had to be saved. Tell the French ambassador that you saw me here."[68]

In a single stroke, the unconditional surrender both saved lives and put an end to the idea of a "third segment" or "third component." With a military victory, there was no longer a need for a "third segment" to reconcile forces within a coalition "government of national concord." On 2 May 1975, the new government ordered the dissolution of all political organizations that had come into existence under the ancien régime.[69] All others that could be considered civil society organizations, such as the Women's Movement for the Right to Life, disbanded because, as the group's cofounder Ngo Ba Thanh explained, there was no need for such an organization after the war.[70]

There was still hope that the PRG, which was itself a coalition of many organizations, would transform itself into a new transitional government in the south. But continued U.S. hostilities quickly closed off the option for two separate governments in Viet Nam while the ensuing "Third Indochina War" helped increase the power of the hardliners in the government of the unified Viet Nam for the next decade or so.[71] The economic and social difficulties created by the war did finally force the government to relax some bureaucratic controls over the economy, but no new institutions were ever created to help the Vietnamese people struggle against the authoritarian nature of the Communist Party and the state.[72]

It has often been surmised that economic growth will bring about more economic and political participation and that this, in turn, will make regimes less authoritarian. Moreover, it has been surmised that increased integration into the global market will help create the kind of institutional changes that hasten democratization in societies under authoritarian rule. However, authoritarianism seems to have been on the increase in Viet Nam in the past decade even as the country has enjoyed unprecedented economic and trade growth. Authoritarianism has manifested itself not only in repressive measures by the central government but also by widespread abuses of power at all levels of society. Some of the roots of this sorry state of affairs go back to the dislocations, the polarization, and the repression of social and political movements outlined in this chapter. Had the repression of the Third Force not occurred from 1973 to 1975, the political legacies of the war might have been quite different for postwar Viet Nam.

Notes

1. "Transcript of Kissinger's News Briefing to Explain Vietnam Cease-Fire Agreement," *New York Times*, 25 January 1973, 19.

2. Porter, *A Peace Denied*, 186.

3. Thieu made similar statements repeatedly for the next two years: see, e.g., the reports of his speeches in *Dien Tin*, 14–15 April 1974, 13 November 1974, and in the

pro-Thieu and pro-U.S. daily *Chinh Luan*, 14 November 1974. All translations from Vietnamese sources are mine.

4. *Chinh Luan*, 28 April 1973.

5. The two quotes are from the reports in *Dien Tin*, 3 October 1973.

6. Statement by Minister Nguyen Van Hieu, 28 June 1973, in *Journal of Contemporary Asia* 3, no. 3 (1973): 383. This issue reprinted the entire statement, which is several pages long.

7. Hassler, "They Call It a Third Solution," 202; Luce and Sommer, *Vietnam*, 123; Pomonti, *La rage d'être vietnamien*, 242.

8. Jacques Decornoy, "'Tombeur' de Diem et ennemi de Thieu," *Le Monde*, 27–28 April 1975.

9. Even Ambassador Averell Harriman, who had been the chief negotiator for the United States in Paris, denounced Nixon's "Vietnamization program" in language about as strong as could be expected from one in his position. "The Administration's program of Vietnamization of the war is not in my opinion a program for peace, but it is a program for the continuation of the war. . . . Furthermore, the Vietnamization of the war is dependent on an unpopular and repressive government": Harriman, *America and Russia in a Changing World*, 140.

10. According to *Tin Sang*, published daily by a group of Catholic deputies in Saigon's National Assembly, South Vietnam had 1.1 million regular soldiers and 4 million "popular defense" forces: *Tin Sang*, 3 August 1971. According to statistics released by the U.S. Information Service on 3 January 1972, the Nixon administration had supplied the ARVN with 910,000 small arms (i.e., submachine guns and machine guns), 775 airplanes, 2,100 pieces of artillery and tanks, 940 naval boats, and 45,000 military vehicles. Of the seven million tons of high explosives delivered on all fronts in Indochina during the previous three years, only about three million tons had been delivered by air. The rest were delivered by artillery strikes and other means, mostly in South Vietnam and by ARVN soldiers.

11. Trinh Pho, a Vietnamese officer in the Political Warfare Section of the ARVN, explained in the long article "The Mobilization of Soldiers in a New Sweep," *Quan Chung*, 5 September 1969, 1–2, that the main reason for drafting so many people into the army was to keep them under government control.

12. *Tin Sang*, 26 June 1970.

13. Takashi Oka, "Thieu Denounces 'Immediate Peace,'" *New York Times*, 16 July 1970, 9.

14. Ibid.

15. *Tin Sang*, 16 July 1970.

16. Quoted in Burchett, *Grasshoppers and Elephants*, 143.

17. The declaration was published in *Tin Sang, Xay Dung* (Constructiveness), *Dai Dan Toc* (The Greater Populace), and *Hoa Binh* (Peace) on 6 February 1971.

18. Ho Ngoc Nhuan, "Invasion of Laos, What Next?," *Tin Sang*, 11 February 1971, 1.

19. Nguyen Van Trung, *Dan Chu Moi* (New Democracy), 26 October 1971, 1.

20. Flora Lewis, "Thieu Foe in Exile Suggests New Regime," *New York Times*, 7 September 1972, 4. Ngo Cong Duc had been a Catholic deputy in the Lower House of the National Assembly in Saigon; he was also a nephew of the archbishop of Saigon. In January 1972, he had produced a detailed study of the prison system in South Vietnam and gave a breakdown of the 200,000 political prisoners in various prisons there. I was the director of the Vietnam Resource Center in Cambridge, Massachusetts, at the time. I translated the study and made it available to the press, research institutions, and various congressional offices. Later on, the study and many other documents were compiled by the Vietnam Resource Center and National Action/Research on the Military-Industrial Complex, a project of the American Friends Service Committee, in the monograph entitled "After the Signing of the Paris Agreements: Documents on South Vietnam's Political Prisoners." That publication was widely distributed beginning in June 1973.

21. Viet Tan Xa, 16 November 1972.

22. Quoted in *Doan Ket* (Unity), 31 March 1973. *Doan Ket* was a biweekly published by the Association of Vietnamese in France.

23. Quoted in Ngo Vinh Long, "Thieu Refuses to Discuss Prisoner Situation," *Boston Phoenix*, 26 June 1973.

24. *Doan Ket*, 26 May 1973.

25. Quoted in Long, "Thieu Refuses to Discuss Prisoner Situation."

26. All of the quotes from Senator Kennedy's speech are from *Boston Phoenix*, 26 June 1973.

27. "Relief and Rehabilitation of War Victims in Indo-China, Part IV: South Vietnam and Regional Problems," *Hearing before the Subcommittee of the Committee on the Judiciary to Investigate Problems Connected with Refugees and Escapees*, U.S. Senate, 93d Congress, Washington, D.C., 1973, 8.

28. Daniel Southerland, "Saigon Curbs Homeward-Bound Refugees," *Christian Science Monitor*, 16 March 1973.

29. Frances FitzGerald, "How It Is Now with the People of My Lai," *New York Times*, 4 May 1973.

30. Thomas W. Lippman, "'Let Us Go Home,' Viet Villagers Ask," *Washington Post*, 23 November 1973.

31. Seymour M. Hersh, "200,000 New Refugees Reported Since the Truce," *New York Times*, 28 February 1973, 10.

32. Thomas W. Lippman, "Saigon Fights to Regain Land, People," *Washington Post*, 30 September 1973.

33. Fox Butterfield, "Saigon Starting to Resettle 100,000 Refugees Far from Home," *New York Times*, 22 March 1973, 12; Joseph B. Treaster, "Saigon Is Moving Refugees to Get Broader Control," *New York Times*, 5 July 1973, 1.

34. *Hoa Binh*, 6 June 1973; Henry Kamm, "Horde of Ghost Refugees Get U.S. Food in Vietnam," *New York Times*, 8 March 1973, 1.

35. *Washington Post*, 25 July 1973; Fox Butterfield, "Corruption and Laxity Demoralize Vietnam City," *New York Times*, 4 August 1973, 3.

36. *Washington Post*, 11 September 1973.

37. "United States Aid to Indochina," House Committee on Foreign Affairs, July 1974; "Vietnam—The Changing Crucible," House Committee on Foreign Affairs, 15 July 1974.

38. *Dai Dan Toc*, 18 May 1974.

39. *Dien Tin*, 1 July 1974.

40. *Chinh Luan*, 25 July 1974. Details on the usurpation of land are in ibid., 17 July 1974.

41. A reprint of the interview with Pham Van Dong by Jean Lacouture can be found in the "Documents" section of *Vietnamese Studies* 39 (1974): 47–48. The quarterly *Vietnamese Studies* was edited by the famous Nguyen Khac Vien and published by the Foreign Language Publishing House in Hanoi.

42. Young, *The Vietnam Wars*, 286–89.

43. "Dong Chi Le Duc Tho noi ve mot so van de tong ket chien tranh va bien soan lich su quan su [Comrade Le Duc Tho discusses a number of questions on the general assessment of the war and the writing of military history]," *Tap Chi Lich Su Quan Su* (March 1988): 1–10.

44. Porter, *A Peace Denied*, 188.

45. "Fiscal Year 1974 Authorization for Military Procurement, Research and Development, Construction Authorization for the Safeguard ABM, and Active Duty and Selected Reserve Strengths," *Hearings before the Committee on Armed Services*, U.S. Senate, 93d Congress, pt. 3, Authorizations, Washington, D.C., 1973, 1383.

46. Porter, *A Peace Denied*, 187.

47. Subcommittee on U.S. Security Agreements and Commitments Abroad, *Staff Report*, 11 June 1973, 33.

48. James M. Markham, "Where Vietcong's Roots Go Deep," *New York Times*, 18 February 1974, 1; James M. Markham, "Paris Accords Exalted in Area Held by Vietcong," *New York Times*, 19 February 1974, 1.

49. "Vietnam: May 1974," staff report prepared for the use of the Committee on Foreign Relations, U.S. Senate, Washington, D.C., 5 August 1974, 22.

50. "Bao Cao Dien Bien 21 Nam Khang Chien Chong My va Nhung Bai Hoc ve Toan Dan Danh Giac cua Long An [Report on developments in the twenty-one years of resistance against the Americans and the lessons of the entire population fighting the enemy in Long An]," Ban Tong Ket Chien Tranh Tinh Long An (Committee on Assessment of the War in Long An Province), Long An, 1985, 127–30.

51. *Dien Tin*, 7 August 1973; *Chinh Luan*, 7 August 1973.

52. For detailed reports on the economic blockade, see *Congressional Record*, 20 May 1974, 4 June 1974.

53. *Dai Dan Toc*, 30 August 1974, 30 September 1974; *Dien Tin*, 6 September 1974.

54. *Dong Phuong*, 11 October 1974.

55. *Dai Dan Toc*, 16 October 1974.

56. *Dien Tin*, 20 September 1974.

57. Ibid.

58. Ibid., 22 September 1974.

59. Ibid., 22 September 1974, 24 September 1974.

60. *Dai Dan Toc*, 8 August 1974.

61. *Manchester Guardian Weekly*, 31 August 1974.

62. *Chinh Luan*, 25 September 1974.

63. *Washington Post*, 2 November 1974.

64. *Hoa Binh*, 27 September 1974.

65. *Washington Post*, 7 October 1974.

66. James M. Markham, "Vietcong Assail Thieu Opponent," *New York Times*, 24 November 1974, 13.

67. On 25 April 1975, the *Far Eastern Economic Review* reported that, according to a report from Tokyo, the United States "knew in advance of Saigon's plans to withdraw its troops from part of the north of the country. . . . Japanese financial leaders were reportedly told by sources close to U.S. Secretary of State Henry Kissinger in early February that the Americans were prepared to condone a South Vietnamese military 'redeployment' from the north in order to form a new, stronger defense perimeter nearer Saigon." "Intelligence: Japan's Early Warning," *Far Eastern Economic Review*, 25 April 1975, 5.

68. *Le Monde*, 2 May 1975.

69. Ibid., 3 May 1975.

70. Ibid., 12 May 1975.

71. For details, see Westad and Quinn-Judge, *The Third Indochina War*.

72. For the situation in the southern half, see Long, "The Socialization of South Vietnam." See also Fforde, "Rethinking the Political Economy of Conservative Transition," 126–46.

Walter L. Hixson

Viet Nam scarcely exists in American history or memory. "Vietnam," on the other hand, has left an indelible imprint on American history and memory. Thus, for most Americans, Viet Nam is not so much a country in Southeast Asia as it is a cultural phenomenon of their creation. Indeed, one might argue that the most important historical lesson of the "Vietnam War" (more properly the Second Indochina War or the American War) is that for Americans the conflict had little to do with Viet Nam itself.[1] Indochina, rather, functioned as a site, one of many through a long history of intervention, in which the United States carried out the drives of its militant national identity. American cultural imperatives drove the decision to intervene, the conduct of the war, and the torturous path to exit the country and come to grips with its shattering impact and legacy.[2]

For several years now, the historiography of the American War has been trending toward de-emphasizing the notion that the United States "had to" intervene in Indochina as part of the Cold War struggle against world communism. Fredrik Logevall, Mark Bradley, Kathryn Statler, and Andrew Preston, among other scholars, emphasize that rather than being driven into the conflict by the mandates of the Cold War, the United States *chose* to enter into the war, often despite warnings from allies. Just *why* it made that decision has not been so fully explored.[3]

Diplomatic historians tend to focus on individual decision makers, including key figures in allied nations, but especially on U.S. national security elites and, above all, on President Lyndon Johnson. The obsessive focus on Johnson reflects the traditional top-down methodology of diplomatic history as well as the subdiscipline's focus on government documents, to the exclusion of theoretical and cultural approaches. Bradley has shown how the two might be combined to good effect, but while scholars continue to take up residence in Washington and make the pilgrimage to the LBJ Presidential Library in Austin, not enough conceptual, cultural, or comparative work is being done on the war and certainly not enough on its impact and legacy in Indochina.[4]

Clearly, the Cold War influenced the U.S. response to the decolonization of Indochina and the imminent triumph of the Vietnamese Communist Party under Ho Chi Minh. For many scholars the conflict begins there, but this begs the question of probing more deeply into the reasons for the profound U.S. investment in the Cold War itself. Just how was it that the United States could decide that its "national security" authorized and made rational an expansive intervention in an obscure nation nine thousand miles from Washington and on the Chinese border? I would suggest that the causation of the intervention penetrates much more deeply into American culture than the Cold War alone and certainly more deeply than the Oval Office and other offices in Washington, D.C., and in foreign capitals.

The United States pursued an atrocious strategy (literally as well as figuratively), but no strategy would have worked, as the Indochina intervention was doomed from the outset. The massive "nation-building" that the United States orchestrated in Viet Nam, flowing out of modernization theory and the academic security complex, failed to create a viable "South Vietnam." The corrupt little fiefdom in Saigon, which became bloated with black markets and brothels to service the foreign intervention, could not make the transition from trope to viability. As David W. P. Elliott succinctly explains, the bottom line in this unwinnable postcolonial war was that "the Vietnamese non-communists could not have won without the United States, but could not have won by dependence on the United States either."[5]

Beginning in 1964, the United States thoroughly militarized the conflict, which meant that it could only kill and destroy but never win the war. The illusion that the answer lay in greater exertions of military force flowed from "can-do" American arrogance; dismissal of the lessons of previous postcolonial wars, including the First Indochina War; and ignorance of Viet Nam's history and culture—its deep-seated Confucian and Buddhist traditions, even its tenacious one-thousand-year (ultimately successful) resistance of China. Americans viewed the Vietnamese through an Orientalist lens and badly underestimated them. But mostly Americans did not think much about the Vietnamese at all. "It is striking," Bradley notes, "how little most Americans in and out of the corridors of power really knew about Vietnam."[6]

It was hardly surprising, then, that U.S. military strategy proved to be an abject, albeit horrifyingly destructive, failure. The United States sought to implement counterinsurgency doctrine by pursuing "pacification," which led to indiscriminate slaughter while driving survivors off their ancestral lands and thus further alienating their "hearts and minds." Search-and-destroy operations, artillery strikes, chemical warfare, and a bombing campaign unprecedented in human history savaged the Indochina region. Taken as a whole, the United States conducted a coldly lethal campaign of annihilation, killing at least 1 million Vietnamese in 1965–75.[7]

By the late 1960s, the inability to win, combined with the sheer destructiveness and the mounting *American* body count, created psychic turmoil in the United States. As democracy, under God, was supposed to be ever on the march, a teleology that placed the United States and other modernized, white, Western nations at the vanguard, there was no cultural space to accommodate defeat. Haunted by the specter of the nation rendered "a pitiful helpless giant," President Richard Nixon and National Security Adviser Henry Kissinger exerted manly credibility by escalating the U.S. bombing and waging the war for an additional four years. By the time it finally ended in April 1975, the long American war had "undermin[ed] the forces of moderation" that Ho Chi Minh had once personified, thus ushering in a hardened Soviet-style regime as the government of Viet Nam.[8]

History and Memory

The struggle to reconcile failure in Viet Nam with traditional American "victory culture" best explains the ways in which the Vietnam War history and memory evolved in the postwar era. While history ultimately is the stuff of narrative and discourse, no amount of linguistic manipulation could erase the fact that the United States pulled out of Viet Nam and its hapless client collapsed so quickly as to shock even the victors. American culture could and did, however, function to obscure the reasons for the American defeat, to ensure that few lasting lessons were learned from the conflict, to elide the unprecedented devastation it had heaped upon the region, to blame critics for the defeat, and thus to make possible the next wave of U.S. foreign intervention less than a generation later. Most U.S. citizens "still remembered Vietnam as a 'bad war' that we didn't win and probably shouldn't have gotten into," Lynda Boose explains. "But the key ideological issues that had constructed the opposition—just why Vietnam was a 'bad war' . . . had receded into oblivion."[9]

The traumatic cultural impact of defeat began to appear even before defeat had been consummated. The failed Nixon-Kissinger quest for "peace with honor" featured détente, troop withdrawals, and unprecedented saturation bombing while at the same time going on the offensive against the media and the antiwar movement on the home front.[10] The domestic side of the campaign fueled what would become an American obsession with prisoners of war (POWs). As Edwin Martini explains, the POW/MIA issue "came to define the matrix of the American war on Vietnam in the production of both foreign policy and cultural representations."[11] Nixon emphasized to the public that any negotiated settlement for U.S. withdrawal must entail the return of American POWs, implying that the Vietnamese had other plans or had threatened to keep the Hanoi Hilton running in perpetuity. The Vietnamese revolutionaries had given no indication that they would pursue a course other than routine repatriation of POWs in the wake of an American withdrawal. In fact, they had already unilaterally released several POWs to the custody of U.S. groups advocating an end to the war.[12]

The growing preoccupation with the nonexistent threat that U.S. POWs would not be returned reinforced imagery of the ruthless "gook" enemy that deserved all of the air strikes and destroyed villages that Nixon and Kissinger might choose to heap on them. Moreover, the POW/MIA myth carried over into the postwar era and would become so indelibly entrenched that in 1990 a poll showed that a stunning 84 percent of Americans believed that Viet Nam still held American captives. Even though Viet Nam abided by the Paris Peace Accords and returned all of the U.S. POWs, the myth prevails widely well into the twenty-first century that the perfidious Asian foe maintained secret detention and deprivation camps for Americans missing in action.

For the record, no remotely credible evidence exists that the Vietnamese held back any American prisoners—unless one counts Hollywood films as part of the evidence. Indeed, these films *are* evidence of the cultural production of popular "knowledge" about the history and memory of the Vietnam War. While only a small minority of Americans have read a basic history of the Vietnam War, tens of millions of them have seen the *Rambo* films or the Chuck Norris *Missing in Action* series. Many of these viewers undoubtedly recognize kitsch when they see it and surely did not interpret the films as gospel, yet these productions, complemented by doctored photographs of MIAs, hoaxes of "actual sightings," and the tireless efforts of fundraising groups and a handful of pandering politicians supposedly determined to "bring our boys home," all combined to create a broad cultural perception that American troops were indeed being held for years after the end of hostilities.

This mythology flourished in a cultural climate of the 1980s in which Ronald Reagan came to symbolize the nation's rebirth from defeat not only in Indochina but also from the humiliating 444-day Iran hostage crisis and the Soviet invasion of Afghanistan. Reagan's claim that the United States had not been defeated in Viet Nam—it had merely vacated the country—and that the struggle was a "noble cause" resonated in a culture that had suffered severe psychic blows through defeat in the war and the demasculinizing hostage crisis carried out by Islamic clerics and "students" chanting hate-filled slogans and burning the American flag outside the U.S. Embassy in Tehran.

Reagan understood "traditional American values," especially love of country, and he meant to bury the debilitating "Vietnam syndrome." "The truth is we did have victory [in Indochina]," the Great Communicator declaimed in 1985. "We continue to talk about losing, [but] we didn't lose that war. We won virtually every engagement."[13] Reagan thus elided that the conflict was a postcolonial guerrilla war in which the United States fought against the grain of postwar history. Moreover, even as the war became more conventional after the Tet Offensive of 1968, the United States never succeeded in driving the People's Army of Viet Nam out of "South Vietnam." Finally, Reagan affirmed the misperception that had led to defeat—namely, that wars are decided by military means alone. Reagan was a reader of *Reader's Digest*, not Clausewitz, but his view resonated in a culture striving for an explanation that was compatible with the national mission and victory culture.

Appropriately enough, Hollywood complemented the Reagan-era

cultural revival, as the *Rambo* and *Missing in Action* films came out in the early to mid-1980s. As the Reagan administration invaded Grenada, orchestrated a mercenary war in Nicaragua, and bolstered death squads in El Salvador, triumphant narratives appeared not only in film but also on television, in magazines, in pulp fiction, and even in children's toys. Representations such as *Top Gun*, *Red Dawn*, *The A-Team*, *Soldier of Fortune* magazine, Tom Clancy's clichéd techno-thrillers, and a new even more masculinized version of GI Joe all echoed the "America Is Back" revival in the 1980s.

Nothing has quite defined American culture both at home and abroad like Hollywood. Hence, the Vietnam films had a profound impact. Well before the missing-soldier kitsch appeared, a spate of ambitious and acclaimed films with major stars and directors had initiated the cultural process in which "Vietnam" would prevail over Viet Nam in American history and memory. The Academy Award–winning films *Coming Home* and *The Deer Hunter*, both released in 1978, and *Apocalypse Now*, released in 1979, were major artistic and commercial successes. None adopted an explicitly pro-war or apologetic message, and, indeed, all contained themes and vignettes that cast a negative light on the U.S. intervention.

The three Vietnam epics, joined in the 1980s by other substantial films such as *Platoon* (1986) and *Full Metal Jacket* (1987), established a cultural frame in which "Vietnam" centered almost exclusively on the undeniably traumatic experiences of American veterans. The major films scarcely even depicted the Indochinese, and when they did, they depicted them as vicious "gooks" (*Deer Hunter*) or crazed, face-painted natives (*Apocalypse Now*). The lone female sniper in *Full Metal Jacket* offered interesting allegorical possibilities, but the theme went undeveloped and paled in comparison with the riveting story of the humiliations of basic training and the battle for Hue. Even a critical film such as *Casualties of War* (1989), which centered on the rape of a Vietnamese woman, ultimately was a story, like *Platoon*, of struggle among the American grunts. The Vietnamese people and the actual country of Viet Nam remained a sideshow.

With their focus almost exclusively on Americans, the Vietnam War films advanced the cultural project of forgetting what American militarism did to Indochina in favor of an overwhelming focus on the victimization of the U.S. men and, occasionally, women (*China Beach*, 1988) who served there. Gone were overt antiwar films such as *Catch-22* and *M*A*S*H*, both released in 1970 and neither focused explicitly on Indochina, or the often overlooked *Go Tell the Spartans* (1978), a film that actually did humanize the Vietnamese. While the PBS series *Vietnam: A Television History* (1983), based on the popular history by the journalist Stanley Karnow, did often reflect critically on the war, it also came under attack from advocacy groups such as Accuracy in Media for being "biased" against the United States. Certainly, no overtly antiwar documentaries, like the hard-hitting and award-winning *Hearts and Minds* (1974), were being produced in the 1980s.[14]

The design and erection of "the Wall"—the Vietnam Veterans Memorial dedicated at the Washington Mall in 1982—underscores the cultural reframing of "Vietnam." Following the authorization of funds to build a Vietnam memorial on the mall, Maya Lin, a twenty-one-year-old architecture student at Yale University, won the design competition. The simple black granite wall met the competition criteria, itself revealing that the memorial was to be overtly apolitical and that it would contain the names of the American dead from the war. The genius of Lin's design, however, as has been made abundantly clear in subsequent years, lies in the interactive potential of the Wall, which reflects back on its visitors and invites them down into the sunken memorial to literally touch the names; take imprints; or leave flowers, letters, and ruminations on the war, all of which have been done by the millions.

The Wall reflects the cultural shift toward "Vietnam" in that only the American names and symbolism of American loss appear at the site, but even more instructive was the controversy that erupted over the selection of Lin's design. An Ohio native who understandably thought she was an American, Lin found, much to her shock, that her Asian American identity became a key issue. The *Washington Post* inaccurately and inanely labeled her "an Asian artist for an American war." As reporters, politicians, and the Vietnam veterans and others involved in the memorial project revealed anxiety about her racial identity, Lin suddenly "realized that people were having problems with the fact that a 'gook' had designed the memorial. It left me chilled."[15]

Critics wanted no hint of Asia in the "Vietnam" memorial. They immediately sought to undermine the design committee's selection, which the Reagan administration accommodated by delaying the groundbreaking. A proposed compromise—which showed a primitive understanding of what constitutes art—called for adding a heroic statue, a flagpole, and patriotic inscriptions to the existing design. In a compromise over the compromise, the statue of the veterans in each other's grasp and the flagpole went up at a nearby but separate site, preserving the integrity of the original design. Reagan declined to attend the dedication of the Wall in 1982 but turned out two years later for the dedication of the combat bronze. Bludgeoned by the controversy, Lin attended neither the groundbreaking nor the dedication for her own winning design.

Condemnation of the "liberal media," while simultaneously ascribing it with blame for defeat in Viet Nam, emerged as a crucial element in the mainstreaming of the right wing under Reagan. The process actually began with Nixon and Vice President Spiro Agnew, who memorably assaulted the media and other "nabbering nabobs of negativism." Nixon targeted the "liberal press" for opposing "wars of the Vietnam type . . . in defense of freedom and our country."[16] Nixon and Agnew dug their own corrupt political graves; hence, it was not until the 1980s that blame for defeat in Viet Nam began to be broadly associated with "negative" reporting by the "liberal media." While news reports especially on television in the wake of the Tet Offensive did have an impact on the public, the media did not lose the war. It merely began reporting more accurately on a war that was being lost without their help.

Closely associated with vilification of the media was the successful cultural project of discrediting the antiwar movement and blaming it, too, for the Indochina debacle. This stab-in-the-back thesis suggested that insufficiently patriotic forces at home—at best, "a misguided minority opposition . . . masterfully manipulated by Hanoi and Moscow," as General William Westmoreland put it—had undermined the nation's fighting men in the field.[17] A consensus began to take hold that "caricatured the antiwar paradigm by associating it with a flag-burning, America-hating procommunist radical fringe."[18] As a corollary, another remarkable national myth emerged to the effect that hundreds, if not thousands, of Vietnam veterans were spat on by uncivilized, long-haired protesters virtually from the moment they disembarked from their airplanes. Research by the Vietnam veteran Jerry Lembcke failed to unearth evidence that such sordid events ever actually occurred. However, he did find that "the spit almost always flew from pro-war right-wingers onto antiwar activists."[19]

By the end of the 1980s, the cultural repackaging of "Vietnam" had begun to establish hegemony over the history and memory of "America's longest war." As the war had now been depicted as noble, and defeat blamed on poor strategy, liberal reporting, and antiwar opposition, the original "lessons" of the war became marginalized. The reconstruction of Vietnam memory began with Jimmy Carter, who initially had condemned the war, which he blamed on the nation's "inordinate fear of communism." However, Carter at the same time set the tone for the ensuing decade of revisionism by asserting that the United States had pursued altruistic goals in Indochina. Moreover, Carter elided the unprecedented violence the United States had delivered in Indochina by declaring, "The destruction was mutual."[20]

As the history and memory of "Vietnam" were being repackaged, the United States resumed its normal interventionist course in foreign policy. Within five years of the U.S. defeat in Viet Nam, first Carter and then more aggressively Reagan intervened to roll back reformist governments in Central America. Despite the popular bumper-sticker warning "El Salvador Is Spanish for Vietnam," Reagan backed "death squads" in El Salvador and the "Contras," consisting mostly of remnants of the Somoza police-state regime in Nicaragua. Ultimately, the Iran-Contra scandal—and not the lessons of the failed Indochina intervention—slowed down the interventionist campaign to empower right-wing regimes in Central America. A similar pattern unfolded with respect to Afghanistan, as first Carter and then Reagan provided expansive military support to the mujahedin—Islamic reactionaries known as "freedom fighters" under U.S. national security discourse.

Thus, "Vietnam" brought no meaningful change in U.S. foreign policy. The United States did not send its own forces into either Central America or Afghanistan, but the nation had traditionally employed indirect and often covert means rather than direct intervention whenever possible. Indeed, the United States had long sought to contain communism in Indochina by indirect means until the situation in "South Vietnam" had deteriorated to the point at which direct intervention appeared requisite.

Any hope that the disastrous intervention in Indochina might fundamentally redirect U.S. foreign policy in a nonmilitary direction died in the desert sands of Iraq and Kuwait. George H. W. Bush unwittingly foreshadowed the revival of direct intervention by declaring in his inaugural address in 1989, "The final lesson of Vietnam is that no great nation can long afford to be sundered by a memory."[21] As the United States mobilized for the Persian Gulf War following Iraq's invasion of Kuwait in August 1990, the "lessons" of "Vietnam" surfaced immediately. Revealingly, however, those lessons augured for the more immediate and merciless use of military force, in contrast with "Vietnam incrementalism." The lesson of "Vietnam" was that the United States had been insufficiently militant. Other Vietnam lessons were at play, as well—notably, a policy that restricted the news media's access to the battlefield while simultaneously policing antiwar protesters on the home front.

As the massive U.S. invasion of Iraq unfolded, the nation's "smart bombs," their work graphically displayed by television networks that now functioned as tools of the militant state, completed the task of rehabilitating war within American culture. The boys returned home to glory rather than protest after crushing Saddam Hussein's forces. "By God," Bush exulted, "we finally kicked the Vietnam syndrome once and for all."[22] As in Indochina, of little interest to patriotic Americans was the devastation of Iraqi society, which would grow worse as the United States turned power back over to Saddam Hussein while maintaining the economic sanctions that contributed to the deaths of hundreds of thousands of Iraqis.

Viet Nam itself was quite familiar with geopolitical isolation and economic sanctions, having endured them at the behest of a vengeful America for more than twenty years. The United States froze Viet Nam's assets, precluded the International Monetary Fund and other agencies from lending money to Hanoi, and even tried unsuccessfully to keep Viet Nam from taking its seat in the United Nations. In 1979, when the Third Indochina War erupted, with Viet Nam and the Soviet Union aligned against China and the genocidal Cambodian regime, the United States backed the Khmer Rouge. Throughout the 1980s and well into the 1990s, elected officials who called for normalizing relations with Viet Nam risked being denounced by the POW/MIA lobby and challenged in the next political campaign.

The U.S. Congress remained meekly compliant throughout the 1980s but finally put the POW/MIA myth to rest, although the triangular black-and-white flag that it spawned can still be seen outside federal buildings and at other sites across the nation. In 1993, a thoroughgoing and bipartisan congressional investigation reported there was no evidence that "North Vietnam" had ever held prisoners following the Paris Peace Accords of 1973. The press summoned the nerve to weigh in, as the *Washington Post* reported that only "a handful of distressed and angry Americans" were holding up normalization.[23] As the dot-com age of globalization dawned, a consensus materialized that enabled Bill Clinton (though a "liberal draft dodger") to lift the U.S. economic embargo and move to normalize relations. Opposition remained, including from Clinton's opponent in 1996, Senator Robert Dole, but with the soft-drink and fast-food companies and other businesses eager to plunge more deeply into the Southeast Asian market, normalization prevailed at last. "Vietnam" remained a campaign issue well into the current century, however, and probably cost the Vietnam veteran and former antiwar activist John Kerry the presidential election in 2004. While Kerry shied away from his own antiwar past, fellow "swift boat veterans for truth" savaged him in television commercials on behalf of George W. Bush, who had used his father's political clout to flout the Selective Service System in Texas. The election in 2004 may have marked the high point—and, simultaneously, the low point—in the cultural process of sowing confusion and erasure in public memory of the Vietnam War.

While most Americans no longer think about Viet Nam, scholars and journalists are revealing disturbing new evidence of the depth of American malice there. It is becoming increasingly clear that we are being liberated from the hegemonic representations that viewed "Vietnam" only as a place where U.S. soldiers became victims while the people of Indochina remained invisible. For many years, vilification of the U.S. media and of the antiwar movement obscured the devastation of Indochina during a prolonged and viciously destructive war. Spurred in part by the Cambodian genocide, human rights consciousness and activism have grown steadily over the past generation. Genocidal violence in Cambodia, the former Yugoslavia, Rwanda, and Darfur has prompted the United Nations and nongovernmental organizations to analyze, condemn, and attempt to punish indiscriminate violence and crimes against humanity.[24]

Scholars and journalists operating in a climate more conducive to examining indiscriminate violence have focused attention on U.S. atrocities in Indochina. While most U.S. servicemen did not engage in atrocities (90 percent did not even engage in combat), and many were appalled by them and duly reported them, it is no longer possible to treat "My Lai" as an aberration. Research based on long-submerged military investigations is inexorably revealing that sexual assault, executions, and indiscriminate slaughter of Vietnamese civilians were far more widespread than previously acknowledged.

Despite myriad rapes, summary executions of both combatants and noncombatants, and other violations of the laws of war, virtually no one was prosecuted.[25] Legal challenges to prosecution existed, to be sure, but the larger concern was that prosecution of individual soldiers for war crimes would inevitably reveal that these crimes occurred in the context of orders to rack up body counts under the "mere gook rule" in which *any* dead Vietnamese was to be counted as an enemy combatant. Prosecution of U.S. war crimes thus would have implicated military and civilian officials at the highest levels and would have served as an indictment of the war itself in history and memory. To the twenty-year-old grunts, placed in an untenable combat role and under extreme psychic duress, distinctions among Vietnamese might quickly erode. The resort to extirpative war ensued, killing tens of thousands of Vietnamese and ruining the lives of many of the U.S. veterans who encountered extreme challenges in moving on with their lives after engaging in, witnessing, or being associated with the atrocious wartime conduct.[26]

An increasing research focus on the impact of the American war on Indochinese society will shed more light on bombing, artillery strikes, and the use of defoliants in the U.S. campaign of chemical warfare.[27] More and more scholars are going beyond Washington, Austin, Paris, and London and are taking up residence in Hanoi, Ho Chi Minh City, Beijing, Moscow, and Phnom Penh, as well as in the homes of U.S. veterans and of Vietnamese villagers. More cultural, comparative, and conceptual work will follow as scholars move beyond reliance on government documents alone.

As we begin to learn more about the impact of U.S. violence in Indochina, we can begin to rewrite the American cultural history of "Vietnam." In so doing, there is the hope that we can replace erasure and apologia with reckoning and reconciliation so that we might learn from the past and transcend its brutal legacies.

Notes

1. Along these same lines, David W. P. Elliott has noted, "For America, the Vietnam War was never about Vietnam, but always about some larger abstraction of concern to the United States": Elliott, "Official History, Revisionist History, and Wild History," 295. See also Franklin, *Vietnam and Other American Fantasies*; Hagopian, *The Vietnam War in American Memory*. To cite a revealing example of how the phenomenon can play out culturally, Scott Laderman's analysis of the comment books at the War Remnants Museum in Ho Chi Minh City revealed that many visi-

tors from the United States had so thoroughly internalized their own nation's hegemonic discourse of "Vietnam" as a crusade for freedom, which had primarily victimized *Americans*, that many appeared shocked at what the museum's exhibitions showed had been done to Indochina. "So marginalized had the deeper imperialist critique of many historians become in American popular discourse," Laderman notes, "that many visitors appeared to be simply unaware of it": Laderman, "The Other Side of the War," 194.

2. I elaborate on this argument in Hixson, *The Myth of American Diplomacy*.

3. The literature on U.S. intervention is, of course, huge, and much of it is redundant. Some of the more useful works on the origins and escalation of the American War are Bradley, *Imagining Vietnam and America*; Statler, *Replacing France*; Lawrence, *Assuming the Burden*; Rotter, *The Path to Vietnam*; Logevall, *Choosing War*; Preston, *The War Council*.

4. A notable recent exception focused on the postwar era is Martini, *Invisible Enemies*.

5. Elliott, "Official History, Revisionist History, and Wild History," 292. See also Prados, *Vietnam*.

6. Mark Bradley, "Introduction," in Bradley and Young, *Making Sense of the Vietnam Wars*, 10.

7. Hirschman et al., "Vietnamese Casualties during the American War."

8. Quinn-Judge, "Through a Glass Darkly," 131.

9. Quoted in Kaplan and Pease, *Cultures of United States Imperialism*, 583. See also Keith Beattie's stimulating study, *The Scar That Binds*.

10. For an account of the apogee of American violence from the air, and the indifference of Nixon and Kissinger to the destruction, see Randolph, *Powerful and Brutal Weapons*.

11. Martini, *Invisible Enemies*, 43.

12. Allen, *Until the Last Man Comes Home*. See also Franklin, *M.I.A.*

13. Quoted in Hixson, *Myth of American Diplomacy*, 258.

14. For a comprehensive overview of the Vietnam films, see Devine, *Vietnam at 24 Frames a Second*.

15. Martini, *Invisible Enemies*, 207.

16. Beattie, *The Scar That Binds*, 21.

17. Ibid.

18. McMahon, "The Vietnam War and American Society," 175.

19. Lembcke, *The Spitting Image*.

20. Herring, *America's Longest War*; McMahon, "The Vietnam War and American Society," 166–68.

21. Martini, *Invisible Enemies*, 162.

22. Hixson, *Myth of American Diplomacy*, 171.

23. Martini, *Invisible Enemies*, 194.

24. From an extensive literature, see Kiernan, *Blood and Soil*; Power, "A Prob-

lem from Hell"; Mann, *The Dark Side of Democracy*. On human rights, see Ishay, *The History of Human Rights*; Donnelly, *Universal Human Rights in Theory and Practice*; Moyn, *The Last Utopia*.

25. On this point, see Barnett, *Atrocity and American Military Justice in Southeast Asia*, as well as the works cited in the next endnote.

26. See the devastating accounts in Greiner, *War without Fronts*; Nelson, *The War behind Me*; Sallah and Weiss, *Tiger Force*; Turse, *Kill Anything That Moves*. My Lai has spurred a vast literature. Two of the best, with divergent perspectives, are Bilton and Sim, *Four Hours at My Lai*; and Oliver, *The My Lai Massacre in American History and Memory*.

27. On Agent Orange, see Martini, *Agent Orange*.

CHAPTER 3

"The Mainspring in This
Country Has Been Broken"
America's Battered Sense
of Self and the Emergence
of the Vietnam Syndrome

Alexander Bloom

In April 1975, the same month that Saigon fell and the Vietnam War came
to an end, Americans tuned in for one of the first major events of their bicentennial celebration. President Gerald Ford came to Massachusetts for
the commemoration of the Battle of Lexington and Concord. Ford hung
a lantern in the belfry of Old North Church. He reviewed a contingent
of citizens dressed in colonial military uniforms marching on Lexington
Common. But the end of the Vietnam War was as much on his mind as
the beginnings of the American Revolution. "It is time to place the hand
of healing over the heart of America," he told a crowd in Concord.[1] Yet,
despite his own hopes, Ford later told the American Society of Newspaper
Editors that "the United States did not carry out its commitment in supplying military hardware and economic aid" to the South Vietnamese.
"If we had," he argued, "this present tragic situation in South Vietnam
would not have occurred." Mike Mansfield, the Democratic Senate majority leader, responded that Ford's accusation was "a distortion so immense that it borders on the irrational."[2] The fighting in Viet Nam might
have ended. The war, at least at home, would go on.

As the nation looked to celebrate its two-hundredth anniversary, the
contrast between the idealism embodied in the Bicentennial and the
dispiriting mood created by Vietnam and the Watergate scandal embodied the internal uneasiness of the nation. "If the Bicentennial helps

us focus on the contrast between our idealism and our crimes," the *New Republic* editorialized, "so much the better."[3] For Daniel Ellsberg, the coincidence of these events was even stronger: "It was the will of the American people, expressed to Congress, that ended this war now. That's the best possible celebration of the Bicentennial of the American Revolution that I can imagine."[4]

OVER THE LAST QUARTER OF THE TWENTIETH CENTURY and the first decade of the twenty-first century, the shadow of Vietnam continued to hang over American life, from U.S. foreign policy and domestic politics to the personal attitudes of individual American citizens. This haunting aura of the war in Indochina took on a name of its own—the "Vietnam syndrome"—describing the cynical, frustrated, and pessimistic sense with which America approached the world. This troubled Americans deeply, as they feared that their vaunted sense of mission had given way to feelings of limitations and hesitancy. Every subsequent international success was hailed not only for its own achievement, but also as a demonstration that the nation had finally put Vietnam behind it. But as William Faulkner had written years before, "The past is never dead. It's not even past." This was never so true as after Vietnam.

While it took some time for the notion of a "Vietnam syndrome" to coalesce within the culture, it is clear that the first stirrings of this attitude began almost immediately with the end of the war. Elements were even beginning to emerge before American troops had come home for good. "Back in another America, people used to dance in the streets when a President declared the end of a war," *Newsweek* observed in May 1975.[5] Instead, after Vietnam a random and impressionistic, but heartfelt, array of observations emerged about a nation trying to cope with a loss Americans once could not have envisioned but that nonetheless now stared them squarely in the face. Those responses contained the first signs of a perspective that would dominate the national mood for the next three decades.

THE UNITED STATES HAD NEVER CONCLUDED A WAR the way the one in Viet Nam ended. There was no victory, not even a sense of relief. For some, the end seemed inevitable; for others, desirable. No one was surprised. The time that Americans expected victory or thought their military was invincible had long since passed. "Perhaps long ago in the early days of the war," David Halberstam wrote in 1975, "there was some element of misguided idealism for the war. But that was long ago."[6] For years Americans had watched the nightly news, with its images of a war they could not win. For years public opinion surveys had registered the criticisms of a majority of American citizens about the war effort. The impact of the war and the debate about its meaning had spread across the American landscape.

Now it was over, and Americans began the task of trying to figure out what it all meant. Dean Rusk, secretary of state under President John F. Kennedy and President Lyndon B. Johnson and one of the war's central planners, observed, "It may take twenty-five or thirty years before one can make a real judgment where the course of wisdom lay, either in getting in or getting out." Political and cultural analyst Garry Wills thought differently: "It will take some people twenty-five or thirty years to discover what was always wrong about our presence there. . . . It should have taken about twenty-five minutes."[7]

It was not just the politicians and the military planners who struggled to make sense out of the end of the war. Vietnam veteran Don Parrish recalled that "on the day that Saigon fell, I got a real empty feeling. . . . That really took the wind out of the sails, and I had lots of problems with it. . . . We knew it was happening, it was gonna happen, and it did happen, but I still couldn't believe it."[8] Former POW Dennis Chambers concluded, "We blew it. . . . We should not have ended up on the roof of the goddamned American Embassy. . . . We got our ankles kicked by a bunch of midgets."[9] Fred Terhune, a wounded former Green Beret, put it succinctly: "the mainspring in this country has been broken."[10]

> My grandfather's generation fought in the war to end all wars.
> My father's generation fought in the war to rid the world of fascists.
> My generation fought in Vietnam to—to what?
> —W. D. Ehrhart, *In the Shadow of Vietnam*, 49

LONG BEFORE SAIGON FELL, long before Richard Nixon declared that America had achieved "peace with honor," American soldiers had been coming home from Viet Nam. Soldiers fought in Viet Nam as they had fought no previous American war. During the Second World War, one enlisted or was drafted for the duration. In Viet Nam, a stint in the Army was two years, with one year "in country." As soon as they arrived, soldiers began counting down the days until they would leave — and envying those who went home sooner. "I always stand and watch a 707 make that beautiful left bank and take off. I know it's going home, 200 GIs aboard, all of them reborn."[11] But it was an unexpected rebirth they would encounter. The juxtaposition between war zone and home town often proved disconcerting. "I was killing gooks in the Delta, and seventy-two hours later I'm in bed with my wife," one veteran recalled.[12] Jan Scruggs, who would later lead the movement to build the Vietnam Veterans Memorial, has summarized the experience of returning home: "They put you on an air conditioned plane with smiling stewardesses, and suddenly the war was over." He tells of one young soldier's experience: "'Wash up,' [his] mother said. 'Your welcome-home dinner is just about ready.' He looked at his hands. Mud from Vietnam was still under his fingernails."[13] This new form of military engagement and disconnection would create a very different battlefront and home-front situation for the veterans, their families, and all of the citizens back home. Young soldiers always seemed to be going off to war or coming home from war. And they were.

AMERICAN SOLDIERS HAD, OF COURSE, come home from wars before, sometimes even during the fighting. Furloughed soldiers during the Second World War often found it difficult to talk about their experiences. There was "the 'silent soldier' tradition after the last war," historian Dixon Wecter noted in 1944. "On the other hand, parading his memories before those who obviously do not understand is even worse. . . . Often he feels a curious sense of guilt, found only in the furloughs of wartime: here he is, being made much over, wasting time, escaping from danger and death, while his buddies in the foxholes or in the thick of flak continue to take it." However, Wecter concluded, "Most of these irritants are of course short-lived, and once the war is over will evaporate even more quickly, as returnees forget in the sheer happiness of being home for good."[14] Vietnam veterans often felt exactly the opposite.

Part of the overall American mythology of its wars extended beyond the nation's commitment to fight only just wars and to do so only when called on to save others. Sometimes, in this glorified history, the war saved young Americans, as well. War made boys into men, decidedly *American boys* into *American men*. "He makes a good fighting man, but rarely loses amateur standing," Wecter concluded in 1944. He remained "a homesick hero" bound "by what Lincoln called the mystic chords of memory to the old farm and village and hearthside." And most important, "Once the job is done, a few months out of uniform probably erase most of the marks, heal the bruises and scars, of his service. He is not quite the same fellow as before, but more resemblances appear than differences." In fact, the chance to go to war might fix the small problems that had cropped up in adolescence. "Many a veteran's return from war means a fresh start in life. . . . If he had been a loafer, the local no-good, he may find his slate wiped more or less clean."[15]

These images remained strong throughout the Second World War and into the postwar years, reinforcing all of the other myths about the meaning of that war. Even an experience like the Korean War, which might have reconfigured the popular stereotypes created by the Second World War, was quickly forgotten. The Second World War had been the good war, providing Americans with an image of virtue and victory they would carry into the Cold War era. Americans might have learned lessons from Korea that would have aided the reactions to Vietnam. Instead, they chose to ignore what they might have learned. If considered at all, Korea came to be seen as an odd aberration in the postwar world of American exceptionalism.[16]

What could have been avoided from the Korean experience was unavoidable with Vietnam. For Vietnam veterans, rather than "wiping the slate clean," as Wecter suggested the Second World War had done for its soldiers, Vietnam became a badge—and not a particularly positive one—pinned to these young men. Rather than "irritants evaporating," the postwar home-front experience only magnified the alienation and difficulty many began to feel while still in Vietnam. And even within the world of American war veterans, the Vietnam soldiers often felt slighted. One Vietnam veteran recalls sitting among Second World War vets at an American Legion Hall. "I found myself listening to middle-aged men telling me how it was in a 'real war.' They didn't know or care about what we went through."[17] Another vet recalls how discussion of this topic went beyond lack of interest or patronization. "Why," he was asked by one Second World War vet, "didn't we just drop an A-bomb on the chinks and get it over with? Everyone seemed to agree." The Vietnam vet recalled being a little tired, and possibly a little high; he told the fellow to shut up. . . . So he started telling them about what he had seen—about the long lines of refugees, what white phosphorous and gunships and napalm really did. Suddenly one of them reached across the table and hit him below the eye, on the cheek. Another jumped him and held on while the first man hit him again and again. Then both of them picked him up and threw him outside. His nose was running blood and his face hurt badly. "Too bad you weren't killed over there, you fucking Red," one of them said.[18]

One veteran summarized the comparative experiences of the Second World War and Vietnam veterans: "Our war was different. They didn't know how I felt about it; besides, when they came home, bands played and there were parades."[19]

> I had thought there would be a parade with banners when
> I returned. . . . I thought confetti would be thrown. . . .
> [T]hat's what I had dreamed about.
> —Eddie Graham, quoted in Mark Gerzon, *A Choice of Heroes*, 44

THE NOTION OF THE VIETNAM VETERANS returning home without a victory parade became both an actual and a symbolic way to describe their homecoming experience—actually a metaphor for the entire experience. There were some parades, and many veterans came home to warm family and community welcomes. But most recall leaving Viet Nam, even as the war raged beneath them, with a sense of relief and joy. "The second that bird lifted off the ground," one soldier recalled, "about 160 people just shouted—we were so happy."[20] Instead of a parade, a number of soldiers recall shedding their Vietnam identity as quickly as possible: "We got home and went into the airport. We went into the bathroom and there was uniforms scattered all over. Guys were just leaving them there. We threw ours away, put on civilian clothes and never mentioned Vietnam again." Another recalls seeing "40 uniforms stuffed in the urinals and toilets with Silver Stars on them, Purple Hearts, it didn't matter."[21]

For most soldiers, it was a steak dinner and then home, minimal gestures that proved empty. "You walked in and got your steak and your baked potato. That's your thanks from the United States government— you get a steak, cooked just the way you want it! So you ate your steak, and went back, and smoked some more pot, because everyone had more pot."[22] For another, the steak dinner seemed to epitomize all that was wrong with the American approach: "So when you first got off the airplane . . . there's a sign that sets up there . . . it says, 'Welcome Back, Soldier, America's Proud of You.' Huh? That's incredible that sign. 'Cause that's all there is—that sign. That's all there are—those words. And they're empty. And no steak dinner and no amount of words written in red are going to prove anything different."[23]

Myra MacPherson concluded in 1984, from her numerous interviews with Vietnam vets, that one theme "encountered in every veteran I have ever met is searing anger at their homecoming—of being shunned, of having to expunge the most indelible year from their lives, of having to become 'closet' vets. And for many there is the depression that comes from the feeling that it was all a waste."[24]

For many of these vets, the postwar experiences could be summed up in the mundane, as well as the dramatic. One vet described what, finally, the end of the war meant to him: "Peace for the ordinary servicemen . . . has involved waiting in an employment line; a runaround from public agencies while trying to get a job; getting into and paying for school; and avoiding the war news in the newspapers."[25] By 1980, just before these vets would become part of the Reagan-era attempt to revise the history and meaning of the war, pollster Louis Harris surveyed American military veterans, finding that half of the younger veterans reported that they were "not always proud to wear [their] uniform in public places." In an odd twist, Harris discovered in 1979 that antiwar activists had warmer feelings toward Vietnam veterans than congressional leaders.[26]

These young men and women had gone off with a vague notion of defending America and its values, although the direct threat was never that clear, and the values were hardly reinforced in Viet Nam. Instead, they returned to an America they often did not recognize. Veteran Allan Wyscarver described this disorientation using popular culture termi-nology: "America and Americans somehow seemed to have changed. I couldn't put my finger on just exactly what was different, but I felt like I was an alien from another planet. People seemed less friendly, less open, and less human. They would stare at you as if you were possessed. I even thought a couple of times that I wasn't actually heading home—that I was in the 'Twilight Zone,' and that I would wake up and be back in Vietnam."[27]

"We went to Vietnam as frightened, lonely young men," remembers

William Jayne. "We came back, alone again, as immigrants to a new world."[28] America had become a different place, largely transformed by the Vietnam War experience itself. Ironically and perversely, the veterans of that war felt they had little place within this new world.

> The disastrous events of the last month in Southeast Asia are not only an appalling human tragedy for the peoples of Cambodia and South Vietnam, they are the most serious defeat of Western Christendom in a generation, and the final requiem of the United States as a great power.
> — Alexander McColl, *Soldier of Fortune*, in James William Gibson, *Warrior Dreams*, 28

FOR MUCH OF ITS HISTORY Americans proudly proclaimed that the United States had never lost a war. Once they knew they had, Americans, as a people, had no national vocabulary with which to phrase the discussion. This might have left them speechless. Instead, Americans said lots of things. In different ways and from different perspectives, political analysts and cultural commentators all chimed in on the basic premise that something about the country was terribly broken. What needed repair, as well as how to fix it, became the first topic of analysis.

In the immediate aftermath of the fall of South Vietnam, it seemed that everyone was called on to offer some assessment, to measure the damage, and to suggest where the nation was headed. Daily newspapers, weekly newsmagazines, and journals of political and cultural opinion were filled with postmortems. Reporters interviewed policymakers and average citizens, soldiers who had returned from Southeast Asia, and individuals who had fought against the war at home. There seemed no area of American life that had not been affected and that would not be altered in the future because of the Vietnam experience.

For some, the end was comparable to other great defeats in history. "It was like being at Waterloo," CBS reporter Ed Bradley later recalled of the last days of the war. "Nothing else in my lifetime was as important as . . . Vietnam. It was such a tragedy."[29] For historian Christopher Lasch, writing in the left-leaning *New York Review of Books* in June 1975, the meaning of the loss would shape the future identity of the United States: "Any lingering illusions that this was to be the American century have been shattered by the collapse of anti-communism in Southeast Asia."[30] At the other end of the political spectrum, the view was no better. In the conservative *National Review*, Anthony Bouscaren observed that "America has become a simpering, defeatist, isolationist nation. The damage done to America by the Vietnam debacle is inestimable." The future looked bleak to Bouscaren: "America is going into a national eclipse, and it is going away willingly. . . . America has lost its honor, and no one cares about that either."[31] *Newsweek* opined, "Such is the legacy of Vietnam: a bitter remembrance of things past that is sure to haunt the future."[32]

A few voices were unequivocal, if disappointed. General William Westmoreland, the former American commander, noted, "It was a sad day in the glorious history of our country. . . . We failed. We let an ally down." William Bundy, a foreign-policy adviser in the Kennedy and Johnson administrations, cautioned against overdoing the self-criticism: "Because we lost we shouldn't beat our breast. It was a close choice with moral factors on both sides."[33] But the chorus of critical analysts drowned these voices out. *Time* magazine editorialized what many Americans were feeling: "It is now almost universally conceded that the American intervention in Vietnam was a mistake—a mistake that involved four Presidents, many of the nation's top statesmen." The fault, *Time's* editors argued, lay with "an American inability to accept defeat, or a hypnotic preoccupation with the models of previous, simpler wars. There was no precedent to quote, no guide book to lead the way out."[34]

Calling Vietnam a "mistake," however, was only one way to assess the situation, perhaps the kindest of the criticisms. In the first outpouring of analysis, many of the general themes that would be sounded over the next twenty-five years found their initial articulation. Some moved well beyond the idea that Vietnam was a "mistake" to much harsher conclusions. Journalist J. M. Cameron believed that "the lesson of the war is not that it turned out to be a mistake," but instead that "it was a vicious and immoral war in which the means employed bore no proportion to the (variously and incoherently stated) objectives of the war." Objecting to those who said that the United States had shown restraint in Viet Nam, Cameron contended that, while "North Vietnam wasn't bombed back into the Stone Age . . . , the reasoning behind the talk of restraint is curious. If a superpower does not use nuclear bombs or if it doesn't use conventional weapons to bring about the total destruction of civilian lives and property it is said to be exercising restraint. The corruption of the mind and heart represented by such an argument is the worst consequence of the war for the United States."[35]

During the war, many people in the growing opposition had fastened on to the views of J. William Fulbright of Arkansas, chair of the Senate Foreign Relations Committee. Fulbright's televised committee hearings had helped awaken the American public to the realities of Vietnam war policy and offered moderate critics a forum to express their reservations about the war. Fulbright increasingly spoke about the limitations imposed by our national arrogance and, in the days immediately following the collapse of South Vietnam, reiterated that notion: "Americans have assumed a certain godliness, a certain feeling that everything we did was just wonderful while everyone else was either bad or questionable." Part of that arrogant attitude was also tinged with racist cultural views, "a contemptuous, supercilious attitude—calling the other side 'gooks' and 'charlies.'"[36] In the pages of the *New Republic*, Anthony Lewis, a columnist for the *New York Times*, echoed Fulbright's worries about the costs of American arrogance. Americans had to come to terms, Lewis argued, with the "painful awareness of our hubris—the overweening arrogance that made us persist for so long in pursuit of folly, and to make policy not in terms of horror visited on the people of Indochina but in terms of our image, our face."[37] This second general theme—that of a nation failing because of its blind commitment to its own self-image and notions of how the world should operate—found many adherents in the postmortems of 1975.

A major element of the arrogant American attitude about the rest of the world came to be understood as its ignorance of the cultures and histories of other, especially non-Western peoples. Twenty years later, Robert McNamara would admit as much in his memoirs, but in 1975 this idea was only beginning to work its way into American consciousness. The noted China scholar John K. Fairbank wrote in 1975 what McNamara would only publicly admit in 1995: "The root cause of our Vietnam failure was thus the profound American cultural ignorance of Vietnamese history, values, problems, and motives when we originally went to the aid of the French in Vietnam after World War II." To Fairbank, "The worst evil of such ignorance was that it left Vietnam faceless and speechless, an almost meaningless object to be manipulated by us for our own power-politics purposes." This myopia had serious consequences. "This cultural ignorance leads on to imperialistic exploitation," Fairbank contended, "disregarding the interests of the local people as they see them in their cultural terms and imposing upon their situation our view of the world as seen in our cultural terms. . . . Lesson two: Our values are not those of everyone."[38]

Conversely, there were also hints of emerging counterarguments, certainly less prominent and finding fewer sympathetic ears in the wake of the defeat, but there nonetheless. One analyst cautioned against an emerging "rightwing myth, being promoted by Barry Goldwater, among others, that civilians would not allow the military to win the war." This would find renewed articulation in the 1980s as part of the attempt to revise the history of the war in the Reagan years.[39] Another observer cautioned that "the very people who warned us most solemnly about the peril of a rightwing backlash should we 'bug out,' are now busy trying to provoke it."[40]

The final thread to emerge in the end-of-the-war discussion came not from critics or supporters who wanted to remember the lessons of Vietnam but from those who wanted to forget. This may have been strongest among the soldiers themselves. "It is not really surprising that those who fought in Vietnam no longer . . . care what happened there," Ronald Steel wrote in the *New Republic*. "They want to expunge it from their minds, to be done with it, to pretend . . . that it never happened."[41]

AMID THE RELIEF, the exhaustion, and its unfulfilling resolution, the Vietnam postmortems laid out in random, impressionistic, and, despite academic or legalist phrasing, emotive styles the ideas of a nation coming out of something it never fully understood. Hints of debates to come could be found in all of these expressions. These were merely the first step. "Now the next question becomes real to us," Norman Mailer concluded. "Do we recover from Vietnam? The answer is most certainly yes. We will recover. . . . But we will never be the same."[42]

> The age of innocence is over now, and no one—not even Gerald Ford—
> still claims to be able to see a light at the end of the tunnel.
> —Adam Yarmolinsky, "Myths and Interests," *The New Republic*,
> 3 May 1975

BETWEEN THE ELECTIONS OF 1972 AND 1976, America went reeling. The fighting in Viet Nam came to an end—for the U.S. soldiers, with the "peace with honor" withdrawal in 1973, and for the Vietnamese, with the surrender of Saigon a little more than two years later. Compounding the loss, both the president and vice president of the United States resigned in disgrace. The scandal that enveloped the president obsessed the nation for twenty months, as the crimes of Watergate unfolded before Americans' eyes. As the United States prepared to enter its bicentennial year with citizens' morale at low ebb, "doubt, gloom, pessimism and suspicion clouded and colored collective thinking," observed reporter Kandy Stroud.[43] Pollster Pat Caddell, surveying American attitudes on behalf of several political candidates, found that basic values had been battered. "Perhaps most important," Caddell concluded, "the overriding belief that we were a nation of special people, that we could always bend events to our will, that things in America always got better. . . . [t]oday, most people no longer accept that cherished notion."[44] The first post-Vietnam era had begun.

Maybe that cherished notion could have been saved in 1968. Maybe if Robert Kennedy or Eugene McCarthy had won the presidency and withdrawn the troops. Maybe if Richard Nixon's "secret plan" had been an actual end to the war instead of merely turning the ground fighting back over to the South Vietnamese. Maybe if all of the other blows and tragedies had not followed one upon the other in the wake of the end of the war in Southeast Asia. Had Watergate not tainted the domestic political scene. Had the vice president not also resigned in disgrace. Had the economy not begun to sour in 1970. Had Americans not watched as energy prices skyrocketed and then had they not had to sit in long lines during the few hours each day when service stations sold gasoline. Maybe without all these blows, or if the troops had been brought home five years earlier, Americans could have come out of the Asian war less battered, less self-critical, less cynical, less pessimistic. But they didn't. By the time the troops and the POWs came home, by the time the South Vietnamese leaders had fled the country, by the time North Vietnamese tanks drove into Saigon, American attitudes had taken on a new tone. And it was not a happy one.

Everywhere people looked, they found signs of Americans' disenchantment with their government, with their leaders, with the institutions of the society, and even with the possibilities of their own futures. At the center of this growing cynicism was the Vietnam experience. Assessments ranged from academic analysis to the views of people on the street. Sheldon Wolin of Princeton University concluded at the end of the war that America faced "a dramatic and qualitative break in [its] history. We have moved from a society of free choice and opportunity to a society shaped by necessity."[45] A car salesman in Riverdale, New York, told journalist Peter Osnos, "The war weakened the cement that has always bound us together, the mortar has been kind of jarred loose by this war. The general faith in institutions of our country has been shaken." Osnos summarized his numerous interview responses: "Vietnam had caused considerable disillusionment with government and other 'institutions'— particularly diminishing belief in the wisdom and truthfulness at the top levels of Washington officialdom."[46]

The Survey Research Center at the University of Michigan had been studying public opinion during each of the election cycles from 1964 to 1970. Political scientist Arthur H. Miller brought these data together in 1974 in the article "Political Issues and Trust in Government." His general conclusion of "widespread discontent" also found that "distrust of the government is not related to party identification but to policy dissatisfaction." The solution did not lie with the return to power of one party or the other. Republicans and Democrats were equally responsible. The cynicism cut across class lines, race differences, regional divides. "What is startling," Miller concluded, "is the rapid degree of change . . . over a period of six years."[47] Those were the very years Americans began to turn against the government's policies on Vietnam.

Things did not improve in the early 1970s, either. A Harris Poll taken in 1973 found that the number of Americans feeling "alienated" and "disaffected" had climbed from 29 percent in 1966 to 50 percent. The number jumped to 55 percent after Gerald Ford pardoned Richard Nixon a year later. A *New York Times* survey concluded that, by 1975, Americans felt "a substantial decline in optimism about the future."[48] "There was in Riverdale," Osnos concluded about the people he spoke with in one community, "an unmistakable sense of disillusionment, a tarnished view of America and a new—or at least redoubled—wariness of the instruments and personalities responsible for the nation's destiny."[49]

GERALD FORD SENSED THIS ANGST, although he never expressed it with the philosophic or religious rhetoric that others, such as Jimmy Carter, would later employ. President Ford's favorite word during his first months in office in 1974 was "healing"; he would later title his presidential memoir *A Time to Heal*. Ford entered the White House to a collective sigh of relief from the American people. During his first weeks he strove, through symbolic moments, to give Americans a sense of a fresh breeze blowing through Washington. In contrast to the closed and guarded style of the

Nixon administration, Ford seemed open and available. Ford let reporters follow him through a typical day, the public seeing him toast his own English muffin for breakfast or take his daily swim in the White House pool. In the days just before and after Nixon's resignation, reporters camped outside Ford's home in suburban Washington, D.C., filmed him coming out in his bathrobe and slippers to bring in the morning papers. His first White House dinner, just days into his administration, found former Nixon critics on the guest list. Ford and his wife, Betty, danced into the night to "Bad, Bad, Leroy Brown" and other popular songs. Republican Senator Mark Hatfield, a prominent critic of the Vietnam War, yelled out during the dancing, "Happy New Year!"[50]

The honeymoon lasted a month. On 8 September, Ford announced "a full, free, and absolute pardon" of Richard Nixon. Overnight, Ford's approval ratings dropped from 66 percent to 49 percent. His reputation never fully recovered.

> America lost her virginity in Vietnam
> (And she caught the clap, too)
> That's nothing—so did I
> I did too, but now I watch who I go out with
> So should America
> —Graffiti on a latrine wall in Viet Nam, John Clark Pratt,
> *Vietnam Voices*, 15

NO ASPECT OF AMERICAN LIFE SUFFERED as serious a blow as a result of Vietnam as American foreign policy. In the post–Second World War years, the United States had trumpeted its system and its values as the path to follow in the modern world. Its communist adversaries were totalitarian and duplicitous. The United States stood for virtue, democracy, and self-determination. Communists were portrayed as murderers; Americans saved lives. Communists subjected populations; Americans liberated them. America was about openness; the Soviets and their client states were about secrecy. The American system was the one that would best serve the people of the underdeveloped world. The American flag was the flag flown in heaven.

Vietnam proved a sobering wake-up call. Presidents lied. Optimistic proclamations contradicted pessimistic behind-the-scenes assessments. Failed policies led to countless and unnecessary American deaths. For many, if the United States were to venture into the world again, it should be with the chastened awareness that Vietnam provided. "We must recognize," Chester Cooper, a former member of the National Security Council staff, wrote in May 1975, "that American military assistance cannot compensate for fatal political weakness. And before we once again commit our troops to battle, we must reckon the total cost of the war: the maimed, the dead—and the prisoners."[51]

Americans turned away from their post–Second World War willingness to intervene, even to spend American dollars abroad. Opinion polls found hesitancy on the part of the American people to become involved in the ways they had before. A Harris Poll of 1975 suggested that 65 percent of Americans opposed military aid abroad "because they feel it allows dictatorships to maintain control over their population." Other surveys suggested an unwillingness to come to the aid of foreign countries, even when attacked by outside forces. Noting that Americans were now unwilling to fight to protect an ally, South Korea, Senator John Culver of Iowa concluded, "Vietnam has taken a mighty toll on the national will of the American people."[52]

Secretary of State Henry Kissinger, a holdover from the Nixon administration, felt that what the nation needed was not a revised foreign policy vision; it needed to "carry out an act somewhere in the world which shows its determination to continue to be a world power." Kissinger's view resonated with that of Ford's Secretary of Defense James Schlesinger, who was reported to be "generally gloomy," feeling "the world no longer regarded American military power as awesome."[53]

On 12 May 1975, just weeks after the fall of Saigon, Kissinger, Schlesinger, and their boss, Gerald Ford, got their chance to reassert American power in the world. Sailing between Saigon and Thailand, a private American merchant vessel, the *Mayagüez*, was seized by the new Khmer Rouge government in Cambodia and forced to a remote sea island port. Ford, likely still smarting from a denial of funds for continued assistance in Viet Nam, declared resolutely, "I can assure you that, irrespective of Congress, we will move." The National Security Council debated the nature of the response, with Kissinger and Vice President Nelson Rockefeller suggesting B-52 bomber strikes on the Cambodian mainland. Schlesinger, arguing that this would be excessive, counseled only a rescue mission, without bombings. Ford opted for a middle path, with American planes attacking

Cambodian patrol boats in the area, a few strikes on the mainland to prevent reinforcements from sailing to the island, and a Marine rescue mission to free the ship and its forty-member crew. Before the troops could initiate this mission, however, the Cambodians released the crew.[54]

In the immediate wake of the Vietnam debacle, the voices of praise rang through the nation. "It's good to win one for a change," exulted Representative Carroll Hubbard of Kentucky.[55] Ford's poll numbers rose. The *New York Times* editorialized that Ford had "no alternative but to employ direct military means. . . . This he did with exemplary speed."[56] One newsmagazine called the action "a daring show of nerve and steel."[57] The influential *New York Times* columnist James Reston concluded, "The Administration almost seems grateful for the opportunity to demonstrate that the President can act quickly. . . . Officials here have been bridling over a host of silly taunts about the American 'paper tiger' and hope the Marines have answered the charge."[58] "It was wonderful," Senator Barry Goldwater of Arizona declared. "It shows we've still got balls in this country."[59]

What could not be known in May 1975 was that the reaction to the *Mayagüez* incident initiated a pattern that would emerge in nearly every foreign policy encounter Americans would undertake over the next quarter-century. At each of these moments, the success of a mission was declared, usually with words of hyperbole that went well beyond the significance of the immediate incident. In addition, each encounter would be proclaimed as not only resolving a particular situation, but as the cure for the disaster of Vietnam. America would "win one for a change."

Yet Vietnam would haunt the analysis of any action, just as it framed the responses. After noting Kissinger's curious statement about the *Mayagüez* incident—"We are not going around looking for opportunities to prove our manhood"—journalist Lucy Komisar concluded, "Our leaders did it all over again, in miniature and in caricature, landing troops on a tiny island and bombing the Cambodian mainland to erase the 'humiliation' to this country."[60]

The story of the *Mayagüez* only grew worse as details of events unfolded. Diplomatic efforts, it turned out, were well under way when Ford ordered the landing of the U.S. Marines. Those negotiations, not the threat of American power, had led to the release of the crew. The island chosen for the rescue mission turned out not to be the one where the crew was being held. A helicopter, bringing troops into position for the landing, crashed, killing twenty-three soldiers. In the end, forty-one Americans died and forty-nine were wounded in an unnecessary effort to save forty Americans, who were sailing to freedom when the military actions began.

Four months later, assessing the entire incident, journalist Walter Pincus concluded that "President Ford and his spokesmen tried to make a silk purse out of a sow's ear when they described the *Mayagüez* affair as a regenerative turning point in the country's post-Vietnam recovery of national confidence." In fact, he concluded, the encounter could best be seen as a "botched military operation in which the world's strongest nation lucked out against the world's newest and probably weakest."[61] At the first anniversary of the incident, columnist Anthony Lewis, writing in the *New York Times*, concluded that "Ford and his men were not interested in the facts—or in the lives they might lose. They were interested in flexing American muscles. They wanted to use the occasion for a show of 'strength.' That is why they used a sledgehammer, hastily, to crack a peanut."[62]

During Vietnam, Congress had passed restrictions on the president's war-making abilities, including requiring congressional authorization for many military actions. It had failed to hold the Ford administration to these requirements. Lewis called Congress "spineless" in the *Mayagüez* encounter. After the fact, Congress initiated a study of the incident. The report, published in the fall of 1976, reaffirmed all of the critical assessments that had emerged since the actual events. The best reply the administration could muster to the report was the comment by Ford's press secretary that the administration "disagreed" with the conclusion and the accusation by Kissinger's deputy, Lawrence Eagleburger, that the timing of the report was intended to aid the Democratic nominee, Jimmy Carter, and embarrass the president on the eve of a presidential debate about foreign policy.[63] Thus, in the first moment that Americans stepped into the world after the fall of Saigon, their best intentions turned again into their worst nightmare. American planning seemed ill advised. American soldiers died unnecessarily. The power of the United States in the world was made to look weak. And the American people were once again provided with the specter of their government proclaiming great victories and a reassertion of American prestige, only to have actual events prove the conclusions exaggerated, the details less admirable, and the results only compounding American cynicism. Unfortunately, the *Mayagüez* would only be the first of a long series of these kinds of foreign policy moments.

> This may be the first time in our history when it is better to run for
> President as a peanut farmer from Plains, Georgia than as a United States
> Senator from Washington, D.C.
>
> —Jimmy Carter, *A Government as Good as Its People*, 106

DURING 1975, JIMMY CARTER set out to run for president the next year with
an approach new to American politics—an approach, as he noted, that
might work only in this pivotal year. This would be the first presidential
election after the end of the Vietnam War and the scandals of Watergate.
The desires of the American people were different from what they had
ever been before. Buffeted by crisis and defeats, Americans looked for
leadership that would help heal their wounds. "We have been through too
much in too short a time," Carter asserted.

> Our national nightmare began with the assassination of John Ken-
> nedy, and went on to include the assassination of Robert Kennedy,
> and of Martin Luther King, Jr., and the wounding of George Wallace.
> We watched the widespread opposition to the war in Vietnam, and the
> division and bitterness that war caused, and the violence in Chicago in
> 1968, and the invasion of Cambodia, and the shootings at Kent State,
> and revelations of official lying and spying and bugging, the resigna-
> tions in disgrace of both a President and a Vice President, and the dis-
> closure that our top security and law enforcement agencies were delib-
> erately and routinely violating the law.
>
> No other generation in American history has ever been subjected
> to such a battering as this. Small wonder then that the politics of 1976
> have turned out to be significantly different from years past.[64]

The election of 1976 changed the nature of American presidential politics. In the past, candidates had sought to build on the achievements of
the past, to carry on the expansion and furthering of the American dream.
They had proposed New Deals, Fair Deals, New Frontiers, Great Societies.
Now they would not talk about what they would do that was new, about
keeping the nation moving forward. Now they would talk about what had
been lost in the wake of all the recent troubles. "We can now agree," Carter
declared, "to come together and seek a rebirth of patriotism in which all
our citizens can join. We must bind up our wounds. We simply cannot afford to let them fester any longer."[65]

Something essential had disappeared from American life, vanishing in the jungles of Southeast Asia, erased along with Watergate tapes. The job of the next president, whoever that was to be, would be to bring back that which had gone. "We have lost some precious things that historically have bound our people and our government together," Carter asserted. "We feel that moral decay has weakened our country, that it is crippled by a lack of goals and values, and that our public officials have lost faith in us."[66] What Carter or any political analyst could not have known in 1976 was that this new style of campaigning, election-year promises to reconstruct or resurrect that which had disappeared from American life, would mark presidential elections for the next thirty years.

AS CARTER BEGAN TO PLAN FOR HIS RUN for the White House, the developing strategy fell into two areas—substance and style. Patrick Caddell, his young pollster, had highlighted the growing sense of pessimism among Americans. The details only strengthened the overall perception. Forty-two percent said they thought economic hard times were "still ahead of us." Fifty-six percent thought the nation's energy problems were "primarily the result of greed on the part of oil companies." And a whopping 68 percent believed that over the previous decade "America's leaders have consistently lied to the American people."[67] Thus, one of Carter's most quoted promises became "I'll never lie to you." This is remarkable, in and of itself. It seems obvious that a politician running for office would promise never to lie. What politician would not make that statement? Yet Americans felt so bruised and battered by the crimes of Watergate, the lies of Vietnam, the duplicity revealed in the Pentagon Papers, that the mere promise of truthfulness became a positive badge for a presidential candidate.

When it came to a campaign style, Carter's symbolic actions reinforced this sense of a decent man working hard for the American people. The trappings of the imperial presidency, as critics had begun to call America's highest office, were being stripped away even as Jimmy Carter ran for it. Campaigning around the country, Carter carried his own bags, traveled by sedan and not limousine, stayed in the homes of supporters, and made the bed in the morning. Reporters photographed him at home in Plains, Georgia, working in his peanut fields, dressed not in the suit and tie of the campaign trail but in workingman's blue jeans.

Carter talked about the "tragedy of Vietnam" in nearly every speech, but that was about as far as discussion of the Asian war went. Vietnam was surely one of the collection of evils that had created the current American sense of cynicism and pessimism. Beyond this identification, there was little direct discussion of the war by either candidate in 1976. This corresponded to the initial way Americans attempted to move beyond the Vietnam experience. It had been a bad experience; now it was over. They felt shaken but determined to move on. This attitude would have serious implications for the returning veterans, as well as for the overall sense of American personal identity. But in the short term, the hope was that if Americans could not sweep the memories of Vietnam entirely under a rug, at least they could pay it quick acknowledgment and move on. In 1976, the candidates obliged.

> The war was, among other things, a social thermometer for this country. Its opening years reflected our confidence, our reliance on technology. . . . Its middle time showed a dying of confidence, disguised by a tendency to soothe ourselves with lies. . . . Our confidence, once it crumbled into lying, led us to fear—an anticipation of violence by pre-empting violence: Kent State was a domestic My Lai.
> —Garry Wills, "The Meaning of Vietnam," 1975

A GOOD DEAL OF SOCIAL AND POLITICAL ANALYSIS in the wake of the end of the Vietnam War took a sweeping national approach. Why did we lose? What did it mean for the nation? The world? Our future? But an array of ground-level assessments also followed. What had the war done to Americans, not as a nation, but as individuals? As citizens? As participants in a democracy that had conducted a losing and, as many thought, an immoral war in Asia? Just as there was no vocabulary for describing national loss, none existed for this kind of individual American failure. American soldiers had always done the right thing because American citizens had always sent them into just wars with moral intentions, and together they had prevailed. They experienced none of this in Viet Nam. In fact, the reactions to the war were expressed in terms of emotional wounds as well as national defeats. American wars had once united the nation, brought out its best attributes, and ended with its values reaffirmed. None of these feelings emerged in 1975. Matching the wounds of the injured soldiers were the emotional scars individual Americans experienced.

As they tried to assess the meaning of the war's end, America's two major weekly news magazines, *Time* and *Newsweek*, each worried about the psychic damage Vietnam had caused. *Newsweek* feared the impact on America's young. "Perhaps the cruelest intrusion of Vietnam upon America," the editors argued, "was what it did to a generation of American youth. It sent thousands of men fleeing into self-imposed exile and turned their neighbors and their nation against them. It turned thousands of others into radicals. . . . [I]t claimed the lives of 55,000 American men."[68] *Time* worried about the impact on the nation as a whole. "One of the war's victims was the national conscience, which was never able to reconcile America's lofty intentions with the slaughter that appeared every evening on the TV screens." This regular viewing of the horrors of a war that we had come to oppose "damaged the fabric of American society." Insult was added to psychic injury as "leaders first deceived themselves and then deceived the public."[69]

At the heart of the Vietnam postmortems were several extremely troubling questions about Americans themselves. This was, after all, the most widely covered war in American history. Nightly news footage provided Americans with a fuller sense of the fighting than ever before. Antiwar rallies and congressional hearings offered more alternatives and critiques than they had ever experienced in wartime. The culture was alive with arguments, coming from everywhere—government officials, newspaper columnists, entertainment figures, professional athletes, people on the street. Yet, despite this wealth of information and the unparalleled access, the United States had persisted in a losing and frustrating effort for years, even after the country had demonstrated in polls, elections, and civil actions its discomfort with the undertaking. Much had been made, even during the war, of how little Americans had known of the beginnings of U.S. Southeast Asian policy, of America's role in the French war, or in the establishment of the regime of Ngo Dinh Diem. "The war was invisible at the outset, from mere ignorance," Garry Wills noted in the *New York Review of Books*. "This ignorance had become part of the national story Americans came to share." However, the shared story continued: *America woke up one day and discovered thousands of American soldiers, placed in harm's way, taking over the fighting of a war that many believed should have never taken place.* But, why did they persist, then, once they knew what they knew? The war was "invisible" when it was a back-burner foreign policy activity in the 1950s and early 1960s. But as Americans came to know more and more, Wills noted, "We kept it invisible by an ever-more difficult willed ignorance." What were the implications of this kind of denial? What had Americans done to avoid the hard questions about the war until late in the game? And how did this add to the overall meaning of the war experience itself?[70]

Finally, deeper than worries about self-delusion or lack of political clarity were the feelings of what the war showed about American intentions and values as a people. Previous American wars had meant the victory of virtue, the triumph of the good, the eradication of evil. The defeat of Hitler and fascism had been the preeminent model for the twentieth century. Framing the Civil War as the means by which slavery was abolished or the American Revolution as the path by which democracy was established further reinforced the idea that Americans fought wars for higher values. But, as former Army chaplain and Episcopal priest William Mahedy would later put it, "The Vietnam war provided no transcendent meaning by which the national purpose could be reinterpreted and transposed into a new key." Instead, and shockingly, "War was, for the first time in American history, experienced by great numbers of its participants as sin."[71] This was as burdensome an emotional weight to bear as any. Over its history, many had called the United States "God's country"; the American flag, some believed, was the flag flown in heaven. Religious or not, patriotic or not, soldier or demonstrator, hawk or dove—Americans knew the Vietnam War put them on the side of sin more than it put them on the side of the angels. This was not where Americans were used to seeing themselves.

An editorial in the *Christian Century* of May 1975 framed the discussion in religious terms but echoed sentiments that resonated through the society. The Vietnam War "has cut deeply into our soul and divided us as a nation." Calling on "all Americans to work for our rehabilitation as a people," the journal prayed that "God cleanse us not only of our arrogance of might, but also the arrogance of righteousness."[72] On a more secular plane, Sheldon Wolin identified a similar undertaking. "A history has begun to take shape in which we can scarcely recognize ourselves," he observed. "By some terrible irony, we have been forced to enter history a second time, in this our bicentennial year. The first time we entered proclaiming our independence and liberty, the second time frantically trying to conceal our dependence and servitude."[73] This was, as one contemporary analyst concluded, "a massive disjunction in American culture, a crisis of self-image. If Americans were no longer winners, then who were we?"[74]

Time magazine hoped that there would not be "an infinite cycle of protests, recriminations and guilt. The U.S. has paid for Vietnam—many times over." Looking to the future, it contended that "a new phase of American history has finished. It is time to begin anew."[76] This would be easier to wish for than to achieve.

EVEN BEFORE AMERICANS came to know the phrase "Vietnam syndrome," they knew its components and felt its impact—in politics, in foreign relations, and in their sense of their nation and of themselves. The United States had begun its Vietnam adventure in another time, when Cold War priorities and an unquestioned sense of America's mission and righteousness had led it to believe that the people of the world awaited a chance to replicate the American experience and that the aim of American foreign policy was to give those people just such an opportunity.

The Vietnam experience shattered many illusions, these included. In the first year after the war, rumblings of a new American sensibility began to emerge. Cautiousness, cynicism, and confusion replaced the sense of mission and altruism. These feelings would fester and grow over the next few years, coalescing into a mindset that would shape the nation and its dealings with the world—a Vietnam syndrome. Americans grew uncomfortable with this new reality yet could not escape their state of discomfort and wariness. The power of the Vietnam experience and its unsatisfactory conclusion on so many fronts would prove impossible to overcome. From this post-Vietnam mindset, whose elements we can see beginning to emerge as early as 1975, Americans would confront their nation and their world for the rest of the twentieth century—and after.

Notes

1. Gerald Ford, "An Irony of History," *Newsweek*, vol. 85, 28 April 1975, 16–17.

2. Ibid., 17.

3. "On the Disaster," *New Republic*, vol. 172, no. 18, 3 May 1975, 3.

4. Daniel Ellsberg, "After the Fall: Reactions and Rationales," *Time*, vol. 105, 12 May 1975, 20.

5. "The End of an Era," *Newsweek*, vol. 85, 15 May 1975, 20.

6. David Halberstam, "My Turn: Why It Never Worked," *Newsweek*, vol. 85, 14 April 1975, 11.

7. Garry Wills, "The Meaning of Vietnam," *New York Review of Books*, vol. 22, 12 June 1975, 24.

8. Wilson, *The Sons of Bardstown*, 172.

9. Engelmann, *Tears before the Rain*, 147.

10. Fred Terhune, "It All Seems a Waste," *Newsweek*, vol. 85, 14 April 1975, 34.

11. Quoted in Polner, *No Victory Parades*, 70.

12. MacPherson, *Longtime Passing*, 64.

13. Quoted in Scruggs and Swerdlow, *To Heal a Nation*, 10.

14. Wecter, *When Johnny Comes Marching Home*, 511.

15. Ibid., 457, 460.

16. There was much Americans could have learned from the Korean experience. After some initial victories, the war bogged down in a stalemate that lasted for more than three years. More than 140,000 Americans and one million South Koreans were killed or wounded. Harry Truman's popularity tumbled, most precipitously when, in April 1951, he relieved General Douglas MacArthur of his command. Six years after the end of the Second World War, the invincible United States was stuck in an Asian war.

Even at the time, Korean War veterans were compared unflatteringly with their Second World War counterparts. An article in the *New York Times Magazine* depicted the Korea veterans as possessing "an almost robot-like disinterest . . . that is in disturbing contrast to the assertive individualism of the World War II soldier." They had no "special link" with their "'old outfits' in the sweat-and-strain-and-buddy sense felt by veterans of World War II." Two of the article's conclusions, although written in 1953, resonate powerfully across the years, back to the Second World War and forward to Vietnam. "Tons of paper," the article argued, have been used to "explain the reasons for the Korean war to the guy fighting it. But he didn't get it. And he still doesn't." For the nation, as a whole, "there is not the personalized concern in the war that the nation's masses shared in World War II." As a result of both of these concerns, "not many in the United States think that anything very good or anything very bad can come out of the Korean War, it's not easy for a soldier to lose his heart in that kind of fight." George Barrett, "Portrait of the Korean Veteran," *New York Times Magazine*, 9 August 1953, 12, 24–27.

The "younger brothers" who had fought in Korea did not measure up to their older siblings who had vanquished the Germans and the Japanese. These were the soldiers who remained the model for postwar America. Movies set during the Korean War proved few and far between, while films about the Second World War continued to roll out of the motion picture studios. Korea became the forgotten war.

17. Quoted in Polner, *No Victory Parades*, 9.

18. Quoted in ibid., 57.

19. Quoted in ibid., 10.

20. Quoted in Figley and Leventman, *Strangers at Home*, 10.

21. Richard Moser, "Talkin' The Vietnam Blues: Vietnam Oral History and Our

Popular Memory of War," *The Legacy: The Vietnam War in the American Imagination*, ed. Michael D. Shafer (Boston: Beacon, 1990), 108, quoted in ibid., 11.

22. Quoted in *Strangers at Home*, 11.

23. Quoted in ibid., 11–12.

24. MacPherson, *Longtime Passing*, 5–6.

25. Quoted in Severo and Milford, *The Wages of War*, 357.

26. See MacPherson, *Longtime Passing*, 54–55; Lembcke, *The Spitting Image*, 75.

27. Quoted in Greene, *Homecoming*, 65.

28. Quoted in Capps, *The Unfinished War*, 96.

29. Quoted in Engelmann, *Tears before the Rain*, 176.

30. Christopher Lasch, "The Meaning of Vietnam," *New York Review of Books*, vol. 22, 12 June 1975, 28.

31. Anthony T. Bouscaren, "All Quiet on the Eastern Front," *National Review*, vol. 27, 20 June 1975, 658.

32. "The End of an Era," 22.

33. Westmoreland and Bundy, quoted in Ellsberg, "After the Fall," 20.

34. "How Should Americans Feel?," *Time*, vol. 105, 14 April 1975, 27.

35. J. M. Cameron, "The Meaning of Vietnam," *New York Review of Books*, vol. 22, 12 June 1975, 32.

36. Ellsberg, "After the Fall," 20–21.

37. Lewis, "Hubris, National and Personal," *New Republic*, vol. 172, no. 18, 3 May 1975, 17.

38. John K. Fairbank, "The Consequences of Cultural Ignorance," *Current*, vol. 174, July–August 1975, 48. See McNamara, *In Retrospect*.

39. Adam Yarmolinsky, "Myths and Interests," *New Republic*, vol. 172, no. 18, 3 May 1975, 14.

40. Stanley Hoffman, "The Sulking Giant," *New Republic*, vol. 172, no. 18, 3 May 1975, 16.

41. Ronald Steel, "Lies and Whimpers," *New Republic*, vol. 172, no. 18, 3 May 1975, 21.

42. Norman Mailer, "The Meaning of Vietnam," *New York Review of Books*, vol. 22, 12 June 1975, 21.

43. Stroud, *How Jimmy Won*, 423.

44. Caddell, quoted in ibid., 169.

45. Sheldon Wolin, "The Meaning of Vietnam," *New York Review of Books*, vol. 22, 12 June 1975, 23.

46. Quoted in Lake, *The Vietnam Legacy*, 67, 72.

47. Miller, "Political Issues and Trust in Government," 965, 970.

48. Cited in Zinn, *The Twentieth Century*, 256.

49. Quoted in Lake, *The Vietnam Legacy*, 72.

50. Mieczkowski, *Gerald Ford and the Challenges of the 1970s*, 28.

51. Chester L. Cooper, "The POWs," *New Republic*, vol. 172, no. 12, 3 May 1975, 12.

52. Cited in Zinn, *The Twentieth Century*, 240, 249, 256.

53. Quoted in ibid., 249–50.

54. Mieczkowski, *Gerald Ford and the Challenges of the 1970s*, 295.

55. Ibid., 296.

56. Anthony Lewis, "A Famous Victory," *New York Times*, 10 May 1976.

57. Lucy Komisar, "You Won't Have Uncle Sam to Kick around Anymore," *New York Times*, 30 June 1975.

58. Quoted in Zinn, *The Twentieth Century*, 251–52.

59. Quoted in Carroll, *It Seemed Like Nothing Happened*, 168.

60. Komisar, "You Won't Have Uncle Sam to Kick around Anymore."

61. Walter Pincus, "The Four Days of Mayaguez," *New York Times*, 28 September 1975.

62. Lewis, "A Famous Victory."

63. "Mayaguez Operation Criticized in Report," *New York Times*, 6 October 1976.

64. Stroud, *How Jimmy Won*, 139.

65. Ibid., 152.

66. Ibid., 127.

67. Ibid., 197.

68. "The End of an Era," 21.

69. "How Should Americans Feel?," 27.

70. Wills, "The Meaning of Vietnam," 24.

71. William P. Mahedy, "'It Don't Mean Nothin': The Vietnam Experience," in Capps, *The Vietnam Reader*, 34.

72. "Cleanse Us of Arrogance," *Christian Century*, vol. 92, 7 May 1975, 462.

73. Wolin, "The Meaning of Vietnam," 23.

74. Gibson, *Warrior Dreams*, 10.

75. "How Should Americans Feel?," 27.

CHAPTER 4

Heonik Kwon

Cold War in a
Vietnamese Community

Some conceptual contradictions prevail in the existing interpretation of the Vietnam War, particularly in relation to the interpretation of the Cold War. On the one hand, the Vietnam conflict is discussed as being part of the progression of the bipolar global political confrontation of the second half of the twentieth century and, indeed, as a formative episode of the global Cold War. This is evident in the scholarship on Cold War global history and in that of modern international history more broadly. On the other hand, there is also a tendency to leave the Vietnam War out of the discursive domain and conceptual parameters of Cold War history, especially in depictions of the Cold War that center on modern European history. Moreover, the incongruity between Cold War history and the history of the Vietnam War is strongly marked in representations of the war as it arguably was experienced in Viet Nam and by the Vietnamese people.

This incongruity is not merely due to the fact that Cold War history usually centers on international and diplomatic history, thereby taking on a scale of description and analysis that is different from the representation of the Vietnam War as a national or social history. The reasons are much more structural, in the sense that the uneasiness between Cold War history and Vietnam War history arises from the very structures and patterns of interpretation embedded in these thematic domains. Furthermore, the place of the Vietnam War in the international history of the Cold War and the problem of the Cold War in the social history of the Vietnam War are closely interrelated analytically. This essay reflects on these as yet unresolved issues in our understanding of the Cold War as globally waged yet locally specific and divergent. It also aims to show that these issues concern not merely Cold War international history but also the research parameters of the social history of the Vietnam War. To this end, I begin by introducing the idea of parallax vision, which I believe is useful for thinking through the Cold War as both international and social history.

Parallax Vision

In the dominant view of the outside world at the time of the conflict, the Vietnam War was one of the major "limited wars" of the Cold War era fought between communist forces backed by the Soviet Union and the Chinese in the north and the regime supported by the United States in the south. In Viet Nam, the war is referred to as the American War (lit., the war against America) and thus is officially considered an extension of the collective struggle against colonial domination (i.e., the "French War") and part of the long march toward achieving a fully sovereign, united nation-state. These two contradictory identities of the war—as postcolonial and as bipolar—have been a key issue of historical research and a point of paradigm shift.

Many distinguished scholars of modern history have delved into this contradiction. Marilyn Young begins her seminal history of the Vietnam War with the troubled episode of the U.S. Merchant Marines who in 1946 were charged with bringing American troops home from the Pacific. Their vessels were ordered to ferry thirteen thousand French combat troops to Saigon and thus, against the protest of many sailors, to assist France in its attempt to reoccupy Viet Nam in the name of protecting its old colony from the threat of communism.[1] Odd Arne Westad foregrounds the dynamics of decolonization in the history of the global Cold War.[2] In his accounts, the anticolonial and postcolonial political movements of Africa, Asia, and Latin America, and the competition between the superpowers, appear to have shaped each other in myriad interpenetrating ways.

Bruce Cumings approaches the bipolar-postcolonial contradiction as a parallax effect embedded in modern geopolitics.[3] Parallax vision, a key concept in early astronomical sciences, addresses "the apparent shift in an object's position when viewed alternatively from different vantage points."[4] Cumings extends this principle, originally applied to gauging the distance to stars, to an understanding of American foreign politics of the mid-twentieth century—in particular, the question of how, after the war, the United States could "[repudiate] the values underlying the liberal construction of World War II as the democratic war against racism, fascism, and colonialism."[5] Radical political movements in Asia changed after the Second World War ended from a positive force moving toward a postwar world of free nations into a negative, menacing force serving the expansion of Soviet power. Cumings explains that this identity shift was a parallax effect that arose from a change of position at the geopolitical center rather than from any change in the peripheral regions. In other words, according to Cumings, when the American power moved from membership in the anti-Axis alliance to the position of preeminent leader in the global anticommunist crusade, it imposed on the Asian political movements an illusory translocation to the Soviet side.

Cumings discusses the geopolitical parallax within the broad context of post–Second World War U.S. policy toward East Asia and Southeast Asia, including the occupation of Japan, the occupation of the southern half of the Korean peninsula, and the intervention in Viet Nam. The positional shift in U.S. foreign policy that Cumings discusses took place amid a tremendous shift in American society, according to Eugenia Kaledin, from collective commitment to the war effort in the 1940s to the early stirrings of the Civil Rights Movement in the 1950s.[6] Mark Bradley explores early Viet Nam–American diplomatic history, partly developing these ideas based on extensive archival research in Viet Nam, the United States, and Europe.[7] He confirms that, following the surrender of Japan in August 1945, Viet Nam's revolutionary leaders anticipated that their push for national independence would be endorsed by the United States, whose attitude toward the non-Western world they considered different from that of the European imperial powers. The Vietnamese revolutionaries were encouraged by Franklin Roosevelt's denunciation of French colonialism, and with this and other related background issues, their leader, Ho Chi Minh, opened Viet Nam's Declaration of Independence in September 1945 by quoting Thomas Jefferson.[8] Bradley shows how this initial convergence in diplomatic vision between Viet Nam and America concealed their leaders' radically divergent expectations, which were to become manifest in violent clashes in the following decades. He proposes that the origin of the Vietnam War is unintelligible without relating the horizon of bipolar geopolitics to the field of postcolonial visions and "the visions and assumptions of the imagined Vietnam and America of Vietnamese revolutionaries and U.S. policymakers in a mutually constitutive fashion."[9] The Viet Nam–American War, he concludes, was the pursuit of a postcolonial future in the era of the Cold War.

The orientation of Bradley's persuasive study is called "postrevisionism" in Cold War historiography. It inherits, and partly attempts to move beyond, the revisionist approach in international history that, disillusioned with orthodox interpretations of the Cold War's origins that put all of the blame for the escalation of hostility on the Soviet side, turned to examining the active role played by the United States. Revisionism has developed into the currently dominant postrevisionist approach, which attempts to reassess East-West relations as a mutually constitutive "joint venture" and to further decenter the Cold War's origins, partly thanks to the new accessibility of archival material in Eastern bloc countries.[10] Revisionist scholars examining revolutionary movements in the peripheral regions have contributed to the understanding of the rise of bipolar confrontation within the wider historical context of decolonization. Following Cumings's visual metaphor, we may say that the core of the revisionist school in this sphere of research was to refuse analytically the positional shift that resulted in the geopolitical parallax. In other words, it sought to tell a different story of the Cold War in the Third World by placing the horizon of the bipolarizing modern world firmly within the spectrum of the decolonizing traditional societies.

Although I fully endorse this approach—and, indeed, spent part of my youth trying to digest some of the explosive ideas in Cumings's seminal work on the origins of the Korean War—I also feel obliged to point out the limit of this perspective in comprehending bipolar modernity in a multidimensional, multifocal way—that is, from the inside out, as well as from outside in, and from above, as well as from below.[11] There is an irony that, in taking into account the view of peripheral actors, the very strength of this approach turns out to be its main weakness because it renders the view unrealistically homogeneous. To understand the political process in the bipolarized postcolonial periphery, our attention must shift in new directions, including one that is opposite from the one for which revisionist historians have called—namely, to consider postcolonial visions within the field of bipolarized historical experience. The Cold War's parallax was not merely geopolitical or diplomatic; it created a further parallax between state and society. When a revolutionary movement turned into a revolutionary state, its postcolonial vision could also turn into a doctrine to be imposed on the diversity of communal experience.

Divided Family History

In the communities of southern and central Viet Nam (what was South Vietnam before 1975), kinship rarely constitutes a politically homogeneous entity. These communities' genealogical unity is crowded with the remains of wartime political bifurcation. In the customary practices of *ve chau to* (to return to the place of origin and gather to serve the ancestors), people face not only the heritage of meritorious ancestors who contributed to the nation's revolutionary march to independence but also the stigmatizing genealogical background of working against the revolution. As in Sophocles's epic tragedy of Antigone, which inspired Hegel in his philosophy of the modern state, many people in these regions were torn between the familial obligation to attend to the memory of the war dead related in kinship and the political obligation not to do so for those who fought against the revolutionary state. It is very common in this region for a family to have both revolutionary martyrs from the American War to commemorate and close relatives of those martyrs who were killed on the opposite side of the war's frontier to account for. The commemoration of the former group had been a legitimate and, in fact, highly encouraged and organized activity by the state hierarchy of the unified Viet Nam; that of the latter group had not. Thus, in the ancestor worship of this region, the dead are at once united in kinship memory and bipolarized in political history, a disparity that has emerged as a critical social issue in southern and central Vietnamese communities in recent years.

In December 1986, the Sixth National Congress of the Vietnamese Communist Party legislated the general initiatives for socioeconomic reform that later became known as *doi moi* (renovation). The report of the party congress at the time focused on economic issues, including changing the organizational basis of agricultural production from collective to private units, opening the border to foreign capital investment, and building managerial skills within the state's political and administrative apparatus.[12] In the cultural arena, it highlighted investment in education to prepare the younger generation to become a skilled industrial workforce and the continued need to oppose "vestiges of feudal, colonialist, and bourgeois cultures [and] superstitions and other backward customs and practices."[13] Despite this official warning, the reform sparked a forceful revival of ancestor worship and other ritual activities in local communities that previously were classified as "feudal vestiges" and "backward customs and practices."[14]

Throughout the 1990s, Vietnamese communities engaged in an intense, sometimes competitive, mobilization of human and financial resources to rebuild *nha tho toc* (family and lineage ancestral shrines) and *dinh* (village communal houses). This largely voluntary popular activity of *viec ho* (work of family ancestor worship), or what Hue-Tam Ho Tai calls "commemorative fever," was less a return to old, "backward customs" than the rise of a distinct way to demonstrate economic development.[15]

In the central Vietnamese villages near Danang with which I am familiar, a large number of former partisan fighters of the American War took an active role in reviving rituals of ancestor worship, and their participation contributed to the communal initiatives' being tolerated by the state. In a letter to the district Communist Party office requesting permission to construct a lineage temple, a prominent war veteran and senior member of a lineage group argued, "It is according to the principle of our revolution to share wealth and happiness with the generations of war dead who knew nothing but poverty and suffering. The nation's prosperity should benefit all the generations of Viet Nam, not merely those who are alive."[16]

Ordinary Vietnamese villagers may not express their interest in family affairs so eloquently, but those I knew nevertheless were cognizant of the particular idea of human rights or justice embedded in the veteran's statement: just as the living have a right to subsistence and a right to pursue economic prosperity, so do the dead. In the popular Vietnamese conception, subsistence for the dead means ritual commemoration, which guarantees their inalienable right to social existence. The idea of justice in this moral economy is founded on general social intimacy with the memory of the dead in Vietnamese cultural tradition, and it throws critical light on militant secularism and the coercive enlightenment drive of revolutionary state politics. The statement of the former partisan leader offers good dialectical reasoning to these two forces—tradition and revolution—and grafts creatively traditional norms to the tree of revolutionary morality by using the new reform-era language of national economic prosperity.

Grafting has been a principal metaphor in historical imagination (about old and new, foreign and native) in modern Vietnamese intellectual history since the very early colonial era.[17]

The revival of ancestral rituals was a generalized phenomenon throughout Viet Nam but had added complexity in the southern and central communities. Patricia Pelley argues that, after taking power in 1945 in the northern half of the country, the revolutionary Vietnamese state sought to divert ancestral rituals from the family and community to the state.[18] Describing the same process, Shaun Malarney explains how the state penetrated into domestic and communal lives and turned ritual space into an instrument of social integration and political control.[19] Whether the state moved into family ritual life or the ritual moved into the hands of the state, the focus of these scholars commonly is on the politics of war heroism, a central and familiar element in the process of modern nation-building.[20] The Vietnamese state has put great emphasis on the civic moral duty to commemorate the sacrifices made by revolutionary patriots in wars of liberation, and it has invested enormous administrative resources in instituting the national memory of war. The result, at the local level, has been the establishment of war cemeteries and monuments at the center of villages' public spaces and the substitution of hero worship for traditional ancestor worship.

In this new organization, Vietnamese villagers were encouraged to relate to the memory of young volunteer soldiers and eminent party activists in the same way that they previously had related to the founding ancestors of a community or of a family line. In domestic life, people replaced the memorabilia of ancestors with state-issued death certificates of revolutionary martyrs and mass-produced portraits of national leaders. Despite the formal similarity, however, there was a considerable semantic difference between the old and the new "ancestor worship." The old worship practices strengthened communal solidarity on a local scale, whereas the new ones were meant to contribute to integrating these parochial local relations to the sacred community of the nation.

Following reunification in 1975, the institution of hero worship was forced on southern Viet Nam as the principal instrument to bring the region into moral and political unity with the established revolutionary north. Unlike in the north, however, in the south, the imposition of ritual political institutions has created formidable social problems related to the political complexity of genealogical memory mentioned earlier and, ultimately, to the question of what George Mosse has called "the myth of national experience" in war memory.[21] Jay Winter and Jean-Louis Robert have shown, extending Mosse's insights, how the First World War was experienced differently not only by Paris and London, but also by various residential districts within Paris. They suggest that the history of the Great War should be approached in terms of multiple "convergences" and "divergences" rather than according to a unifying, mystifying scheme of national or European experience.[22] The same is true of the history of the American War in Viet Nam.

The institution of hero worship made sense in the context of northern Viet Nam, where the memories of the war dead predominantly were of "voluntary" soldiers who had left their homes to fight on distant battlefields. The communities to which these soldiers belonged handed over to the state their precious offspring, and the state sent their bodies back to the communities and honored their memory. It is not easy to extend this classical relationship between civil society and the national state to the postwar situation in the southern regions. The war effort there did not consist of a clear division between a home front of war economic production and the distant horizon of battlefields. It was instead a *xoi dau*, the popular expression for "village war" among southern Vietnamese, which turned the spheres of secure communal life into a vicious, confusing battleground.[23]

Xoi dau is a familiar expression for people of the war generation in the southern and central regions of Viet Nam. It refers to a ceremonial Vietnamese delicacy made of white rice flour and black beans. Used as a metaphor, however, the term conveys how the people of these regions experienced the Vietnam War. In that context, xoi dau refers to the turbulent conditions of communal life during the war, when the rural inhabitants were confronted with successive occupations by conflicting political and military forces: at night, the village was under the control of the revolutionary forces, and during the day, the opposing forces took control. Life in these villages oscillated between two different political worlds governed by the two hostile military forces. The people had to cope with their separate yet absolute demands of loyalty and with the world changing politically from day to night, over many days and nights, to the extent that this anomalous world sometimes almost appeared normal. "Xoi dau" conveys the simple truth that when you eat the delicacy, you must swallow both the white part and the black part. This is how xoi dau is supposed to be eaten, and this is what it was like living a tumultuous life in the brutal dynamic reality of Viet Nam's civil and international war.

I heard many painful stories about living in "harmony" with thundering bipolarity and just as many creative stories about subverting the zero-sum logic of the situation. One very common story is about how one brother joined "this side" (*ben ta*; the revolutionary side), and another brother (usually a younger one) was dragged to "that side" (*ben kia*; the American side). The situation is tragic, and the result is often painful: neither returns home alive, and the younger brother cannot easily return home even in memory. Yet it also has a creative side: how, for instance, the family hoped to have at least one of the brothers survive the war by having them on different sides of the battlefield and that the brother on the winning side might be able to help the brother on the losing side to rebuild his life if the family had extraordinary luck and both returned home alive.

The ancestral altar in the home of a stonemason living south of Danang displays two framed pictures of young men. One man wears a military uniform, and his name is inscribed on a state-issued Hero's Death Certificate hanging above the altar. The other man, dressed in a high school uniform, also fought and died in the war; his death certificate, issued by the former South Vietnamese authorities, is carefully hidden in a closet. In 1996, the family's matron decided to put the two soldiers together. She took the Hero's Death Certificate down from the wall and placed it on the newly refurbished ancestral altar. She then laid the photograph on the right hand side of the altar, which is usually reserved for senior members of the family. She invited friends, her surviving children, and their children over for a meal. Before it was served, she held a modest ceremony, in which she said she had dreamed many times about moving the photograph of her younger son, which she had kept in her bedroom, to the altar next to his elder brother. She addressed her grandchildren:

> Uncle Kan admired Uncle Tan. Uncle Tan adored the Little Kan. And the two were sick of the thought that they might meet in a battle. I prayed to the spirits of Marble Mountains that my two boys should never meet. The goddess listened. The boys never met. The goddess carried them away to different directions so that they cannot meet. The gracious goddess carried them too far. She took my prayer and was worried. To be absolutely sure that the boys don't meet in this world, the goddess took them to her world, both of them. We can't

blame the goddess. So, here we are. My two children met finally. I won't be around for much longer. You, my children, should look after your uncles. They don't have children, but they have many nephews and nieces. Remember this, my children. Respect your uncles.

Another family living near Danang has a similar yet deeper history of displacement and reconciliation. In 1937–38, the French colonial authorities in Indochina conscripted numerous laborers from the central region of Viet Nam and shipped them to the great Mediterranean city of Marseilles. There, two thousand Vietnamese were brought to the powder mill of Marseilles. The conscripts manufactured gunpowder for the French army and, under the Vichy regime, for the German army. A number of these Vietnamese labor soldiers objected to their situation and joined the French Resistance, while others continued to endure the appalling working conditions at the powder mill. Returning home in 1948 after sharing with French citizens the humiliating experience of the German occupation, these foreign conscripts found themselves in a highly precarious situation. The cadres in the Vietnamese revolutionary movement distrusted them; indeed, they looked upon them as collaborators with the colonial regime. The French took no interest in their past service to the French national economy or in their contribution to the resistance movement against the German occupiers. Many of these returnees perished in the ensuing chaos of war, and many of their children joined the revolutionary resistance war against America in the following era.

The family's grandfather, a former labor soldier of the French colonial army, was one of these returnees and had an extraordinary survival story to tell. He had twice rescued his family from the imminent threat of summary execution—first, in 1953, by pleading with French soldiers in their own language, and again in 1967, thanks to the presence of an American officer in the pacification team who understood a few words of French. The man's youngest brother had died unmarried and without a descendent, and so the man's eldest son now performs periodic death-anniversary rites on behalf of the deceased. His brother was killed in action during the Vietnam War as a soldier of the South Vietnamese army, and his eldest son is a decorated former partisan fighter of the National Liberation Front.

This Vietnamese family has a multiple history of cooperating with the wrong side of the political divide, according to how this is defined by the postwar political community. The family's grandfather worked for the French colonial army, and his brother fought in opposition to the Vietnamese revolutionary movement. This history of collaboration coexists in a family with a history of patriotic contribution, such as that embodied by his eldest son, and these two histories interact with each other within the family in ways that differ from how they play out in the wider society: the man's experience of working in France helped to save his family from annihilation; his son's record of revolutionary merit helped to rescue his family from the stigmatic status of a collaborator or "reactionary" family, which many other families had to endure in postwar years.

These Vietnamese generations can help each other to overcome the bipolar structure of enmity—even, as in the case of the brothers of the stonemason's family, if they are both dead. This imaginative reciprocity has been one of the prominent aspects of the recent ritual revival in the southern regions. Just as the active involvement of revolutionary war veterans helped to legitimize communal initiatives to reconstitute their ritual basis, so did the presence of a revolutionary death certificate at home in assimilating the stigmatized genealogical memory to the domestic ritual space. In the greater Danang area in the second half of the 1990s, it was clear that the residents were conducting their regular ancestral rites more publicly than before and hoping to hold death commemoration rites within a more open circle of relatives. The latter involved identities—in particular, the war dead from "that side"—who once would have been labeled *phan dong* (counterrevolutionary). In the places I observed, this regionally specific aspect of ritual revival was first brought into action by families with a meritorious revolutionary credential (and there were many of them in the area). It was apparent to me, in studying the domestic space, that the fact that certificates for revolutionary death were present at home facilitated bringing home the memory of the unrevolutionary death into a demonstrative coexistence with the former. The positive moral value of the former contributed to neutralizing the negative political value of the latter.

This political economy of ancestral worship, which is particular to southern and central Viet Nam, has not yet been properly addressed in existing studies on Vietnamese social development. Yet in my opinion, it has far-reaching implications not only for Viet Nam's future but also for comparative studies of Cold War history and culture. Here I will confine the discussion to the second issue.

Postcolonial Cold War

The stories of struggle for survival I have introduced here are hardly uncommon among Vietnamese villagers, but they remain unfamiliar in the
existing histories of the Viet Nam–American War, which have focused
primarily on the international, diplomatic dimension of the war's historical reality. On the front of social history, existing accounts are strongly
biased in favor of the Vietnam War as American history. Stories of un-
healed wounds and enduring pains from the Vietnam War abound in
bookstores, yet these stories are predominantly about the sufferings of
American participants in the conflict and the troubling memories of this
failed war as they are felt in American society. Recently, however, there
have been some notable public and scholarly efforts to change this situation and to look at the Vietnam War experience from Vietnamese perspectives, through their historical knowledge and experiences.

Christina Schwenkel's *The American War in Contemporary Vietnam*,
for instance, is a pathbreaking contribution to the growing trend of paying both attention and respect to the other side of the Vietnam conflict.[24]
Her rich ethnography of contemporary Vietnamese war commemoration
and monumental arts follows the canonic ethos of modern anthropological research, which may be called the commitment to represent the
native's point of view. She is rightly critical of how in the previous era this
viewpoint was ignored, simplified, and distorted. She also shows how distorted understandings of the Vietnamese struggle for national liberation
and for a politically independent, unified postcolonial national community unfortunately persist today. Those who harbor these distorted views
appear in her book with diverse identities, including U.S. lawmakers and
American tourists to Viet Nam. However, the main target of Schwenkel's
critical commentary is the broad realm of public discourse about the
meanings of the Vietnam War in contemporary American society. According to Schwenkel, even many years after Viet Nam and the United
States opened diplomatic relations, these two countries, which fought one
of the longest armed conflicts in the modern world, have not yet found
a point of mutual recognition about the conflict's origins and characters
through which a meaningful closure of the past may become possible.
For the United States, efforts to come to terms with the Vietnamese side
of the war fall far short of efforts to bring Viet Nam into the global market
economy; for Viet Nam, its justified cause of keeping alive the legacy of its

collective heroic struggle against a foreign power now must confront the market-driven propensity to drop the value of past history to make room for the value of future prosperity. Schwenkel courageously confronts the dynamic and turbulent changes that are taking place in the meanings of the Vietnam War in national and transnational contexts. She describes these changes in diverse settings and through the voices of diverse groups of actors, both Vietnamese and American, who not only observe and experience the changes but also are involved in making them.

This commendable project to look at the legacies of war from the native point of view starts with the categorical distinction between the American War (for Viet Nam) and the Vietnam War (for America) in terms of a national liberation war versus a Cold War episode—the dual postcolonial-bipolar scheme that is familiar in the existing literature of the Vietnam War. The problem, however, is that the actual American experience of the Vietnam War cannot be relegated solely to the Cold War paradigm. The Vietnam War is remembered in American society as being akin to a civil war, albeit primarily an *American* civil war. This means that the interpretative conflicts over whether the Vietnam War was a victorious postcolonial struggle or a sorry episode of the Cold War are not outside American public history but, rather, embedded in it. Otherwise, the very notion of the Vietnam syndrome, which is still talked about today, would not make much sense.

The same applies to the history of the American War. Contrary to what Schwenkel claims, I do not believe that the bipolar paradigm of political history is alien to Vietnamese society. True, the externalization of this paradigm from national memory is fundamental to Viet Nam's official war memorial art and to the state's postwar efforts to integrate the confused southern and central regions into a unified national community based on a single, homogeneous national narrative of war. This does not mean, however, that diverse Vietnamese regions and societies experienced the American War in the same way and in the same spirit. We must not confuse the native's point of view with the state-instituted "national" point of view, especially against the background of a civil and international war that involved the extreme polarization of communal life as part of an enduring postcolonial struggle. This last situation is what the xoi dau metaphor tries to covey. The meaning of the idiom, although clearly not the same as the meaning of the "Cold" War, nevertheless becomes intelligible when we question all received wisdoms about the meanings of the

American War, as well as those about the Vietnam War, and start focusing more closely on the lived realities of these wars. If we do so, we come to see how the histories and meanings of these two kinds of war were actually intertwined in human experience, as was the family history of the former labor soldier south of Danang.

The postwar Vietnamese politics of heroic war death is based largely on a prevailing postcolonial vision. Its commemorative art, including the monumental forms found in many villages or districts, clearly renders the sacrifices in the American War in continuum with earlier struggles against colonial occupation, often looking even further back to ancient battles against Chinese intrusion. The change of perspective in the historiography from the dominant, singular Cold War framework to the alternative framework of disjunctive parallax effects between decolonization and bipolarization was an important, constructive paradigm shift. The postcolonial paradigm is superior, in anthropological language, in representing the "native's point of view" to the orthodox Cold War paradigm proper. The relative strength of the postcolonial perspective, however, becomes a weakness when the analysis turns its attention from the domain of international history to that of local history. Whereas the postcolonial perspective is attentive to the intentions and historical particularities of the peripheral other (unlike the geopolitical perspective, which tends to be oblivious to them), it also has the tendency to be analytically oblivious to the fact that the peripheral national other, in Cold War conflicts, has already assimilated the bipolar geopolitical worldview and therefore cannot be reduced to a homogeneous, unifying identity.

We must approach the idea of a "global experience" of the Cold War conflict cautiously.[25] The same is true, as noted earlier, about any assumptions about "national experience" in the conflict. In the fields where the conflict took a violent form and involved the radical bifurcation of social forces, the assumption can be especially problematic. The postcolonial historical perspective has not yet come to terms with the ironic progression of bipolar history in which the very "native's point of view" it tried to represent has turned into a locally hegemonic force, thereby ruling against divergent experience and memories.

The revival of ancestral and death-commemoration rituals in southern and central Viet Nam should be considered partly in view of these historical questions—as a creative local response to the place of the postcolonial vision in a changing global structure of power. The practice of reuniting brothers away from their bifurcated history of death is primarily a family affair, but it is at once an initiative to change the existing, towering political hierarchy of war death to a more historically accountable, socially democratic form. The voluntary cultural movement is in line with a growing intellectual movement in Viet Nam—among writers, in particular— that is attempting to reconfigure the history of the American War, using mainly fictional and poetic forms of communication, from a coherent, unified historical narrative of self-determination into a relatively less coherent, divergent experience of a "domestic conflict."[26] This rising "civil war" perspective on the history of the war, as Marilyn Young indicates, is not a negation of the foreign and international dimension of the conflict.[27] On the contrary, I argue elsewhere that the perspective is an expression of the civil society in the process of being empowered: if the war was a communal conflict as well as an international one, it means that the community should play as active a part as the state actors and international organizations in bringing the conflicts to end.[28]

THE LAST POINT BRINGS THE DISCUSSION BACK to the issue with which I began this essay: Cold War history as social and communal history. In the context of southern Viet Nam, I have located the cultural sphere of death commemoration as a site of major communal initiative for the resolution of bipolar conflicts and the milieu of what Robert Hertz would have called morally "ambidextrous" social practices. It is partly thanks to Hertz, whose promising intellectual life ended prematurely in the fields of mass mechanical slaughter during the First World War, that anthropological research has been exploring the close analytical relations between social attitudes to death and the structure of political power. Hertz was interested in how societies construct hierarchies biopolitically and explored the question through his investigation of a traditional mortuary cultural complex in Southeast Asia that expresses the moral hierarchy of "good death" versus "bad death" by means of their symbolic association with the "right hand" and the "left hand."[29] These ideas require close examination; for the purpose of our discussion, it suffices to introduce the notion of "symbolic ambidexterity" that Hertz coined at the end of his classic *Death and the Right Hand* as an alternative to the prevailing moral and hierarchical polarity between the symbolic properties of the right and of the left. Hertz believed that the preeminence of the right hand is the inscription of the principles of social hierarchy (including "good death" versus "bad death") on the human body, and he expressed his political vision using the same symbolic language: "The distinction of good and evil, which for long was solidary with the antithesis of right and left, will not vanish from our conscience. . . . If the constraint of a mystical ideal has for centuries been able to make man into a unilateral being, physiologically mutilated, a liberated and foresighted society will strive to develop the energies dormant in our left side and in our right cerebral hemisphere, and to assure by an appropriate training a more harmonious development of the organism."[30] The moral symbolic bipolarity in traditional societies that Hertz wrote about is clearly not an issue of the same nature as the ideological bipolarity in modern politics with which we are dealing here: the former relates to questions of social hierarchy within a given society, whereas the latter, in conventional wisdom, is principally about a contest between contrary social formations and ideologies. Nevertheless, we have seen how these two separate issues of bipolarity can make a critical association in the historical field of the Cold War waged in violent forms.[31] If we reduce the history of the Cold War to a "test of wills" between two superpower actors to mutually deter an "alien way of life," the two forms of bipolarity will probably have no meaningful relationship. If we confine our knowledge of the history to the narrow meaning of the "Cold" War and within the centrality of the dominant Western experience of the conflict, it is difficult to imagine how the two bipolarities can be intersected. This experience was more about the fear of mass annihilation of human lives than about the reality of mass death and displacement. If we attend to bipolar history elsewhere, as well as here, and include in it the experience of violent political confrontations within local and national communities, which is what the global Cold War actually meant in much of the world in the past century, the political bifurcation of the human community and a moral polarization of death become closely interrelated phenomena. In the history of the global conflict in the latter sense, communities were driven to select politically "good death" from the mass of other war death and extract an ideologically coherent genealogy out of the enmeshed history of violence across the ideological border.

When we decenter our position in this way, we need also to decenter the history from a geopolitical to a social history so we can include in the history the enduring locally specific legacies of the global conflict and the creative everyday practices of conflict resolution arising from this milieu.

Otherwise, the horizon of the Cold War's mass death will remain only a series of tragic and unfortunate events in the past, with no transformative values meaningful to the present time.

On a closing note, I add a few more lines to the family history of the former labor soldier in Danang. Shortly before he returned to his home village at the end of 1948, the man's grandmother died in a tragic incident. At that time, she was living alone in her bamboo house. She had lost her husband in 1936 and her children shortly after, and her orphaned grandchildren had left the village for an urban ghetto or farther away. She survived on a small plot of land where she grew vegetables; the neighbors regularly helped the lonely woman with rice and fish sauce. On the fifth day of the eleventh lunar month of 1948, she spotted a group of French soldiers conducting a house-to-house search. She was ill at the time and waved at the soldiers for help. The soldiers came, pushed her back into the house, closed the shutters, and set fire to the bamboo house. In the following era, the spirit of this woman came to assert her vitality through various apparitions, which eventually led the villagers to erect a small shrine in her memory on the site of her destroyed home. The locals then started calling her Ba Ba Linh, or Powerful Grandmother.

Throughout the chaos of the Vietnam War, her humble shrine attracted steady visits by local women who came to pray to the old woman for their family's safety. During the day, some Saigon soldiers saw the village women kowtowing to the shrine, heard the story, and prayed for their own wishes at the site. At night, the peasant militiamen, coming to survey the area, heard the same story. The village women saw that some of these partisan fighters were praying to the shrine before they hurriedly joined their group to move to the next hamlet. When people returned to the village after evacuation during the critical period of the Vietnam War at the end of the 1960s, they recall that there was nothing standing in the hamlet except the humble wooden shrine dedicated to Ba Ba Linh. Today, the old woman's shrine continues to attract prayers for other aspirations and desires.

Notes

1. Young, *The Vietnam Wars*, 1–2.
2. Westad, *The Global Cold War*.
3. Cumings, *Parallax Visions*.

4. Hirshfeld, *Parallax*, xii.

5. The quote is from Kuznick and Gilbert, *Rethinking Cold War Culture*, 4.

6. Kaledin, *Daily Life in the United States*.

7. Bradley, *Imagining Vietnam and America*.

8. The Vietnamese declaration opens with, "All men are created equal. They are endowed by their Creator with certain inalienable rights; among these are Life, Liberty, and the pursuit of Happiness": ibid., 4. See also Luong, *Revolution in the Village*, 129–31.

9. Bradley, *Imagining Vietnam and America*, 178.

10. The expression "joint venture" is from Kaldor, *Global Civil Society*, 62. On decentering the origins of the Cold War, see Hunter, *Rethinking the Cold War*, 8–16.

11. Cumings, *The Origins of the Korean War*.

12. Stern, *The Vietnamese Communist Party's Agenda for Reform*.

13. Duiker, *Vietnam*, 189.

14. On ritual revival in contemporary Viet Nam, see Luong, "Economic Reform and the Intensification of Rituals in Two North Vietnamese Villages"; Taylor, *Goddess on the Rise*.

15. On the activity of *viec ho*, see Viet, *Viec ho*. The quote about "commemorative fever" is from Tai, *In the Country of Memory*, 1. On the described interpretation of ritual revival, see Malarney, "Return to the Past?"

16. Kwon, *After the Massacre*, 114.

17. Jamieson, *Understanding Vietnam*.

18. Pelley, *Postcolonial Vietnam*, 168.

19. Malarney, *Culture, Ritual, and Revolution in Vietnam*, 56–72.

20. Anderson, *Imagined Communities*; Gillis, *Commemorations*; Rowlands, "Remembering to Forget"; Werbner, *Memory and the Postcolony*; Winter and Sivan, *War and Remembrance in the Twentieth Century*.

21. Mosse, *Fallen Soldiers*.

22. Winter and Robert, *Capital Cities at War*, 20–24.

23. Trullinger, *Village at War*.

24. Schwenkel, *The American War in Contemporary Vietnam*.

25. Borneman, *Subversions of International Order*, 3.

26. Bradley, *Imagining Vietnam and America*, 189–92; Duiker, *Vietnam*, 191; Jamieson, *Understanding Vietnam*, 321–22.

27. Young, "Epilogue," 516.

28. Kwon, *After the Massacre*, 174–75.

29. Hertz, "The Pre-eminence of the Right Hand."

30. Ibid., 22.

31. The "ambidextrous" commemorative practice in central Viet Nam has a further dimension relating to its ritual organization that is constituted by gods and ancestors placed in the interior of the house and anonymous ghosts commemorated in the exterior. The typical ritual action in this concentric-dualist structure con-

sists of kowtowing to the placed identities and turning to the opposite side to repeat the action on behalf of the placeless beings that are imagined to wander about in the exterior environment. This organization makes the identities unassimilated to the interior ritual space, including the politically troubled memory of the dead discussed in this essay, categorically ghosts. A proper understanding of the relationship between moral conceptual polarity and political bipolarity in the Vietnamese context, therefore, ought to include popular Vietnamese beliefs and imaginations about ghosts of war, with which this chapter does not deal: see Kwon, *Ghosts of War in Vietnam*.

CHAPTER 5

The Ambivalence
of Reconciliation
in Contemporary
Vietnamese
Christina Schwenkel | Memoryscapes

In a postreform era of global market integration and increasing prosperity for certain segments of the population, it is easy to lose sight of
the extent to which Vietnamese individuals and wider society remain ad-
versely affected by the legacies of war. As Rosalind Shaw has observed in
the context of the African slave trade, long after mass violence subsided,
landscapes continued to bear the traces of traumatic histories in varied
and, to the casual observer, often indiscernible ways.[1] More than thirty-
five years after reunification, visual reminders of the war in Việt Nam's
built and natural environment—from monuments and martyrs' cemeteries that dot the countryside to reforested woodlands and bomb-crater
fish ponds—have reconfigured postwar topographies of suffering into
dynamic landscapes of memory, what I refer to in this chapter, borrow-
ing from Shaw, as memoryscapes. For Shaw, the presence of invisible inhabitants—such as the malevolent spirit forces that haunt sites of historical trauma—are also symbolically constitutive elements of postviolence
memory that form menacing and, at times, dangerous spiritscapes.[2] In
his research on postwar spectral landscapes in central Việt Nam, Hoenik
Kwon has likewise demonstrated the important role that spirit geogra-
phies play in people's everyday lives as they attempt to work through a
traumatic past under present conditions of economic reform.[3]

In this chapter, I build on the work of these scholars to examine Vietnamese memoryscapes as dynamic zones of memory interaction and interchange between people, the built environment, and the spirit world. I emphasize *intersections* as a means to transgress the rigid boundaries that are often drawn between communities of memory, meaning, and practice. This approach allows me to make certain claims about the mutability of contemporary memoryscapes in Việt Nam. First, Vietnamese memoryscapes are shaped and traversed by multiple state and nonstate actors, both national and transnational, who are differently positioned and involved in memory-making activities that diverge and intersect at particular moments. This is important to recognize because it allows for the blurring of "borders" between national histories and unsettles the binary logic of official and vernacular memory that typically associates the Vietnamese state with secular and ideological forms of remembrance and "the people" with more spiritual ritual practices. This chapter then reaffirms Hue-Tam Ho Tai's important observation that "official history and public memory . . . are as likely to coexist in symbiotic fashion as to be in tension with each other."[4]

Attention to memoryscapes as zones of transformation and intersection further reveals how memories of the war are produced both through spontaneous, individual acts of recollection and through encounters between people (living and nonliving), objects, and sites associated with mass trauma.[5] The changing, often transnational, forms of memorial expression found on the landscape suggest that commemorative practices are by no means consistent and uniform in meaning or intent. And although deeply marked by histories of violence and suffering, these landscapes increasingly bear signs of healing and recovery in ways that signify new and profoundly meaningful memorial gestures and sentiments. Friendship forests planted in defoliated regions and martyrs' temples constructed to honor the dead attest to the diverse and often collaborative commemorations practiced by both American and Vietnamese citizens, despite being bound up with lingering feelings of ambivalence and even bitterness.[6]

Based on two years of anthropological fieldwork conducted between 1998 and 2004, this chapter examines intersecting histories and commemorative practices at two sites of war memory located in southern and central Việt Nam. In the absence of officially sanctioned mechanisms for working through unresolved pasts, symbolic acts of reconciliation took place at both sites through encounters with the spirit world. Such acts of engaging with and remembering the war dead, at times inconspicuously, represented culturally effective strategies to resolve historical suffering. In the first section, I journey with Trung, a veteran of the Army of the Republic of Việt Nam (ARVN) to a large martyrs' cemetery for fallen revolutionary soldiers on the outskirts of Hồ Chí Minh City. As a member of a divided family caught on both sides of the war (and as a young man who fought on the "losing" side), Trung's complex relationship to the past and his desire for social reintegration demanded he find a balance between active forgetting and strategic remembrance. His participation in memorial rituals at the cemetery, including a state ceremony for three Vietnamese MIAs whose remains had recently been recovered, worked to both affirm an official commemorative hierarchy and to restore family and social harmony, even as the haunting presence of other noncommemorated pasts hung heavily over our journey. In the second section, I examine the remaking of the Khe Sanh Combat Base in Quảng Trị Province on the edge of the former demilitarized zone (DMZ) into a transnational tourist site and museum that attracts both domestic and international tourists. U.S. and Vietnamese visitors, especially veterans, who journeyed to the remote location close to the Lao border, responded to the on-site exhibitions and memorial productions with marked ambivalence on account of the conflicting historical memories and experiences represented at the site. At the same time, visitors' diverse cultural engagements with the spirit world produced surprising solidarities through joint commemoration of the lives lost across enemy lines. In both locations—Khe Sanh and the martyrs' cemetery—sites of official memory became spaces of symbolic interaction with "the Other," including spectral beings and battlefield adversaries, that both complemented and complicated meanings intended by the state. Such interactions also engendered expressions of empathy and a deeper understanding between former enemies based on recognition of a shared traumatic history. This recognition of history, and of the Other's humanity through his or her commemoration, suggests the possibility for a new politics of empathic reconciliation to take place.

On Pasts Remembered and Forgotten in an Urban Cemetery

It was a cloudy autumn morning in Hồ Chí Minh City when Trung and I began our journey to Biên Hòa, a rapidly industrializing city in the nearby province of Đồng Nai. We intended to locate the former military cemetery of the Republic of Việt Nam (RVN), forcibly abandoned and partially dismantled in a symbolic demonstration of regime change during the late 1970s. Trung had not visited the site since 1979, when, at the request of the newly reunified government, he had transferred his older brother's remains from the cemetery to a family burial plot in the Mekong Delta. As we drove, Trung informed me that he had expanded our itinerary to include a few additional memorial sites that he felt were important for me to visit to understand the complexity of the war and its impact on his life.

Born in 1944, Trung had been a university student in the early 1960s when Buddhist demonstrations against the government of Ngô Đình Diệm began to intensify. In 1963, he joined friends who identified as either communists or nationalists to protest Diệm's repression of Buddhists and to demand the withdrawal of the United States from Việt Nam. As a university student, Trung had avoided universal conscription until one year later, when he was unable to continue his studies and was subsequently required to join the military. He chose the army and spent the next eleven years fighting the war, much of it alongside U.S. forces until their withdrawal. This was not an easy choice for Trung to make, yet he saw himself and the rest of his generation largely as victims of geography. "I was in Sài Gòn and had to follow the law. I had no choice," he said. "The government worked with Americans, and I had to, as well. Had I lived in the countryside, I would have been forced to follow the communists." Trung openly and enthusiastically discussed his experiences working with U.S. troops as a communications officer, although when it came to the *liberation* of Sài Gòn—a term he used in accordance with conventional state discourse—the conversation abruptly ended. "What did I do on April 30, 1975?" he replied to my question. "I don't want to talk about that day. I was an officer who had access to a lot of classified information. When the war ended, I had big problems."

Trung subsequently served three years in a re-education camp. Soon after his release, his father, who had fought with the Việt Minh against the French and with the revolutionary forces against the United States, died. Trung informed me that after our trip to the RVN military burial grounds where his brother had been interred, we would proceed to Hồ Chí Minh City's civilian cemetery to visit his father's grave in an elite section for decorated party members who had served their country. But first, he told me, we would make a brief, unplanned stop on the outskirts of the city at the region's largest and most important martyrs' cemetery.

Located in District 9, Nghĩa trang Liệt sĩ Thành phố Hồ Chí Minh (Hồ Chí Minh City Martyrs' Cemetery) contains the graves of thousands of soldiers from the greater metropolitan area who fell during the wars for independence from France and the United States, as well as in the "Southwest Campaign" against the Khmer Rouge in the late 1970s.[7] Construction on the site began after City Regulation 29, which set aside 51.6 hectares of land for the project, was passed on 3 April 1984.[8] Over the next two decades, the number of graves grew to exceed fourteen thousand.[9] This expansion reflected an increase in both demand for state burial spaces following a spike in the discovery of MIAs' remains and requests to relocate the graves of the nation's war dead from distant, rural burial sites and cemeteries.

The layout of the Hồ Chí Minh City Martyrs' Cemetery mirrors the general design of national cemeteries in other parts of the country: beyond the main gate, a path that divides the grounds into symmetrical halves leads to a grand central monument atop an elevated platform. Built by the sculptor Nguyễn Hải, who is known for his public and monumental works of commemorative art, the main monument in Hồ Chí Minh City, Bà Mẹ Tổ Quốc (Mother Việt Nam), stands thirty meters high and is flanked on each side by potted trees and socialist realist statues honoring both male and female combatants. To the front of Mother Việt Nam, who holds a draping flag of the country tightly to her chest, an armed female soldier stands guard (see figure 5.1). In 1998, to mark the three-hundred-year anniversary of the founding of Hồ Chí Minh City, a copper relief spanning several hundred meters and depicting the nation's history of battlefield victories was assembled along the back edge of the platform. This expansive open area remained vacant for the duration of my visit, and no incense burned in the faded blue urn at the base of the monument.

The design of the grounds, on the other hand, is seemingly atypical of Vietnamese war cemeteries. Ordinarily, graves are arranged in a uniform and linear manner in tight rows, with little space between each plot. In an effort to "democratize" death, there is nothing to distinguish one grave from the next, and all are positioned to face the same direction (usually the front gate) in an orderly and aligned manner (see figure 5.2). Martyrs' cemeteries are often empty—they do not typically draw daily traffic but do attract crowds for state commemorative ceremonies, during the lunar New Year, and on the anniversaries of deaths when those dates are known by family members.[10] The Hồ Chí Minh City Martyrs' Cemetery, how-

FIGURE 5.1. *Bà Mẹ Tổ Quốc* (Mother Việt Nam), sculpture by Nguyễn Hải,
Hồ Chí Minh City Martyrs' Cemetery, 2000. Photograph by the author.

FIGURE 5.2. Trường Sơn National Cemetery, Quảng Trị
Province, 2000. Photograph by the author.

ever, introduced a unique design aesthetic that encourages more regular
and meaningful interactions between the living and the dead. Arranged
according to urban districts, graves are positioned in a circular fashion
in groups of eight (an auspicious number), often around a small tree or
a bed of flowers (see figure 5.3). "It's like the dead are joined together for
talking," Trung commented. This arrangement provides wider spacing
between the graves, allowing family members to picnic on the grounds
next to the resting place of loved ones. Though uniform in size, many of
the tombstones were individualized with a small round photograph of the
deceased at the head of the tomb, giving a more specific sense of person-
hood to the general "martyr" identity.[11] And unlike the "cold" altar at the
Mother Việt Nam monument, most of the graves were attended to with
incense, fruit, or fresh flowers. The grounds were also well maintained
with abundant green foliage, colorful gardens, and freshly mowed grass.
This atmosphere created a peaceful and inviting park-like environment,
and during my visit with Trung on an ordinary Sunday morning, the
cemetery was bustling with families tending to graves, as well as couples
posing for wedding photographs.

When we arrived at the cemetery, Trung and I proceeded to the reception area, where we met and drank tea with the managing curator, a

FIGURE 5.3. Circular arrangement of graves, Hồ Chí Minh City
Martyrs' Cemetery, 2000. Photograph by the author.

migrant from northern Việt Nam. On the right-hand side of the room, a
family consulted a thick black book and map that listed the names and
gravesite locations of each interred war dead. An elaborate altar and three
small coffins draped with national flags stood in the middle of the room
under the eternal gaze of a bust of Hồ Chí Minh (see figure 5.4). On each
side of the bust hung a sign extolling the virtuous sacrifices of the martyrs:
"Sống Anh Hùng" (Live as Heroes), "Chết Vinh Quang" (Die Glorious).
The curator gestured in the direction of the altar and announced that we
had come on a special occasion: a memorial service was in process for
three MIAs whose recently unearthed remains were to be buried by party
officials and family members later that day. It was this altar, and its insistence on mourning and spiritual practice, that altered the officialdom of
the secular space and blurred the lines between state memorial and private ritual practice (see figure 5.5). Offerings of tea, fruit, money, incense,
flowers, and candles, along with a banner that read, "Vô Cùng Thương
Tiếc Liệt Sĩ" (Eternal Grief for Martyrs), broke with state ideologies of
collective moral heroism to also recognize individual loss and grief, as
well as the important role that cultural beliefs and values play in commemorating and communing with the war dead.

After drinking our tea, Trung walked toward the altar, lit three joss sticks, raised them above his head with his palms together in prayer, bowed three times, stood for a moment in silence, and then called me over as he placed the burning incense in an urn. "These are the remains of three soldiers. [He read their names.] They have been missing since 1968 when a unit of eight men went on a mission together and died. Only now, more than thirty years later, have three sets of their remains been found. Like me, they worked in communications."

At first, I was unsure how to interpret Trung's actions at the altar and thought perhaps it had been a means for him to publicly affirm his re-education and devotion to the socialist nation under the watchful gaze of the curator. I wondered if Trung believed, like Nietzsche had argued, that a delicate balance between refined remembrance and complicit forget-

FIGURE 5.4. Reception room and altar at Hồ Chí Minh City Martyrs' Cemetery, 2000. Photograph by the author.

FIGURE 5.5. Repatriated remains of three soldiers, Hồ Chí Minh
City Martyrs' Cemetery, 2000. Photograph by the author.

ting was necessary for human existence, for the growth and development
of an individual, a culture, and a nation.[12] Clearly, with his stigmatized
past, Trung had learned how to live both historically and unhistorically —
that is, how to remember and forget certain pasts in particular times and
spaces. Yet as we talked, I saw that it was not simply the burden of a non-
commemorated RVN past that overshadowed Trung's acts. As he reflected
on the intersecting histories and commonalities he felt he shared with the
deceased "liberation soldiers," such as their similar backgrounds and as-
signments during the war, I recognized that far deeper meanings and desires were attached to his public and yet very intimate commemoration
of former "enemies."

In his work on mass death and collective memory, Kwon examines
the lingering presence of specters of war that haunt Việt Nam's contemporary landscapes. In the afterlife, he argues, ghosts continue to feel the
pain and trauma of their violent deaths, although they no longer recol-
lect the ideologies and hostilities that led to their suffering. "There is no
enmity in the cemetery," Kwon quotes a popular Vietnamese proverb,

suggesting the possibility of reconciliation in the afterworld.[13] Indeed, in the Vietnamese village where he conducted fieldwork, Kwon found an assemblage of wandering spirits that cohabit with the living, including a U.S. officer, an Algerian conscript from the French War, a southern Vietnamese soldier, and PAVN war dead. Like the villagers' offerings to wandering souls in Kwon's research, Trung's ritual observance of the MIAs' remains was a moral act of memory intended to reconcile and transcend social and political divides through recognition of a shared humanity and traumatic history that left him with a profound sense of connection and camaraderie.

Trung's offering of incense at the altar likewise reaffirmed the transformation of homeless and hungry MIA souls without graves into settled and satiated ancestors dutifully tended to in their new "homes" by reverent family members.[14] A popular saying in Việt Nam stresses the importance of the grave as a home for the dead: "sống cái nhà, chết cái mồ" (a house is to the living what a grave is to the dead). Like families who invest large amounts of money in the construction of beautiful homes that flaunt their rising socioeconomic status, so, too, does the size and design of the tomb serve as a status referent. Superstitious beliefs concerning the interconnections between homes and graves abound in Việt Nam. A large, ornate grave that is properly maintained and geomantically positioned is believed to ensure an auspicious future. "If a grave is beautiful and quiet [i.e., tended to], the family will develop well," one research respondent explained, pointing to the promise of health, prosperity, and longevity. An improperly constructed or unmaintained grave, on the other hand, may have an ominous effect on the living. Respondents with family members suffering from illness or failing in business who consulted with diviners were advised that their misfortunes could be linked to problems with family graves. Once resolved (in one case, the removal of an animal that had burrowed under the tombstone), health or economic well-being readily improved. Given the significance of the grave as a mediator of relations between the living and the dead, the lack of a "home" due to missing remains is of serious moral and spiritual concern to families, as the spirits of their loved ones are believed to wander aimlessly with hunger through the afterlife.

With an estimated 300,000 Vietnamese MIAs from the war with the United States, an official statistic that does not include RVN soldiers, there is widespread anxiety about locating these remains and giving them a proper burial place. In interviews, veterans recollected how the dead were buried quickly in makeshift graves with temporary markers next to streams or distinctive trees for easy identification and exhumation after the war. Today, these burial places are almost impossible to recognize due to radically altered postwar landscapes. In recent years, however, as the economy has improved and prohibition of superstitious practices has waned, families and government officials have intensified the search for MIAs. Journeys to former battlefields to locate the remains of loved ones was a focus of intense public interest during my research. The mass media also became an important tool to stir survivors' memories about sites of death and burial locations. On Việt Nam Television, a twenty-minute nightly army newscast entitled *Nhắn Tìm Đồng Đội* (Search Mission) displayed photographs and sketches of missing soldiers with information including name, year born, village, army unit, rank, and approximate date and place of death. "If anyone knows the current location of this grave, please contact . . . ," the male and female narrators, clothed in military uniforms, beseeched viewers.[15] Consulting with clairvoyants to locate MIAs has also become popular in recent years, and the high success rate reported in the press has even persuaded the military to engage in such practices.[16] Stories of mothers and veterans who devoted the last years of their lives to seeking and returning remains have captivated the nation, as thousands of distressed families, at long last, have been able to bury loved ones and propitiate their spirits in culturally and emotionally gratifying ways.[17]

These activities have further altered Việt Nam's memoryscape as increasing numbers of individual and mass graves are excavated and the remains of MIAs are transferred to family burial plots or state martyrs' cemeteries, where they can be ritually attended to as ancestors and heroes. As Shaun Malarney has argued, a primary concern of Vietnamese families is to "car[e] for the souls of the war dead and ultimately integrat[e] them into the benign realm of family ancestors."[18] For this to take place, the repatriation and reburial of remains are often necessary. Such was the case for a family I met during my visit to the Hồ Chí Minh City Martyrs' Cemetery. While strolling the grounds, Trung and I came upon a middle-aged son and daughter, with their aging mother, who were picnicking at the site of their father's grave. They invited us to sit down and partake in their meal. Incense was burning at all of the graves in the circle, while offerings of fruit, cigarettes, flowers, and rice wine had been placed on the father's tomb. Trung lit eight joss sticks, inserted one into a small ceramic vase that adorned each grave, and then took a seat next to me on the grass. The daughter presented us with an apple and orange—*lộc* (merit) from the father's altar—while the mother told the story of the search for his remains. After the war, she spent ten years attempting to find her husband's burial site. In 1985, with the aid of information she received from residents in an area of Long An Province, where he reportedly fell, she managed to locate his grave and subsequently interred his remains in a Long An martyrs' cemetery. For five years, she and her family made the long journey to care for his grave but eventually requested repatriation and reburial closer to their home. Officials agreed, and in 1990, his remains were once again transferred, this time to the martyrs' cemetery in Hồ Chí Minh City.

The ritual veneration of the spirits of the father and his comrades in an official site of secular memory demonstrates how intersecting state and religious practices jointly reaffirm a moral commemorative order marked by the transformation of hungry and wandering MIA ghosts into settled and nurtured ancestor-heroes. Trung's commemorative acts toward former adversaries likewise revealed his own moral desires to properly honor pained souls that had made the long journey "home" to their final resting place in a martyrs' cemetery. Such gestures can also be understood as reconciliatory acts of "forgetful forgiveness,"[19] aimed at healing his own painful and unreconciled memories of a divided social body. "These men are also my brothers," Trung proclaimed in a display of fraternal camaraderie meant to transcend political-ideological division and reinforce national and familial unity. "We were all born of the same dragon and fairy," he continued, referring to the origin myth of Âu Cơ and Lạc Long Quân. "It's time to forget the past and look only to the future.... After the end of the war we still had families and neighbors, so how could we continue to hate each other? Many families were divided, including mine, with sons and a daughter who followed the RVN and a father who went with the communists, but today we have to forgive and forget."

After we said goodbye and took leave of the site, Trung and I proceeded to the former Biên Hòa burial grounds of the RVN military, whose dilapidated state and ransacked ruins contrasted sharply with the well-cared-for grounds of the Hồ Chí Minh City Martyrs' Cemetery (see figure 5.6). Trung was silent; it was a painful return for him, as well as for our driver, who also had served in the ARVN. As we slowly and silently made

FIGURE 5.6. Former Biên Hòa military cemetery of the
Republic of Việt Nam, 2000. Photograph by the author.

FIGURE 5.7. Former entrance to the Biên Hòa military cemetery
of the Republic of Việt Nam, 2000. Photograph by the author.

our way around the cracked and toppled tombstones to where Trung's brother had once been interred, the burning joss sticks that locals had carefully and surreptitiously placed around the site's perimeter and in the crevices of the stairs leading to the once-ornate, pagoda-style entrance (see figure 5.7) revealed the ongoing work of mourning for the war's non-commemorated souls and the unresolved pasts that are not yet forgotten or fully reconciled.

Intersecting Memoryscapes at Khe Sanh/Tà Cơn Airfield

The DMZ has played a central and enduring role in U.S. historical memory and contemporary imagination of the war in Việt Nam. Established in 1954 to demarcate the temporary division of the country into the Democratic Republic of Việt Nam (DRV) and the State of Việt Nam (later the RVN), during the war this strip of land came to signify and naturalize for U.S. troops a legitimate boundary between presumably sovereign territories. Yet because this "border" remained unrecognized by Hà Nội and the population of the DRV, the DMZ is not a historical-geographical construct that plays any significant role in northern Vietnamese social memory.[20] In fact, it is all but absent.

In this section, I examine the making of the DMZ into a war tour for international consumption in the 1990s and its subsequent remaking, also for a broader domestic audience, in the 2000s. During the war, some of the most decisive and devastating battles took place in areas in and around the DMZ, where U.S. combat bases had established a strong presence. In the mid-1990s, a selective "re-Americanization" of the landscape took shape as "DMZ tours," primarily targeting U.S. tourists and returning veterans, were organized to battle sites and abandoned bases that resonated strongly in U.S. historical memory.[21] A decade later, however, a more pronounced trend toward "Vietnamization" had occurred, both in terms of the people and the memories represented at the sites. To demonstrate such shifts, I focus on Khe Sanh Combat Base, known in Việt Nam as Sân bay Tà Cơn (Tà Cơn Airfield), and the site's reconstruction in 2003. As an example of "difficult heritage"—that is, heritage associated with violent destruction rather than creative construction[22]—Khe Sanh/Tà Cơn holds strong emotional and historical meaning for visitors from all sides of the war. And not unlike the intersecting histories at the martyrs' cemetery, Khe Sanh/Tà Cơn is also a site for diverse and ambivalent expressions of memory that are reconciliatory, on the one hand, and irreconcilable, on the other.

For international tourists who come to Việt Nam in search of battle sites and artifacts of war, the DMZ offers what the journalist David Lamb once called a "living war museum,"[23] complete with deserted military bases, underground tunnels, bomb craters, deforested landscapes, scattered war relics, unexploded ordnance, standing ruins, and other lingering signs of a violent history. Yet, the term DMZ invokes a specific set of historical experiences and geographical imaginaries that form a distinct U.S. landscape of war memory. Very few of my research respondents in Hà Nội, for example, were familiar with the *khu phi quân sự* (DMZ), although all identified important historical and memorial sites in the area. In keeping with the spatial construct of the DRV as whole and continuous (i.e., no recognition of a "North" and "South" Việt Nam), "Quảng Trị Province" served as an important geographic referent rather than "the DMZ." In the words of one intellectual in 2000, "The *khu phi quân sự*? [ponders for a long moment] Oh yes—the *khu phi quân sự*. No, this has no commemorative significance for us. 'The DMZ' [using the English term] is part of U.S. memory, not Vietnamese. Mostly foreigners go there. There are other places of historical significance in our memory, such as Quảng Trị citadel where thousands of people lost their lives in a long and violent battle."[24] War sites and battlefields with differing historical and commemorative value thus constituted very different, though at times overlapping, "U.S." and "Vietnamese" memoryscapes that also reflected competing geospatial boundaries of the postcolonial nation-state.

These divergent topographies of memory likewise influenced the development of the area's tourism industry into separate markets to cater to distinct domestic and international needs.[25] During visits to the DMZ in 1998–2000, these markets rarely intersected and, with the exception of the Vịnh Mốc tunnels, Vietnamese and foreign tourists seldom crossed paths on their journeys. Compared with its international counterpart, domestic tourism at this time was quite nascent, and touristic motivations differed significantly. For example, consumption of the war as spectacle—what fueled much international tourist interest in the DMZ—was not a domestic practice. Rather, Vietnamese journeys were often motivated by a desire to alleviate suffering through the fulfillment of cultural obligations that included the search for MIAs' remains or visits to the graves of loved ones buried in the national martyrs' cemetery at Trường Sơn. Moreover, because Vietnamese tourists traveled not to "the DMZ" but to the province of Quảng Trị, their itineraries included destinations that typically were unfamiliar to foreigners but significant in Vietnamese memory. Mai, a tourist from Hà Nội, recalled her trip to the area in 1999, which was similar to the Vietnamese tour I undertook a year later:

> In Quảng Bình, we stopped at the house of Mother Suốt and then continued on to Vĩnh Linh base in Quảng Trị, which had been an important supplier of goods for the Hồ Chí Minh Trail.[26] From there we visited the Vịnh Mốc tunnels, where residents lived underground during U.S. bomb attacks, and then we stopped at the temporary border at Bến Hải River to take pictures. We traveled along Highway 9 to the Trường Sơn National Martyrs' Cemetery to find my uncle's grave and then made a brief stop at the headquarters of the Provisional Revolutionary Government before ending the tour at the citadel in Quảng Trị.

Such domestic tours were often state-sponsored for *ưu tiên* (priority) families of martyrs and war veterans, and they differed considerably from the more commercialized and sensationalized excursions to "the DMZ." Those tours targeted a nondomestic market of tourists who were well versed in U.S. popular culture and cinematic memory.[27] In such tours, the memoryscape was "Americanized" through visits to sites important in U.S. military history and through the presentation of U.S. experiences and historical knowledge, as younger Vietnamese guides born after 1975 integrated American veterans' recollections into their tour discourse.

During my fieldwork, the twelve-hour "DMZ Tour" began each morning at six in neighboring Huế City.[28] The sites were grouped into two clusters — Highway 9 (east-west) and Highway 1 (north-south) — allowing busloads of tourists to diverge and then reconvene for lunch at the crossroads before continuing the journey. Along Highway 9, the bus traveled to Camp Carroll (eventually removed from the itinerary), and then to the "Rockpile," a 230-meter-high limestone formation that served as a firebase and observation point. Somewhere to the southwest, a guide explained, passing around a laminated map and pointing to a distant mountain range, is "Hamburger Hill." The next destination was an impoverished "Montagnard" community of Bru-Vân Kiều people, whose land had been devastated by chemical defoliants. A path through the village that allowed tourists to peer inside the stilt homes to get an "inside" view of ethnic minority culture ended at the Cuban-built Đa Krông Bridge, which marked the start of a branch of the Hồ Chí Minh Trail. The last stop on Highway 9, close to the international border with Laos, was the Khe Sanh Combat Base, site of the infamous seventy-seven-day siege by PAVN forces in 1968.[29] After lunch at the DMZ Hotel, the second leg of the tour continued along Highway 1. There, tourists made brief stops at the "skeleton cathedral" (the ruins of a bombed Catholic church) and the Hiền Lương Bridge, which spans the Bến Hải River and marked the "former border" at the Seventeenth Parallel. Tourists then briefly traveled to "the other side," to visit the Vịnh Mốc tunnels, where they edged their way slowly through the narrow underground pathways built by villagers to escape U.S. bombing. Until the mid-2000s, this was the only zone of contact between international and domestic tourists, and the relative lack of Vietnamese people encountered on the tour up to this point reinforced a sense of U.S. ownership of, and rights to define, the memoryscape.

Nestled among coffee trees in a new economic zone, the Khe Sanh Combat Base was a highly anticipated stop on the tour. As the site of one of the most significant and debatable battles in the U.S. history of the war, it is also the best known in popular memory. According to Stanley Karnow, the protracted two-month battle and siege of Khe Sanh by PAVN forces in 1968 was "daily fare for American television viewers."[30] Over a period of nine weeks, he reported, more than seventy-five thousand tons of bombs were dropped on enemy troops, the "deadliest deluge of firepower ever unloaded on a tactical target in the history of warfare."[31] In the 1990s, little remained of the original base, except for traces of the airstrip, scattered rounds of spent ammunition, and rusted scrap metal from U.S. planes ("Not much to see," complained one tourist). When the tour buses pulled in, a small group of vendors hurriedly approached visitors to sell unearthed relics from the base, such as rusted and misshapen forks, spoons, razors, coins, medals, pins, lighters, and dog tags. "Don't wander off the path," guides warned tourists, pointing to the danger of land mines.

The postwar built environment at Khe Sanh included a two-room administration building that also housed a small exhibition of war artifacts, photographs, and maps of PAVN attack plans. A decaying historical marker provided a brief and, for many U.S. tourists and veterans, controversial synopsis of the "liberation" of Tà Cơn, claiming that more than one hundred thousand U.S. and "puppet" (*nguy*) troops had been killed, injured, or captured, and close to two hundred U.S. aircraft had been shot down. Khe Sanh, the text stated, was a Điện Biên Phủ for the

United States, a reference to the siege and defeat of the French in 1954.[32] In 1997, a new monument was erected to replace the crumbling marker and soften what some foreigners took to be a triumphalist tone (see figure 5.8). Rather than celebrating the number of casualties, the new inscription, engraved in black marble in both English and Vietnamese, emphasized the strategic location and significance of the Tà Cơn Airfield for U.S. forces. On 8 February 1968, it stated, PAVN troops, together with local militia forces, attacked and lay siege to the area, turning the landscape into a "hell on earth and a terrible obsession for American troops" until they abandoned the base and the surrounding district was liberated on 9 July. "Ultimately we had to retreat," the monument's text read, quoting U.S. Secretary of Defense James R. Schlesinger. Such conflicting accounts of history (a seventy-seven-day siege or a five-month siege?) and claims to victory unsettled many international—particularly, U.S.—tourists accustomed to very different historical truths.[33] Many complained about "biased" and "inaccurate" information in comment books, interviews, and online travel blogs. For some, discontent with the assessment and celebration of U.S. "defeat" contributed to a lingering cynicism and sense of irreconciliation as the Khe Sanh Combat Base evolved into a transnational space of contested history and memory.

By the mid-2000s, a larger and more diverse group of visitors was traveling to Khe Sanh/Tà Cơn. Several factors contributed to this shift. The first was the notable growth in domestic tourism. As more families and veterans had the resources to invest in the search for MIAs' remains or to travel to former battlefields, memoryscapes that had been distinct became increasingly entangled. Second, veterans of the armed forces of the RVN also began to appear more frequently on the scene. In neighboring Huế City, operators of DMZ tours, aware that many Western tourists preferred guides who were former RVN soldiers rather than graduates of state training programs, began to advertise "Veteran Guides."[34] Some of these men, also aware that their history had become a desired commodity, offered independent DMZ tours on the back of their motorbikes. The resulting assemblages of memory that became manifest at Khe Sanh/Tà Cơn gave shape to a unique transnational "community of trauma" that engaged in culturally meaningful and often spontaneous acts of commemoration and reconciliation, despite lingering tensions.[35]

When I returned to Khe Sanh in 2004, the area was no longer a vast, unbounded space for imagining an embattled U.S. marine base. Rather,

FIGURE 5.8. Khe Sanh/Tà Cơn monument,
2004. Photograph by the author.

FIGURE 5.9. Highway 9–Khe Sanh Victory Museum, 2004. Photograph by the author.

the grounds had been fenced in and renovated to include outdoor exhibits and a newly built museum. After paying the $1.50 entrance fee at the gate to the clearly marked "Di tích Sân bay Tà Cơn" (Vestige of Tà Cơn Airfield), I proceeded to the Highway 9–Khe Sanh Victory Museum that had opened in 2003 on the anniversary of the area's liberation. According to the curator, the museum had been designed in the architectural style of Bru-Vân Kiều houses, which typically are positioned on top of supporting columns or stilts (see figure 5.9). Although the dominant narrative conveyed was still that of "total victory," curators had organized the exhibit in such a way as to provide insights into the diverse wartime experiences of American and Vietnamese troops, including those of ethnic minorities. This was done, for example, through the display of weapons, equipment, and uniforms of U.S. and RVN forces. Images borrowed from the U.S. press offered views of everyday life inside the base. U.S. troops were shown working, organizing, strategizing, fighting, panicking, fleeing, dying, and grieving. The siege of Khe Sanh, according to the exhibit, produced much disorder and misery for U.S. troops and undermined their confidence and military might. Images by Vietnamese photojournalists, in contrast, showed the courage and determination of the liberation forces. While the tragic result of these intersecting histories—namely, the death and injury of U.S. soldiers[36]—was given strong representation, compassionate acts carried out across enemy lines amid the violence of war were also woven into the narrative, including an image of a PAVN military doctor tending to a badly wounded American prisoner, thus publicly reaffirming Việt Nam's moral superiority and commitment to its official "humane policy" (*chính sách nhân đạo*).³⁷

The grounds outside the museum had also undergone significant renovation to include an open-air military exhibition that extended beyond the newly landscaped gardens and concrete walkways to the dusty red earth at the site's more unkempt borders. On the perimeter, concealed amid tall fescue grasses, U.S. bunkers had been re-created from sandbags to convey a sense of the makeshift conditions under which troops had lived and fought (see figure 5.10). Close by, a collage of broken wings, propellers, and other sections of U.S. aircraft jutting out from the earth stood as silent testimony to the number of planes destroyed in combat. Just steps away from the monument, a simple concrete shrine had been erected in traditional architectural style to commemorate those who had died at the base (see figure 5.11). Given the poverty of the area, the offerings were less elaborate than those made at the Hồ Chí Minh City Martyrs' Cemetery—just a package of biscuits, a few sticks of incense, and two battery-operated candles left "burning." Still, as at the martyrs' cemetery, this small shrine complicated and transformed a site of secular national memory into a space of ritualized care for the souls of the war dead, irrespective of side, ideology, or nationality.

Such practices demonstrate how visitors have actively reconfigured the dominant meaning of Khe Sanh/Tà Cơn through their work of mourning and remembrance. Yet commemoration played out differently for American and Vietnamese visitors, from candid religious expression and spontaneous memorial acts to discreet superstitious practices. Comment books in the museum, for example, became an impromptu memorial as visitors from the United States composed mournful eulogies and tributes to the war dead. Veterans' entries, in particular, commemorated specific men, identified by name and military unit, or the veterans composed more general dedications to the memory of "friends," "comrades," and "fallen brothers." These tributes were often transnational and transpolitical in scope as the books became a means to recognize the immense suffering and loss experienced on all sides of the war. For example, in 2004, a retired U.S. Army lieutenant wrote, "To all the soldiers who served here. Both sides fought valiantly for their countries." Other memorial dedica-

FIGURE 5.10. Reconstructed bunker, Khe Sanh/Tà Cơn, 2004. Photograph by the author.

FIGURE 5.11. Altar to commemorate the war dead at Khe Sanh/Tà Cơn, 2004. Photograph by the author.

tions were explicitly religious in content, calling for God to bless or have mercy on the souls of "all the warriors" or "all combatants." American visitors thus used the comment books as a tool to reconcile traumatic histories and past hostilities, as well as to recognize the common humanity of all troops who lost their lives in the war, even while some of the entries made clear the anguish of unresolved suffering.[38]

Vietnamese visitors, on the other hand, had their own form of spontaneous commemorative practice that, like the dedications to "all warriors" in the comment book, also can be understood as a particular cultural approach to remembering and reconciling with the dead, including those who once occupied the position of "enemy." In addition to the altar that tended to the souls of Khe Sanh's war dead, visitors had inconspicuously placed incense sticks along the site's perimeter, not unlike what I observed at the RVN cemetery. Clearly, in both cases, these memorial acts were not intended to be a publicly displayed offering. Particularly in the case of officially noncommemorated RVN war dead, such acts might be viewed with contempt and suspicion. Yet they were also not concealed. At Khe Sanh, joss sticks had also been placed at the entrances to the reconstructed bunkers and at the base of the museum's flight of stairs. When I spoke with the groundskeeper about this practice, he laughed and explained, "Such are the spiritual beliefs of the Vietnamese! There were many soldiers who died here. If people do not light incense, their souls will cause problems for the living." "It's a sign of respect for the dead," a tour operator likewise informed me. Similar to Trung's commemoration of the three sets of MIA remains, these sundry ritual offerings (words of tribute, incense, biscuits) can be viewed as moral and cultural acts of remembrance that transcend political and national boundaries to incorporate *all* of the war dead into a community of memory.[39] The groundskeeper reaffirmed the ontological settling of the past through commemorated and cared-for souls when I inquired about the presence of troublesome ghosts from the war. He smiled and replied, "There are no longer hungry ghosts around here."

Commemoration as Hopeful Reconciliation

Scholars of social memory have long been attentive to the diverse ways in which experiences and knowledge of the past are sustained and communicated not only through written and oral expression, but also through objects, images, and performative acts.[40] Traumatic histories, in particular, are often considered incommunicable or difficult to narrate.[41] As Rosalind Shaw argues, memories of violence often take nondiscursive form in visual and ritual practices that transform topographies of terror into complex memorial landscapes.[42] The case studies in this chapter have shown how memoryscapes in Việt Nam are continually shifting in form and meaning, tied to individual and broader social practices of healing: monuments, cemeteries, and museums are constructed (and in some cases, demolished); MIAs' remains are brought home or moved to new burial grounds; and new, often transnational, relations with the dead are built and sustained through memorial rites and acts of veneration. These examples speak to the heightened role that memory work plays in societies like Việt Nam that are undergoing rapid socioeconomic change, when the tensions and boundaries between remembrance and forgetting shift in response to new actors on the scene (such as returning American veterans) and new opportunities and desires to confront, engage with, and settle the past.

The diverse commemorative acts performed and witnessed during visits to Khe Sanh and the Hồ Chí Minh City Martyrs' Cemetery not only demonstrate the mutability of postwar landscapes of memory.[43] They also reveal the transformation of traumascapes into dynamic topographies of recovery. To commemorate is to seek resolution and relief from historical suffering; acts of remembrance enable—and, indeed, often demand—selective, if not willed, forgetting. Thus, Trung, an ARVN veteran, made ritual offerings at a state martyrs' cemetery to restore and reaffirm family and social unity while neglecting the trauma of postwar re-education and social marginalization that continue to shape his life today, and U.S. veterans at Khe Sanh wrote brief tributes to the war dead to express sentiments of shared loss and camaraderie, often setting aside lingering feelings of animosity. These affective practices can also be understood as symbolic reconciliatory gestures that hold the promise of a less divisive and more integrated future. Commemoration is thus the enactment of a politics of hopeful and empathic reconciliation.

In his work on the Truth and Reconciliation Commission in South Africa, Richard Wilson cautions that ideas and understandings of "reconciliation" are neither fixed nor culturally uniform, and that healing mechanisms such as "truth telling" may not have the best interests of traumatized populations equally in mind. He asks, for whom is reconciliation sought and for what intent and purpose?[44] Likewise, in Việt Nam much ambivalence and tension involved in the work of reconciliation remain, particularly when it comes to contested moral claims to victimhood. As I have argued elsewhere, the term *reconciliation* itself carries distinct social and cultural meanings for different groups of people involved in the war—for some closure and healing, for others, prosperity and new economic opportunities.[45] Such complexities notwithstanding, when Vietnamese visitors to Tà Cơn lit incense for the souls of U.S. war dead and when U.S. veterans honored the deaths of "all warriors," commemoration became a transformative, ethical act that conferred the status of humanity on the former enemy and likewise deemed the Other worthy of remembrance.

The intimate ritual practices and interactions between people, the landscape, and the spirit world at Khe Sanh and the war cemeteries reveal how local and transnational actors have both facilitated and inhibited the ongoing work of reconciling unsettled pasts, for underneath the possibility of resolution and recovery lies the specter of obligatory forgetting. Is social progress and peace better served by amnesia and willed forgetfulness, as Nietzsche once asked and as Trung's actions seem to suggest?[46] Does the survival of a nation depend on the effacement of an inglorious past, as Ernest Renan surmised?[47] "We shouldn't remember the South," a friend who grew up during the time of the RVN commented to me during the celebration of the twenty-fifth anniversary of the "liberation" of Sài Gòn in 2000. "Things are better now. If we remember the South, it will only stir up resentment." Like Trung's "forgetful forgiveness," here social forgetting suggests also a particular cultural strategy of reintegration and social coexistence. Public remembrance of the past, in this person's view, risks undermining such processes by perpetuating a cycle of hostility and perhaps even violence.[48]

Yet those assigned to national oblivion—such as Trung's brother, who remains outside the realm of official memory—continue to cast a dark shadow over Việt Nam's economic reform process as a politics of postwar remembrance increasingly shapes and is shaped by global capitalism. Thus, a Honda plant built on the site of another RVN war cemetery that Trung and I tried to locate one day had effaced all traces of the former burial grounds, now lost to the expansion of industry. In recent years, more open discussion has taken place among Vietnamese intellectuals about extending the right of remembrance, and even state benefits, to RVN war dead and their families. But until such ideas become national policy (and many are doubtful they ever will), the small but significant memorial gestures, such as those performed by local people at the RVN cemetery, serve as a call to engage in commemorative acts as a moral practice that dismantles an entrenched hierarchical order of memory and recognizes "the inalienable rights of the dead" to be remembered and mourned.[49]

Notes

1. Shaw, *Memories of the Slave Trade*, 46.

2. Ibid., 50.

3. Kwon, *Ghosts of War in Vietnam*. See also Gustafsson, *War and Shadows*.

4. Hue-Tam Ho Tai, "Introduction: Situating Memory," in Tai, *The Country of Memory*, 7.

5. Halbwachs, *On Collective Memory*.

6. Schwenkel, *The American War in Contemporary Vietnam*, 42–44.

7. Because the term *martyr* (*liệt sĩ*) as currently used in the Socialist Republic of Việt Nam (SRV) refers to soldiers who fought on the side of the revolution, it excludes military war dead from the RVN, who were also referred to as "martyrs" during the era of the republic.

8. "Nghĩa trang Liệt sĩ TPHCM mất gần 20 ha đất!" [Hồ Chí Minh City Martyr's Cemetery to lose twenty hectares of land!], Xa Lộ News, adapted from *Sài Gòn Giải Phóng* [Sài Gòn Liberation], 2 March 2008, available online at http://tintuc .xalo.vn/00-725456839/nghia_trang_liet_si_tphcm_mat_gan_20_ha_dat.html (accessed 30 December 2009).

9. Ibid.

10. Schwenkel, *The American War in Contemporary Vietnam*, 103–5.

11. This practice was also found at the RVN cemetery in Biên Hòa. Tombstones in martyr cemeteries typically list the name of the deceased, year and place of birth, and year "sacrificed" (*hy sinh*).

12. Nietzsche, *On the Advantage and Disadvantage of History for Life*, 8–9. Writing in the same era, Ernest Renan similarly pointed to the role that both remembrance and forgetting play in the construction of national history and national identity: see Renan, "What Is a Nation?"

13. Kwon, *Ghosts of War in Vietnam*, 27.

14. For a detailed examination of the categorical transformations of ghosts into ancestors, heroes, and deities: see also Kwon, *Ghosts of War in Vietnam*, chap. 6.

15. Nhắn Tìm Đồng Đội also has a comprehensive website that tracks current search efforts and numbers of comrades found: see http://www.nhantimdongdoi .org/?ssoft=1&item=1&sid=Ssoft223990375954368184466972 (accessed 18 July 2009).

16. Consulting with mediums is generally considered superstitious activity that

is frowned on by the party. One officer explained to me that neither the military nor families of martyrs have been condemned for consulting with mediums because such work strengthens, rather than undermines, the nation-state: see also Schlecker and Endres, "Psychic Experience, Truth, and Visuality in Post-war Vietnam."

17. See, e.g., Vũ Toàn, "20 năm và 10,000 ngôi mộ liệt sĩ trong rừng sâu" [Twenty years and ten thousand martyr graves in the deep forest], *Tuổi Trẻ* [Youth], 1 December 2004, 7. Fraud has also been reported, particularly in relation to the search for remains: see P. V., "Những trò lừa bịp mới thông qua dịch vụ 'tìm mộ liệt sĩ'" [New tricks and scams in the service of "locating martyr graves"], *An Ninh Thế Giới* [World security], 7 December 2000, 1, 4–5.

18. Malarney, "The Fatherland Remembers Your Sacrifice," 47.

19. Seong-nae, "Mourning Korean Modernity in the Memory of the Cheju April Third Incident," 199.

20. For example, maps of the Democratic Republic of Việt Nam showed its territory as encompassing the entirety of the country rather than demarcating a "North Việt Nam," as cartographically represented in the West.

21. This also included the revival of certain U.S. military vernacular such as "China Beach," and "Hamburger Hill" to attract visitors already familiar with such locations: Schwenkel, "Recombinant History," 7.

22. Logan and Reeves, *Places of Pain and Shame*.

23. David Lamb, "Monument to Perseverance May Fall," *Los Angeles Times*, 21 May 1999, 5.

24. Here the respondent refers to the protracted, eighty-one-day battle at the ancient Quảng Trị citadel in 1972 that, despite devastating losses, Vietnamese official history identifies as having contributed to "total victory" (*toàn thắng*) in 1975.

25. For a similar process at the Củ Chi tunnels in Hồ Chí Minh City, see Schwenkel, "Recombinant History."

26. Mẹ (Mother) Suốt, or Nguyễn Thị Suốt, is a national hero known for rowing soldiers across the river in her old age during bombing raids. A picture of Mẹ Suốt standing in her boat is commonly found in museum exhibits on the war.

27. Considerable commercial hype surrounds tours of the DMZ, and local entrepreneurs have been quick to capitalize on their popularity. For example, after completing the tour, visitors can retire to the DMZ Hotel or relax at the DMZ Bar wearing their DMZ T-shirts and baseball caps.

28. In 1998, the DMZ tour cost $25 per person. One year later the price dropped to $12 and continued to decrease in increments until it reached $8 per person in 2004.

29. The seventy-seven-day siege, according to U.S. historians, took place between 21 January and 8 April 1968, although as Peter Brush points out, these dates are rather arbitrary: Brush, "Recounting the Casualties at Khe Sanh." According to Vietnamese history, the battle against "Tà Cơn" lasted until 9 July 1968 when the base was fully "liberated."

30. Karnow, *Vietnam*, 552.

31. Ibid., 553. Karnow also reports a death rate of fewer than five hundred for U.S. troops and more than ten thousand PAVN forces. Although active in the battle, the number of ARVN combatants killed in action at Khe Sanh is not provided.

32. General Westmoreland and the U.S. press also made this analogy during the battle, despite obvious differences: see ibid., 552–54.

33. Conflicting claims reflect differing criteria for assessing victory and defeat. While Vietnamese claims to victory centered on the closure of the base and liberation of the surrounding area, U.S. claims had largely to do with body counts. See Brush, "Recounting the Casualties at Khe Sanh"; M. Young, *The Vietnam Wars*.

34. Schwenkel, "Recombinant History," 19–20.

35. Morris, "About Suffering."

36. All of the dead and injured displayed in museum photographs were "enemy troops."

37. See also Schwenkel, "From John McCain to Abu Ghraib."

38. For example, one woman wrote in 2004, "I am making this trip for my brother who served here in Vietnam for two years and has spent thirty years since living with the trauma."

39. On remembrance as cultural and moral practice, see Lambek, "The Past Imperfect."

40. See esp. Connerton, *How Societies Remember*.

41. Scarry, *The Body in Pain*.

42. Shaw, *Memories of the Slave Trade*, 63.

43. See also Tai, *The Country of Memory*.

44. Wilson, *The Politics of Truth and Reconciliation in South Africa*, 99.

45. Schwenkel, *The American War in Contemporary Vietnam*, 33–47.

46. Nietzsche, *On the Advantage and Disadvantage of History for Life*.

47. Renan, "What Is a Nation?"

48. In her work on postwar Sierra Leone, Rosalind Shaw argues that grassroots practices of forgetting as a means to reconcile and reconstitute community have largely been ignored by truth commissions that place greater emphasis on the therapeutic benefits of verbally expressed memories of trauma and violence, a practice that has its roots in Western psychotherapy. Shaw, "Rethinking Truth and Reconciliation Commissions."

49. Kwon, *Ghosts of War in Vietnam*, 163.

CHAPTER 6

**Remembering War,
Dreaming Peace**

On Cosmopolitanism,

Compassion, and

Viet Thanh Nguyen | Literature

All wars are fought twice, the first time on the battlefield, the second time in memory. So it is with what Americans call the "Vietnam War" and what Vietnamese call the "American War." The significance of this war for the United States and the way it would be remembered is expressed in Martin Luther King Jr.'s prophecy of 1967: "if America's soul becomes totally poisoned, part of the autopsy must read 'Vietnam.'"[1] From the perspectives of many artists working on the war, the American soul was indeed poisoned, but not fatally. It would be art's task both to perform the diagnosis and to provide the treatment for the American body politic, wounded and staggered by its failures in Southeast Asia. The fact that this treatment would hardly be a cure is borne out by the current symptoms displayed by the American body politic, its wars in Iraq and Afghanistan, telling indicators of a persistent and ongoing American syndrome, the bellicose urge for violence and domination.

Faced with this syndrome, writers who remember the war explicitly insist, or implicitly show their readers, that some of the tools of the literary trade are the same habits of the spirit that the American body politic needs to temper its aggressive disposition. These tools and habits are compassion and cosmopolitanism, without which literature would be dead on the page. Human beings who are neither compassionate nor cosmopolitan would appear like some of the characters and authors of such an uninteresting literature, able to imagine only very circumscribed worlds. Writers fighting the war again in memory make great use of compassion and cosmopolitanism, with part of their purpose being to illuminate a path to peace for their readers. This path is an unpaved road whose visibility is dim, whose route is perilous, and whose destination is unknown. Literature's fitful light provides some guidance, so long as we do not overestimate what literature can do, which is the tendency of writers and literary critics, or underestimate it, which is the tendency of people who do not read literature.

Not surprisingly, King's prophecy provides a place for literature and the arts. An autopsy of the American soul is not possible, he said, unless Americans hear the voices of common Vietnamese people, without which there is "no meaningful solution."[2] Literature is one way to record, imagine, or transmit these voices, and literature is one way to prepare audiences to hear the voices of others. In both cases, what is necessary for writer and reader is compassion. But compassion and its related emotions—empathy, sympathy, and pity—are hardly feelings that direct us or shape our narratives with any political or moral certainty. While invoking compassion may allow us as individuals to feel the pain of others, it may also facilitate injustice and inequality by permitting us to do nothing to alleviate that pain.[3] For some of compassion's critics, compassion is always inherently conservative, since our evocations of feeling for the other might really only mean a demand for attention to our own capacity for sympathy. Our pity for the other's broken body only reminds us of the wholeness of our own.[4] Here, compassion is a sign of false consciousness or even political manipulation, as in the slogan from the George W. Bush era calling for a "compassionate conservatism," or in the ways that a "community of compassion" built by Americans for themselves after 9/11 became a "patriotic community" for the purposes of waging war.[5] Therefore, when King asked us to hear with compassion those unheard Vietnamese voices, we could be excused for being wary of his religious calling. Perhaps those other voices might simply be used as choir and chorus for a well-rehearsed American drama telling of how a house divided between black and white—as well as between left and right—is nevertheless unified when confronted with foreign threats.

Nevertheless, a healthy skepticism should not mean giving up on compassion just yet. While compassion has significant limits in politics and economics, where sympathy and pity amount to small change indeed, it has greater currency in art. Here, empathy and sympathy are compassion's cousins. If sympathy is identifying with someone, then empathy is identifying as someone.[6] While sympathy may compel pity and objectification, it may also breed a sense of shared suffering. This fellow feeling may urge us toward action, as empathy may also do in its ability to make us identify with an "other." This empathetic identification may take place through our relationship to works of art, particularly those in which we find narratives of compassion. Even here, however, action is not certain, for these narratives ask readers to be witnesses to scenes of suffering that may purge readers of the need to take political action, rendering them passive, except for the pleasure of their emotions, in the face of injustice.[7] But compassion is like every technique in an artist's repertoire or every rhetorical trick up a politician's sleeve—the meanings not absolute but only evident in use. As Susan Sontag reminds us, "Compassion is an unstable emotion. It needs to be translated into action, or it withers."[8]

Gesturing toward translation means acknowledging that different translators will render compassion and its cousins in varied ways. When it comes to the American War and its literary aftermath, what is noticeable is how differently construed these emotions are by the powerful versus the weak, the wealthy versus the poor, and men versus women. In what follows, I pursue this idea that our feelings not only have structure, as Raymond Williams argues, but that they also have different styles.[9] Even emotions are tainted, or tinged, by our historical and contemporary identities, by our social and economic classes. Unifying these differences is the overarching structure and style of feeling that give compassion and its related emotions meaning in the larger world, cosmopolitanism—an endeavor dating back to ancient Greek efforts to create citizens of the world who would strive for conversations and human contact across all kinds of borders. Literature, able to offer stories besides the ones that justify war, plays a key role in cosmopolitanism's efforts to imagine peace and cope with war's long half-life in memory.[10] Here, wars remain emotionally radioactive, disfiguring the living well after the ceasefires are signed and the shooting has stopped. Against this disfigurement, and against the state-sponsored machinery of war, cosmopolitanism offers a fragile shelter where writers and readers together can plot the long struggle to peace.

Cosmopolitanism Now (and Then):
What a Difference Race Makes

The American War in Viet Nam's history is retold perhaps most memorably by Hollywood's cinema-industrial complex, which has waged a campaign of virtual shock and awe in a celluloid Viet Nam. But regardless of whether American war stories are cinematic, literary, political, or historical, the dominant tales are melodramas of traumatized white manhood. These melodramas of beset manhood substitute the experience of the white male combat soldier, journalist, or politician for the experiences of the nation and its multitudes. War stories such as these return more than just white American men to center stage; they also reaffirm the dominance of that stage and its productions as an American one, a theatrical bill accepted by American audiences, critics, and scholars. But what if we narrated the war from the perspectives of those shadowy figures in the wings and background of an American production? Would the starring role of "America" be cast differently? Would the drama bear the same name? The war's diverse cast was international and multicultural, including American soldiers of color, South Korean soldiers for hire, South Vietnamese civilian refugees, Japanese journalists, American female intellectuals, and many more. Their oral histories, novels, films, reportage, and photojournalism are war stories, too, providing vivid evidence for how the war and its aftermath must be read from a cosmopolitan point of view that broaches the boundaries of nation, gender, and race.

But since whiteness has been the screen for American film fantasies, I focus here on other colors of the American spectrum—those imprinted on Asian Americans and Latinos. They have long occupied ambiguous places in American society, seen by other Americans as foreigners and strangers. Not surprisingly, Asian Americans and Latinos produce ambivalent war stories, lashed by conflicting feelings of patriotism and revulsion. In *China Men*, Maxine Hong Kingston writes about a pacifist brother who must choose between going to Viet Nam and fleeing the United States. He decides that the "United States was the only country he had ever lived in. He would not be driven out."[11] His is a different kind of war story, not unusual but relatively unknown. Having reluctantly volunteered for the U.S. Navy to avoid the inevitable draft that might turn him into a combat soldier, the brother spends his tour watching bombers go on missions but never having to drop a bomb or fire a missile himself. Kingston makes it clear that the line separating a Navy bureaucrat and a civilian at home going about her or his everyday activities was thin. Whenever "we ate a candy bar, when we drank grape juice, bought bread (ITT makes Wonder bread), wrapped food in plastic, made a phone call, put money in the bank, cleaned the oven, washed with soap, turned on the electricity, refrigerated food, cooked it, ran a computer, drove a car, rode an airplane, sprayed with insecticide, we were supporting the corporations that made tanks and bombers, napalm, defoliants, and bombs. For the carpet bombing."[12]

In Kingston's vision, the war is a total one, for in a military-industrial complex, where armed might defends capitalist right, the American civilian serves his patriotic purpose through unquestioning consumption. One antidote to civilian complicity is, implicitly, the power of the (anti) war story that Kingston tells about her brother's passive resistance, ending this way: he "had survived the Vietnam war. He had not gotten killed, and he had not killed anyone."[13] The brother's story is unlike the typical war story, whose climaxes involve a soldier's experience in killing and surviving. The banality of her brother's experience is Kingston's subversive point about how not all war stories need involve violent, and masculine, action and climax.[14]

Kingston's war story is different from the dominant Vietnam War story in other ways, too, most noticeably in how she compassionately gestures at the Latino presence in the U.S. Army. Before the war, her brother teaches remedial students, one of whom is Alfredo Campos, a Mexican immigrant in school to "get a job away from the grape fields." Campos volunteers for the war, and in Viet Nam all of his buddies are "Latins."[15] He has a Vietnamese girlfriend, who wears a leopard miniskirt in the picture he sends home. Kingston's brother screens a slideshow for Campos's classmates, and I imagine that what they see is Campos the tourist and traveler, someone learning what Paul Gilroy calls "vulgar cosmopolitanism."[16] Vulgar cosmopolitanism is worldliness without a passport, an unlicensed sophistication that threatens official representatives of any culture and guards of any border, an unintended consequence of the U.S. policy of shipping poor soldiers of color to fight overseas wars.

While compassion and empathy for the Vietnamese were not always the outcomes of these soldiers' time in Viet Nam, the oral histories and writings of working-class black and Latino soldiers shows them much more likely to feel empathy for the Vietnamese than their working-class white counterparts.[17] For white soldiers, empathy for the Vietnamese was usually a corollary to an existing tendency toward an elite cosmopolitanism. The most memorable literary incidents of such compassion among U.S. soldiers are found in high literary forms such as novels, memoirs, and poetry, and even there they are exceptional, written by a handful of highly educated war-veteran authors such as Tobias Wolff, Robert Olen Butler, Tim O'Brien, and Yusef Komunyakaa. If elite cosmopolitanism is necessary to cross over the racial difference between whites and Vietnamese, then the racial similarity between poor Americans of color and the Vietnamese was one stimulus for a vulgar cosmopolitanism seeded among the wretched of the earth.[18]

Aztlán and Vietnam, George Mariscal's collection of writings by Chicanos who went to war or who protested at home, illustrates this working-class capacity for a vulgar cosmopolitanism. For Mariscal, a "structure of recognition" enables many Chicanos to identify with the Vietnamese and to see in Vietnamese lives a reflection of their own. This structure of recognition is a mode of empathy and compassion that serves to heighten political consciousness among some Chicanos as they develop a sense of solidarity with the oppressed racial other.[19] But if some soldiers of color recognized in the Vietnamese a kinship based on the hard work of surviving poverty and colonization, others did a different kind of dirty work by participating in American atrocities, including the My Lai Massacre. By doing so, they forged what King called a "brutal solidarity" between white and black soldiers.[20] This fraternity's rituals of initiation involved both warring and whoring. What took place on the battlefields and in the brothels of Viet Nam reminds us that the oppressed of one country can swiftly become the oppressors in another country. In a telling footnote, Mariscal says that perhaps "the Chicano GI's recognition of his own situation in the Vietnamese, rather than leading to a heightened critical awareness, in fact produced exaggerated forms of violence, [with] possible dynamics of self-hatred."[21]

The Chicano soldier's capacity both to empathize with the Vietnamese and to murder them is hardly surprising, no matter how unsettling. Neither is it a surprise how American conduct of the war pivoted constantly between sympathy and slaughter, expressed, for example, in the vacillating U.S. rhetoric between "winning hearts and minds" and establishing "free-fire zones."[22] Compassion turns into murder, and vice versa, because they are faces of the same coin, one flipped every time a soldier encounters danger or the perception of danger. Because of this unpredictable element of chance and randomness, the individual emotions of compassion and empathy cannot stop a war machine's momentum. In the chiaroscuro of a battlefield, compassion and empathy dwell uneasily in both shadow and light. In shadow, compassion and empathy facilitate the killing by making us traumatized witnesses to mayhem, but in the most generous light, compassion and empathy enable the battlefield's conscientious objectors.

An Architecture of Empathy: Compassion in the Making of Art

Two antiwar novels illustrate how compassion and empathy have more of a fighting chance when wars are fought again in memory. Takeshi Kaiko's *Into a Black Sun* is a semiautobiographical account of a Japanese journalist in Viet Nam during the early years of the American War, while Ahn Junghyo's *White Badge* tells the story of South Korean soldiers fighting for the U.S. government, their services bought. But any kind of Asian racial empathy that might exist between Japanese, South Koreans, and Vietnamese does not necessarily lead to peaceful relations. The Japanese were at least partially responsible, during their occupation of Viet Nam in the Second World War, for a famine that killed an estimated one million to two million Vietnamese. Later, during the American War in Viet Nam, South Korean soldiers fashioned a reputation for brutality so widespread that Vietnamese civilians feared them more than U.S. soldiers. Yet in both novels, the portraits of South Vietnamese, who come off poorly in most American accounts, are empathetic. What the novels show is that a useful architecture of empathy is composed, as are all structures and styles of feeling, from many elements. Here, a mix of racial and cultural similarity is cemented by political consciousness, reinforced by intellectual and aesthetic cosmopolitanism.

Into a Black Sun illustrates the contradictory uses of compassion and empathy vividly. The narrator feels like someone who "had eyes only for atrocities."[23] The key moments for him are when he witnesses two public executions of young men accused of being Viet Cong terrorists. During the first execution, the narrator identifies empathetically with the executed and is sickened, but during the second execution, the narrator views the killing with cool objectivity. The fluctuation between the two moments of spectatorship is the movement between identifying with the victim and with the victimizer, a move that also characterizes the Japanese public's relationship to the war in Viet Nam. Scenes of warfare in Viet Nam provoked significant antiwar sentiment by reminding the Japanese public of its own status as victim of U.S. warfare and victimizer of other Asians.[24] Kaiko's novel constantly brings up moments of such identification, as the narrator sees how the Vietnamese now were so much like the Japanese of the Second World War, suffering under U.S. bombardment or enduring postwar starvation. But such compassionate identification may only mask the pleasure one finds in witnessing another's suffering or obscure the complicity of everyday Japanese in an economy that supported the American War. Kaiko illustrates this problem in an episode in which the narrator's desire to overcome being a spectator leads him to accompany Vietnamese troops into the jungle, where guerrillas ambush them. Facing a mortal threat to his life, the narrator discovers that his empathy for the Vietnamese dying around him is inconsequential next to his own desperate desire for self-preservation.

While Kaiko focuses on the subjective effects of complicity, *White Badge* deals with both a narrator's complicity and a nation's collusion. The narrator calls U.S. payments to the South Korean government for the use of its troops "blood money," which "fueled the modernization and development of the country. And owing to this contribution, the Republic of Korea, or at least a higher echelon of it, made a gigantic stride into the world market. Lives for sale. National mercenaries."[25] As in *Into a Black Sun*, the narrator in *White Badge* constantly sees a visual reminder of his own experience during the Korean War: "in these people I saw Korea twenty years ago," starving, begging, despairing, dying.[26] Unlike Kaiko's narrator, this narrator not only fluctuates between identifying as victim and victimizer, he is also a killer. His one moment of killing an enemy terrifies him, requiring him to obliterate the soldier with hand grenades, the physical equivalent to the way the narrator cannot identify with the man he is killing. Instead, he reserves his identification, in these moments of death, for other Korean soldiers.[27] Under pressure of his own possible demise, the narrator, like Kaiko's narrator, rapidly runs out of compassion for the Vietnamese and turns to preserving his own self and those most like him.

The experiences of these Japanese and South Korean narrators show compassion's conservativeness. Our empathy for others finds its inspiration in the way these others mirror our selves and move us in their resemblance, but that movement reaches a limit when the other's survival threatens our own self. This conservatism of compassion is, as Bruce Suttmeier argues, spectatorial.[28] We see the other's suffering from a distance that allows us to do absolutely nothing in the world or on the battlefield. We should not forget, however, that for the Vietnamese during wartime, and even afterward, national interest and self-interest often are not even hidden behind the rhetoric and practice of compassion. If the narrators of *White Badge* and *Into a Black Sun* clothe their self-interest in garments of empathy, some of the Vietnamese they encounter feel no need to do the same, so naked and abject is their suffering. In *White Badge*, a Vietnamese elder who leads a village of refugees forcibly displaced by South Korean soldiers tells the narrator, "We don't feel a sense of affinity with you"; this refusal of empathy exists because of the Koreans' foreign status in a country haunted by a thousand years of foreign occupation.[29] But regardless of their status as victims, the Vietnamese should not be exempt from the demands of ethical behavior by privileging their own victimization and forgetting their capacity to victimize.[30] The Vietnamese example reminds us that in looking at victims, or in feeling victimized ourselves, we often wrongly construe compassion and empathy as extravagances, luxuries from which the suffering are mistakenly and condescendingly excluded by right of their pain.

Imagined as necessary extravagances, however, compassion and empathy trim the distance between us and our others in ethical, political, and aesthetic ways that are not easily dismissed, particularly in the realm of memory and its reworking through art.[31] In both *Into a Black Sun* and *White Badge*, Vietnamese characters speak of their lives and histories in ways that are rare in American literature. In *Into a Black Sun*, for example, the narrator's Vietnamese translator tells him with bitterness that "no one really seriously sympathizes with us, because if they did they couldn't bear this country for another day."[32] The translator recognizes the superficiality of the Japanese narrator's compassion and how it literally does not move the narrator enough. But paradoxically, it is the Japanese narrator's sense of compassion that allows him to depict his own inadequacy in regard to an other who speaks back to him.

Still, despite compassion's limitations, we can argue that as a style of feeling, compassion inflects the style of art, itself a luxury no less needed. Through these necessary extravagances of compassion and empathy realized in art, the "America" in these works is not the same "America" in

American cultural work about Viet Nam. One major reason is that the Vietnamese who appear in these Asian novels and American minority reports are not the same Vietnamese who disappear in American literature. Their appearance demands that our discourse about the war be transformed from an American monologue into a conversation among many equals. Even if this conversation does not stop killing or complicity in wartime, it is measurable in its impact on how we talk about a war in its aftermath. Kaiko gestures at the importance of such conversation in the biblical verse from 1 Corinthians 13:12 with which he begins *Into a Black Sun*: "we see now through a mirror / in an obscure manner, / but then face to face. / Now I know in part, but then / I shall know even as I have been known." The promise of compassion and empathy for an other is thus this glimpse of self-consciousness, an always shadowy knowledge that is necessary before the work of recovering from war and constructing peace can begin.

Cosmopolitanism as a Structure of Feeling

Do cosmopolitanism and compassion make a difference in the world at large? Do they have any effect in leading toward Immanuel Kant's call for "perpetual peace"? In understanding cosmopolitanism's possibilities and limits, looking toward Williams's suggestion that emotions are felt individually but produced socially is helpful.[33] Feeling is never simply individual, and it is never unique. But since we may take our feelings to be only our own, their structural dimension is difficult to detect or articulate, even though it is the thing that would connect us to others and make us feel at home with them. The new "semantic figures" of these structures must be reinterpreted by a later generation of critics, who can approach them "at a reduced tension . . . the intensity of experienced fear and shame now dispersed and generalized."[34] From the perspectives of artists, critics, and audiences, cosmopolitanism is fundamentally important as a structure that allows individual feelings to connect to shared social feelings through a work of art.

But cosmopolitanism has another structural dimension built in with the aesthetic, found in the political, and here much of the controversy around cosmopolitanism, and the usefulness of compassion, is found. Cosmopolitanism's critics have amassed a powerful set of objections, for even if cosmopolitanism can cultivate a greater compassion for others and strangers, many doubt that it can compel people to action in meaningful ways beyond the individual for the following reasons: cosmopolitanism imagines a world citizen, which is impossible without a world state; even if such a world state existed, it would in effect be totalitarian, with no competing power to check it; cosmopolitanism underestimates the enduring power of nationalism and the nation-state in determining cultural identities, political rights, and economic benefits; cosmopolitanism is an abstraction that cannot compel real love or compassion, which must be rooted in the visceral attachments of people to the local, not the global; cosmopolitans are rootless people with no loyalty, more inclined to love humanity in the abstract than people in the concrete; cosmopolitanism is Western in origin and not easily transposed to non-Western societies, which may be opposed to cosmopolitanism's global ambitions and belief in individual rights and liberties; cosmopolitanism has no philosophy of solidarity, which is necessary for mobilizing political alliances to struggle for a cosmopolitan world; some of the diasporic, mobile, migrant peoples that cosmopolitanism favors are actually committed to the global capitalism that some cosmopolitans disavow; and cosmopolitan literature may do more to enhance the reputations of cosmopolitan writers than to help the poor or exotic populations whose stories populate the literature.[35]

Given a world dominated by the World Trade Organization, the Group of Eight, the World Bank, the International Monetary Fund, Google, the Hollywood film industry, and so on, most of them led and staffed by fairly cosmopolitan people, the cosmopolitan sensitivities described here in writing and reading literature seem anemic. The cosmopolitan's sympathy for strangers may do more to pleasure the cosmopolitan than to change the deep structures of inequality that make travel, conversation, and consumption possible for certain classes, including the managerial elites of global political and financial organs. Thus, Elaine Scarry argues that cosmopolitan ideals are meaningful only if enacted beyond the realms of education, culture, and the aesthetic, in institutions that have political, economic, and legal impact on people's lives. The test for "imaginative consciousness," she writes, is not a "pleasurable feeling of cosmopolitan largesse" but a "concrete willingness to change constitutions and laws"— an argument that echoes Kant's proposal for a federation of cooperating nations to ensure peace.[36] But Scarry is one of cosmopolitanism's more generous critics, for while recognizing its limits, she also argues that works of the imagination can expand human consciousness. Still, she marks those limits clearly, saying that "the human capacity to injure other people is very great precisely because our capacity to imagine other people is very small."[37] Art and literature, as representatives of peace, simply do not have enough power to transform the world, or so the anti-cosmopolitan argument goes, stating, essentially, that cosmopolitanism is too much about individual feeling and not enough about social structure.

These criticisms indicate cosmopolitanism's weaknesses and limits, but they do not invalidate cosmopolitanism altogether, unless we insist on some diametrical opposition between "abstract" cosmopolitanism and something like "concrete" patriotism or nationalism. As the debate around Martha Nussbaum's polemic on behalf of cosmopolitanism suggests, patriotism and cosmopolitanism are like other seemingly diametrical opposites, deeply dependent on each other despite evident antagonism.[38] Without love of one's own country, one cannot love the countries of others, and without the love of humanity, the love for one's own kind appears shriveled. But since the love of humanity seems to be in much shorter supply than the love people feel for their own kind, cosmopolitanism has the advantage of urgency and priority for those looking for ways to cultivate peace. Without cosmopolitanism's demand to empathize with others who are not like us—to see oneself as another, and the other as oneself—we are left with a dangerously circumscribed empathy, which does have political use and structural impact. This is evident in President Jimmy Carter's assertion that the war in Viet Nam enacted "mutual destruction" on both countries. Mutual here implies equal, an equation one can accept only if one ignores the vastly unequal damage inflicted on the United States and Viet Nam, not to mention Cambodia and Laos. This equation of mutual destruction shows how compassion and empathy can be used in art and politics to render people equally human in ways that ignore how people are not equal in terms of their capacity to inflict suffering on others. If compassion and empathy circumscribed by nationalism can have a political and economic impact, then why can't compassion and empathy unleashed by cosmopolitanism have an impact as well?

Because, cosmopolitanism's critics would say, nationalist empathy has a vehicle for harnessing emotion, the nation-state, while cosmopolitan empathy has no such structure to turn compassion into action. Yet the necessity of grounding cosmopolitanism on the soil of real places has already taken place in partnership with nationalism, articulated in Kwame Anthony Appiah's version of cosmopolitanism. On the one hand, his cosmopolitanism values conversation with strangers, where conversation is "a metaphor for engagement with the experience and the ideas of others." On the other hand, he says that "there are limits to cosmopolitan tolerance. . . . [W]e will not stop with conversation. Toleration requires a concept of the intolerable."[39] Although Appiah never mentions how tolerant cosmopolitans will deal with the intolerable, perhaps they will conduct what Gilroy calls an "armored cosmopolitanism," one that not only confronts "terror" but also resurrects the imperial mission of benevolent conquest in a style better suited to culturally sensitive global capitalists.[40]

Although cosmopolitanism's exploitation by nationalism and capitalism may invalidate it for some, perhaps this exploitation is actually a sign of hope, for if the powerful can take up cosmopolitanism, it must mean that cosmopolitanism is useful politically, contrary to what its critics have argued. Without overstating the case for cosmopolitanism, literature, or art, and while acknowledging the necessity of changing laws, policies, and institutions, I find it clear that cosmopolitanism as a feeling is required to change structures. Just as warfare needs patriotism, the struggle for peace needs the cosmopolitan imagination of a utopian future. Without such an imagination, and without the expansive deployment of compassion beyond the borders of our own kin, we are resigned to the world we have inherited, one that we are in danger of destroying through self-interested habits of aggression and heedless consumption. Gayatri Spivak argues for the "supplementation of collective effort by love" and the "mind-changing one-on-one of responsible contact," both part of the cosmopolitan creed of compassion and conversation.[41] Spivak reconfigures cosmopolitanism's urge for intimacy, the need to put distant people in touch with one another in the name of revolutionary solidarity. But since the ability to travel and to meet distant others is not available to all, cosmopolitanism makes a difference when it brings us closer in the imagination to distant others. The structure of feeling in this case is imaginary, but no less potent, for in some cases people may prefer to know each other from a distance rather than in proximity (and conversely, physical intimacy may only breed contempt, and worse). In this context, Nussbaum's defense of art's political and social purpose is convincing, when she says that art, particularly narrative art, facilitates a "cosmopolitan education" that allows us to see others empathetically and to see ourselves from the other's perspective.[42]

This cosmopolitan education works not just in direct encounters with works of art, great and small, and not just in schools, where art is used for pedagogy. In fact, cosmopolitan education works environmentally, seeping into our minds and our emotions through a set of assumptions that our own cultures create about which other cultures are civilized and human. An average American need never have gone to England or to a university to know Shakespeare's name and hence to feel, however dimly, a human connection with English culture. Even American tendencies against intellectuals, the elites, and the French would not prevent an average American from feeling that the French have done something worth being saved (or so I hope). In the absence of this cosmopolitan education about certain others that is enacted on the student (in the classroom) and the citizen (through mass culture), a vacuum is created in the human soul when it comes to those others not represented in a given society's cosmopolitan education. Those who are not represented are more likely, in times of war, to be subjected to a violence whose ferocity is far bloodier than that practiced on enemies we consider to be more human. Violence can be measured and tempered, and cosmopolitan education is fundamental to limiting violence on those we see as closer to us on the human scale and justifying ever greater violence against those we see as further away on the animal horizon.

We can measure our cosmopolitan sympathies for others via the bomb test. How many bombs are we willing to drop? Where will we drop them, and on whom? What kinds of bombs will we use? Much has been made of how the United States dropped more bombs on Viet Nam, Cambodia, and Laos during the American War than were dropped on all of Europe during the Second World War, and how the total tonnage and indiscriminate bombing of soldiers and civilians was a measure of the war's brutality. This brutality would not have been possible if Americans were not already predisposed to consider Southeast Asians inhuman. Another bomb test is, obviously, the nuclear one. In *The English Patient*, the novelist Michael Ondaatje depicts the atomic bombing of Hiroshima from the perspective of one of his characters, the Indian sapper Kip, a soldier in the British Army whose hazardous specialty is defusing unexploded bombs. Hearing of the atomic bomb's detonation, Kip has a flash of understanding: the bomb would never have been dropped on a white country. For Kip, the harsh illumination provided by the bomb begins his decolonization through his recognition of the racism in Western civilization that allows Western technology to be used against non-Western people. As a novel, *The English Patient* both depicts what happens when one culture does not recognize another culture as equally human and is, itself, as an artistic artifact, evidence against the underlying logic of Eurocentric racism, one strand of which is the belief that only whites can write.[43] *The English Patient* proves Kingston's claim in *The Fifth Book of Peace* that "war causes peace" by producing revulsion on the part of war's witnesses, who lead not only antiwar movements but also write antiwar literature.[44]

Still, writing back against racism, empire, and war, as Ondaatje does, takes place not on the universal scale but on the intimate scale of the individual artist and work. Without these individual artists and works, cosmopolitan education on a universal scale cannot take place. Yet the criticism of cosmopolitanism advanced by Scarry points to the inadequacy of individual works of art and how rare it is to find one that enacts significant change, such as Harriet Beecher Stowe's *Uncle Tom's Cabin* or E. M. Forster's *A Passage to India*. My suspicion is that many people share Scarry's view about art, although with a less generous spirit. Those suspicious people who do not read literature may be skeptical about whether it has any purpose or use, questions not normally directed toward the law or business or government. But does the average lawyer or businessperson or bureaucrat make more difference, inflict more damage, or do more good than the average writer? The average writer and the average book need to be measured against their equivalents—average people in average jobs—not against daunting standards of making a universal difference or changing the world. Against such high standards, most of us would count as failures, too, not just the average work of art or the average obscure writer. So let the midlist novelist be compared to the vice president of a regional bank; let Shakespeare be compared to Bill Gates; let the novel be compared to the computer; let cosmopolitan education be compared to war. Only with the appropriate comparisons can we say whether art, and the cosmopolitan impulse to see art as a means to peace, make a difference. As Kingston says, "Peace has to be supposed, imagined, divined, dreamed."[45] This kind of dreaming will not happen without cosmopolitanism and its persistent, irritating reminder that it is easier to wage war than to fight for peace.

Conclusion: Compulsory Empathy and the Enemy's Voice

Without cosmopolitanism's call for an unbounded empathy extending to all of humanity, we are left with nationalism's compulsory empathy, enacted in its own structures of feeling. For contemporary American audiences, "the Vietnam War" names a structure of feeling that tunes out empathy for the other and helps Americans forget that "Viet Nam" is the name of a country, not a war. "The Vietnam War" is expressed through art most affectively in the Hollywood subgenre called the Vietnam War movie, exemplified in films such as *The Deer Hunter*, *Platoon*, and *Apocalypse Now*. These films individually demand empathy for the U.S. soldiers who are the protagonists of their narratives. Collectively, though, the films create a system of compulsory empathy imposed on American audiences as a whole, in two ways. First, audiences are compelled to empathize with the United States since these soldiers and their suffering—both as victims and victimizers—stand in for the emotional, cultural, and psychic devastation wreaked on the United States by the war. Of course, not every American will feel the same degree of empathy toward American experiences, and some Americans will resist empathizing with these films. But compulsory empathy works even more effectively in a second, negative fashion, by providing American audiences few other options for empathy besides the stories featuring Americans. In the absence of stories or news featuring others, the moral imagination of Americans is inevitably stunted, since a compulsory system offers very limited alternatives to the thing that it makes normal. Thus, if one is not straight in a regime of compulsory heterosexuality, one risks being labeled queer; if one does not feel for American experiences in a system of compulsory empathy, one skirts charges of betrayal, as was the case in the early years after 9/11. In that climate, it was both outrageous and courageous for the novelist Barbara Kingsolver to publish an article only days after 9/11 in which she both mourned for its victims and reminded her fellow Americans that bombings of that scale were hardly unusual and that Americans were often responsible for them. "Yes, it was the worst thing that's happened, but only this week," she wrote. "Surely, the whole world grieves for us right now. And surely it also hopes we might have learned, from the taste of our own blood . . . that no kind of bomb ever built will extinguish hatred."[46]

Kingsolver's perspective is possible because she refuses the compulsory empathy of nationalism, remembering the plight of others who have been bombed and seeing the United States from their anguished eyes, in a way that recalls another portion of King's speech: "here is the true meaning and value of compassion and nonviolence, when it helps us to see the enemy's point of view, to hear his questions, to know his assessment of ourselves. For from his view we may indeed see the basic weaknesses of our own condition, and if we are mature, we may learn and grow and profit from the wisdom of the brothers who are called the opposition."[47] King labels the other not a stranger or a foreigner, as is the tendency in most versions of cosmopolitanism, but the enemy, a word that compels us to ponder how we use violence on the enemy and the violence with which the enemy threatens us. Turning to the enemy's perspective is a crucial step in eradicating the sentimentalism and idealism that weakens cosmopolitanism, for such a move reminds us that the other is not likely to see us from a generously compassionate point of view. Indeed, the other—the enemy, the terrorist—is likely to be subject to his or her own version of compulsory empathy. To arrive at any hope of a compassionate conversation, cosmopolitanism must therefore negotiate between competing systems of compulsory empathy produced from communities demanding attention to their own grievances. Appiah and Nussbaum underestimate the difficulty of achieving such a conversation by forgetting to remind us how histories of violence and inequity render entry into these conversations so difficult for women, the colonized, and the minority. Shut out of these conversations, these populations may turn to violence to speak. Appiah calls such gestures anticosmopolitan intolerance, and so they may be in some cases, but in other cases some may feel that violence is the only tolerable alternative to confront unjust power. Understanding that our enemies are motivated not only by hatred but also by compassion and empathy—in other words, by love—allows us to understand the partial and prejudiced nature of our own compulsory emotions.

Western tourists in Viet Nam routinely encounter compulsory empathy of another kind, the one fostered by revolutionary idealism and displayed in the battlefield memorials and the historical, political, and military museums frequented by such tourists. How tourists react to such displays—whether they reject them as propaganda or recognize them as another nation's emblems of compulsory empathy—is determined to a large extent by their recognition of, attachment to, or reflection on their own systems of compulsory empathy.[48] But for those readers who have never been to Viet Nam, I will use *Nhật Ký Đặng Thùy Trâm* (The Diary of Dang Thuy Tram) as my concluding example of the complexities involved in hearing the enemy's voice. Dang Thuy Tram was a young North Vietnamese doctor who served in South Vietnam during the American War and who was killed by U.S. troops in 1970, at twenty-seven. She kept a diary of her two years of service, which was recovered by a U.S. military intelligence officer, Frederick Whitehurst, who kept it for decades before he found the chance to return it to Tram's family in 2005. It was published in Viet Nam later that year and sold some 430,000 copies in a country in which the average print run is one thousand to two thousand copies. Critics have attributed the phenomenal success of her diary to the idealistic, romantic, vulnerable personality on display; the readiness of a postwar generation to revisit a war that many young Vietnamese do not remember and do not understand; and the willingness of the government to allow a wider discussion of the war than via the narrower terms set in the past.[49] The epic story of the diary's disappearance and reappearance also played a part in the book's marketability and its eventual translation into more than a dozen languages.

For the English version, Tram's family and the publisher selected the title *Last Night I Dreamed of Peace*, extracted from two occasions in the diary in which she mentions dreaming of peace.[50] In the United States, the title of the book has helped to shape its marketing and reception as a book that offers hope for peace and the reconciliation between enemies. In reading the book, however, what becomes noticeable is not the desire for a reconciliation between enemies—in fact, there is no such desire, only "hatred" as "hot as the summer sun" for the U.S. and South Vietnamese militaries—but for a peace that arises from victory and the defeat of the enemy, whom she calls "bandits," "vicious dogs," and "bloodthirsty devils" and against whom she dreams not of peace but of revenge for all whom they have killed.[51] What is a cosmopolitan to make of this enemy's voice?

While the publisher's framing of the book as a call for "peace" steers the audience's reading in a certain direction—and demonstrates that "peace" can be turned into a commodity as much as war—my suspicion is that the diary's power for American readers comes not so much from the gestures at peace but from the highly recognizable narrative of compulsory empathy offered by Tram of herself. What is memorable about her is the depth of her compassionate feeling for her patients, her comrades, and her fellow Vietnamese. "It's not my love for a certain young man that makes me feel and act the way I do," she writes. "This is something immense and vibrant within me. My longings extend to many people. . . . What am I? I am a girl with a heart brimming with emotions."[52] The diary vividly records her willingness to sacrifice youth, romantic love, and even her own life for the revolution, her affections for the "brothers" that she adopts among her comrades (and their more romantic ardor for her), her fear of being misjudged by other revolutionaries, her contempt for the petty politics and jealousies among members of the Communist Party, and her struggles with what she depicts as her bourgeois inclinations. Her diary makes clear that romantic love and revolutionary love share roots, as do compassion for one's comrades and compassion for the nation. Of a soldier who has just died, she writes, "Your heart has stopped so that the heart of the nation can beat forever," and she describes feeling that she and her adopted brothers share "a miraculous love, a love that makes people forget themselves and think only of their dear ones."[53] But in the same entry that describes how she is "profoundly compassionate" toward her wounded comrades, she also mentions "American bandits."[54] The model of emotion she offers is therefore not so different from the very one that Kingsolver criticizes, the deep feeling for one's own that is shored up by hatred for the other, the harnessing of individual empathy for the greater cause of patriotic war. As Tram says, "This diary is not only for my private life. It must also record the lives of my people and their innumerable sufferings, these folks of steel from this Southern land."[55]

An American audience's ability to extract sentiments of peace from Tram's diary is possible not in spite of the hatred for Americans on display but because of it; ironically, Tram's patriotic hatred for Americans is understandable to Americans who have patriotically hated others. But it is also the passage of time that makes American audiences willing to reconcile with a past enemy, to recognize in the enemy's sentiments of love and hatred a set of twinned emotions felt by Americans, as well. But as far as American audiences are indeed in search of reconciliation with their former Vietnamese enemies, what does "peace" mean? Does it mean simply getting over a war or recognizing that the struggle to end war continues? King's analysis of the war in Viet Nam is again prescient when he connects his present of 1967 to our present, saying:

> The war in Vietnam is but a symptom of a far deeper malady within the American spirit, and if we ignore this sobering reality . . . we will find ourselves organizing "clergy and laymen concerned" committees for the next generation. They will be concerned about Guatemala and Peru. They will be concerned about Thailand and Cambodia. They will be concerned about Mozambique and South Africa. We will be marching for these and a dozen other names and attending rallies without

end unless there is a significant and profound change in American life.[56]

The wars in Iraq and Afghanistan constitute the present from which we look back toward Viet Nam. Thus, in reading Tram's diary in an American context today, the English title—*Last Night I Dreamed of Peace*—might provoke a sense that we should be able to reconcile with our current enemies if we can do so with our former enemies. So it is that the English title of the diary, inaccurate as it is in foregrounding a relatively insignificant theme in Tram's writing, nevertheless signals hope for a broader peace than the one Tram imagined.

But the fact that we are still at war forty-six years after King's speech and forty-three years after Tram's last words may mean that the compassion called for by King is inadequate. Or it may mean that the compassion called for by King, one that inspires nonviolence rather than violence, never truly came into existence. After all, our efforts to speak of the wars in Iraq and Afghanistan are still inadequate and inarticulate, and at least one major reason is the paucity of Iraqi and Afghan stories. Invoking the voices of enemies, others, or strangers is hardly innocent or unproblematic, as numerous critics have shown and any study of the American demand for Vietnamese voices will make evident. Nevertheless, the presence of those voices and the problems they articulate are preferable to their absence and erasure. Complicating the task of attending to those voices is the ongoing work of understanding our place in past and present structures of feeling. For Williams, a structure of feeling in its own present exists "at the very edge of semantic availability," which in retrospect may be seen as part of a "significant (often in fact minority) generation."[57] Looking back to the war in Viet Nam and the stories that have emerged from it, what we witness are a minority of authors using cosmopolitanism and compassion both to challenge American representations of the Vietnamese and to call for a peaceful alternative to the American War. If the call for peace by these authors is oftentimes inarticulate, it is because it is uttered like the same call today, in what Gilroy calls a state of "hopeful despair," an apt description of cosmopolitanism itself.[58] In this fragile structure of feeling that is cosmopolitanism, peace exists, but only on the edge of semantic availability, on the tips of our tongues.

Notes

1. Carson and Shepard, *A Call to Conscience*, 144. Throughout this chapter, I will normally use "Viet Nam," which is how the country's name is written by the Vietnamese. When I use "Vietnam" or "the Vietnam War," these words denote the American point of view on Viet Nam. My thanks to audiences at Texas Tech University, Ohio State University, Rikkyo University, and Harvard University for their questions and comments that helped me to refine my arguments, and to Frederick Aldama, Lawrence Buell, Nicholas Donofrio, Yuan Shu, and Adena Springarn for arranging some of these talks. A longer version of this chapter appeared in *Japanese Journal of American Studies* 20 (2009): 1–26.

2. Carson and Shepard, *A Call to Conscience*, 149.

3. Lauren Berlant argues this in "Compassion (and Withholding)," in Berlant, *Compassion*, 1–13, as does Suzanne Keen in Keen, *Empathy and the Novel*, 35.

4. This argument is advanced in Edelman, *No Future*; and Suttmeier, "Seeing Past Destruction."

5. Yui, "Perception Gaps between Asia and the United States of America," 71. Keen agrees that empathy for one's own does not lead to an "ethics of compassion" for others: Keen, *Empathy and the Novel*, 164.

6. These distinctions between sympathy and empathy come from Song, *Strange Future*, 87–90. Similarly, Keen argues that empathy is feeling with another "as opposed to feeling *for* another, or sympathy." Keen, *Empathy and the Novel*, xxi.

7. This, Kathleen Woodward argues, is Berlant's reading of *Uncle Tom's Cabin*, which Woodward calls the "ur-text" for what she defines as "liberal narratives of compassion" in her essay "Calculating Compassion," in Berlant, *Compassion*, 59–86.

8. Sontag, *Regarding the Pain of Others*, 101.

9. The chapter "Structures of Feeling," in Williams, *Marxism and Literature*, is more suggestive than exhaustive. Williams does gesture briefly at the relation of "differentiated structures of feeling to differentiated classes" but does not explore how different classes may have different feelings. Besides class, the only other form of differentiation to feeling that he discusses is generational.

10. Concerning storytelling and peace, Gayle Sato argues that "it is the process of narrative reenactment—a process of returning to the same ground to remember and retell it yet articulate it anew each time, a process that creates an incremental and always partial narrative recovery of the past—that contains the possibility of an ethical, community-building practice of pacifism": Sato, "Reconfiguring the 'American Pacific,'" 114.

11. Kingston, *China Men*, 283.

12. Ibid., 284.

13. Ibid., 304.

14. Kingston revisits her brother's experiences in Kingston, *The Fifth Book of Peace*.

15. Kingston, *China Men*, 281–82.

16. Gilroy, *Postcolonial Melancholia*, 67.

17. See Mariscal, *Aztlán and Viet Nam*; Terry, *Bloods*.

18. Komunyakaa is the only nonwhite writer in this group. I include him here to emphasize how cosmopolitanism, class, and whiteness are usually aligned among American veteran authors. Komunyakaa is the exceptional African American author who proves the rule that dominant stories of the war are usually told by white men.

19. Mariscal, *Aztlán and Viet Nam*, 39.

20. Carson and Shepard, *A Call to Conscience*, 143.

21. Mariscal, *Aztlán and Viet Nam*, 311.

22. The Catch-22 of American attitudes is expressed most infamously, but perhaps apocryphally, by the American major who said, "It became necessary to destroy the town in order to save it." The quote was reported by Peter Arnett in the *New York Times* in February 1968, but it apparently has been difficult to corroborate.

23. Kaiko, *Into a Black Sun*, 71.

24. See Suttmeier, "Seeing Past Destruction."

25. Junghyo, *White Badge*, 40.

26. Ibid., 53.

27. Ibid., 76, 189.

28. Suttmeier, "Seeing Past Destruction."

29. Ibid., 91.

30. I elaborate on this point in Nguyen, "Speak of the Dead, Speak of Viet Nam."

31. The dialectic of necessity and extravagance comes from Kingston, *The Woman Warrior*, and Sau-ling C. Wong's critical appropriation of that dialectic to describe the workings of Asian American literature in Wong, *Reading Asian American Literature*.

32. Kaiko, *Into a Black Sun*, 151.

33. Williams, *Marxism and Literature*, 131–32.

34. Ibid., 134.

35. The commentary on cosmopolitanism is extensive. For a few sources, see Appiah, *Cosmopolitanism*; Archibugi, *Debating Cosmopolitics*; Brennan, *At Home in the World*; Cheah and Robbins, *Cosmopolitics*; Clifford, *Routes*; Derrida, *On Cosmopolitanism and Forgiveness*; Douzinas, *Human Rights and Empire*; Gilroy, *Postcolonial Melancholia*; Hollinger, *Postethnic America*; Kant, *To Perpetual Peace*; Kaplan, *Questions of Travel*; Nussbaum, "Patriotism and Cosmopolitanism"; Srikanth, *The World Next Door*; Vertovec and Cohen, *Conceiving Cosmopolitanism*.

36. Scarry, "The Difficulty of Imagining Other People," 105.

37. Ibid., 103.

38. See the essays in Nussbaum, *For Love of Country?*.

39. Appiah, *Cosmopolitanism*, 85, 144.

40. Gilroy, *Postcolonial Melancholia*, 59–60.

41. Gayatri Spivak, "Cultural Talks in the Hot Peace: Revisiting The 'Global Village,'" in Cheah and Robbins, 340.

42. Nussbaum, *For Love of Country?*, 6.

43. Ondaatje, *The English Patient*.

44. Kingston, *The Fifth Book of Peace*, 227.

45. Ibid., 61.

46. Barbara Kingsolver, "A Pure, High Note of Anguish," *Los Angeles Times*, 23 September 2001, available online at http://articles.latimes.com/2001/sep/23/opinion/op-48850 (accessed 12 September 2008).

47. Carson and Shepard, *A Call to Conscience*, 151. But it is important to reiterate here that empathy has no inherent political meaning and can be deployed as much to fight a war as to end it. Keen quotes from Secretary of Defense Robert McNamara in Errol Morris's film *The Fog of War* about the need to "empathize with your enemy"—or, as McNamara goes on to say, about how "we must try to put ourselves inside their skin and look at us through their eyes, just to understand the thoughts that lie behind their decisions and their actions": Keen, *Empathy and the Novel*, 105.

48. For more on American tourists' reactions to Vietnamese war memorials and museums, see Edmundson, "In the New Vietnam"; Laderman, *Tours of Vietnam*; Schwenkel, *The American War in Contemporary Vietnam*.

49. For more on the history of the book, see Fox, "Fire, Spirit, Love, Story"; Vo, "Memories That Bind"; Vuong, "*The Diary of Dang Thuy Tram* and the Postwar Vietnamese Mentality."

50. Tram, *Last Night I Dreamed of Peace*, 27, 111.

51. The quotes are from Tram, *Last Night I Dreamed of Peace*, 47, 74, 83, 114, the English-language edition of the diary, although I have cross-checked the translations with the original Vietnamese edition, *Nhật Ký Đặng Thùy Trâm* (Hanoi: Nhà Xuất Bản Hội Nhà Văn, 2005).

52. Ibid., 96.

53. Ibid., 83, 86.

54. Ibid., 104.

55. Ibid., 158.

56. Carson and Shepard, *A Call to Conscience*, 156.

57. Williams, *Marxism and Literature*, 134.

58. Gilroy, *Postcolonial Melancholia*, 75.

CHAPTER 7

Mariam B. Lam

Việt Nam's Growing Pains
Postsocialist Cinema Development and Transnational Politics

What the rest of the world knows of Việt Nam today includes the global Phở noodle soup phenomenon (with T-shirts playfully declaring "I ♥ U Phở -ever" and "What the Phở?"), the bit-by-bit cultural matriculation of celebrity adoptees of Julie Andrews and "Brangelina" (Brad Pitt and Angelina Jolie), and George W. Bush donning his inadvertently subversive transgender sky-blue silk *aó daì* tunic at the Asia-Pacific Economic Cooperation Summit in Hà Nội in November 2006. For those who do not enjoy "ethnic" food, Hollywood entertainment propaganda machines, and political follies news programming, we still have *the movies* proper.

As we have seen in countless Vietnam War films, the continuous stream of Cold War historical manifestos, and the renewed rhetoric of multinational corporate investment, the military-industrial imaginary of "Vietnam" is also still very much alive in many people's hearts and minds.[1] On the diasporic shores of every continent now, we find thriving ethnic enclaves, uneven upward socioeconomic mobility, and the lingering dramas of anticommunist protest against particular areas of Socialist Republic governance. In recent years, these transnational communities have managed to involve their political leaders—ambassadors to Việt Nam and members of Congress in the United States, for example—in efforts to draw international attention to particular policies and practices "back home" in Việt Nam.[2] These diasporas include those who make use of their new political capital, as well as their own personal venture capital, to push for improvement in the sociocultural conditions of both extended kin and country; they also include those with more individualistic pursuits.

How do we in the "international community" make sense of these circulating transnational cultural-economic identities and ideologies? How does the socialist state of Việt Nam make sense—and cents—of them? In addition to the migration of peoples across borders, cultural "traffic" currently flows within Việt Nam, throughout Asia, and across oceans in very concrete material forms.[3] Examining these processes, their forms, and their participants furthers the internationalization of the field of Vietnamese cultural studies to reveal the unique ways in which Vietnamese cultural history challenges existing theoretical and methodological approaches to film studies, Việt Nam studies, and area studies.[4] This chapter will map out the intersecting arenas within which "the nation," its diaspora, and global capitalism are collaborating, competing, and compromising in the development of contemporary Vietnamese cinema.

Further, as a result of the relatively recent rise in Việt Nam's gross national product and the heightened international visibility that has come with membership in the World Trade Organization, the state has necessarily become more attentive to its reputation in the global media. The world is now looking beyond the Vietnam of the war years to a revived economy with hopes of new and lucrative cultural dynamism. Vietnamese cultural-policy makers and cultural producers alike, then, must both conform to and negotiate a more salient sociocultural *politics of pressure*—a combined top-down and bottom-up politics of international, national, and interpersonal pressure. Such pressure comes in the form of international governmental and economic collaborative ventures; transnational professional, intellectual, and social networks; mainstream international perception and media accounts of the development of film education in Việt Nam; and Việt Nam's deepening industrial interdependence. Foreign film festivals and tours, college graduates who want more than tourist-sector jobs, and increasing diasporic presence all infect the contemporary study of Vietnamese advancement in cultural education. This chapter will therefore also explore and highlight what does *not* fit neatly into the growing curriculum and repertoire of film education, and what does *not* get taught or analyzed in national cinematic history and criticism, to provide the historical backdrop for the current developments.

Finally, in the current postsocialist leaning of Việt Nam's neoliberal market practices,[5] "culture" has become an increasingly instrumental import-export commodity, just as it has served the United States well as its leading export commodity in recent decades.[6]

The growth and familiarity of information technology in cross-cultural contact ushers in the desire to adopt and participate in the imagined "world culture." Foreign people, distant exotic places, and globally repackaged commodities become imbued with economic and cultural value and social cachet, even within the socialist state and certainly for its young population.[7] Culture and media are the new terrains of contemporary ideological battlegrounds over such (in)visibility.

Some critics bemoan the widening chasm between the haves and have-nots or the inaccessibility of social media, the Internet, domestic education, and professional occupational placement for all citizens. World-wide fads and pop culture such as *Dancing with the Stars* and *American Idol*–style entertainment, Yahoo! 360 pages, and Facebook (intermittently banned or firewalled in Việt Nam) encourage a "Me" generation in which personal celebrity reigns as the best path to economic and social success. Others fear for Việt Nam's global cultural assimilation, lamenting the absorption of local cultural forms and outlets into multinational corporate sectors and World War II service industries (a hybrid breed of a global middleman managerial class and economic-processing zone). These production skills, which cater to international markets, soon become more individually and nationally profitable than historically "traditional" Vietnamese arts, crafts, and cultures. With global commercial consumption comes the sense of anticipated loss of diversity in ethnicities, cultural practices, and languages. Greater permanent outmigration by export laborers, skilled professionals, and intellectuals, as well as those on the economic and social margins in search of gold-mountain dreams, reflects internal developmental contradictions. Within this dense context of globalization described by critics such as Arjun Appadurai, David Harvey, Fredric Jameson, and Saskia Sassen, the study of *culture* and its processes of globalization must be understood anew on all sides of the Pacific and by scholars of Vietnamese and of Việt Nam–U.S. history, politics, and economics.

The presentations and broadcast displays of more worldwide sporting events in, increased travel and tourism to, and hosting of international pageants and economic summits by Việt Nam, for example, all project an image of progressive multiculturalism toward greater awareness and understanding between diverse peoples and politics. Vietnamese film criticism, then, likewise needs to move beyond close readings of specific scenes or characters, and beyond simple quotes by film auteurs, toward a more political-economic approach to film production and thematic content if it is to teach us anything significant about cinema's role on these ideological cultural-nationalist battlegrounds. The domestic penetration of Hollywood blockbusters and Korean pop music and melodramas into Việt Nam, together with the popularization of local Vietnamese cuisine internationally (e.g., by the food critics Anthony Bourdain and Andrew Zimmern) and of remote beach resorts beyond the country's borders (e.g., features about Nha Trang on cable television's Travel Channel), diverts attention from the discrepant and discordant spaces of rapid national economic growth—that is, Việt Nam's growing pains.

Vietnamese Cinematic History

The historical irony of these newly rhetoricized cultural models is not lost on the diasporic Vietnamese communities that have pushed for deeper and more thorough cultural education in Việt Nam over the past three decades.[8] While these critics tend toward cynicism and skepticism, they continue to exert pressure on the postsocialist state to follow through on its new promises—promises the diasporic communities now share with their extended network of kin and professional collaborators inside Việt Nam. If in the early years of protest politics there was suspicion that the diasporic communities were dismissive of the interests of the Vietnamese people, such charges are now quieted. The political pressures by diasporics and nationals are now in global ideological alignment. Historically, the impetus for the collective compulsion within the diaspora to participate in Vietnamese domestic issues has been partly a response to disavowals of the expatriates' love of, and loyalty to, Vietnamese nationalism in the postwar decades and the historical amnesia that has attempted to sever their cultural lineage and allegiance to the nation. Harsh critics of diasporic political angst often also forget or omit that much of the expatriates' investment in "homeland politics" has resulted directly from very material contributions in the form of sending pharmaceuticals and remittances, as well as working with international nongovernmental organizations (NGOs) in Việt Nam after 1975.

To trace some of this nearly forty-year ideological alignment that has slowly formed by way of filial and social networks and professional linkages, I focus here on one unique development that has been fostered over time with collective transnational capital and a mutually respectful spirit of domestic and diasporic industrial collaboration. Today, various academic and popular narratives circulate about the history of Vietnamese cinema. Each chronology spins a different story of Vietnamese cultural history. One version of the tale highlights the current leadership's creation myth of sorts—that is, that the modern Vietnamese film industry originated in Hồ Chí Minh's founding of the Việt Nam Cinema Association in 1953 and his signing of the "Decree on Founding the National Agency of Cinema and Photography."

However, looking further back into the nation's colonial history as rendered in postcolonial French scholarship, one finds that the first cinema houses in Việt Nam were established in urban areas before World War I. French (and later, American) films were shown in French-owned cinemas, while imports from Hong Kong and China were shown in theaters run by the Chinese. It is difficult to disinter this anthropological and architectural history, but we know that the total number of theaters in Việt Nam head reached sixty-three by 1939. Roy Armes explains a more narrowly defined nationalist Vietnamese film history:

> After the coming of sound . . . the majority of Vietnamese films were based on Vietnamese literary sources and were presented as Vietnamese productions, but "in reality, the Vietnamese were only a minority amongst the film crews. The basic work, shooting, editing, sound, copying, series production, etc. was undertaken by foreigners." . . . All this activity stopped completely after the French surrendered to the Japanese in 1940. Vietnamese filmmaking was reborn as a guerrilla cinema during the struggle against the French, but Vietnamese critics like to date the birth of an "authentic" national cinema at the Decree of March 1953 by Hồ Chí Minh, which set up the National Society for Film and Photography.[9]

Two films, *Cánh đồng ma* (The Ghost Field) and *Trận phong ba* (The Storm), are believed to have been made in Hong Kong employing Vietnamese actors in the late 1930s. Socialist films from the midcentury that have survived include *The Battle of Đông Khê* (1950), *Chiến thắng Tây Bắc* (North West Victory; 1952), *Việt Nam on the Road to Victory* (1953), and the most easily accessible, *The Battle of Điện Biên Phủ* (1954).

By the end of the First Indochina War and the partition of the country into "North Vietnam" and "South Vietnam," there were two distinct Vietnamese film industries. It is significant that this differentiated cultural lineage is thoroughly absent in the current neoliberal, reconciliatory global cultural history. The Hà Nội film archives report the establishment of Hà Nội's Việt Nam Film Studios in 1956 and of the Hà Nội Film School in 1959, as well as the production of hundreds of Democratic Republic of Việt Nam–produced newsreels, war documentaries, scientific films, features, and animated films during this period. Occasional trips to the Moscow Film Festival by the films' producers were also reported. The film industry of this era based in Sài Gòn, by contrast, is mentioned only as an afterthought in the academic literature, if it is mentioned at all. Its productions tend to be relegated to the status of U.S. military and propaganda films or imitations of Hong Kong action films. Notable American films that remain in this cultural history might include Joseph Mankiewicz's adaptation of Graham Greene's *The Quiet American* (1957) and Marshall Thompson's *A Yank in Viet-Nam, or Year of the Tiger* (1964).

In fact, while rarely referenced in Vietnamese film criticism, the years 1954–75 were a highly dynamic period of cultural production in the south. Similar to the case of the Philippines under the dictatorship of Ferdinand Marcos, the dynamism resulted from a number of factors: the abundance of economic resources for local artists and filmmakers aided by the U.S. presence, the existing infrastructure of film studios and talent in Sài Gòn, the emotional tumult and political chaos of life in the Army of the Republic of Việt Nam (ARVN) under the U.S. military presence, and the nature of intense cosmopolitan cultural contact. I have seen personal collections and found footage of experimental cinema from this period that range from Yoko Ono–like abstract videos to films that tackle contemporary issues of sexuality, drugs, religious practices, peace, music, miniskirts, and the military-industrial complex. Yet they are nowhere to be found in the current cultural history; nor are they included among accessible archival materials. Following the reunification of the north and south in 1975, some attention was paid to studios in the former Republic of Việt Nam. Although little reason is given for this shift in focus, it is not difficult to surmise that the best-equipped and best-maintained studios remained standing in the south after the war.

During the third period of Vietnamese film history, from the late 1970s to the early 1990s, melodramatic socialist realism and heroic revolutionary tales came to dominate Việt Nam's burgeoning nationalist film industry. The domestic film industry had four distinct arms in this period: (1) Hồ Chí Minh's Việt Nam Cinema Association, which showcased domestically produced film; (2) the Cinema Department of the Ministry of Culture and Information, which authorized projects and funded and distributed productions; (3) Fafilm, which held exclusive rights to import, export, and distribute both Vietnamese and foreign films; and (4) the Institute of Cinematographic Art and Conservation, which archived eighty thousand reels of film.[10] All four of these arms were under the control of the Ministry of Culture and Information during this time. After đổi mới in 1986, a censorship bureau remained that had the authority to inspect film scripts both before and after production and to send staff to oversee scenes and shots. Việt Nam has had only twenty-five censorship-free years in its entire history, during its modernist period in the 1920s to the 1940s. Today, Vietnamese film directors and critics themselves often serve as members of the censorship board.

I date the beginning of Việt Nam's contemporary cinematic period to 1994, when the U.S. economic embargo of nearly twenty years was lifted. While the Ministry of Culture and Information guided native filmmakers toward works that depicted war victimization and destitution, evoking global sympathy and remorse, its funding for national cinema began to diminish as a whole, while domestic Vietnamese audiences longed for something different—anything that reflected their contemporary lives, interests, and experiences. Curiosity and overly determined empathy may have led international audiences to seek pathos-filled glimpses of the Vietnam War's aftermath. Young people in Việt Nam, however, began expressing discontent with such depressing cinematic reminders of their postwar developing nation-state.

At the time, only a handful of documentary films by diasporic Vietnamese and feature films by mainstream French auteurs were being given license to shoot in Việt Nam—for example, Tiana Thi Thanh Nga's *From Hollywood to Hanoi* (1993), Hien Duc Do's *Việt Nam: At the Crossroads* (1994), Régis Wargnier's *L'Indochine* (1992), and Jean-Jacques Annaud's *The Lover* (1992). Trần Anh Hùng, the French diasporic director of *The*

Scent of Green Papaya (1993), filmed his second feature, *Cyclo* (1995), on location in Hồ Chí Minh City with the leading Hong Kong actor Tony Leung Chiu Wai, and the Vietnamese American brothers Tony and Timothy Bùi shot features with American stars, including Harvey Keitel, Patrick Swayze, and Forest Whittaker, in Việt Nam.

It also was not until the mid-1990s that domestic Vietnamese filmmakers began to reach further aesthetically with their craft and to develop domestic film scholarship. As a result of the simultaneous growth of native and diasporic film production and because the films produced and distributed overseas are more easily accessible, the diasporic, not the domestic, films made during this period have often come to represent Vietnamese cinema in the West. The confusion—and conflation—of native and diasporic projects did, however, succeed in bringing more international attention and curiosity to domestic Vietnamese filmmaking abroad, as well as interest in diasporic cinema "at home." Several of the most culturally penetrating films from this early contemporary period are Vũ Xuân Hưng's *Giải hạn* (Misfortune's End; 1996), Nguyễn Thanh Vân's *Đời cát* (Sand Life; 2000), Đặng Nhật Minh's *Mùa ổi* (Guava Season; 2001), and Phạm Nhuệ Giang's *Thung Lũng Hoang Vắng* (Deserted Valley; 2002).[11]

As domestic and diasporic practitioners began to interact with one another at international film festivals and on projects being produced in Hồ Chí Minh City, recognizably talented Vietnamese actors began to receive foreign acclaim in multiple geopolitical registers, allowing them to promote their own celebrity according to a familiar international star system. The director Lưu Hùynh's film *Passage of Life* (1999) introduced the Vietnamese model and actress Trương Ngọc Ánh, who went on to star in Đòan Minh Phượng's and Đòan Thành Nghĩa's *Hạt mưa rơi bao lâu* (Bride of Silence; 2005), Lưu Hùynh's *Áo luạ Hà Đong* (The White Silk Dress; 2006), and the French diasporic filmmaker Othello Khanh's *Saì Gòn Nhật Thực* (Sài Gòn Eclipse; 2007). Trương Ngọc Ánh has now established her own production company. The older, more seasoned Vietnamese actress Như Quỳnh, who has also appeared in Trần Anh Hùng's films, finds consistent televisual and cinematic work and promotional endorsements.

Another provocative feature of these new transnational ventures is increasingly savvy placement of Vietnamese film at Asian and Southeast Asian film festivals, as well as at select European, Canadian, and American film festivals such as Cannes and the Berlinale. Not only do these festivals serve as networking sites for future collaboration, but the promotional value of the venues is clear from any glance at recent advertising posters for films. The biennial Vietnamese International Film Festival (ViFF), funded and run voluntarily out of Southern California, is primarily driven by women and is diasporic in organizational composition, while the annual domestic Vietnamese Liên hoan phim festival and awards ceremony is state-driven and predominantly composed of men.

Media journalism in Việt Nam has also begun to offer outlets for high-quality film critique by young, alternative film critics and filmmakers, such as Lê Thị Thaí Hoa, a female reporter who has written for the daily newspapers *Thanh Niên News* and *Tuổi Trẻ*; Châu Quang Phước, a contributing writer for the newsmagazine *Tia Sáng*; and Phan Gia Nhật Linh (a.k.a. Phanxine), who writes a cinema column and maintains a blog about Vietnamese and international filmmaking. Linh Phan was a Ford Foundation fellow in the Cinema Department at the University of Southern California (USC) while he maintained his "Góc Phanxine" (Phanxine Corner) column in the glossy celebrity magazine *Giải trí Điện ảnh kịch trường*. He recently directed his first short film, *Thằng chó chết* (Dog Day; 2010); assisted in the continued transnational flow of Vietnamese film and production students to USC for training under the direction of Michael Uno; and returned to Việt Nam to establish film blogs, alternative online film festivals (YCineFilmFest), and other collective projects.

Generous financial assistance from the Ford Foundation has brought progress to Việt Nam in the field of cultural anthropology, particularly in the areas of religion, ethnology, and cinema. The foundation committed a total of $1.4 million from 2005 to 2011 to developing the Vietnamese Film Studies Program founded at the University of Social Sciences and Humanities in Hà Nội.[12] The program was put under the direction of Dean Wilson, who wrote the initial grant proposal and who, among his other responsibilities, coordinated the residencies of the film and media professionals David James (School of Cinematic Arts, USC), Park Kwangsu (Korea National University of the Arts and Pusan Film Commission), Apichatpong Weerasethakul (Kick the Machine, Bangkok), Chris Berry (Goldsmiths College, London), and Ed Guerrero (Tisch School of the Arts, New York University), as well as of Vietnamese and diasporic Vietnamese writers, producers, and directors such as Phạm Nhuệ Giang (*Deserted Valley*), Trần Anh Hùng (*The Scent of Green Papaya*), Charlie Nguyễn (*The Rebel*),

Stephane Gauger (*Owl and the Sparrow*), and Vy Vincent Ngo (*Hancock*). Wilson also taught seminars on film styles, genres, theories, and histories; production models; screenwriting; and methods of research.[13]

Most of the Film Studies Program's two-year curriculum involves bringing the students up to date on film-production standards and global cinematic aesthetics, form, and content. Less attention appears to be devoted to cultural studies methodologies that would train them to combine interdisciplinary analytical skills in political economics, aesthetic theory, international cultural theory, and close textual reading. Students familiarize themselves with David Bordwell's introductory textbook *Film History* in Hà Nội, and some receive Ford Foundation funding for additional training at USC that also includes instruction in film production, direction, and storyboarding but relatively little training in social and cultural critique and analysis, despite USC's strengths in teaching both areas.

Before it closed its branch office in Hà Nội in 2008, the Ford Foundation also established a two-year program film studies program in Hồ Chí Minh City similar to the one it funds in Hà Nội. It is directed by the leading Vietnamese film critic Ngô Phương Lan and housed at the University of Social Sciences and Humanities. However, there is very little interaction between this program and the one in Hà Nội in terms of curricula, administrators, instructors, or students. Also, instead of attending that program, most filmmakers from southern Việt Nam come out of the Hồ Chí Minh City College of Theater and Cinema, which receives little to no state funding or assistance.

According to alumni and graduates, film students in southern Việt Nam do not have access to the same film festival circuits, training and funding opportunities, and academic resources as their counterparts in Hà Nội. They produce their student films and postgraduate films collaboratively with other students and friends, receiving only occasional recognition at the national Golden Kite Awards and virtually no international attention, except when diasporic friends introduce their work outside Việt Nam.

The Vietnamese director Bùi Thạc Chuyên (*Sống trong sợ hãi* [Living in Fear]; 2007 and *Chơi vơi* [Adrift]; 2009) and his frequent screenwriting collaborator Phan Đăng Di (*Bi, đừng sợ* [Bi, Don't be Afraid]; 2009) have done a great deal to create a burgeoning film community in their native Hà Nội. Bùi Thạc Chuyên founded and contributes to the Centre for

Assistance and Development of Movie Talents, providing weblog news, as well as professional and social networking on Facebook. Marcus Vũ Mạnh Cường of Hà Nội, an energetic economics student pursuing a doctorate in Germany and the cofounder of Yxine.com, maintains a public blog in Vietnamese, as well as an online short-film competition. These forums provide news, visibility, and promotion, but they are still finding their way to film analysis and criticism very much in isolation. Currently, there is little sense of Southeast Asian regionalism, despite the academic advances in Southeast Asian cinema in recent decades.

Also, while the existing Vietnamese film studies curriculum as a whole looks to world (predominantly European and some Soviet) cinematic history and current Vietnamese film *production*, there is little evidence of extensive study or scholarship devoted to Vietnamese national film *history*. Other than several popular Vietnamese paperback books (now out of print) highlighting famous actors and actresses, only one critical compilation, funded by the Ford Foundation, exists. It was published in 2008 only in Vietnamese and is extremely difficult to acquire, even within Việt Nam, according to my graduate students.[14]

These increasingly complex and trenchant transnational industrial cooperatives and relationships compel continued revitalization and constant change both in the domestic Vietnamese film industry and in its cultural critique. The scholarship on such rapid cultural development needs to evolve from relying on one educational model of film history. Vietnamese film education remained centralized in the north in Gerald Herman's Hà Nội Cinémathèque archive, theater, and café, for at least the first five years of its development; it expanded to the south only recently, in 2008–9, with the initial student cohort at the University of Social Sciences and Humanities in Hồ Chí Minh City. This is a welcome development, as potential film students from central and southern Việt Nam could not afford to relocate to Hà Nội to pursue such a highly speculative educational and career path, and because most of the diasporic and transnational film production in recent decades has been centralized in the south rather than in the north. The re-emergence of the southern Vietnamese film industry encourages local and national demand for even more cultural education, as locals, expatriates, transnationals, and diasporics all invest in the country's reborn and blossoming visual, musical, and literary arts scene.

New Directions for Vietnamese Film Criticism

The weakest area in the development of film studies in Việt Nam is film criticism and cultural analysis—or, in more popular parlance, critical thinking skills. This weakness is also partly a product of polemical transnational politics in cultural training. At a film salon in Hà Nội in 2008 hosted by the journalist Julie Phạm Hoài Hương of the diasporic *Người Việt Tây Bắc* (Northwest Vietnamese News), several Vietnamese attendee-respondents at a screening of *The White Silk Dress* focused their comments on how "accurate" Lưu Huỳnh's depiction of rural life in the Vietnamese countryside appeared to them. Comments soon turned toward the expatriate director's biography to elucidate how much he might or might not know about Vietnamese rural life, despite the fact that he was born and raised "in country" and had returned to spend the previous dozen years of his life there. Uncritical and non-self-reflective notions of historical "facticity" and "cultural authenticity" resulted in an easy charge to make against a diasporic filmmaker who chose to reside permanently in Việt Nam to help grow the local film industry.

While such negligible understandings of critical and creative subject positionalities and of the *fiction* genre of feature film should not necessarily reflect the national film studies curriculum as such, these comments do register the distance national cultural awareness of film, and of arts education in general, has yet to travel. Critical analytical training requires a diverse methodological repertoire that goes beyond training in production techniques and occasional contact with international auteurs. Of the filmmakers and scholars who have been invited occasionally to teach as guests in Hà Nội, only a few have had that diverse critical training.[15] Further, if the state wants to amass a critical audience and a loyal following internationally, additional problems of lack of access to the films and related difficulties in distribution and circulation also will need to be resolved.

Returning to Vietnamese film research and writing, the visual anthropologist Lee Ngo describes the work of the leading Vietnamese film scholar Ngô Phương Lan:

> *Modernity and Nationality in Vietnamese Cinema* is, ironically, a product of the very subject it attempts to explore, and in many ways it can be regarded as the quintessential book on the government-approved

Vietnamese perspective on Vietnamese film. . . . [H]er general analysis is simultaneously descriptive and prescriptive: "In the evolution of cultural values, nationality meets modernity. Culture, art and literature will enjoy steady development if harmony is created between nationality and modernity." . . . It is no surprise that Ngô Phương Lan's *Modernity and Nationality in Vietnamese Cinema* has garnered so many accolades from the Vietnamese academic community, warranting its translation into English. It is a very well-researched book . . . presenting an alternative to the hegemony of Euro-American cultural critique. The book, however, assuming it represents Ngô Phương Lan's own formal position in the state's film industry infrastructure in some capacity, offers the more general perspective of the Vietnamese state and its increased interest in film production.[16]

Further describing this text and the critical anthology *Le cinema vietnamien*, edited by Philippe Dumont and Kirstie Gormley, Ngo writes, "While both books leave something to be desired, particularly in their shared dearth of analysis, clarity, and content, they certainly inspire more attention to this very exciting topic that continues to unfold. . . . [I]n the case of *Le cinema vietnamien*, the stakes of the conversation are apparent and understood across disciplines and cultural backgrounds, but the quality of the conversation must be raised in order for more people to take the matter seriously."

Meanwhile, the number of films in globalizing Hollywood genres such as horror, action, and romantic comedy is growing exponentially within Việt Nam's domestic film industry. Korean pop (or K-pop)—which initially signified forms of popular music, such as boy bands, but has now extended to other forms of popular culture, including gangster and horror films of the "Korean Wave," soap operas, and game shows—has translated culturally very well to upwardly mobile and hungry global-culture-consuming Vietnamese urban youths. Under the prominent phenomenon of sensationalizing celebrities, the same promotional strategies and national public relations work are called on to turn figures as different as the pop star Ngô Thanh Vân and the martyred revolutionary war doctor Đặng Thùy Trâm into cultural icons.[17] In countermeasure, as independent diasporic Vietnamese filmmakers, including Gauger, have encouraged, "Independent film is really about the 'spirit' of making films outside of the box. . . . Whether it's a genre film . . . or a character-driven film . . . , these films must have a distinct vision that stays away from the cookie cutter."[18]

The rest of this chapter explores provocative films and cultural phenomena that *do not* fit neatly within the current model of cultural education available in Việt Nam but that need to be examined more thoroughly. They include such Korean-Vietnamese coproductions as the horror movie *Mười: The Legend of a Portrait* and two more recent films by Đặng Nhật Minh. A rigorous political-economic analysis of the history of Korean-Vietnamese cooperative ventures and coproductions, which also include the popular Korean television series *Cô dâu vàng* (Golden Bride) and the Vietnam War film *Sunny/Someone Dear Is Far Away* (2008), thus is part of the cultural redevelopment, or "re-education," that I hope to see in Việt Nam's future.

The past three decades have witnessed parallel struggles by South Koreans, Korean Americans, Vietnamese, and diasporic Vietnamese to contend with their conflicted relationships to transnationalism and globalization; modernity and "homeland" economic development; war memory and trauma; and new forms of agency, subjectivity, and resistance. Both nation-states—the Republic of Korea and the Socialist Republic of Việt Nam—continue to wage internal and international ideological battles with their own histories of war, cultural memory, partition and possibilities for reunification,[19] and global capitalist interactions with "the West." Transnational marriages and mail-order brides from Việt Nam to Korea, shared international adoption patterns, the Phở noodle soup craze throughout Korea and its diaspora, and Korean tourism in Việt Nam have all contributed to more investment by the South Korean state in cultural media in Việt Nam. Patterns of cultural consumption lead to evolution in the film industry that is worthy of academic investigation; they also gauge future climates for economic cooperation. The various forms of internal, or domestic, colonization of cultural forms that continue long after reunification or "liberation" have lasting effects. The traumatic recovery work of transnational arts networks and other collaborations are just the beginning. For example, when queried about the global concept of "cultural citizenship" in Việt Nam by colleagues in the United States, Europe, and Latin America, I am compelled to explain how such a concept would be politically loaded and used very cautiously, if at all, by a diasporic academic in Việt Nam. Yet it is one of the most crucial concepts to the development of Vietnamese film and cultural education.[20]

Ahead of the learning curve, the transnational arts exhibition "Trans-POP: Korea Vietnam Remix," by the artists and academics Yong Soon Min and Viet Le, toured Seoul, Hồ Chí Minh City, San Francisco, and Irvine, California, from October 2007 to March 2009. The visual artists and artworks featured in the exhibition variously engaged "interconnections between the two countries, including the intersections of history, trauma, and contemporary popular culture."[21] Viet Le, an assistant professor of Visual and Critical Studies at California College of the Arts, asks, "In what ways does mass media, particularly film, create a space of interaction and intelligibility in which national discourse and traumatic memory is relived, rearticulated, reconciled? . . . How are traumatic pasts subsumed into often hopeful narratives of modernity and progress? . . . How do varied forms of popular and visual culture in Việt Nam (emerging art market and films), South Korea ('Korean Wave' pop culture phenomen[a]), and the West (war films, Hollywood blockbusters) offer complex reads on the legacies of trauma?"[22]

Many of my academic colleagues in Korean studies over the years, and several of the Korean artists during the first leg of the "TransPOP" exhibition in Seoul, showed great concern about the role played by Korean soldiers, or "mercenaries," who fought in the Vietnam War. They described social political movements and citizens' petitions calling for redress in the form of an apology by the Republic of Korea to the Socialist Republic of Việt Nam, and theorized a sense of collective guilt over the nation's participation in the war. They wondered whether a national apology was something the Socialist Republic of Việt Nam awaited from the Republic of Korea, and I was forced to inform them that Việt Nam is more invested—historically, politically, and economically—in obtaining an apology from the United States and a visit from Barack Obama at this time. Economic and social relations between Việt Nam and Korea are already quite strong. Nevertheless, at least two Korean films have fictionalized the experience of Korean soldiers for hire in Việt Nam. The first, White Badge (1994), directed by Ji-yeong Jeong, is the film adaptation of a novel based on the author's war experiences that had problems with the Korean government when it was published in the mid-1980s. It follows Sergeant Han as he suffers from post-traumatic stress disorder after the Vietnam War; having led a Korean infantry unit fighting alongside American allies behind enemy lines, Sergeant Han feels responsible for the deaths in his platoon. With a huge budget and the controversy that surrounded the first film shoot in Việt Nam by a Korean filmmaker since the war, *White Badge* stands as Korea's first national attempt to forge a transnational collective consciousness. The second, *R-Point* (2004), directed by Su-chang Kong, is set in January 1972, during the Vietnam War, and is about a South Korean Army base in Nha Trang that begins receiving mysterious radio transmissions from a patrol that has been missing for six months. The commanding officer and his unit are sent into the ominous stretch of land known as R-Point to investigate the whereabouts of the missing soldiers; they have five days to retrieve either the soldiers or their dog tags. The horror/suspense psychological thriller was a huge international hit, as well as Korea's highest grossing horror film in the year it was released. Thus, in the ten years between 1994 and 2004, genre appeal proved more profitable than trauma and recovery.

In celebration of the sixteenth anniversary of the establishment of diplomatic relations between Korea and Việt Nam, the Second Korean Film Festival was held in Hà Nội on 8–10 May 2008 and drew in hordes of film fanatics. According to one sponsor, the *Seoul Daily News*, approximately forty thousand advance tickets to the screenings were sold. The Korean Embassy, the Korean Cultural Center in Việt Nam, and the Vietnamese Ministry of Culture, Sports, and Tourism cosponsored the festival. The grand opening ceremony was attended by top Korean pop stars and such illustrious film directors as Lim Soon-rye, whose *Forever the Moment* (2008) opened the festival. Lim had remarked on the increasing visibility of Vietnamese cinema in Korea at the Jeonju International Film Festival earlier that year, and the Korean pop star Bada, who performed her hit songs at the opening event, "expressed her fondness of Vietnam and how she always ate phở or Vietnamese rice noodles at least once a week."[23]

Also at the festival's opening ceremony, the Korean starlet Lee Young-ah and the veteran Vietnamese actress Như Quỳnh reunited for the first time since Lee appeared as Quỳnh's daughter in *Golden Bride* (2008). Lee told journalists that she had learned Vietnamese for her role as a foreign bride in Korea and that she was often asked by fans if she was, indeed, ethnically Vietnamese or partly Vietnamese. (She is not.) The televisual drama series was the first mainstream production to tackle the issues of international marriage and *lai Đại Hàn* children (라이따이한 in Korean), or the offspring of Vietnamese women impregnated and abandoned by South Korean soldiers during the Vietnam War.

The current phenomenon of Vietnamese women traveling to Korea for marriage has led to situations that often involve domestic violence, a subject that has attracted sociological scholarship and has been featured in two compilations of documentary short films produced by women's non-profit community organizations in Seoul attempting to aid these transnational brides. The films feature vignettes of Vietnamese brides, but because the organizations receive some funding from the Korean government, they tend to veer toward more positive personal narratives. In transnational labor and marriage migration circles, East Asian host countries such as Korea and Taiwan are viewed as having harsher and more disciplinarian employers and husbands than neighboring Southeast Asian nations such as Singapore and Malaysia, to which many Vietnamese also migrate. Vietnamese American and Vietnamese Australian nongovernmental organizations (NGOs) have sent volunteer groups consisting of diasporic mental-health professionals to several of these host countries to help the large number of women who have fled from husbands whom, the women claim, have stolen their immigration papers and otherwise abused them. Because many of the women do not speak the language of the host country in which they are living, they have nowhere to turn but to churches, temples, and shelters for counsel.

The Singaporean filmmaker Mirabelle Ang's excellent documentary *Match Made* (2006), about a Vietnamese marriage service based in Hồ Chí Minh City, follows the process of outmigration for marriage as a business from the perspectives of both a Singaporean man searching for a Vietnamese wife and the young Vietnamese woman whom he ultimately selects.[24] The film was chosen for screening at the ViFF in Southern California and at festivals in Venice, London, and Singapore in 2009, but it has never been screened at a film festival in Việt Nam, where it might have the biggest cultural impact and the most sociological utility.

A third Korean film production, *Hardship Brings Dollars: A Diary Account of the Lives of Vietnamese Migrants in South Korea*, produced and directed by two women—Kim Seonju and Cheong Seura—with the support of Migrant Workers Television (a media-production NGO based in Seoul that has explored relationships between migration, media, and class since 2006), documents the everyday life of unskilled Vietnamese male migrant workers. The film follows a young female Korean reporter as she chronicles the routines and struggles of the transnational Vietnamese laborers Mr. Pong and Mr. Tun, who provide cheap labor to small and midsize companies and face poor treatment, class and ethnic discrimination, and language barriers. In an insightful review of the film, Kyuri Kim, Jimisha Tolliver, and Verenice Torres write:

> As early as the 1200s, several thousand Vietnamese fled to Korea after the exile of the Vietnamese Lý Dynasty. Today, descendants of these people have mixed with Koreans and are found in both South and North Korea. In the modern period after the division of Korea and the Korean War, the Vietnamese had various contacts with both North and South Korea. Today, the Vietnamese are the second largest group of foreigners, after the Chinese, who migrate to South Korea, mainly as agricultural and industrial workers and also as brides. Vietnamese migrants play a conspicuous part in the increasing transformation of South Korea into a multiethnic and multicultural nation. . . . South Korea now has an epochal chance to interact and engage with a mass of people of multiple ethnicities and nationalities and to considerably expand its international cultural exchanges that would ultimately benefit the country. While hope for the new era of reconciliation, harmony, and co-prosperity endures, one cannot deny that for now hardship is what brings dollars.[25]

The reviewers insightfully frame the two men's journeys as a search for the new "Korean Dream," rather than the clichéd American Dream. Korea's attempts to come to terms with its own changing socioeconomic needs and ethnic demographics require it to turn toward a familiar rhetoric of multiculturalism. After sociological studies in transnational migration and marriage, cinematic arts are one of the only other scholarly areas that have shed light on this global economic trend. Kim and her colleagues and Mirabelle Ang artfully contextualize the transnational politics between these two countries in ways that no industry participants or film historians have done.

Returning to the celebration of the sixteenth anniversary of Korean-Việt Nam diplomatic relations, Việt Nam's Minister of Culture, Sports, and Tourism Hoàng Tuấn Anh was quoted as telling reporters during the Second Korean Film Festival in Hà Nội that the event "showcased the advancement of the Korean film industry and . . . strengthened the positive impression the Vietnamese people have of Korea and Koreans." Hoàng also spoke about a possible joint-project with the Korean Film Council.

The Vietnamese government drew up a [$450 million] budget to build a large film studio in Việt Nam that would be six to seven times the size of Korea's Namyangju studio. It was to be completed by 2012, and talks with Korean partners have been completed. "It's a natural phenomenon that two countries sharing common attitudes toward history, culture and lifestyle influence each other," he was quoted as saying by the local press, and "[A]s much as we understand Koreans' deep love for their traditions, there can be no criticism about *hallyu* (the Korean wave)."[26]

As the minister hoped, Lotte Cinema, a major Korean film distributor and theater chain, opened its first branch office in Hồ Chí Minh City in 2008 and became the second-largest exhibition provider in Việt Nam (behind CGV, another South Korean firm) when it bought Diamond Cinema Joint Venture Company (DMC), a Korean-owned media circuit that operates six multiplex theaters in Hồ Chí Minh City and Đà Nẵng. Even though CGV and Megabox, a rival Korean media corporation, already had theaters in China and seemed primed for expansion into Việt Nam, Lotte had an advantage because it was already running the fast food chain Lotteria, which had the popular shrimp burger, in urban Việt Nam. Lotte bought the multiplex theaters run by DMC and converted them into two three-screen theaters in Hồ Chí Minh City and Đà Nẵng, signaling "the implementation of Korea's savoir-faire in multiplex movie experiences," according to the critic Lee Hyo-won, and "the theater in [Hồ Chí Minh City] also marks the opening of Lotte Mart to provide 'one stop entertainment' in movies and shopping."[27]

In July 2011, however, CJ-CGV was not to be outdone by Lotte and paid $73.6 million to purchase a 92 percent stake in Envoy Media Partners (the 2005 registration was based in the British Virgin Islands), which in turn owns 80 percent of Việt Nam's largest cinema operator, MegaStar Media Company. CGV was able to maneuver this acquisition by partnering with CJ Media, which controlled much of the Vietnamese televisual sector. Some of the remaining shares are owned by Phuong Nam Corporation, a locally based Vietnamese publisher. The only other leading local player, the privately owned Thiên Ngân Film (Galaxy Studio), is involved in the full range of industry business, including film distribution, production, and home entertainment, operating two multiplex theaters in Hồ Chí Minh City. MegaStar opened its first movie theater in Hà Nội in 2006 and currently operates seven multiplexes with fifty-four screens throughout Việt Nam, including Hồ Chí Minh City, Đà Nẵng, Hải Phòng, and Đồng Nai. MegaStar is also the local operator of four "Hollywood" production houses, making it the leading film distributor in Việt Nam. In 2010, MegaStar had revenues of $23 million, accounting for some 60 percent of the nation's movie box office. The theatrical market grew from annual revenues of $2 million in 2006 to $25 million in 2010, of which only an estimated $5 million could be attributed to Vietnamese titles.[28]

These statistics raise the highly problematic and contested issue of the spread of American movies into developing nations. While Vietnamese filmmakers work to create a new audience base to help their national film industry, Korean distributors work as middlemen for Hollywood, inundating Việt Nam with Korean and Western films and limiting the number of Vietnamese films they show in their theaters. This industry control creates a unidirectional foreign production–domestic consumption pattern that will have negative consequences for the Vietnamese film industry in the future. According to the *Film Business Asia* reporter Patrick Frater, in 2010 Việt Nam's Competition Administration Department launched a probe into MegaStar's distribution operations based on a claim by four local companies (including Galaxy) that it was abusing its formidable position to impose high-minimum ticket prices beyond what the market could take (rigging), and others accused MegaStar of selling multiple films as a bulk unit to theaters (block booking). Although the investigation is ongoing, CGV continues to acquire properties in Việt Nam and to consolidate Korean ownership of the country's movie theaters. "With a population of 90 million and a steady growth rate at the box office that recorded more than a 20% increase" in 2010, a CJ-CGV spokesperson told a Korean business magazine, the Vietnamese film industry "is going into a long-term growth period." The Korean company plans to use its multiplexes as a "bridge for introducing Korean culture in Southeast Asia."[29] The current state of Vietnamese film education provides no space for an analysis of the fascinating phenomenon of Korean-Việt film development.

Meanwhile, in September 2009, five poignant Vietnamese films—*Ba Mùa* (Three Seasons; 1999), *Mê Thảo, thời vang bóng* (Once upon a Time; 2002), *Mùa len trâu* (Buffalo Boy; 2004), *Chuyện của Pao* (Pao's Story; 2006), and *Rừng đen* (Black Forest; 2008)—were screened at the National Museum of Korea in Seoul.[30] The goal of the event, which was billed as the "Good Morning Việt Nam Cultural Smorgasbord" in South Korea, was to "promote friendship relations and cultural exchanges between Việt Nam and the Republic of Korea."[31]

The ultimate Korean-Vietnamese transnational cooperative film venture is *Mười: The Legend of a Portrait* (2008). It charts the path of a young Korean writer who travels to Việt Nam in search of a plot line for her next novel. There, a mystery centering on a century-old vengeful spirit named Mười (played by the Vietnamese actress Anh Thư) is slowly revealed to her and she is drawn deeper and deeper into the legend. A brief opening sequence in South Korea introduces the audience to the young creative writer Yun-hee (played by the Korean actress Jo An), who then visits her old friend Seo-yeon (the Korean actress Cha Ye-ryeon) now living in Việt Nam, who helps Yun-hee investigate the legend of Mười. By the end of the film, Korea and Việt Nam bond over urban legends and patriarchal realities—and, of course, gore.

The film, which cost $3 million to produce, was financed by IM Pictures and coproduced by Phước Sang Entertainment, receiving support from both the Korean Film Council and Việt Nam's Ministry of Information and Culture. South Korea's Kim Tae-kyung, who directed the midsize hit *Yoo Ryung* (Ghost; 2004), was placed at the helm. Providing advance publicity for the film, in an article in 2007, *Variety*'s Seoul correspondent Darcy Paquet explained that the cast would include the well-known Vietnamese actresses Anh Thu and Hong Anh and the popular Korean stars Jo An (*Wishing Stairs*) and Cha Ye-ryeon (*Voice*), and elaborated that "Việt Nam was one of the first countries to embrace the so-called Korean Wave, and Korean pop culture remains highly popular there."[32] Richard Kuipers, an early reviewer of *Muoi*, noted after the film's release in Korea, "Whether or not the pic can spark genre activity in Việt Nam is in the hands of the country's censorship officials. . . . [T]hough [it is] widely available on pirated DVDs, 'Muoi' has yet to be given the nod for release by authorities, known for their reluctance to approve films with supernatural themes."[33] Kuipers had nothing to fear. The film was released in Việt Nam after the censorship board cut out several gory death scenes, much to the chagrin of the occasionally confused Vietnamese audiences. Kuipers also observed that the film "moves swiftly and looks great. . . . Lovely exteriors around the picturesque town of Da Lat won't do the tourist biz any harm," adding that the "results are encouraging enough to suggest there's a lucrative V-horror category just waiting to be born."[34]

The Vietnamese director Nguyễn Võ Nghiêm Minh has called attention to what he fairly views as Orientalist tendencies in the international film industry and among film critics. Out of the sea of positive reviews for his critically acclaimed film *Buffalo Boy* in 2004, only a handful—by Magnohla Dargis of the *New York Times*, Giovanna Fulvi of the Toronto International Film Festival, and a few French reviewers—actually provided a "cogent review without provoking the exotics of the setting or the culture," he says, noting that he found reviews from India and Bosnia particularly "thought-provoking and eloquent."[35]

More alarming, however, is the lack of penetrating critiques of films even by leading Vietnamese auteurs such as Đặng Nhật Minh. His feature *Guava Season*, cowritten by Đặng Nhật Minh, Bùi Bài Bình, Nguyễn Lan Hương, Phạm Thu Thủy, and Lê Thị Hương Thảo, but based on an original story by Đặng ("Ngôi nhà xưa"), portrays Hà Nội in the period from 1954 to the late 1980s, a period of revolutionary change for the city from the perspective of a mentally challenged man named Hòa, who suffered a traumatic brain injury when he fell out of a guava tree at thirteen. Now a middle-aged man, Hòa's perception and memories are stuck in his childhood and he is attached to the colonial villa that was the family home in his youth, even though the house was seized by the state and given to another family years earlier.[36] The villa's new residents retain the guava tree, which Hòa continues to climb each day without the homeowner's knowledge. When the homeowner's daughter, Loan, a university student, discovers what Hòa is doing, she shows pity and allows him to enter his childhood residence. Before long, however, the family patriarch returns and kicks Hòa out of the house, and he once again enters both internal and national domestic displacement.

Over the course of the film, the viewer learns that Hòa's father—once a lawyer (possibly a law professor) who was gradually pushed out of his profession, sent for re-education, and compelled by regime changes to give up the house—had designed and built the family home thirty years earlier. Hòa's older brother has emigrated to Germany with his family to find work, while his younger sister, a teacher named Thủy, takes care of Hòa when she can. Loan's family is also scattered: her parents and siblings stay in Hồ Chí Minh City, where her father is in business, while she remains in the north to complete her education. Hòa is perceived as crazy because he lives in his memories, such as that of his first waltz, piano playing, hopscotch, thunderstorms against the guava tree, and his mother's death, all of which are anchored in the house; Thủy, by contrast, has repressed all memory of the house and of their family history. In the film's climax, memory and repression are reversed as Hòa and Thủy experience another jarring reopening and reignition of their family's personal historical trauma.

In a side plot of sorts, the film also stages Hòa's marginalized life as a model at a fine-arts school. Lan, a young rural-to-urban migrant worker, also models in the nude to earn extra income to help her hospitalized mother. The camera work frequently lingers during scenes of Hòa's and Lan's visual consumption by the class and by the film viewers, ourselves. Đặng Nhật Minh uses the cinematography, the audience's discomfort, neoimperial erotic desire, and the embedded socioeconomic class disparities operating in these scenes to mount a subtle, manifold sociocultural critique.

In *Guava Season*, Đặng weaves a strikingly touching analysis of visual cultural work and national historiography while considering the potential role of aesthetic pedagogy and the arts in Việt Nam under its current political and economic conditions. The film explores the interconnected relationships among the house as a monument and memorial of social history, the economic sustainability of an intellectual aesthetic citizenship, and the differing vantage points and communications of one generation that lived through a war and another that is immersed in the pleasure of new popular cultural forms. It challenges its viewers to consider the role of cultural education in Việt Nam, the role of the international spectatorship of touring Việt Nam cinema, and the writing of cultural criticism informed by national history and social economic realities, all with a quietly penetrating story of two Vietnamese families and their personal histories. The film sees nearly no circulation today in Việt Nam and is available for viewing at only two locations in the United States — on VHS cassette at the University of Washington, Seattle, and at the American Museum of Natural History in New York. Meanwhile, Đặng's highly problematic *Thương Nhớ Đồng Quê* (Nostalgia for the Countryland; 1995) is available for purchase worldwide.[37]

I conclude this chapter with a similarly complex rendering of Vietnamese postsocialist cinema: Đặng's most recent work, *Đừng Đốt* (Don't Burn It; 2009), a filmic adaptation of the Vietnamese bestseller *The Diary of Đặng Thuy Trâm* (2005). Đặng employed the state's biggest budget to date for any single feature film to create the tale of complex reconciliation.[38] *Don't Burn It* is a tearjerker, as expected, but it also includes moments of penetrating potential analytical and cultural insight. During scenes in which the young revolutionary heroine appears to internally challenge or question the political ideological positions of the war machine on her own revolutionary side and the behavior of her superior cadres, she is chastised as giving in to her "bourgeois" upbringing and tastes. Soldiers of the ARVN are also characterized generously in their depictions, a nearly unseen portrayal in socialist and postsocialist Vietnamese cinema since 1975.

When asked whether the censorship board had made any editorial cuts in the film, Đặng replied, rather instructively, that if a screenplay is based on a "factual" document with which the state cannot take issue, and the document is already in circulation, there is no reason for censorship.[39] Of course, Đặng's coy answer overshadows the fact that a filmmaker who was not already so trusted within the national film industry would have been subjected to more scrutiny. Since the film's release in Việt Nam and abroad, it has generated very little discussion, criticism, or appreciation, except at the Golden Kite Awards in 2010, and even then, far more controversy resulted from the festival's slighting of the London-based French Vietnamese diasporic actress Phạm Linh Đan's ambiguously queer portrayal in Bùi Thạc Chuyên's *Adrift*.[40] The honoring of diasporic directors, actors, and actresses with awards—or, rather, the lack thereof—had been a sticking point for the state and its film commissioners over the several previous years of the Golden Kite Awards, leading up to its biggest slight that year. From 2010 on, relatively more appreciation was shown toward diasporic and expatriate filmmakers and thespians, including a Best Actor award for the Vietnamese American actor, director, and writer Dustin Trí Nguyễn for his portrayal of a mentally challenged martial artist in Lưu Huỳnh's *Huyền thoại bất tử* (*The Legend Is Alive*).

The parallel ironies of "reconciliation" politics displayed in the award selections and in Đặng's *Don't Burn It* are indeed calibrated to the political-economic initiatives and social-cultural ambivalences in which the state is entrenched. Within the current context of cultural education in Việt Nam, however, even the works with the greatest global cultural resonance and highest quality by the most "nationalist" and prolific of state-sponsored film auteurs can be undervalued, because the state, critics, and new film audiences do not yet have the critical vocabulary to engage in the kinds of cultural discourses that currently are circulating about the development of postsocialist Vietnamese film.

It is therefore important to find Vietnamese film analysis that is anchored in, but not shackled to, national film histories and industry developments. The films that are produced today in Việt Nam have been deeply affected by the history of the international Cold War and are part and parcel of that thick traumatic legacy. Producers and practitioners of cultural education, as well as the burgeoning Vietnamese film industry I have discussed here, cannot be easily assimilated to existing theoretical and methodological practices in Vietnamese studies. Việt Nam now must deal with the United States, Korea, and many other players in the so-called global village, and it must do so with more conscientious attention to complex, polemical, and multidirectional transnational relationships and diasporic triangulations. Historiographical writing, general cultural education, tourism, diplomacy, and amnesty all inflect the contemporary study of Vietnamese literature, film, and arts. My larger goal is to delineate how a rapidly growing global cultural tourism that requires the interdependence between the new transnational circulation of cultural forms—such as Vietnamese film, print and broadcast media, and education—and the state's rhetoric of its postsocialist economic needs reveal ways in which academic approaches make manifest complex constructions of social memory and world cultural memory.

Notes

1. Throughout the chapter, I have used the spelling "Vietnam" to denote the globally pervasive mainstream depictions of the imagined country during and following the Cold War, while I use the spelling "Việt Nam" in reference to the nation-state in its formal monosyllabic form with proper diacritics.

2. The development of national systems of social infrastructure increasingly relies on the presence and direction of international NGOs more familiar with global public policy and law, including humanitarian aid, rescue, and rights. These transnational NGO collaborations include everything from assistance to victims of Agent Orange/dioxin, disaster relief, voluntary medical missions to foreign and domestic adoption agencies, HIV/AIDS prevention programs, and sexuality-based needs assessments by community-based organizations. They include both foreigners and returning Vietnamese expatriates. Indeed, while the socialist state often views the diasporic communities as insensitive to the needs of a developing nation in their critiques of particular state social policies, many of the earliest NGOs that brought

assistance to Việt Nam after 1975 were in fact diaspora-based organizations. For this history and reference listings, contact the Southeast Asian Resource Action Center.

3. See, e.g., Iwabuchi et al., *Rogue Flows*; and Erni and Chua, *Asian Media Studies*.

4. Việt Nam was absent from cultural studies critical anthologies even in 2005: see, e.g., Abbas and Erni, *Internationalizing Cultural Studies*, 1. See Miller et al., *Global Hollywood 2*; Stokes and Maltby, *Hollywood Abroad*.

5. For provocative cultural discussions of postsocialist and neoliberal transitions and practices, see Laderman, *Tours of Vietnam*; Nguyễn-võ, *The Ironies of Freedom*; Schwenkel, *The American War in Contemporary Vietnam*; and Zhang, *Postsocialism and Cultural Politics*.

6. See Miller et al., *Global Hollywood 2*; Stokes and Maltby, *Hollywood Abroad*.

7. The postwar median age in Việt Nam is 26.4, and more than half the population is younger than 35, according to the Central Intelligence Agency's *The World Factbook 2007*.

8. For a more complete discussion of this abbreviated cinematic history, see Lam, "Circumventing Channels"; Lam, *Not Coming to Terms*.

9. Armes, *Third World Film Making and the West*, 146–47.

10. Norindr, "Vietnam," 46.

11. Alternative titles for *Guava Season* are *Guava House*, *Season of Guava*, and *The Season of Guavas*.

12. Dean Wilson completed his doctorate in French in 2007 at City University of New York; his dissertation, written in English, is "Colonial Viet Nam on Film: 1896 to 1926." From his appointment in 2005 to 2011, he designed the full-time, graduate-level program and curriculum; wrote the grant proposal obtaining Ford Foundation support for those six years (a total of US$1.4 million); recruited and trained established directors and writers in Hà Nội to teach film and media courses in the Vietnamese language; organized and implemented administrative operations, office staff, enrollment, program library, and infrastructure; and generated guidance texts, schedules, procedures, professional networks, career development, and study abroad programs. He continues to serve as a consultant to the Film Studies Program.

13. For more information about Wilson and the program initiatives, see http://tinvanonline.org/2009/07/22/dean-wilson-phd.

14. I thank Julie Phạm Hoài Hương for providing a copy.

15. Among the filmmakers, there is the possible exception of the Vietnamese female director Phạm Nhuệ Giang, who has done intensive research screenings of all of the holdings at the Hà Nội Cinémathèque archive over the course of an entire year. I thank Mike DiGregorio for this information.

16. Lee Ngo, double-feature book review, *Journal of Vietnamese Studies* 5, no. 2 (June 2010): 251–55.

17. For a lengthier discussion of this phenomenon, see Lam, "Circulating War Memories."

18. Interview with Stephane Gauger, Palm Springs, Calif., 1 February 2008. For more on the dominant history of independent filmmaking, see Levy, *Cinema of Outsiders*; Merritt, *Celluloid Mavericks*.

19. The most useful and telling parallel postcolonial historical example of partition is India and Pakistan, while the most useful historical postsocialist example of the difficulties of reunification is arguably East Germany and West Germany.

20. I have had to rehearse all of the possible literal translations of this global notion of cultural citizenship in Lam, *Not Coming to Terms*, as there currently is no equivalent concept in the Vietnamese language that captures all of its English significations and connotations.

21. "TransPOP: Korea Vietnam Remix," exhibition and symposia program materials, Seoul, Hồ Chí Minh City, Irvine (Calif.), and San Francisco, October 2007–March 2009.

22. Viet Le, "Love Is a Battlefield: Trauma, Pop, and Korean and Vietnamese Relations in *White Badge* and *Bride from Hà Nội*," paper presented at the Annual National Conference of the Association for Asian American Studies, Honolulu, April 2009. I am indebted to Yong Soon Min and Viet Le for intensely generative discussions about Korea–Việt Nam relations from January 2008 to the present.

23. Lee Hyo-won, "Cinema Bridges Korea, Việt Nam," *Korea Times*, 19 May 2008, available online at http://www.koreatimes.co.kr/www/news/art/2009/10/141_24414 .html.

24. Mirabelle Ang, dir., *Match Made* (in English, Chinese, and Vietnamese, with English subtitles), on the Singapore-Asian Film Archive DVD collection *Singapore Shorts, Volume 2*, 2008.

25. Kyuri Kim, Jimisha Tolliver, and Verenice Torres, "The Untold Stories of Vietnamese Migrants in South Korea," *Asia Pacific Arts*, 17 September 2010, available online at http://asiapacificarts.usc.edu/w_apa/showarticle.aspx?articleID=1566 5&AspxAutoDetectCookieSupport=1 (accessed 18 July 2011).

26. See Lee, "Cinema Bridges Korea, Việt Nam."

27. Ibid.

28. All factual information in this paragraph is from Patrick Frater, "CGV Makes Mega Play in Vietnam," *Film Business Asia*, 8 July 2011, available online at http://www.filmbiz.asia/news/cgv-makes-mega-play-in-vietnam (accessed 18 July 2011).

29. "CJ CGV Acquires Vietnam's Leading Cinema Chain," *Korean Film Biz Zone*, 11 July 2011, available online at http://www.koreanfilm.or.kr/jsp/news/news .jsp?mode=VIEW&seq=1568 (accessed 18 July 2011).

30. "Korea Screens the Best of Vietnam," *VietNamNet/Thanh Nien*, 13 September 2009, available online at http://www.lookatvietnam.com/2009/09/korea-screens -the-best-of-vietnam.html (accessed 13 September 2009).

31. Ibid.

32. Darcy Paquet, "South Korea, Viet Nam Team Up on Film," *Variety*, 4 January 2007, available online at http://www.variety.com/article/VR1117956677.html ?categoryid=13&cs=1 (accessed 13 September 2009).

33. Richard Kuipers, "Muoi: The Legend of a Portrait," *Variety Weekly*, 12 November 2007.

34. Ibid.

35. Personal e-mail correspondence with the director Nguyễn Võ Nghiêm Minh, 2008.

36. Plot details are in the film's description at WorldCat.org: http://www .worldcat.org/title/mua-oi-the-guava-house/oclc/050787344.

37. For an extended analysis of this film, see Lam, *Not Coming to Terms*.

38. This was the state-funded project with the biggest budget until the failed commemorative historical epic film *Lý Công Uẩn—Đường tới thành Thăng Long* (Ly Cong Uan—The Road to Thang Long), directed by Can Đức Mau, which celebrated Hà Nội's millennial anniversary in October 2010 and cost an estimated US$2.66 million.

39. Đặng Nhật Minh, discussion of *Don't Burn It* at the Southeast Asian Studies Program (SEATRiP) Colloquium Series, University of California, Riverside, 29 January 2010.

40. Phạm also portrayed Camille, the daughter of Catherine Deneuve's Éliane, in Wargnier's *L'Indochine*.

CHAPTER 8

Scott Laderman

It was rather late in the brief but sordid history of the U.S.-Vietnamese "catfish wars" that perhaps the most bizarre development in the saga unfolded. In August 2005, several Southern U.S. states banned Vietnamese catfish on the partial grounds that the fish imperiled the nation's bioterrorism defenses. That a food product might represent a bioterror threat would be an explosive charge under any circumstances, but it was one whose timing—it came almost immediately after two consumer surveys delivered devastating news to American catfish producers—struck some analysts as particularly suspicious. Just four weeks before the announcement of the ban, a study by researchers at Mississippi State University found that three out of every four subjects preferred the taste of Vietnamese catfish to that of its North American counterpart.[1] Another survey three weeks later yielded similar, though more evenly split, results.[2] Both polls were deeply troubling to the American catfish industry, which for several years had been waging an unrelenting assault on Vietnamese imports. The widespread charge that Viet Nam provided an inferior product, now seemingly undermined by two *American* studies, had been a crucial component of the domestic producers' campaign.

It thus seemed curious that just weeks after these findings were announced, the state-level ban was issued. In mid-August 2005, Louisiana, Alabama, and Mississippi—which, together with Arkansas, constituted the heart of American catfish country—decreed that retail sales of the Vietnamese fish would henceforth be prohibited.[3] The U.S. Food and Drug Administration (FDA) had detected fluoroquinolones in some of the product arriving from Viet Nam; a number of Vietnamese farmers, it turned out, had added the antibiotic to their feed to prevent fish from becoming diseased. American regulators, concerned that fluoroquinolones might contribute to human antibiotic resistance, had proscribed their agricultural use in the United States. The Vietnamese product was thus banned by the three states. "The apparent intent [of the catfish prohibition] is to protect people from virulent infections and bioterrorism," a fisheries specialist with the Alabama Cooperative Extension System told the press, although, he added, the short-term effect would admittedly be to "create an even playing field" on which American farmers could better compete with the Vietnamese.[4]

Praised by the industry, the decision incensed free marketeers. William Anderson, an economist and adjunct scholar at the Ludwig von Mises Institute, facetiously warned that "some sneaky terrorists might be trying to kill Americans by slipping poisoned catfish into our food supply." After all, he sarcastically reminded his capitalist audience, "Vietnam does have a government that calls itself communist." In fact, Anderson wrote in a more serious vein, the ban had nothing to do with "catfish terrorism"; rather, it was instituted "to protect [the] politically connected owners" of Southern catfish farms.[5] Radley Balko of the Cato Institute echoed his libertarian colleague. With the ban in the American South, he joked, it was "as if Vietnamese Al Qaeda operatives were planning attacks on the [United States] by poisoning the country's catfish exports." The "absurdity of nativist thinking"—the effort to protect American farmers from Vietnamese competition—was "appalling," Balko declared.[6]

Whereas the analysts misinterpreted the "bioterrorism" concern, which they understood to mean fish being immediately used as bioterror weapons rather than gradually contributing to antibiotic resistance—a situation that could prove calamitous in the event of a bioterror attack—they were prescient in noting the suspicious nature of the tri-state ban. While the routine use of antibiotics in livestock is indeed a legitimate concern, the timing of the ban seemed questionable. That a ban was issued, however, was not in the least surprising. From the moment Vietnamese catfish exports began to seriously compete in the United States, American producers and their government allies sought to neutralize the threat emanating from Southeast Asia. Their tactics were diverse, ranging from pressing a linguistic challenge over what constitutes a "catfish" to leveling nakedly xenophobic appeals to American grocers and filing an antidumping petition with the U.S. International Trade Commission.

That this transnational conflict, which has come to be known as the catfish wars, pitted Americans against Vietnamese only lent the issue a special historical resonance. After all, it was just several decades earlier that the United States had laid waste to a fair portion of Southeast Asia. Yet the catfish wars came to represent a different sort of conflict. Although the belligerents may have been familiar, the more recent struggle was not martial. Still, the underlying concerns of Washington in the early twenty-first century echoed those of the 1940s through the 1970s. Whereas the previous conflict involved the threat posed by Vietnamese revolutionary nationalism to the post–Second World War liberal world order sought by the United States, the more recent catfish dispute involved the defense of American capitalism's hegemonic position from the challenge posed by a Third World state undergoing a wrenching capitalist transformation. Vietnamese catfish would come to represent "foot soldiers" in this new but ideologically familiar war.[7] At stake were not only the profits of American catfish producers. Imperiled, too, was the legitimacy of U.S. counsel on the global necessity of capitalist theory. If it was true that "open trade is not just an economic opportunity" but "a moral imperative," as George W. Bush confidently insisted in May 2001, then the catfish wars threatened to expose U.S. economic policy as deeply and profoundly immoral.[8] Once again, it seemed, the plight of distant Vietnamese might force an American self-reckoning.

When, in the decades following its devastating war with the United States, Viet Nam progressively deepened its capitalist transformation under the liberalizing policy known as *doi moi*, its commitment to the sort of model championed by those who sought "structural adjustment" in the Third World only grew. As part of this transformation, Hanoi sought not just Viet Nam's service as a manufacturing platform for large multinational corporations. It also sought, with the encouragement of American trade representatives, to penetrate the international market in agricultural commodities such as coffee and seafood. In the case of the former, Viet Nam's experience proved sobering. The Vietnamese government provided subsidies to farmers in the 1990s to encourage their entry into the global coffee business. Its initial investments appeared promising. Indeed, by 2000 Viet

Nam had emerged as the world's second-largest coffee producer. Things did not, however, turn out as the government had hoped. The flood of low-quality robusta beans pouring out of Viet Nam quickly led to a global glut. Prices plummeted, and Vietnamese farmers soon found themselves facing financial ruin. In the heart of the country's coffee-growing region, the development organization Oxfam reported that, by 2002, farmers dependent solely on their coffee crop were earning "pre-starvation" incomes.[9] The transition to export-oriented agriculture had not delivered the vast benefits that Vietnamese planners had promised.

The same might be said of the capitalist transformation more broadly. Numerous Vietnamese acquired considerable wealth under *doi moi*. But many more did not. Millions found themselves struggling to survive as the idea of socialist revolution became an increasingly distant memory. In the countryside, peasants were uprooted as land ownership became concentrated in fewer and fewer hands. In urban areas, workers suffered exploitation by rapacious corporations seeking ever lower costs. User fees were introduced for education and health services once guaranteed by the state. And obesity became a concern in a country still plagued by widespread malnutrition. By the mid-1990s, in fact, income inequality had become even more pronounced in Viet Nam than in the capitalist West. And, as in much of the West, "ethnic minorities" disproportionately found themselves among those left behind.[10]

Still, economic officials in Hanoi appeared undaunted. At the same time that "market" forces were decimating Vietnamese coffee farmers—while, it should be noted, creating enormous profits for roasters based mostly in the West—Vietnamese in the Mekong Delta were being confronted with a comparable threat to their economic survival. In the 1990s, Viet Nam had begun to emerge as a major seafood producer, and with no product was the country's ascent more pronounced than catfish. Indeed, Vietnamese catfish exports to the United States grew nearly seven-fold from 1999 to 2002, according to U.S. industry estimates, increasing from five million to thirty-four million pounds.[11] By 2002, a year after Washington and Hanoi enacted a bilateral trade agreement signed by the two governments the year before, Vietnamese exports, while still a relatively small portion of the overall catfish market, had captured roughly 20 percent of the market for frozen fillets.[12] American producers took notice. Already they were concerned about the ramifications of the bilateral trade agreement, which had the effect of dropping average tariffs on Vietnamese imports from approximately 40 percent to 3–4 percent.[13] It is perhaps not surprising, then, that when the earnings of American catfish farmers dropped precipitously in 2001, the aquaculturists blamed the Vietnamese for their ills.

Vietnamese diplomats and industry leaders worked quickly to counter the American charge. They cited what they considered powerful evidence: U.S. government data and the findings of research organizations. In a report in October 2001, for instance, Consulting Trends International attributed the drop in catfish prices "primarily" to "higher domestic catfish inventories" in the United States, a development that, according to the *Far Eastern Economic Review*, was due to "increased U.S. pond acreage and lower feed prices."[14] Nguyen Huu Dung, secretary general of the Vietnam Association of Seafood Exporters and Processors, thus insisted that the price decrease reflected only a "normal economic phenomenon in its development cycle" caused by production and consumption patterns in the United States.[15] Still, domestic growers believed that the Vietnamese imports had to be directly challenged. The industry thus initiated a public relations campaign in 2001 intended to persuade both everyday Americans and wholesale buyers to avoid the Vietnamese product.

Part of the campaign relied on one of the most toxic legacies of the war in Southeast Asia. Representative Marion Berry, a Democrat from Arkansas, publicly suggested that Vietnamese fish were endangering the health of American consumers. "That catfish is produced in disgusting conditions on the Mekong River, which is one of the most polluted watersheds in the world," Berry charged. "That stuff [Agent Orange] doesn't break down. Catfish are bottom feeders and are more likely to consume dioxins that were sprayed as defoliants."[16] The American use of Agent Orange in Viet Nam was one of the more controversial—and, today, contested—of Washington's wartime policies. Veterans from all sides claim to have suffered health consequences from their exposure to the chemical spray, while Vietnamese officials, doctors, and scientific researchers attribute many of the cancers, miscarriages, and physical malformations suffered by countless Vietnamese to the Americans' herbicidal agents. Berry's charge thus amounted, in certain respects, to a perfect illustration of how the war has been remembered by much of the United States. Rather than viewing the American use of chemical defoliants as an action meriting redress by Washington, the toxic aftereffects of the chemical campaign were framed as yet another instance of American victimization at the hands of Vietnamese. That there was, as with the POW/MIA myth, essentially no evidence buttressing the congressman's charge, as even the U.S. Embassy in Hanoi conceded, was immaterial.[17] The accusation was simply too convenient.

More durable, perhaps, than the insinuation regarding Agent Orange was a long-running series of advertisements sponsored by the Catfish Institute, an industry-funded promotional organization, in the trade publication *Supermarket News*. The ads, which ran in rotation for well over a year, could not have structured their entreaties in more nakedly xenophobic terms (see figures 8.1–3). They began by imploring their audience of grocers, in large type, to "never trust a catfish with a foreign accent" and to "beware of imposters," suggesting that the Vietnamese product was not a catfish but a "copycat." Such "slippery imported [c]atfish wannabe[s]," the ads cautioned in an appeal laced with stereotypes of the developing world as filthy, unhygienic, and dangerous, have "grown up flapping around in Third World rivers and dining" on "whatever [they] could get [their] grubby little fins on." This was in stark contrast to the American product, the ads maintained, which was "raised in pure, fresh waters and fed a gourmet diet of natural grains and proteins." Moreover, they continued, grocers could be "confident which processing plants meet strict U.S. government regulations and which ones, well, don't." The "lowly imposter[s]" from Viet Nam, the ads warned, were "probably not even sporting real whiskers." Indeed, "those other guys probably couldn't spell U.S. even if they tried." Given that the supposedly pristine waters of the United States offered the "perfect environment for nature's perfect fish"— the American catfish were said to be more "tender" and more "consistently mild and delicate" than their Vietnamese counterparts—why, the ads suggested, would American grocers even contemplate the imported product?[18]

The wholesalers, it turned out, were not biting. By late 2001, an estimated 30 percent of American seafood restaurants were serving Vietnamese catfish.[19] Legislative action thus became necessary, opening up an additional front in the escalating catfish wars. With most catfish farms located in four Southern states—Mississippi, Alabama, Arkansas, and Louisiana—legislators from the South became the industry's most vocal champions. As early as July 2001, several members of Congress had introduced a bill that would have required all fish sold in American retail outlets to be identified by its country of origin. The concern, Representative

Mike Ross of Arkansas notified his colleagues, was that "so-called catfish are being dumped into our markets from Vietnam and sold as farm-raised catfish." The "truth," he continued, "is that it is not farm raised, and I am not even sure it is catfish."[20] As a result, American consumers were purchasing fish under labels that intimated Mississippi Delta origins—"Cajun Delight," "Delta Fresh," and so on—but that in fact originated in Southeast Asia.[21] And Viet Nam, Ross maintained, exploited not only its "cheap labor" but also its "less stringent environmental regulations." The fish were raised in "floating cages in the Mekong River," he explained, "exposing [them] to pollutants and other conditions." Given that the competition was being "unfair and untruthful," legislation would be necessary to ensure that people "in Arkansas and all across America" will know that they are buying "catfish grown by our farm families, not fish grown in a polluted river in another country."[22] The bill sponsored by the Southern representatives failed to pass, but, significantly, it marked one of the opening salvos in a concerted effort to achieve legislatively what the industry had otherwise failed to accomplish: the neutralization of the market-share threat posed by the Vietnamese fish. When the issue resurfaced several months later, it pitted high-profile proponents of "free trade" against a bloc of Southern members of Congress concerned about the decline of an influential local industry.

Regrouping in the fall of 2001, champions of American catfish growers initially focused on what became known as the "labeling dispute." The North American channel catfish had long enjoyed a poor reputation. Consumed for years largely by low-income people in the South, catfish was viewed by many Americans as a dirty bottom feeder with an occasional "off-flavor" taste.[23] A good deal of consumer marketing sought to alter this view, promoting the fish as a healthy, farm-raised food grown by family producers. Indeed, as the catfish wars escalated in 2001, Southern legislators repeatedly stressed the American industry's humble roots. "All the catfish feed mills and processing plants are either family-owned or farmer-owned cooperatives," noted Representative Ronnie Shows.[24] Moreover, continued his colleague Mike Ross, "many of the plants where the catfish are processed . . . hire workers who are making the transition from welfare to work."[25] The "small business men and women" who farm catfish, testified Senator Tim Hutchinson of his Arkansas constituents, were "struggling to survive in an industry that has been one of the bright spots in one of the poorest spots in the United States in the last decade."[26]

Beware of imposters.

US. FARM-RAISED
Catfish.

ACCEPT NO SUBSTITUTES.
LOOK FOR THE SEAL.

Don't get duped by some slippery imported Catfish wannabe.

Try as they might, fish raised in areas like the Mekong River aren't

the same as genuine U.S. Farm-Raised Catfish.

Not by the hair on their chinny-chin-chins. They're not as tender.

They're not as consistently mild and delicate. They're probably

not even sporting real whiskers. Well, enough's enough.

Now you can be certain which fish are raised in pure,

fresh waters and fed a gourmet diet of grains and

proteins, and which ones float around in Third World

THE PERFECT ENVIRONMENT
FOR NATURE'S PERFECT FISH.

rivers nibbling on who knows

what. You can even be confident

which processing plants meet strict U.S.

government regulations and which ones, well, don't.

GRILLED CATFISH
WITH MANGO SALSA

Just do what consumers are doing and look for the official seal. It's the best way ever to

separate us from those phony phish. To learn even more, visit www.catfishinstitute.com.

FIGURES 8.1, 8.2, 8.3 (*above and opposite*). "Beware of imposters," "Catfish or copycat?" and "Never trust a Catfish with a foreign accent." In a series of advertisements that ran for more than a year in the trade publication *Supermarket News*, the Catfish Institute, an industry-backed organization, drew on xenophobia and fear of Third World pollution in an effort to distinguish American catfish from their Vietnamese counterpart.

Rather than as a case of heavy-handed protectionism by the world's most powerful nation against a relatively small, largely agricultural society recently decimated by the United States, the Southern legislators framed the American conflict with the Vietnamese as a principled stand by embattled family farmers working simply to ensure a level playing field. By the time American producers began significantly targeting the Vietnamese competition, they had developed what they considered a successful "brand" — one that was treacherously under attack by deceitful foreign interests. The "blatant mislabeling" of the Vietnamese fish as "catfish" was "causing confusion among the American people and is absolutely destroying our domestic catfish industry," proclaimed Senator Hutchinson.[27] The Americans thus sought to legislate that only the North American variety of catfish could be identified as such.

This was a remarkable step made possible only by the tremendous power Washington enjoyed in the international trade system. Ichthyologists considered both the American and Vietnamese fish catfish, but the Southern members of Congress sought to force a legal change that would preclude the use of the word "catfish"—even if preceded by a qualifier ("Mekong catfish," "basa catfish")—in identifying the Vietnamese product in the United States. The desired change was not, to be sure, rooted in science. When the FDA sought the counsel of Carl J. Ferraris Jr., a global catfish expert with the California Academy of Sciences, Ferraris was unequivocal. "The FDA wanted some indication of whether there was any justification for limiting the term *catfish* to North American catfish," he told the *New York Times*, "and the answer was there's no justification, historically or scientifically, for such a statement."[28]

This hardly swayed the Southern members of Congress, however, who drew on a series of colorful, if misleading, analogies to underscore their point. "This Vietnamese fish that is coming into our country is no closer to a catfish than a yak is to a cow," asserted Senator Blanche Lincoln. Indeed, she improbably stated, it was "no closer to a catfish than you and I."[29] Representative Marion Berry expressed similar outrage. The Vietnamese and American fish "are two completely different products," he insisted. To call the former a "catfish" would be "the same as calling a cat a cow, and we just simply should not allow it."[30] Seeking to protect the interests of local growers, the legislators succeeded in attaching an amendment to an agricultural appropriations bill that would prohibit the FDA from processing any imported fish that called itself "catfish" unless it were of the *Ictaluridae* variety native to the southern United States.

Given that this amendment was inserted just months after Hanoi entered into a bilateral trade agreement with Washington, numerous members of Congress who for years had advocated normalization of relations between the two former enemies were outraged. The "guiding principle of the recently ratified, and historic, U.S.-Vietnam Bilateral Trade Agreement," Senator John McCain reminded his colleagues, "was to open our markets to each other's products." He continued:

> To my deep dismay, a midnight amendment inserted by the managers on behalf of several Senators with wealthy catfish growers in their states violates our solemn trade agreement with Vietnam. With a clever trick of Latin phraseology and without any mention of Vietnam, these southern Senators single-handedly undercut American trade policy in a troubling example of the very parochialism we have urged the

Vietnamese Government to abandon by ratifying the bilateral trade agreement. Vietnamese catfish are no different than American catfish by nutritional and safety standards—but they are different in the eyes of the large, wealthy agribusinesses on whose behalf this provision was slipped into the agriculture appropriations bill. After preaching for years to the Vietnamese about the need to get government out of micromanaging the economy, we have sadly implicated ourselves in the very sin our trade policy ostensibly rejects.[31]

McCain, like a number of his colleagues, was infuriated not only by the amendment's contravention of his longtime efforts to normalize U.S.-Vietnamese relations but, perhaps most significantly, by its implicit rejection of capitalist principles. If "free trade" was "indispensable to our prosperity" and was, globally, "the way out of poverty," as the Republican senator from Arizona maintained, then how could the United States, which viewed itself as a beneficent provider of economic enlightenment, so blatantly fail to adhere to its own trade orthodoxy?[32] Having endeavored for decades to situate all of Southeast Asia solidly within the capitalist camp, Washington, following its recent victory with Viet Nam, was now undermining its historic achievement. The irony was glaring. Despite their protestations, McCain, Senator Phil Gramm, and other members of Congress were unsuccessful in defeating the amendment. The protection of a local industry would trump market ideology. With the passage of the Farm Security and Rural Investment Act of 2002, the change in FDA regulations was made permanent. Vietnamese farmers were henceforth prohibited from calling their product "catfish." Instead, they became known commercially as "basa" and "tra."

But if the American catfish growers thought that a favorable outcome in the labeling dispute would provide them with protection from Vietnamese imports, they were sorely mistaken. The Vietnamese fish, before the change in FDA regulations, had been most ascendant in the frozen fillet market, and those who purchased and sold these fish—importers and wholesalers serving restaurants and retail outlets—were not dissuaded by the sudden change of name. They appreciated that the fish met FDA requirements—according to the U.S. Embassy in Hanoi, there appeared to be no "substance to claims that catfish raised in Vietnam are less healthy than [those raised in] other countries," while, noted Senator McCain, "FDA officials have visited Vietnam and have confirmed quality standards there"—yet was less expensive than the American product.[33] In short, the imports from Viet Nam continued to sell—and to sell briskly. For American producers, yet another tactical maneuver would be required. Having failed to neutralize the threat from Viet Nam by appealing to American grocers and, working through Congress, proscribing the imports' designation as "catfish," the industry, through one of its trade groups, the Catfish Farmers of America, filed a petition with the federal government in June 2002 seeking an affirmative ruling that Viet Nam was unlawfully dumping its fish on the American market. If the U.S. government found in favor of the American industry (and it was the U.S. government alone that would make that determination), remedies—most obviously, substantially increased tariffs—would be imposed.[34]

There was a remarkable irony in the American farmers' initiation of such an action. For a dumping claim to be favorably adjudged, a domestic industry must demonstrate that a foreign producer is selling a "like" product either below cost or at a price higher in its home market than in its exports to the United States. This presented, for the Catfish Farmers of America, something of a conundrum. After all, the industry had just worked diligently with its congressional allies to prohibit the identification of Vietnamese basa and tra as "catfish" on precisely the grounds that it was entirely dissimilar from the American product. "It is a different species; it is a different order; it is a different fish," Senator Tim Hutchinson had maintained as the labeling issue was being debated.[35] Yet to argue the antidumping case successfully, the industry needed to demonstrate that it was being harmed by a foreign "like" product. If the Vietnamese imports were a "wholly different kind of fish," as Senator Lincoln had insisted only months before the filing of the petition, then American *catfish* producers could not reasonably claim harm.[36] After all, the Vietnamese had ceased calling their product "catfish." But no matter. The industry opted not to address this logical inconsistency, and the government failed to pursue it. The Vietnamese imports henceforth became known in official American parlance as "certain frozen fish fillets from Vietnam."[37]

Prior to the filing of the petition, proponents of the labeling ban had repeatedly indicated that it was not their intention to halt the importation of the Vietnamese fish.[38] Rather, they said, they simply wanted to ensure that it was identified accurately. "This is not a free trade issue," Senator Hutchinson explained in late 2001. "This is a fair trade issue. It is a truth-in-labeling issue. It is calling Vietnamese basa what they are—basa—and allowing that term 'catfish,' which has been part of an important educational and nutritional campaign in this country, to not be kidnapped by those importers that seek to make a quick buck."[39] American consumers, in other words, had to feel confident that they were actually purchasing what they thought they were purchasing. Yet with the decision to file an antidumping petition, the industry's tune quickly changed. The Vietnamese product, that is, could no longer be considered a "wholly different kind of fish."

And so—for the Americans, at least—it was not. When the matter was heard before the United States International Trade Commission (ITC) in 2003, the first person to testify on behalf of the domestic industry was Senator Lincoln. Having faced withering criticism from free traders horrified by what they considered a blatant contravention of capitalist theory, Lincoln attempted to establish an appropriate discursive framework for the dumping dispute. The conflict, her comments suggested, was not a trade offensive waged by the United States against Viet Nam—a sort of economic reprise of the devastating shooting war between the two countries several decades earlier. Rather, in an echo of that previous war, it was framed as a self-defensive necessity in the face of unwarranted Vietnamese aggression. "Catfish is not simply an important component of Arkansas' rural economy," she noted. "In some counties, where unemployment rates have spiked to levels much higher than the national average, the industry serves as one of the sole sources of employment. . . . Unfortunately, due to the surge of imports of Vietnamese fish, our producers have suffered greatly." Those victimized by the Vietnamese imports were among the nation's most vulnerable people. "Some 70 percent of the employees in this industry are in their very first job," Lincoln emphasized. "Many, in fact, are mothers coming off government assistance, single moms who have never had a job before, breaking a cycle of poverty." The threat from Viet Nam was not just economic, in other words. It also imperiled "changes that we want to make socially in order to remove that cycle of poverty among many of our low income families." Still, the economic repercussions were terrible. The fact that imports from Viet Nam cost less than domestic farm-raised catfish, Lincoln asserted, had led to a "significant decline in catfish prices," and this was something that affected her entire state. "It's hurt local banks, whose loan portfolios consist of catfish farms and the processing plants that service this industry. Also, the corner grocery store, the farm implement dealers, the service stations and local retailers of all stripes. Even local schools suffer because of the erosion of the local tax base."[40]

Something had to be done. It was only a year and a half earlier, in December 2001, that Senator Lincoln had offered assurance that she and her congressional colleagues sought to address "the unfair trading practice where it occurs—at the labeling stage."[41] By the time of the commission's hearing in June 2003, however, she had discovered, it seems, that the "unfair trading practice" was in fact much broader. "Some people on the other side of the debate like to point out that Congress passed a labeling law which mandates that only genuine catfish can be sold as such," Lincoln noted of the petition's various Vietnamese and American critics. "While this law has been important both to the industry and to consumers alike, because it requires the product to be sold under a truthful label, it has not been and was not meant to be a solution to the dumping problem." For that, she told the commission, "we have the trade laws, which I strongly urge you to enforce today."[42] In her numerous comments during the labeling dispute, which involved "*the*"—that is, not *an*—"unfair trading practice," she said, Senator Lincoln had not once mentioned a "dumping problem."[43] By 2003, however, the "suffering" of American catfish farmers had become a "direct result" of Vietnamese imports "dumped into our domestic market."[44]

The Vietnamese, of course, objected to this attribution of blame. How, they asked, could they be responsible when their exports were not even a "like" product? Whereas the American industry had fought vigorously in 2001 to obtain legislation proscribing Vietnamese basa and tra from being identified as "catfish"—an effort opposed by the Vietnamese industry, which argued, consistent with scientific opinion, that its exports *were* in fact catfish—by 2003, when the Americans' antidumping petition necessitated that the imports be sufficiently similar, the Vietnamese opted—for pragmatic reasons, one presumes—to reverse themselves. "We believe the good senators had it right," an attorney for the Vietnam Association of Seafood Exporters and Producers (VASEP) told the ITC. "Basa and tra are indeed different from U.S. catfish."[45] And even if the American and Vietnamese products did compete, a Vietnamese trade official emphasized, the Vietnamese industry had done nothing improper. On the contrary—and consistent with capitalist principles—it had achieved a "competitive advantage" through "focused development of an integrated production process."[46]

That official, Nguyen Huu Chi, expressed Viet Nam's disenchantment with the American position. Bilateral trade, he noted, "embodies the aspirations of the people of both countries to replace the conflicts of the past with the promises of a future of prosperity." What did it portend for the notion of universal adherence to a global trade regimen if Washington could "use and abuse" its antidumping laws to "protect" American firms? History, in this instance, was instructive. Since 1975, the United States had placed repeated barriers in the path of normalized bilateral relations. As the Vietnamese would meet demands laid out by Washington, new demands would be made. From the perspective of Hanoi, the goalposts, to borrow an American colloquialism, were constantly being moved. In 2003, things looked little different. The "progress" made since passage of the bilateral trade agreement in 2001 was being "threatened," Chi suggested, by the apparent "commitment of the United States to free trade" only "when it conveniently serves the interest of the U.S. exporters." Let "free market forces" be the "principal regulator" of the trade in seafood, he ironically urged on behalf of the Socialist Republic of Viet Nam.[47] Meanwhile, more than forty thousand fish farmers in the Mekong Delta signed a letter to American officials that protested the U.S. position, declaring that it "ignores the trend toward competition and integration according to established international practices, not to mention the great difficulties it causes our way of life."[48]

To the surprise of few, the federal government, having initially decided that Viet Nam was a "non-market economy" and then ruled preliminarily in favor of the American producers in January 2003, reached a determination that summer that Viet Nam was dumping its product on the United States.[49] It thus slapped tariffs on the Vietnamese fish of 36.84–63.88 percent.[50] The response to the American decision, both at home and abroad, was biting. "It's totally unfair and does not reflect the objective fact," complained Phan Thuy Thanh, a spokesperson for the Vietnamese Ministry of Foreign Affairs. "The application of unfair protective barriers to Vietnam's 'tra' and 'basa' catfish exports to the U.S. over the protest of public opinion—including American opinion—shows the increasing tendency to protect domestic production in the United States."[51] The *New York Times* was similarly indignant: "The fate of Vietnam's catfish offers a warning to poorer nations short on leverage in the world trading system: beware of what may happen if you actually succeed at playing by the big boys' rules."[52] For free marketeers, the ruling heightened their sense of betrayal. Viet Nam had embraced the "Washington consensus" for well over a decade, abandoning its commitment to socialism in favor of the market orthodoxy promoted by the United States. Having adhered to the sort of structural adjustment favored by the International Monetary Fund and other lending institutions, the country now found itself being penalized for enjoying one of the comparative advantages that its low-cost economy enabled. The view of the economist Robert Dunn was typical: "We try to get the Vietnamese to move their economy towards an export-based market approach, and then every time they do it, we slap them down with these countervailing duties and it's become something of a joke."[53]

For thousands of Vietnamese, however, the joke was not amusing. Catfish farmers operating on only the slimmest of margins suddenly found themselves facing enormous losses. The catfish wars were not, it seemed at that time, concluding in Viet Nam's favor. In light of the two nations' shared history, it seems hardly surprising that Vietnamese views of the antidumping ruling would be colored by their memory of the decades-long conflict with the United States. "Our nation has a heavy history, and we try to forget it, try something new based on a spirit of cooperation and free trade," Nguyen Huu Dung of VASEP confided, "but now we are made to wonder whether you wish us ill, as much in the present as you did in the past."[54] Dung was hardly alone in conveying his disappointment. As the vice manager of a Vietnamese export firm complained, "The decision means that they just want Vietnam to be poor forever."[55] In truth, it is doubtful that American officials consciously desired that Vietnamese farmers remain poor. Rather, they likely gave little thought to the Vietnamese at all. Driven by the wish to see American producers succeed, the U.S. officials believed that the fledgling Vietnamese industry was interfering with this objective. Protectionist measures were thus in order. This meant, of course, dispensing with the "free trade" regimen prescribed by capitalist orthodoxy. Enjoying immensely greater power, Washington could simply dictate its bilateral-trade desires. Viet Nam, with its economy a mere fraction the size of that of the United States, would either have to accede to this reality or forgo participation in the American market.

Viet Nam grudgingly acceded to the American reality. But demonstrating persistence reminiscent of that which had frustrated American designs decades earlier, Vietnamese exports continued to find a market. It quickly became apparent that the tariffs simply "didn't help much," noted the *Wall Street Journal*, with Vietnamese catfish exports reaching $77 million by 2008, a substantial increase from the $10.7 million recorded in 2000.[56] Indeed, by 2009 catfish exports accounted for more than 2 percent of Viet Nam's gross domestic product.[57] In what would constitute perhaps the greatest absurdity of the U.S.-Vietnamese saga, by the end of the first decade of the twenty-first century, American producers, having previously worked through Congress to prohibit Vietnamese from calling their product "catfish," were now insisting that the Vietnamese exports needed to be identified as precisely that. The reason was simple. The industry managed to have language inserted in the Food, Conservation, and Energy Act of 2008 by a number of Southern legislators that transferred the regulation of catfish safety—but just catfish—from the FDA to the U.S. Department of Agriculture (USDA).

This was a remarkable development. After all, as one scholar wrote, "An industry call for more government regulation is tantamount to a call for a Spanish Inquisition."[58] But from a strategic perspective, the transition was in fact explicable. The farm bill made catfish the sole seafood regulated by the USDA, which historically has overseen only the meat and poultry industries. Seafood, conversely, has traditionally been regulated by the FDA.[59] This was significant because the USDA requires on-site inspections, not, as is the case with the FDA, simply spot-checking a sample of the imported product. Such a regulatory change would be "potentially disastrous" for Vietnamese farmers, one account noted, for it would require "setting up an equivalent system [that] could take years and effectively cripple their industry." American producers thus optimistically assumed that the regulatory move would amount to a "roadblock" for imported Vietnamese fish.[60] (Even without the change, predicted the editors of *Aquaculture Magazine*, there was an expectation that, given the decreasing value of the U.S. dollar vis-à-vis the Vietnamese dong, the United States would "see a significant drop in imports.")[61]

But, significantly, the law empowered the USDA to determine what species qualified as "catfish." The implications of this definitional issue began to dawn on the American industry. In light of their earlier insistence, codified as a matter of law, that only the American product could be commercially identified as catfish, domestic producers began frantically reversing themselves. "In a scientific sense, pangasius (basa, tra, swai) are in fact Asian catfish, despite labeling and marketing laws" claiming otherwise, insisted one industry official.[62] The government once more found itself facing an awkward dilemma. Congress previously had rejected the scientific consensus in favor of economic protection. Now the Department of Agriculture was being asked to serve those same protectionist ends by reversing the means through which it had earlier acted. In doing so, the government would essentially be conceding that it had previously shirked biological reality for commercial self-interest. Not to backtrack on the designation of the Vietnamese fish would "reek of absurdity from a scientific point of view," pointed out John Friel, a catfish expert and curator of fish at the Museum of Vertebrates at Cornell University.[63]

But those who were benefiting from the low-cost Vietnamese imports—especially manufacturers and sellers of fish sticks and frozen fillets—worried about the narrow priorities of the Southern industry. Vietnamese officials, moreover, raised the prospect of taking the matter to the World Trade Organization.[64] At the Vietnamese Embassy in Washington, the commercial counselor Van Thoah Ngo, denying that Viet Nam allowed the use of banned chemicals, asserted that USDA regulation would establish "a de facto trade barrier."[65] The USDA, having been forced into the unenviable position of deciding whether the Vietnamese fish were in fact "catfish," opted for a policy of stasis. In what turned out to be a nightmare scenario for American producers, the domestic industry found itself falling under the stricter regulatory regime of the USDA while the Vietnamese continued to operate under the pre-2008 status quo. And the USDA continued to punt for years. It still had not ruled on the Vietnamese fish when, in March 2011, Secretary of Agriculture Tom Vilsack indicated that a final ruling might not be issued until 2012.[66] American catfish producers, in other words, found themselves at least temporarily hoist by their own protectionist petard. How long they would stay there remained to be seen.

Few episodes have more starkly evinced the immense chasm that sometimes separates American rhetorical support for universal "free trade" from the naked reality of American xenophobia or protectionism than the confrontation with Vietnamese catfish. In the years after 1975, as the United States suffered something of an imperial decline, Japanese competitors had been subjected to widespread racist derision. The "buy American" campaigns of the last three decades had occasionally tapped into comparable sentiments. In the early twenty-first century, it would be Viet Nam's turn. For a developing nation that took seriously the commitments embedded in its bilateral trade agreement with the United States, the catfish wars marked an era of perceived betrayal. The American campaign "runs counter to the spirit of the [agreement] and the policy to liberalize commerce of the U.S. itself," Deputy Trade Minister Luong Van Tu complained in 2003.[67] For many observers, however, the evident double standard hardly came as a shock. "This is globalization as interpreted by the rich ethnic European countries," Prime Minister Mahathir bin Mohamad of Malaysia noted of the catfish dispute. "They say they will open their markets to us, but they find all kinds of excuses to keep them closed."[68] Subsequent events would only buttress Mahathir's conviction.

Having watched the catfish wars unfold, members of the Southern Shrimp Alliance, a national trade association representing shrimpers in eight Southern states, filed an antidumping petition with the ITC and the U.S. Department of Commerce in late 2003. Their targets were six major shrimp producers: China, Thailand, India, Brazil, Ecuador, and, once more, Viet Nam. And, once more, the developing world would find itself subjected to a U.S. deviation from market principles. Within two years, the petition of the American shrimpers led to the imposition of import duties of 2.3–112.8 percent on the six Asian and Latin American states.[69] American shrimp, like American catfish, would enjoy official protection.

The message for the developing world was clear: The United States need not adhere to the rules it demands of others. Even the corporate press spotlighted the apparent inconsistency. "To those who wish the United States would more faithfully practice the free-trade gospel that it preaches, the [catfish] case is a travesty," the *Washington Post* noted, "illustrating that when it comes to industries with political clout—steel, sugar, and lumber, for example—Washington often finds a way to curtail foreign competition."[70] Viet Nam would again find itself the object of a foreign policy lesson. Having fought a shooting war against the United States several decades earlier, by the early twenty-first century it would be locked in an economic war with its former adversary. How the catfish wars will be resolved remains an open question. But, U.S. determination has stressed thus far, it is not a conflict that the Vietnamese should expect to win.

Notes

1. Janet McConnaughey, "Study Shows Vietnamese Catfish Top U.S.," Associated Press, 18 July 2005. In response to the political ruckus that the study engendered—in particular, the politically awkward fact that a study contradicting the claims of

Mississippi catfish farmers originated in a Mississippi public university—the institution subsequently assured the public that the researchers' findings were merely "preliminary." "We were really using the study . . . to spark academic interest and questions, not to become political or emotional," insisted the head of the Department of Food Science, Nutrition, and Health Promotion. Timothy R. Brown, "Mississippi State Officials Call Catfish Study 'Preliminary,'" Associated Press, 21 July 2005.

2. "Catfish Wars Brouhaha Prompts Another Taste Test," Associated Press, 7 August 2005. In this second taste test, which was undertaken by a marketing company from Baton Rouge, 49.5 percent of people preferred the Vietnamese fish, while 46 percent preferred the American product. Four percent could not detect any difference.

3. Garry Mitchell, "FDA Near Decision on Vietnam Basa Catfish Ban," Associated Press, 18 August 2005.

4. Russ Henderson, "States Ban Vietnamese Catfish," Newhouse News Service, 17 August 2005.

5. William L. Anderson, "The Grave Danger of Catfish Terrorism," Ludwig von Mises Institute, 22 August 2005, available online at http://mises.org/story/1890 (accessed 19 June 2009). The Mises Institute identifies its mission as "advancing the scholarship of liberty in the tradition of the Austrian School." "About Us," Ludwig von Mises Institute, available online at http://mises.org/about.aspx (accessed 9 July 2009).

6. Radley Balko, "Catfish Wars: Why Is U.S. Blocking Capitalist Progress in Vietnam?," FoxNews.com, 2 February 2006, available online at http://www.foxnews.com /story/0,2933,183522,00.html (accessed 18 June 2009). See also Howley, "Catfish Terror," 15.

7. Eric Francis, "Eat Arkansas Catfish . . . If You Can Find Them," *Sync*, 12 January 2011, 14. I am grateful to Jim Levernier for bringing this article to my attention.

8. George W. Bush, "Remarks to the Council of the Americas Conference," 7 May 2001, *Public Papers of the Presidents of the United States: George W. Bush* (Washington, D.C.: Government Printing Office, 2003), 495.

9. Gresser and Tickell, *Mugged*, 10.

10. On Viet Nam's capitalist transformation, see Kolko, "China and Vietnam on the Road to the Market," 431–40; Kolko, *Vietnam*; Laderman, *Tours of Vietnam*, 123–50.

11. Paul Blustein, "Free Trade's Muddy Waters," *Washington Post*, 13 July 2003.

12. Margot Cohen and Murray Hiebert, "Muddying the Waters," *Far Eastern Economic Review*, 6 December 2001, 68.

13. Davis, "Do WTO Rules Create a Level Playing Field?," 239. I am indebted to Davis's article not only for its useful chronological narrative but also for identifying numerous sources on the catfish wars.

14. "Strangely enough," the magazine continued in citing the firm's findings, the

drop in catfish prices also was affected by "declining chicken prices." Cohen and Hiebert, "Muddying the Waters," 68.

15. Nguyen Huu Dung, "Catfish Campaign against Vietnamese Fish," 14 November 2001, available online at http://www.vietnamembassy-usa.org/news/story.php?d=20011114174243 (accessed 30 July 2009).

16. Dan Morgan, "Vietnamese Catfish Rile Southern Lawmakers," *Washington Post*, 10 September 2001.

17. According to the U.S. Embassy, "In the case of catfish, the embassy has found little or no evidence that the U.S. industry or health of the consuming public is facing a threat from Vietnam's emerging catfish export industry. . . . Nor does there appear to be substance to claims that catfish raised in Vietnam are less healthy than [those raised in] other countries." *Congressional Record* [Senate], 107th Cong., 1st Sess., 18 December 2001, 26651. When a number of scientists tested the question of whether the catfish were contaminated by Agent Orange, their data "fail[ed] to support allegations of dioxin contaminated food exports from Vietnam." Schecter et al., "Are Vietnamese Food Exports Contaminated with Dioxin from Agent Orange?," 1401.

18. *Supermarket News*, 12 February 2001, 33; 12 March 2001, 32; 26 March 2001, 40; 9 April 2001, 27; 23 April 2001, 38; 7 May 2001, 114; 21 May 2001, 52; 4 June 2001, 59; 25 June 2001, 27; 16 July 2001, 22; 30 July 2001, 22; 13 August 2001, 24; 27 August 2001, 31; 10 September 2001, 58; 24 September 2001, 32; 8 October 2001, 39; 22 October 2001, 39; 5 November 2001, 37; 19 November 2001, 24; 3 December 2001, 36; 17 December 2001, 30; 25 February 2002, 7; 11 March 2002, 9; 25 March 2002, 48; 29 April 2002, 7; 6 May 2002, 94; 20 May 2002, 33; 3 June 2002, 46; 24 June 2002, 23; 22 July 2002, 90; 9 September 2002, 13; 30 September 2002, 11; 4 November 2002, 28. One of the ads was less definitive about the feeding habits of the Vietnamese fish. They "float around in Third World rivers nibbling on who knows what," it declared.

19. Cohen and Hiebert, "Muddying the Waters," 68.

20. *Congressional Record*, 107th Cong., 1st Sess., 11 July 2001, H3932–H3933.

21. According to a former official in the Office of the United States Trade Representative interviewed by Christina Davis, this "marketing controversy was less the result of Vietnam's exporters than about the American wholesale retailers and supermarkets that were adding labels they thought would make the product sell better." Davis, "Do WTO Rules Create a Level Playing Field?," 241, fn. 73.

22. *Congressional Record*, 107th Cong., 1st Sess., 11 July 2001, H3933.

23. Paul Greenberg, "A Catfish by Any Other Name," *New York Times Magazine*, 12 October 2008, 75. "Off-flavor," Greenberg explained, "happens when blue-green algae predominate in stagnant freshwater and emit geosim—a harmless, muddy-tasting compound that passes easily into fish flesh. Since U.S. environmental regulations limit the amount of water that can be discharged [from catfish ponds], algal blooms are common, and catfish occasionally get that geosim taste." Ibid.

24. *Congressional Record*, 107th Cong., 1st Sess., 4 October 2001, H6267.

25. Ibid., H6268.

26. *Congressional Record* [Senate], 107th Cong., 1st Sess., 18 December 2001, 26642.

27. Ibid., 3 October 2001, 18431.

28. Elizabeth Becker, "Delta Farmers Want Copyright on Catfish," *New York Times*, 16 January 2002.

29. *Congressional Record*, 107th Cong., 1st Sess., 3 October 2001, S10118.

30. *Congressional Record* [House of Representatives], 107th Cong., 1st Sess., 4 October 2001, 18785.

31. *Congressional Record* [Senate], 107th Cong., 1st Sess., 1 November 2001, 21340. The senators who inserted the amendment were Thad Cochran, Blanche Lincoln, Jeff Sessions, Richard Shelby, Tim Hutchinson, and Trent Lott; see *Congressional Record* [Senate], 107th Cong., 1st Sess., 25 October 2001, 20814.

32. "U.S. Senator John McCain (R-AZ) Holds News Conference at the National Press Club," Federal Document Clearing House Political Transcripts, 20 May 1999. In the case of Viet Nam, McCain maintained that American trade resulted in an increase in "daily freedoms" in the country, while the "potential for capitalism" was "advanc[ing] our interest in freedom and democracy there." *Congressional Record* [Senate], 107th Cong., 1st Sess., 18 December 2001, 26651. The Cato Institute scored McCain as one of only eight senators having a "perfect free trader voting record" in the 107th Congress. Daniel T. Griswold, "Free Trade, Free Markets: Rating the 107th Congress," Trade Policy Analysis no. 22, Cato Institute, 30 January 2003, 14.

33. Moreover, McCain informed his congressional colleagues, "U.S. importers of Vietnamese catfish are required to certify that their imports comply with FDA requirements and FDA inspectors certify these imports meet American standards." *Congressional Record* [Senate], 107th Cong., 1st Sess., 18 December 2001, 26641.

34. The conflict of interest is apparent. "Given that the investigation of dumping and industry damage occur under the auspices of domestic law and national administrative officials serve as the judge in a dispute between a national and foreign industry," Christina Davis observed, "there is the possibility for bias in favor of the home industry." Davis, "Do WTO Rules Create a Level Playing Field?," 243.

35. *Congressional Record* [Senate], 107th Cong., 1st Sess., 18 December 2001, 26642. "Importers," he added, "have hijacked the common name of catfish and applied it to a species of fish that is not closely related or similar to what we commonly consider catfish."

36. Ibid., 26645.

37. See, e.g., the documents archived at U.S. International Trade Commission, Completed Investigations: Frozen Fish Fillets from Vietnam, investigation no. 731-TA-1012 (final), available online at http://www.usitc.gov/trade_remedy/731_ad_701_cvd/investigations/2002/frozen_fish_fillets_from_vietnam/finalphase.htm (accessed 26 October 2009).

38. "This provision [the labeling ban] does not exclude Vietnamese basa from

being imported," Senator Tim Hutchinson observed. "Let me emphasize that it does not violate any trade agreements. There can be as many Vietnam basa fish imported into the United States as they can sell if it is properly labeled Vietnamese basa. My objective under the provisions that were included in the [a]griculture appropriations bill was to ensure that labeling is accurate and truthful." *Congressional Record* [Senate], 107th Cong., 1st Sess., 18 December 2001, 26644. Hutchinson's colleague Senator Blanche Lincoln offered a similar, though slightly different, argument. "We are not trying to stop other countries from growing catfish and selling it into this country," she maintained. "We simply want to make sure that if they say they are selling catfish—then that is what they are really doing. It does not violate the 'national treatment' rules in our trade agreements, nor should it violate our bilateral agreement with Vietnam, as some may argue. That is because the language included in the [a]griculture appropriations law applies to anybody who tries to mislabel fish as 'catfish,' whether that mislabeled fish has been grown in Asia or in Arkansas. . . . If our trading partners want to raise catfish of the 'Ictaluridae' family overseas and import it into this country under the label of 'catfish,' then they can do that. Our language does not seek to stop them. It only requires them to deal with the consumer honestly. It only prohibits them from deceiving the consumer." Ibid., 26646.

39. Ibid., 26644.

40. Hearing before the U.S. International Trade Commission, 17 June 2003, "In the Matter of Certain Frozen Fish Fillets from Vietnam," investigation no. 731-TA-1012 (final), Heritage Reporting Corporation, Washington, D.C., 2003, 8–9, 11.

41. *Congressional Record* [Senate], 107th Cong., 1st sess., 18 December 2001, 26646.

42. Hearing before the U.S. International Trade Commission, 11–12.

43. Ibid.; emphasis added.

44. Ibid., 12.

45. Edmund W. Sim, quoted in ibid., 23.

46. Nguyen Huu Chi, quoted in ibid., 15.

47. Ibid., 14–15, 17.

48. Blustein, "Free Trade's Muddy Waters."

49. The determination by Washington that Viet Nam was a "non-market economy," which meant that the United States could disregard Viet Nam's cost and pricing data given the presumption of state interference in Vietnamese economic activity, was opposed by even the U.S.-ASEAN Business Council and the American Chamber of Commerce in Vietnam; see, e.g., Vietnam News Agency, "Vietnam Operates in a Market Economy: Multinationals," *Asia Pulse*, 18 October 2002; "AmCham Backs Local Farmers in Basa Debate," *Vietnam Investment Review*, 21 October 2002.

50. U.S. Department of Commerce, "Notice of Final Antidumping Duty Determination of Sales at Less than Fair Value and Affirmative Critical Circumstances: Certain Frozen Fish Fillets from the Socialist Republic of Vietnam," *Federal Register*

68, no. 120 (23 June 2003): 37116–21; U.S. International Trade Commission, "Certain Frozen Fish Fillets from Vietnam," *Federal Register* 68, no. 154 (11 August 2003): 47608–9; U.S. Department of Commerce, "Notice of Antidumping Duty Order: Certain Frozen Fish Fillets from the Socialist Republic of Vietnam," *Federal Register* 68, no. 155 (12 August 2003): 47909–10.

51. Tran Dinh Thanh Lam, "Vietnam: 'Catfish War' Loss to U.S. Stirs Strong Protests," Inter Press Service, 29 July 2003.

52. "The Great Catfish War" (editorial), *New York Times*, 22 July 2003.

53. Julie Small, "International Trade Commission OKs a 64 Percent Import Tax on Vietnamese Catfish," *Marketplace Morning Report*, 24 July 2003.

54. "The Great Catfish War."

55. Nguyen Dinh Huan, quoted in "U.S. Catfish Trade Ruling Slammed in Vietnam," Deutsch Presse-Agentur, 24 July 2003.

56. Jane Zhang, "Catfishy: Vietnamese Species Embroiled in Identity Crisis," *Wall Street Journal*, 22 December 2009.

57. Shawn Zeller, "When a Catfish Is Also a Competitor," *CQ Weekly*, 8 June 2009, 1298.

58. Santerre, "Catfish Inspection," 164.

59. Ben Evans and Mary Clare Jalonick, "Catfish Wars Heat Up over Inspection Feud," Associated Press, 23 March 2011.

60. Ibid.

61. "Editor's Notebook," *Aquaculture Magazine* 34, no. 1 (January–February 2008): 5.

62. Jeff McCord of the Catfish Institute, quoted in Zhang, "Catfishy." The Catfish Institute is the organization whose earlier advertisements in *Supermarket News* repeatedly dismissed the Vietnamese catfish (pangasius) as "imposters," "conniving copycat[s]," "phony phish," and "catfish wannabes."

63. Zhang, "Catfishy."

64. Zeller, "When a Catfish Is Also a Competitor."

65. Zhang, "Catfishy."

66. Evans and Jalonick, "Catfish Wars Heat Up over Inspection Feud."

67. Vietnam News Agency, "Viet Nam Has Never Dumped Catfish," 3 January 2003, available online at http://www.vietnamembassy.us/news/story.php?d=200301 03103119 (accessed 26 October 2009).

68. Mikhail Raj Abdullah, "P[rime] M[inister] Highlights America's Trade Doublespeak on Vietnam's Catfish Exports," Malaysia General News, 13 August 2003.

69. Associated Press, "Trade Commission Lets U.S. Put Tariffs on Shrimp Imports," *New York Times*, 10 January 2005.

70. Blustein, "Free Trade's Muddy Waters."

CHAPTER 9

Agent Orange

Coming to Terms with

Diane Niblack Fox | a Transnational Legacy

The spraying of chemicals during the war in Viet Nam was controversial from the drawing board. Once the spraying began, the effects of these chemicals, loosely referred to as "Agent Orange," became a matter of often heated debate. As an issue that has persisted for more than half a century, despite various attempts to resolve it through a mix of science and politics, Agent Orange links individual lives to national policies and local issues to global concerns across divides of time and space. Its effects cross borders of nations, class, wealth, gender, and ethnicity. Its meanings shift from person to person and from context to context with a referent that is at times technical, at times experiential, at times metaphoric.

As a topic, Agent Orange has been framed in the languages of medical science, public policy, law, humanitarian concern, history, economics, military ethics, environmental justice, human experience, and story. While each of these perspectives contributes to an understanding of Agent Orange, none is adequate by itself. By exploring some of the frames through which this polyvalent term and its problematic consequences have thus far been approached, this chapter provides an introduction to the use of chemicals in the war in Viet Nam, while working toward a more adequate understanding of what has happened, what is happening, and what is still to be done—in Viet Nam, in the United States, and internationally. The approach of the chapter is to juxtapose the knowledge and questions grounded in individual and community experience to the knowledge and questions generated by the discourses of science, politics, law, and humanitarian initiatives in order to lay a groundwork for dialogue between the stories we tell ourselves about nation building and national security and the stories of people whose bodies and lives suffer the consequences of those processes.

The form of the chapter is meant to reflect the current form of the discussion on the consequences of Agent Orange: separate languages, overlapping and mutually intelligible to a degree, but not yet in full conversation with each other. The chapter begins with a narrative based on an interview with a family in a rice-farming village in northern Việt Nam. It continues with a brief overview of the history of the use of Agent Orange, followed by sections that approach the chemicals and their consequences through science, politics, law, and activist and humanitarian responses.

Why start with stories and their ambiguities? Who can say for certain whether the illnesses of the particular people who tell these particular stories are due to Agent Orange or to some other confounding conditions?[1] I have chosen to begin with a human story because I think that is where *we* start, and where the larger story of Agent Orange and responsibility begins: with human experience, a human search for meaning, and a longing for justice. If telling a human story risks confusion, leaving the story of Agent Orange to science and politics risks diminishing our understanding and our humanity. There is another reason I start with a story: our understanding of Agent Orange has been propelled by these stories and the responses they have elicited from politics and science. Indeed—and it is a point worth pondering—it could be argued that, with the passage of time and the increase in our understanding, the early stories have proven to be more accurate than the early science.

Agent Orange in Stories

The story retold here is based on an interview with a Vietnamese family described by the Red Cross as being among "the poor and disabled, including those who could have been affected by Agent Orange."[2] The setting is the fertile delta land at the mouth of the Red River, in Thai Binh Province, about a three-and-a-half-hour drive southeast of Hanoi. I went to the village with my friend Lang, a native of Thai Binh, under the auspices of the Committee for the Care and Protection of Children (CPCC).

From the committee's office in the district capital of Thai Binh, we drove deep into the delta, through rice fields that stretched green as far as the eye could see under the cold gray winter drizzle. At a small town, we turned off the paved two-lane road onto a dirt lane that dead-ended at a dike. From there we walked a kilometer or so across the top of the dike, along a narrow path. Rows of lettuce and aromatic herbs bordered the path on both sides, growing in the shade of trees that protected them from the withering sun of other days. Ducks swam in the water channeled at the base of the dike; chicken cages dotted its banks.

When we arrived at Mrs. Ha's home,[3] she was cooking lunch over an open fire in the detached kitchen. The family had expected us earlier, but we were late, so they had gone back to work, thinking our plans had changed. Mrs. Ha's husband, Mr. Binh, had gone to the communal warehouse to get wine to sell in the village, and Mrs. Ha had turned to preparing the family meal. She asked us to wait for her husband's return to begin the interview. As we hesitated a moment in the courtyard, family and neighbors began to gather. An old man, giving me a sideways glance, tested my Vietnamese. "What is this in Vietnamese?" he asked. "*Mot ngoi nha*—a house," I answered. He nodded vigorously, and walked up the steps into the new cement house.

It turned out that "house" was indeed a significant word, symbolizing the care given by the extended family. Mrs. Ha's older brother pointed to a mud-walled, thatched-roofed house on a low-lying piece of land across the way. "You see, that house over there was their house," he said. "The relatives got together to loan them money to buy this house." It is a loan the relatives know cannot be repaid.[4]

"My sister and her husband are far too miserable," the brother continues. "I mean, in a year—in roughly twelve months—they had to go to the hospital thirty times, and each time there is only us to count on." I think of what it would take to get a sick person to the hospital from there: down the village lanes to the dike; a kilometer or so along the top of the dike to the small country road; through neighboring villages to the main provincial road, and then an hour or so by car to the provincial capital. But they would not go by car. Would they go by motorbike? I have only seen bicycles in the village. Who would care for the children left behind, look after the house, and tend the crops?

We went into the house and sat on plastic stools around a low table, where Mrs. Ha's brother poured us cups of tea. While we were waiting, Mrs. Ha spoke of her husband's many illnesses, recalling,

> There was a time when the doctors at the hospital in town said, "That's all we can do; let him go home and wait for death. If he craves anything, let him have it." His stomach was swollen like this, and his skin was completely swollen, and he couldn't go to the bathroom. Neighbors, and then other women, and then organizations gave a bit of rice, a few potatoes, and some kernels of corn, and then I had to beg for each nickel and dime.
>
> Then I had a dream about going into the forest to get medicine for my husband, so I "dove through the mud" to get to the forest—all the way to Sa Pa—and there was the medicine to give my husband, folk medicine, and he took it and got better, and did not die.

Lang turned the conversation to strains these illnesses have put on the marriage. "Do you ever get angry or think of leaving?" she asks. "Sometimes I refrain from speaking," Mrs. Ha replies, "and sometimes I argue a sentence or two. Then I reflect, and pity him, and cry, not knowing what to do. He is so thin, his skin is so dark. He is now reaching the time of old age and weakness. His life is like the wind." She turns to speak to the family and neighbors who fill the house, listening to our interview: "when you are happy, do you think you can stay that way forever? We can't be miserable forever, uncles and aunts, grandfathers—can we? That's right— I have to encourage my husband."

When Mr. Binh comes in, he tells us that in 1972, before the Paris Peace Agreements, he was a Special Forces soldier in reconnaissance in Tay Ninh, a heavily sprayed region in the south. Where he was stationed the trees were denuded of leaves; he lived in tunnels, "bare-headed, bare-footed, bare-chested." "Camouflaged by spreading mud on his body," interjects another man. "We saw two hundred liter barrels with yellow stripes," Mr. Binh tells me. "They had three yellow stripes. We had only been through high school, so we could only read the word 'Dio xin,' or 'zio xin,' or something like that. At that time, we thought whoever died, died at once, and whoever lived, lived whole."[5] Mr. Binh came home with many diseases: diseases of the skin, of the nervous system, of the circulatory system, of the digestive system.

"The very regrettable after-effects of that war you see in the first fetus my wife gave birth to," he tells us. "*My* wife, right here. It was like a monster, a monster in a fairy tale. You know, it didn't have a human shape. And a few minutes after it was born, it died. Very, very hard. And my very own wife has many illnesses, most of them women's illnesses. Women also bear the consequences of this war." The couple's second child was slow-witted. He "doesn't know anything," they explain; he just turns from side to side. Their third child, a daughter, was born epileptic and blind, with no pupils. Their fourth child was sixteen at the time of the interview and enrolled in school.

After her daughter was born, Mrs. Ha said to herself, "Enough!" She didn't know if it was because of the war or because of fate, she says, but she went to be sterilized. The procedure, which involved inserting medicine into the fallopian tubes, led to many complications, much loss of blood, and repeated operations. As we spoke, she was in pain, with one half of her stomach swollen. "I only believe in science," she explains.

As for the traditional village healer, I don't dare believe, because my child's brain and eye are very, very important. Therefore, I totally and completely only believe in science. Science says she can't be cured. Then we must bear it, helplessly. What can we do? We can't do a thing.

This all started from giving birth to children like this, and voluntarily going to be sterilized. Then I was unlucky, and the consequence of sterilization was much illness. That made us spend a lot of money, money that a poor family doesn't have . . . very hard, very desperate. But it's all for my husband, all for my children, so I try to overcome the difficulties. Such a hard situation, but I still have to look after my husband, after my children. I know that my life is deeply entwined with his. I link my whole life with my husband and with my children, to 'carry the rivers and the mountains' to my last breath, and only because of war.

Mrs. Ha's brother says he wants to ask me just one more question. "In your country," he begins, "are there children like this?" He gestures around the room. I do not understand his implication, and cannot answer. "Children this strong, this tall, this big—or smaller?" One of the women sitting on the bed laughs and says, "I've seen on TV—they are big. Vietnamese are the smallest." Mrs. Ha's brother continues, "Our life here should be like that of our international friends. But because the war lasted far too long—all our lives—we lost the chance to study, because at eighteen we left school and took up the gun. When the enemy was gone, we came back . . . back to feed our children, but there was not enough, so they are sickly and puny like this. You see?"

"These are the consequences of war," Mr. Binh explains. "What he is saying is that the consequences of war are very great."

Earlier, Mrs. Ha had thanked me, and the American government, for paying attention to them and trying to help. When Mr. Binh again thanks me as a representative of the American government, I explain that I do not represent the government, that I do not know if the government will help, but that I believe ordinary people will. Mrs. Ha's brother replies, "Because everything comes from the people, doesn't it?" When he sees I am again not fully following his meaning, he explains, "Because if the people have sincere hearts and make demands on their government, most governments must execute those policies, because the government is for the people, isn't it?"[6]

Mr. Binh has a request:

I want to ask you to say this to the American people. An unavoidable war broke out between our two countries. In reality, nobody wanted it. Now both sides understand each other, and the two countries are friends, and trade business. Close the past and open the future. The two countries circulate goods. They've exchanged ambassadors already. But what happened before—that is, the consequences of the bombs and bullets, and of the chemicals, outrages the Vietnamese people. Yes, because the result is not to kill a person at once, but the result waits for the children, and for the grandchildren.

So I really hope the American people, together with the Vietnamese people, will demand that the American government not produce those chemicals any longer. Don't take them to make war with any other country. What is banned by international law should not be used. So stop using them. Yes . . . not just I myself in particular, or just the Vietnamese people in particular, but the whole world in general opposes these chemicals."

After his words, we fall silent for a time, each alone with our separate thoughts. Then it is time to pack up and go. Mr. Binh thanks me for trying to bring help. I respond that it is rather late. Yes, he agrees, if help had come earlier, his suffering would have been less. "But I am still here," he adds, "and my wife is still here."

Other people told other stories. There are thousands of these stories, each unique, each a part of a mosaic. As a Red Cross worker in another province put it: "each family, its own set of circumstances." There are stories from the families of men and women in the north who fought in the south and returned home with illnesses of their own and then had children born with birth defects—more birth defects, according to some studies, than the children of their fellow villagers who stayed in the un-sprayed north to fight. There are stories told by combatants in the south, whether they fought on the side of the Saigon regime or on the side of the National Liberation Front. There are stories told by civilians in the south, millions of whom were exposed, including the especially vulner-able groups of pregnant and nursing women and their embryos, fetuses, and infants.[7] There are stories told by Vietnamese Americans, who at times must brave being branded communist for speaking out.[8] And there are the stories told by U.S., Korean, Australian, and New Zealand veterans and by civilians in Canada, Puerto Rico, parts of the United States, and other places around the world where the chemicals were manufactured, stored, transported, or destroyed.

Background

From 1961 to 1971, the United States and the Republic of Vietnam (RVN) used chemicals to defoliate the coastal and upland forests of Viet Nam south of the Seventeenth Parallel, and to destroy a portion of its crops. The six defoliants and herbicides—and sometimes the fifteen other prin-cipal chemicals used during the war, as well—are often generically re-ferred to as Agent Orange. Strictly speaking, however, Agent Orange was a compound of 2,4-D and 2,4,5-T that made up roughly two-thirds of the approximately nineteen million gallons of chemicals sprayed by plane. Agents Orange, Purple, Pink, and Green were contaminated[9] as a by-product of the manufacturing process, with the TCDD form of dioxin—a form that is often referred to as the most toxic manmade chemical in existence. Discussions of the long-term effects of Agent Orange are often more accurately discussions of the effects of TCDD.

The military purpose for the chemicals was to destroy the enemy's pro-tective cover and food supply. While figures vary somewhat, U.S. mili-tary records show that 30–50 percent of the coastal mangroves were de-stroyed, along with roughly 24 percent of the upland forests and 4 percent of the total crops. The ballpark figure given for chemical devastation of the south as a whole is 10 percent; in some provinces, 50 percent of the vegetation was laid waste.[10]

Although there are estimates for the number of people hurt by the chemicals, firm statistics are elusive, given the number of people who have already died, the number who continue to be born, the long lead time for the development of some of the illnesses, the dispersal and subsequent movement of the populations affected, the movement of chemicals in the soil and water and through the food chain, and the slow development of agreement on which diseases and conditions may be linked to the chemicals used and TCDD. The number of people exposed can with some confidence be placed in the millions, however, and of those affected, at a minimum, in the hundreds of thousands.[11]

Evidence of the effects of these chemicals continues to accumulate from dioxin research and hundreds of studies of U.S. and Vietnamese veterans, Vietnamese civilians, and other exposed populations. In the 1970s, the first U.S. veterans who claimed that their illnesses were caused by chemicals were sent to the psychiatric wings of Veterans Administration (VA) hospitals; by 1980, those claims were taken as the topic of serious and hotly disputed studies. In that year, the International Symposium on Halogenated Persistent Organic Pollutants (more popularly called the International Dioxin Conference) was formed, prompted by industrial accidents such as Seveso, rice oil contamination in Japan and Taiwan, and Agent Orange. Also in 1980, in Viet Nam, the National Committee for the Investigation of the Consequences of the Chemicals Used during the Vietnam War was established. The committee was formed in October—hence, its more frequently used nickname, the 10–80 Committee.

A decade later, President George H. W. Bush and Congress charged the National Institutes of Health (NIH) to make a definitive study of the effects of dioxin on U.S. veterans who had served in Viet Nam. Through two decades of research, the list of diseases eligible for compensation by the VA has grown incrementally. By 2010, on the basis of that research, the VA had named fifteen diseases (or sets of diseases) and one birth defect as possibly linked to exposure to chemicals used during wartime in Viet Nam: chloracne, Hodgkin's disease, multiple myeloma, non-Hodgkin's lymphoma, acute and subacute peripheral neuropathy, porphyria cutanea tarda, prostate cancer, respiratory cancers, soft-tissue sarcomas, type 2 diabetes (diabetes mellitus), chronic lymphocytic leukemia, B-cell leukemia, AL amyloidosis, Parkinson's disease, ischemic heart disease, and the birth defect spina bifida. In the children of women veterans, the VA recognizes seventeen other birth defects as linked to the "Vietnam experience" but not specifically to Agent Orange.

In 2002, the director of the experimental toxicology division of the U.S. Environmental Protection Agency (EPA) named TCDD as associated with the following effects on adults: cardiovascular disease, diabetes, cancer, porphyria, endometriosis, decreased testosterone, and chloracne. She cited links to developmental effects in children on the thyroid status, immune status, neurobehavior, cognition, and dentition. Exposure to TCDD also correlates to an altered sex ratio.[12]

Agent Orange in Science

People like Mrs. Ha and Mr. Binh who are thought to be affected by Agent Orange ask questions about survival, questions about responsibility, and questions about meaning: how their families and others like them can find food, shelter, and medicine; who has the ability and the will to cure—or, at least, alleviate—their suffering; what can explain what has happened to them. Science, on the other hand, asks questions about how things work. Through accuracy of measurement, observation, description, analysis, and repetitions of comparisons and experiments, it produces evidence that may strongly suggest, but rarely prove for a given individual, causal links. Since the evidence thus created is by definition always subject to later revision, the time frame of science is theoretically infinite, advancing understanding at a pace incommensurate with human needs and concerns.

A half-century of work on Agent Orange and dioxin, however, has produced enough evidence to shift the scientific telling of the story of Agent Orange from exuberance to caution, and to establish a basis for addressing human needs. Certain scientific milestones mark the stages in this transformation.

The chemicals that would later be developed into Agent Orange were born in the 1930s, a time of infatuation with chemicals and the good things they bring to life.[13] They were first formulated as a help to soybean farmers; the chemicals enabled their plants to be productive in North America, which had a shorter growing season than the bean's native Asia, by altering the hormone system of the plant to force it to grow more quickly. Even in those heady days, however, one researcher issued this warning in a footnote: overdosing with the chemicals would cause the plant to drop its leaves and grow itself to death.[14] It was this very feature that would later appeal to a military fighting against guerrillas who operated under the cover of dense forest.

In the 1940s and 1950s, the story of these chemicals became more complicated as industrial accidents provided the earliest evidence of the hazardous consequences for skin, liver, and the nervous system of exposure to high doses of dioxin.[15] In the 1960s, with the publication of Rachel Carson's *Silent Spring*, the infatuation with chemicals began to give way to caution.[16] In that same decade, the Bionetics Laboratories found teratogenic effects (birth defects) in test animals exposed to Agent Orange, and Dow Chemical called its competitors together to teach them methods for reducing the TCDD contamination in their Agent Orange production. U.S. and Vietnamese scientists, separately, began serious studies.[17] In the 1970s and 1980s, hundreds of laboratory and epidemiological studies were initiated in Viet Nam and the United States, as well as in other parts of the world.

Advances in technology allowed scientists to tell the story of Agent Orange more clearly. For example, developments in gas-chromatography mass-spectrometry made it possible to study the effects of quantities of dioxin particles that formerly had been too small to measure. Scientists learned that minute quantities (parts per billion and parts per trillion) of TCDD still had significant effects. In 1990, understanding of dioxin's multiple effects on the body was advanced by improved understanding of the Ah receptor as the mechanism through which dioxin enters the cell and affects multiple cell functions.

In 1991, as mentioned earlier, George H. W. Bush and the Congress charged the NIH with conducting a "comprehensive review and evaluation" of the Agent Orange studies to date; the previously cited list of diseases veterans may be compensated for was developed from the results of this ongoing study. That list continues to grow.[18] In the 1990s, studies discovered high levels of TCDD dioxin in the soil surrounding former military bases of the U.S. Army and the ARVN and in the fat tissue, blood, and breast milk of people who currently lived on those sites.[19] By 1997, the International Agency for Research on Cancer had concluded that TCDD was a known human carcinogen. In 2000, the EPA released the draft results of its ten-year, more than three-thousand-page study. In addition to the annual international conferences on dioxin begun in 1980, six international conferences approaching Agent Orange through a mix of science, social sciences, and politics were organized by diverse bodies at irregular intervals from 1983 to 2002 in Viet Nam, the United States, Sweden, and France.

Ongoing scientific studies and debates include possible genetic effects; species variation; individual variation within species; timing of critical windows for exposure; the possibility of developing valid exposure assessments; dioxin levels in soil and samples of human and animal tissue (fat tissue, blood, and breast milk); the possibility of male-mediated birth defects that occur years after exposure;[20] the possibility for valid epidemiological study given the passage of time and the absence of baseline data; whether TCDD is an initiator or promoter of damage or a complete carcinogen; and whether there is a threshold level (the shape of the dose-response curve). Recent studies of the role of dioxin in producing epigenetic effects—disruptions of the endocrine, nervous, and reproductive systems that affect more than one generation but are *not* transmitted through the genes—provide another approach to studying the mechanism for what are being studied as possible third-generation effects of exposure to Agent Orange.[21] Debates that mix science and politics include differences of opinion over what the standard should be for regulatory policy when there is scientific uncertainty: "proof of harm," "acceptable risk," or "precautionary principle"?[22]

What does science ask of people thought to be affected by Agent Orange, and what does it offer them? In concrete terms, scientists ask families for samples of blood, breast milk, and fatty tissue; for interviews; and for an inspection of their medical records. Over the course of a half-century, as we have seen, scientific research has accumulated enough evidence about the links of dioxin and diseases that politicians in five countries have been able to use its findings as a basis for arguing successfully to get compensation for veterans and their families for certain diseases.[23] Ongoing research holds out the possibility of eventual support or weakening of additional claims, although perhaps not in the claimants' lifetimes. In some cases, scientists have offered medicine for the duration of a study—help that families found useful and then problematic when the medicines were terminated at the end of the study.[24] In other cases, researchers have promised help, or have been understood as promising help, that never came.[25]

What do these people in turn ask of and offer to science? The families ask science and biomedicine for cures—or, at least, for mitigation of their suffering and for explanations that transform culpability (you are suffering because of your sins or those of your ancestors) into sacrifice (your suffering is part of the sacrifice many made for the independence of your nation). Families offer to science their blood, breast milk, and fatty tissues along with their stories and questions that inspire further research.

The Politics of Agent Orange

Politicians deal with the world in terms of power relations, ethical arguments, logistical possibilities, and the demands of their constituents. For the issue of Agent Orange, that has meant responding to veterans and their supporters and to the nebulous but real power of public opinion, generated in part by narratives like the one recounted by Mrs. Ha and Mr. Binh. This section of the chapter, like the sections that precede and follow it, should be taken as heuristic, as a rough sketch of some of the issues that warrant more complete and careful attention.

The Early 1960s: Decisions and Initial Reports from the Field
The use of chemicals was politically controversial from the beginning, in both military and civilian circles.[26] When experiments at a joint American–South Vietnamese Combat Development Test Center led, in November or December 1961 (accounts vary), to requests that chemicals be used for a "crop warfare program," the United States at first declined, concerned about adverse political affects on the South Vietnamese and about charges of chemical warfare that might be brought by the communists. Arguments within the military and the administration that the use of herbicides and defoliants was banned by the Geneva Protocol and that their use would expose the United States to charges of barbarism were countered by arguments that the concept of chemical warfare applied to people and animals, not plants.[27] Paul Frederick Cecil recalls arguments that killing plants instead of people would blunt guerrilla activity without inflicting direct injury on enemy, ally, or innocent. Another argument was that herbicides were "an economical and efficient means of stripping the Việt Cộng of their jungle cover and food."[28]

In January 1962, President John F. Kennedy authorized the first use of defoliants. The first crop-destruction mission followed on 21 November of that year.[29] Once the herbicides and defoliants were in full use, assessments of their political effects varied, particularly for the part of the program aimed at crop destruction. In 1967, for example, the U.S. Air Force noted success in achieving one of the political objectives of the program, "to separate the [Viet Cong] from the people by forcing refugee movements into GVN [Government of Vietnam, a reference to the government based in Saigon] controlled areas."[30] A study by the Rand Corporation that same year concluded that the program probably was politically counterproductive. Estimating that 325,000 villagers had been affected by spraying operations that destroyed their crops and produced food shortages, the Rand study found that 80 percent of the villagers interviewed blamed the United States and the Saigon government for the destruction of their crops, with 74 percent expressing "outright hatred."[31]

Mid-1960s to Postwar: Science and Politics
Among the first people to raise their voices to publicly question the use of chemicals in war were scientists in both the United States and Viet Nam. How can we classify these challenges? As science? As politics? As an inextricable interweaving? A statement by the Federation of American Scientists in March 1964 read in part:

> We are concerned with reports of the field use of chemical weapons in Viet Nam. Allegations relating to the use of anti-crop agents under American supervision have been officially denied. However, reports that defoliating agents have been used to destroy protective cover have been confirmed by representatives of the Department of Defense. These charges give rise to the broader implication that the U.S. is using the Vietnamese battlefield as a proving ground for chemical and biological warfare. We . . . feel that such experimentation involving citizens of other countries compounds the moral liability of such actions.

The Pacific Division of the American Association for the Advancement of Science (AAAS) echoed these concerns in a resolution passed in June 1966, noting that the biological effect of the agents being used was not known and that scientists had a special responsibility to be fully informed, since the products were the result of scientific research.[32]

In February 1967, five thousand independent scientists, including seventeen Nobel Prize winners and 129 members of the National Academy of Sciences, petitioned President Lyndon B. Johnson to order a stop to the use of herbicides and recommended a review of U.S. policy toward chemical and biological weapons. The Pentagon ordered a review of all published and unclassified literature on the ecological effects of long-term use of herbicides, which was carried out by the Midwest Research Institute and reviewed by the National Academy of Sciences.

In 1969, the United Nations voted to add herbicides and defoliants to the list of banned chemical weapons in the Geneva Protocol. In 1975, President Gerald Ford signed an executive order renouncing first use of these chemicals.[33]

Early postwar discussions of reparations included talk of compensation for the damage caused by Agent Orange. Always politically divisive in the United States, talk of reparations was shelved when Viet Nam attacked Cambodia to stop the depredations of the Khmer Rouge and was then attacked by China, which supported the Khmer Rouge. The United States, solicitous of its renewed ties with China, broke off talks with Viet Nam and extended a trade embargo that lasted until 1994.

The 1970s and 1980s: U.S. Veterans

In the United States, the politics of Agent Orange were fueled by veterans' stories, although at first these stories were dismissed. Claims to the VA that their diseases were caused by exposure to Agent Orange resulted, in the early years, in veterans' being sent for psychological testing. These claims grew in part out of investigations by the VA claims worker Maude DeVictor in Chicago, who noticed unusual symptoms and similarities in the symptoms reported by many veterans returning from Viet Nam and began to ask questions of other veterans, of the Surgeon General's Office, and of Al Young, a U.S. Air Force plant physiologist who told her about health symptoms associated with dioxin exposure. What DeVictor found led her to go to WBBM-TV News in Chicago, leading to the production of an hour-long documentary, *Agent Orange, the Deadly Fog*, that aired on 23 March 1978. The VA dismissed the claims, countering that this information was coming from one city, generated by a woman who was a member of the Black Panther Party.[34]

At roughly the same time, the work of Paul Reutershan was increasing public awareness of Agent Orange and pressure to support U.S. veterans. Reutershan, a twenty-seven-year-old veteran dying of stomach cancer, had made his own connections between his disease and Agent Orange based on lists he had read of diseases some doctors at the time associated with exposure to dioxin and on his memories of a chloracne-like rash. "I got killed in Vietnam—and didn't know it," as he put it. Reutershan spoke wherever he could, including on the *Today* show, and formed a group called Agent Orange Victims International that continued, after his death in 1978, to speak out about Agent Orange and seek legal redress.

The entry of American veterans into discussions about the impact of the chemicals brought the issue a certain legitimacy and political clout among mainstream politicians not eager to offend veterans or their supporters. At the same time, this engagement made allies across formerly hostile lines—between veterans and antiwar activists and, eventually, with Vietnamese as well. In particular, the work of Admiral Elmo Zumwalt, who had ordered the spraying of the river banks in the south where his son was on U.S. Navy boats, did much to raise the respectability of the issue. A book written by father and son, *My Father, My Son*, chronicled the son's terminal battle with two forms of cancer and the birth defects of his own son.

The 1990s to 2000s: U.S.-Vietnamese Relations in Transition
However much politics may have served to legitimate Agent Orange as an issue to be taken seriously in the United States, politics played a quite different role in discussions of the topic between the United States and Viet Nam, where the United States at first considered mention of Agent Orange as a cover for a demand for reparations. A public affairs officer at the U.S. Embassy in Hanoi, describing the U.S. position on Agent Orange in 2001, noted with some heat that he felt the Vietnamese were asking for reparations and that such a demand was a nonstarter. "It's a nonstarter," he repeated, pounding his desk, adding, "It was one of the conditions for re-engagement that there be no reparations. . . . [T]hat was settled long ago." Earlier, he had said that he sensed that Viet Nam would not be satisfied "unless help is labeled 'U.S. assistance to Agent Orange victims.'"

By 2002, Raymond Burghardt, the U.S. ambassador to Viet Nam, was calling Agent Orange the "one significant ghost" that remained from the war, hindering full normalization of relations between the United States and Viet Nam. In 2005, military-to-military cooperation between the United States and Viet Nam was initiated in the form of a joint workshop on dioxin remediation. That summer, cooperation between the EPA, Viet Nam's Ministry of Defense, and the Viet Nam Academy of Science and

Technology was announced, focusing on the cleanup of the toxic remains at the Da Nang airfield. By the spring of 2006, as Viet Nam was poised to enter the World Trade Organization (WTO) and the United States and Viet Nam were recognizing certain shared interests with respect to China and terrorism, Burghardt's successor, Ambassador Mike Marine, was publicly calling for progress on the issue of Agent Orange. In November, when President George W. Bush visited Hanoi to participate in the Asia-Pacific Economic Cooperation summit, a joint statement issued by the two governments enabled that progress. In the statement, President Bush and Vietnamese President Nguyen Minh Triet "agreed that further joint efforts to address the environmental contamination near former dioxin storage sites would make a valuable contribution to the continued development of their bilateral relationship."[35]

In the winter of 2007, when both initial U.S. funding and a Ford Foundation initiative on Agent Orange were announced, Ambassador Marine was quoted by the Associated Press as remarking, "I want to make clear that the United States government understands the concerns of the government of Viet Nam and the Vietnamese people about the impact of dioxin on the environment and human health." At the same time, he noted that since 1988 the United States had spent more than $43 million on aid to Vietnamese with disabilities, whatever their cause, and affirmed, "The United States is committed to supporting the well-being of the people of Viet Nam."[36] A congressional allocation of $3 million for remediation in 2007 was followed by similar allocations for fiscal years 2009 and 2010, for a total of $9 million.[37] Although the sum is incommensurate to the task, it is a great improvement over past denial and intransigence.

The Ford Foundation initiative, spearheaded by Charles Bailey, developed in cooperation with the Aspen Institute into a Track Two effort at citizenship diplomacy, the U.S.-Vietnam Dialogue Group on Agent Orange/Dioxin. In June 2010, the group released a ten-year, $300 million plan of action that targeted both the environmental and human health consequences of Agent Orange: to clean dioxin-contaminated soil and restore damaged ecosystems and expand services to people with disabilities and their families.[38]

In the United States, in Viet Nam, and internationally, to different extents and in differing ways, the politics of Agent Orange has been driven by grassroots efforts that have pushed sometimes reluctant governments to take up the issue. The Vietnamese government was held back in part by its fear that unscrupulous competitors would scare off international markets through misrepresenting the effects of Agent Orange, thus undercutting hopes that agriculture and aquaculture would help lift the country out of poverty. Other political-economic interests that may have added to Viet Nam's initial hesitation include internal difficulties of definition and compensation, as well as its desire first for permanent normal trade relations with the United States, then for acceptance to the WTO, and, finally, for bilateral relations with the United States.

What held back the American government? The arguments most often given are lack of sufficient scientific evidence, fear of liability, and lingering postwar hostility toward Viet Nam. It might also be possible to see in this reluctance an attempt to save face, or to avoid facing what we have done, to save our own self-respect: we are not the sort of country that engages in chemical warfare. To recognize our culpability for Agent Orange would be to challenge our sense of our own decency, threatening our sense of who we are. Unable to face the implications of our actions, we denied their effects, creating in the process ghosts—ghosts, it could be argued, that returned to haunt us in our relations with Viet Nam and with the rest of the world.[39]

Blending politics with humanitarianism as it seeks to put this past behind us, the U.S.-Vietnam Dialogue Group's publicity calls for "Promoting Hope and Dignity: A Long-Term Humanitarian Response to Agent Orange and Dioxin in Vietnam."[40] That the hope and dignity are intended for both countries is suggested in "The Last Battle of Vietnam," by Walter Isaacson, published in *Time* magazine to coincide with the Ford Foundation's announcement in 2007. Isaacson's discussion of the legacies of Agent Orange ends with a call for Americans to live up to their values and show basic decency by following one of the first rules we learn in life: "clean up after yourself."[41]

Legal Approaches to Agent Orange

Law has been turned to in the case of Agent Orange in an attempt to settle questions of responsibility that neither science nor politics can address. Yet advocates for people like Mrs. Ha and Mr. Binh have often been disappointed with its judgments. Once again, this section of the chapter is intended to raise more questions than it answers, as a prompt to further work.

Americans

American veterans, Koreans, and Vietnamese have been among those who have brought legal actions against the U.S. companies that made Agent Orange and the other chemicals used in war. The chemical companies have become the target of the suits in part because the U.S. government as a whole cannot be sued, only individuals within it. The first suit was brought in the United States in 1978 and 1979 by a class of more than 2.4 million U.S. veterans with their wives and offspring, who sued seven chemical companies for injuries they alleged they suffered as the result of exposure to Agent Orange. The case was settled out of court, with the companies agreeing to pay $180 million, the largest award ever made to that date.[42]

Although one of the conditions for the settlement was that the companies would be exempt from future suits by veterans who opted out of the original class-action suit, this condition was overturned by a higher court in 2006 on the grounds that some of the diseases do not develop until many years later, so a veteran who opted out because he believed he was healthy but then later became sick still had a right to sue. New arguments are based not only on the delayed development of disease, but also on the development of scientific knowledge since 1984. A lawyer who works with ongoing veterans' claims describes this early suit as "premature," given what was then known about the effects of dioxin.[43] It was not understood at the time, for example, how dioxin could affect multiple workings of the body. As noted earlier, the mechanism by which dioxin affects multiple cell functions—its binding to the Ah receptor—came to be understood only in 1990. Legal work on behalf of U.S. veterans is ongoing.

Koreans

In 1999, Korean veterans filed suits in Korean courts against Monsanto and Dow, two of the largest manufacturers of Agent Orange, seeking $5 billion in damages. In 2006, the court ordered the companies to pay $62 million to compensate 6,800 of the roughly 20,000 people who had brought the suit. It remains to be seen whether the damages awarded by the court will be paid. In a separate action, South Koreans and U.S. veterans have raised as yet unsettled questions about lingering dioxin contamination at the U.S. Army's Camp Carroll base in Korea, where barrels of Agent Orange were reported to have been buried. In December 2011, the U.S. Army completed a nine-month investigation, issuing an eighty-five-page report that claims no evidence of Agent Orange was found. This claim is disputed by independent environmental experts, one of whom points to the finding of TCDD and 2,4,5-T on the base.[44]

Vietnamese

On 30 January 2004, the Viet Nam Association for Victims of Agent Orange/Dioxin (VAVA) filed a class-action suit in U.S. Federal District Court in New York against thirty-seven manufacturers of the chemicals.[45] Filed under the Alien Tort Claims Act, the suit sought "money damages for personal injuries, wrongful death and birth defects and . . . injunctive relief for environmental contamination and disgorgement of profits" on the grounds of "violations of international law and war crimes, and under the common law for products liability, negligent and intentional torts, civil conspiracy, public nuisance and unjust enrichment."[46]

Although Judge Jack Bertrand Weinstein—the same judge who had presided over the U.S. veterans' suit twenty years earlier—dismissed the lawsuit, he sustained several important points, including that the defendants had the right to sue under the Alien Tort Act, which at the time was coming under attack, and that international law applied in U.S. courts. During the hearing, Weinstein challenged a lawyer for the government who claimed that if the President of the United States ordered his troops to use mustard gas, those troops were bound to use mustard gas, despite international law. No, said the judge; were they to use mustard gas, they would be punishable for war crimes under international law, whatever the presidential order. Other points Weinstein sustained included that the defendants had standing in court and that the statute of limitations had not passed.

Judge Weinstein stated that the suffering of the Vietnamese should not go unaddressed but ruled that nothing could be done in his court, in part because of the internal logic of the law. Laws cannot be applied retroactively. At the time of the spraying, herbicides and defoliants were not classed as chemical weapons; it was only in 1969 that the United Nations thus classified them and only in 1975 that the United States concurred. Further, companies cannot be sued for negligence under the Alien Tort Act. Finally, the judge also ruled that the "government contractor defense" was applicable in this case. Under the government contractor defense, the companies are protected if they can show the government told them to do something and knew at least as much about the dangers as the companies did.

In an appeal, the VAVA plaintiffs challenged the government defense claim. They contended that the chemical companies did not comply with the government's demands, which had specified an herbicide that would not cause harm to people, animals, or the environment. The companies knew that their product contained dioxin, as well as other toxic chemicals, and they knew the quantities of dioxin produced were "unnecessary and preventable had the defendants followed then-existing industry standards for their production."[47] Evidence of this knowledge is a meeting Dow Chemical called in 1965 to share cleaner processing methods with its competitors, warning of possible consequences of a product too highly contaminated by TCDD. But the processing time was longer (four hours instead of forty-five minutes), and the process was not widely adopted. After the appeal was denied in the summer of 2007, the lawyers for VAVA petitioned the U.S. Supreme Court for a hearing. That petition was denied in March 2009, along with a related petition by U.S. veterans.

International

As frustration has grown with what some see as the inability of U.S. courts to render justice in this case, other avenues are being tried. In February 2006, the International Association of Democratic Lawyers announced its intent to bring the lawsuit against the chemical companies to the United Nations High Commission on Human Rights, where the focus would be put on the rights of those who were affected, not on debate over who was responsible.

On 16–19 May 2009, in Paris, an International People's Tribunal of Conscience in Support of the Vietnamese Victims of Agent Orange brought together judges from Algeria, Chile, India, Japan, Romania, and the United States to hear evidence from twenty-seven witnesses in a blend of law and activism. The tribunal found the United States guilty of ecocide and the chemical companies guilty of complicity. It urged Viet Nam to establish an Agent Orange Commission that would assess the amount of compensation due individuals, families, and communities; determine the amount needed for medical facilities and services; estimate costs to clean up the environment; determine the amount due to the state of Viet Nam to indemnify costs already incurred; and set up a trust fund for present and future victims, taking the $1.52 billion the United States spends annually on claims by its veterans as a guide.[48]

Agent Orange as a Humanitarian Concern

While scientists ask for more time to refine our knowledge about the consequences of Agent Orange, politicians respond to the demands of their constituents, and lawyers interpret precedents and legal codes, humanitarian agencies look for ways to bring assistance to people who indisputably need it.

First Responses

A rough sketch of the history of the humanitarian response includes both individual initiatives and organizational responses. In the days that immediately followed the end of the war, what help there was came from extended families and communities, although times were very hard for everyone, and there was little to spare. Friends in Hanoi and Hue told me that on meeting such families, "You just emptied out your purse, emptied out your pockets." Whatever you had, you gave, however small or large. Such help is still vital today. This person-to-person aid has been encouraged by stories in Vietnamese newspapers that give the names and addresses of people who need help. In addition, there has been a variety of government support, ranging from help in reclaiming damaged land for agricultural use to providing subsidies and other medical benefits for people with disabilities.[49] Given the general postwar poverty and manifold urgent needs, perhaps it is less remarkable that these programs have been inadequate to the task than it is that they have been attempted at all.

In the decade after the end of the fighting, Vietnamese doctors began to wonder about the unusual number of birth defects they saw among the children of veterans. By 1990, such observations had led doctors at the Tu Du Maternity Hospital in Ho Chi Minh City to push the Vietnamese government and foreign donors to establish centers to treat these children. By 2000, ten of these centers, known as "Peace Villages," were scattered throughout the country. In some centers, the children stay for varying lengths of treatment and then return home. In others, children and their caretakers (often their mothers) live at the center for a month or so while the children are examined, treated, and taught practical skills appropriate to their ability—sitting up, for example, or eating with chopsticks—and their caretakers are taught techniques of massage and rehabilitation exercises to continue with the child and to share with others when they return to their villages.

One early initiative that drew together Vietnamese and American veterans, along with French, German, and Japanese collaborators, was the Friendship Village just outside Hanoi. According to the history given on its website, when plans for the facility were formalized in April 1992, it was conceived as a residential facility for orphaned children and elderly or disabled adults. By 1998, when the residents were selected, "all of [its] residents suffer[ed] serious health problems attributed to the lingering effects of Agent Orange," notes its website. George Mizo, an American veteran instrumental in conceiving and realizing the work of the village, died from his own Agent Orange–related diseases in 2002.

In 1996, after the normalization of Viet Nam's relations with the United States, attention to the need for humanitarian work on Agent Orange was boosted by the release of two films made by filmmakers at the National Scientific and Documentary Film Center in Hanoi. *Where War Has Passed*, directed by Vu Le My and Luong Duc, was a call to action originally directed to the Vietnamese government. Shocking pictures of disabled children and extreme poverty were punctuated by commentary from veterans from both north and south that highlighted the fact that they had never received any form of compensation for these lingering consequences of war. When American nongovernmental organizations (NGOs) working in Viet Nam translated the film into English, it gained wide international circulation, winning prizes at international film festivals in Japan, Canada, and elsewhere. The second film, *Story from the Corner of a Park*, by the internationally award-winning director Tran Van Thuy, was a gentler meditation on the resilience of one poor family whose two children are disabled. Not made so obviously to shock people, it nonetheless—or, perhaps, therefore—has had a galvanizing effect for humanitarian response.

A key development for a humanitarian approach to the consequences of the chemicals used in wartime was the formation in 1998 of the Agent Orange Victims Fund of the Vietnamese Red Cross. With its creation, a public silence that had had nearly the force of a taboo was broken. More accurately, an English-language silence was broken: the Vietnamese press, as noted earlier, had been writing about the effects of Agent Orange for some years. The fund became a source not only of humanitarian support for people thought to be victims but also of information for international media and humanitarian agencies and groups that passed through its doors. Early in its existence, the fund engaged with the International Federation of Red Cross and Red Crescent Societies (IFRC) in its work on Agent Orange.

In the fall of 1999, the IFRC launched a special appeal to seek international assistance for a group of people it characterized as "caught in the middle of a scientific and political debate which had largely discouraged others from helping them"—namely, people caught in the controversies over Agent Orange. True to its mandate, the appeal continued, the Red Cross would not engage in the debate but would "concentrate on the needs of the individuals and families affected." The appeal referred to the thousands of poor and vulnerable people that Red Cross volunteers met in their daily work, people the appeal characterized as "living with great personal dignity, but in conditions which the Red Cross believes must be improved."[50]

The individuals and families targeted by this program were poor people with a variety of disabilities, including those that have some of the characteristics of spina bifida, cerebral palsy, muscular dystrophy, contractions, malformations, leukemia, blindness, deafness, physical and mental retardation, seizures, several disorders of the nervous system, and a variety of reproductive complications and abnormalities. Not all people with such diseases were classified as possible victims of exposure to Agent Orange. Over the years, criteria were developed on an epidemiological basis, as local and national agencies pooled their findings and reflections. Red Cross and child-welfare doctors compared the children of men and women who had fought in heavily sprayed areas in the south and those who had not, studied family histories of birth defects, examined cases in which healthy children were born to a family before a parent's exposure to the spray but then disabled children were born after that exposure, studied cases of children born to multiple partners of the same person to trace incidences of birth defects, and listened to countless stories.

The IFRC appeal in 1999 was one more step in the slow process of finding assistance for people left in great suffering and need after decades of war, a process at times hindered but not incapacitated by scientific uncertainties and political ambivalence about Agent Orange. It drew initial support for pilot projects in six provinces from the Swedish, Swiss, and

American Red Cross organizations. Working together, the international, national, and provincial Red Cross societies supported local chapters as they used community-based assessment to develop lists of families that included their economic and medical needs and the sorts of grants—or, more often, revolving small loans—that could both ease their burdens and help them be self-sustaining. For the American Red Cross, support for this program was one of the first steps toward establishing an office in Viet Nam. The hammering out of rather awkward phraseology acceptable to all parties allowed the work to go forward: those to be served by the project were called "the poor and disabled, including those who could have been affected by Agent Orange." The work was known informally as the "Disability Program."

Blending humanitarian assistance with political advocacy, VAVA was established on 17 December 2003 as the official representative of Viet Nam's Agent Orange victims. As noted earlier, VAVA was the plaintiff in the court appeal of 2007. Its role is to mobilize material and moral support for the victims, both at home and abroad. Its staff and volunteers support victims in ways that range from home visits to medical and occupational rehabilitation centers and income generation and housing. In addition, VAVA seeks to raise public awareness and support internationally, with particular attention to the United States. By 2010, VAVA had more than 300,000 members in 53 provincial chapters, 312 district chapters, and 2,122 commune chapters throughout Viet Nam.[51]

Activist Groups and Individuals

In the early 2000s, a number of activist initiatives flourished internationally, partly as a result of the attention drawn to the issues of Agent Orange by the Red Cross and other NGOs; by international conferences in Stockholm, in New Haven, and in Paris; and by various Vietnamese-international friendship organizations, as well as by the cumulative impact of an increasing number of personal encounters between international visitors and people thought to be affected by Agent Orange.

In the United States, the Agent Orange Campaign for Relief and Responsibility began its ongoing work of raising awareness by bringing victims for multicity speaking tours of the country and developing legislation to put before Congress. The Fund for Reconciliation and Development (FFRD) organized talks, video screenings, exhibits, and fundraisers at a number of college campuses and community venues, along with briefings on Capitol Hill. In 2006, the War Legacies Project, an outgrowth of the FFRD, was formed to continue and expand this work.

In France, the Franco-Vietnamese Friendship Association organized annual visits to selected villages, bringing supplies and linking donors in France with specific families in Viet Nam in long-term but limited "godparent" relationships, in both person-to-person and village-to-village exchanges. In 2005, Les Enfants de la Dioxine (Dioxin's Children), whose leaders were mostly Franco-Vietnamese, was created in Paris to draw attention and support for affected families in Viet Nam. To give but one example of that organization's approach: Dioxin's Children staged a "die-in" near the Eiffel Tower against the backdrop of a large orange banner that proclaimed "Thirty Years Later, Dioxin Is Still Killing." Taiko drummers and dozens of orange balloons drew the attention of passersby to information the organization was distributing as its demonstrators collected signatures in support of justice for the victims.

In Britain, one dedicated man, Len Aldis, has led the British-Vietnamese Friendship Association to raise funds for wheelchairs and other support for victims, to introduce motions to Parliament, and to create an online petition that by 2006 had gathered nearly 700,000 signatures in support of redress for the victims of Agent Orange. The issue has been brought to the Swiss Parliament. Activists have taken to the streets in Italy and Belgium as well.

Efforts by individuals and small groups have continued and expanded both in Viet Nam and abroad. In Viet Nam, for example, Nguyen Viet Nhan, a doctor at the Hue Medical School, engaged the Vietnamese medical system and foreign visitors with his research, pictures, and visits to families, building, one person at a time, a list of international donors who support medical interventions, small loans, and schools and workshops for people with disabilities. In the United States, Kenneth Herrmann, professor of social work and veteran of the war in Viet Nam, began a project in 1999 that takes students to work with children in the Agent Orange group home in Da Nang, as well as with the elderly in nursing homes, patients in a leper colony and at local clinics, and families who live in a garbage dump. Since 2001, his work has grown to include the Quang Nam Da Nang Fund, which gives direct support to families, and a letter-writing project that invites people affected by Agent Orange to write their thoughts to the United States.[52]

The grassroots and person-to-person activities in Viet Nam are perhaps beyond accounting for, as are the transitory, individual efforts of tourists and other foreigners who organize walks, bicycle tours, and other onetime projects to raise both awareness and funds.

The Second Decade of the Twenty-First Century

At the start of this decade, the Red Cross and VAVA continued to lead the humanitarian efforts to address the human health legacies of Agent Orange. Newer to the field were numerous religious-based (Buddhist and Christian) centers spread throughout Viet Nam, such as the Thien Phuoc Center for Children with Disabilities in Ho Chi Minh City. One newcomer of note, according to the longtime advocate Susan Hammond of the War Legacies Project, is the Children of Viet Nam center based in Da Nang, with its emphasis on "wrap-around care" for the child and the family and on developing social workers in a locally sustainable alliance with the Ministry of Education, the Ministry of Health, and the Ministry of Labor, Invalids, and Social Affairs.[53]

Media appeals, such as Viet Nam Television's "Life Is Beautiful" campaign, which narrates the stories of individual families, have raised significant contributions, both from within the country and from overseas Vietnamese—particularly those who are currently living in what was formerly known as Eastern Europe.[54] Art continues to play an important role in raising public awareness, as seen in the photograph exhibits of Goro Nakamura, whose work has covered Agent Orange for nearly half a century, and Doan Duc Minh; the installations of Debra Kraus and the art of Dinh Q Le; and a number of new films and YouTube postings by Vietnamese and foreigners alike.

The work of the Agent Orange Relief and Responsibility Campaign in the early part of the decade continued, in collaboration with VAVA, with particular emphasis on advocating for House Bill HR 2634, the Victims of Agent Orange Relief Act of 2011, which was intended to address the health needs of affected Vietnamese civilians and veterans, U.S. veterans and their children, and Vietnamese Americans. The War Legacies Project continues its advocacy and educational outreach (of particular interest is its information clearinghouse website), along with collaboration with the Quang Nam Red Cross on family support programs (providing cows and pigs, digging wells, fixing houses), with Dr. Nhan in Hue on his early-intervention center for children younger than six, and with the environmentalist Phung Tuu Boi on reclaiming land that is still contaminated or barren.

The major contributions of U.S. veterans to a variety of these humanitarian efforts also continue. The work of George Mizo in the Friendship Village and of Kenneth Herrmann in Da Nang has already been mentioned. Mike Boehm's peace and reconstruction work at the site of the My Lai Massacre and throughout Quang Ngai Province includes a focus on Agent Orange. Chuck Searcy is sought out in Hanoi not only for his extensive work on unexploded ordnance, but also for his expertise on Agent Orange. The work of the War Legacies Project in Quang Nam was made possible by the will of Robert Feldman, a veteran who, before dying of Agent Orange–related diseases, decided with his wife that his benefits should be given to Vietnamese who had received no such compensation.

As this volume goes to press, USAID is preparing to disburse the second round of the funds appropriated by Congress. The first round went for dioxin removal and health care in Da Nang through the agencies East Meets West, Save the Children, and Viet Nam Assistance to the Handicapped.[55] Applications for the second round of funding were due in early 2012.[56]

As the IFRC appeal put it, "Whilst the issues surrounding the debate remain important, there is little question of the needs of these disabled people in Viet Nam."[57] The questions that humanitarian agencies ask are not about causation but, rather, about what can be done to mitigate human suffering while respecting human dignity. Other questions those who engage in humanitarian work consider are how to discern whether a loan or an outright grant is more appropriate in a given situation; how to support certain families without creating jealousy among others; how to address the legacies of Agent Orange without at the same time creating debilitating fear;[58] and how to lessen the burden Agent Orange puts on the individual, family, and community while not undermining the social cohesion created by the local help given to these families. Then there are questions of funding and logistics.

Another question humanitarian groups consider is how to represent these issues to the public. In pictures shown around the world of children from families such as these, Agent Orange has become a symbol of innocent suffering, intensified and perpetuated by the refusal of those who caused the suffering to take responsibility for their actions. These pictures have taken on a symbolic meaning that exceeds the literal truth claims of these images as representations of the effects of Agent Orange on individual bodies, pointing beyond the physical suffering of individuals to a more general malaise in the body of modern society as well as to the social forces that caused that suffering and shape responses to it.[59]

THE FRAMEWORKS OF STORY, science, politics, law, and humanitarian response presented here are but starting places—brief sketches of some elements of each of these fields. In addition to more complete development of the approaches of each of the fields discussed, many other fields could fruitfully be added to narrate the story of Agent Orange. Economics, for example, could help us understand the corporate profits created by the production of Agent Orange and the losses created by its effects on the rubber, paper, and timber industries, some of the largest sectors of the Vietnamese economy, as well as the costs not only to individual households but also to village, district, provincial, and national social support systems.[60] Through psychology, we might gain some understanding of the webs of trauma that span time and place and generation. Anthropologists have traced reproductive histories, told stories, and recorded the destruction of a belief system as a community interprets the decimation of the forest as a sign that the protective gods of the forest have moved away.[61]

This catalogue of approaches to Agent Orange needs expansion and development, but the discussion thus far is perhaps sufficient to underscore the inadequacy of dealing with Agent Orange solely as a scientific problem to be solved or as a political bargaining chip to be negotiated. In this chapter, I have attempted to open a space for a more adequate understanding of the topic by adding to these two approaches, which have long dominated thought and action on the consequences of Agent Orange, sketches of what must also be taken into account: the long-term economic, psychological, and sociocultural effects of the use of chemicals in war and the humanitarian, legal, personal, and public responses to that use. Agent Orange leaves us grappling with the limits of the tools we have created to understand our world and with ways to act to maintain our humanity in face of those limits. This is a beginning, not an end.

In *The Politics of Storytelling: Violence, Transgression, and Intersubjectivity*, Michael Jackson writes about the power of collective storytelling to rework a traumatic event into a new story that frees both the storyteller and the listener from being stuck in a shattered past. Perhaps a more complete telling of the story of Agent Orange—a telling that embraces rather than denies responsibility—may move us some distance toward reworking our past relations with Viet Nam and toward reclaiming our own national sense of decency and honor. The stories of Mrs. Ha and Mr. Binh turn out to be closely entwined with our own.

Notes

1. While the scientific link between exposure to Agent Orange/TCDD Dioxin has been established firmly enough that the U.S. government compensates its veterans for specific diseases, the link to a given individual is more difficult to establish. The anthropologist Oscar Salemink makes the following analogy: not everyone who smokes gets lung cancer, and not everyone with lung cancer has smoked; nonetheless, scientists have established a link between lung cancer and smoking. Salemink, personal communication, Hanoi, 2000.

2. International Federation of Red Cross and Red Crescent Societies, Programme Update, 2001, 16, available at http://www.ifrc.org/docs/appeals/annua101/01460102 .pdf (accessed 14 November 2012).

3. For that morning, "we" were my friend, a representative of the CPCC, a man I took to be from public security, and myself. The names used are pseudonyms, following American academic convention. However, a friend in Viet Nam who is a writer tells me it is more honest, and more respectful, to use the real name, especially since the stories were being told in a setting where many others observed and participated in the interviews and since the families I have quoted asked that their words be conveyed.

4. The communities that have supported these families for decades are themselves struggling with the consequences of war, whether those consequences are residual chemicals, bomb craters, unexploded ordnance and mines, or several of these at once, and more—to speak only of damage to the land. In Ha Nam Province, the provincial capital was completely razed by bombing except for the skeleton of a church, a doctor from the Red Cross told me. In Thua Thien-Hue Province, the village I visited had been a no-man's land for four or five years; returning villagers were charged with filling in the bomb craters on their own land. How did they even know what land was theirs? I asked. The river was still there, I was told, along with the stubble of clumps of bamboo or sometimes the roots of trees. A grandfather spoke about returning from a "strategic hamlet" to find his shelter full of the bones of people he did not know. Large parts of Dong Nai Province were laid waste by defoliants or contaminated by chemical runoff from the base; villagers moved from place to place "in circles," as a doctor from the Red Cross put it, looking for shelter from the bombs.

5. While this is not an exact description of a barrel of the dioxin-contaminated mix of 2,4-D and 2,4,5-T that was nicknamed Agent Orange, barrels of a variety of chemicals are still being uncovered today and causing death. It is unlikely, however, that the barrel mentioned dioxin. Could it be a misreading of the English "Do not . . ." or, perhaps, "Danger"? This part of the exchange points to the interplay between present preoccupations and memories of the past.

6. At the time, this remark puzzled me, seeming to come straight out of a high school civics course in the United States. Later I learned that shortly before our visit, farmers in Thai Binh had rounded up corrupt local government officials and kept them under house arrest until the central government agreed to replace them.

7. In 1969, when these stories first began to surface, the Catholic newspaper *Tin Sang* was censored by the South Vietnamese government for telling such stories in print.

8. When asked why he chose to risk such branding when there is no hope of compensation, one outspoken Vietnamese American replied, "To see clearly what happened to my life."

9. The herbicides and defoliants were nicknamed for an identifying stripe of color that was painted around each storage barrel, not, as is sometimes assumed, for the color of the chemicals.

10. For discussion, see Buckingham, *Operation Ranch Hand*; Cecil, *Herbicidal Warfare*; Harnly, *Agent Orange and Vietnam*; Lewy, *America in Vietnam*; Stellman et al., "The Extent and Patterns of Usage of Agent Orange and Other Herbicides in Vietnam"; Vo Quy, "The Wounds of War"; Westing, *Herbicides in War*; Young and Reggiani, *Agent Orange and Its Associated Dioxin*.

11. See the painstaking work on exposures in Stellman et al., "The Extent and Patterns of Usage of Agent Orange and Other Herbicides in Vietnam." Based on hamlet census counts coordinated with records of spraying missions, at least 2.1 million but perhaps as many as 4.8 million people would have been present during the spraying of 3,181 hamlets. For another 1,430 hamlets sprayed, it was not possible to estimate population, but it seems safe to assume that this figure would increase. Thus, the percentage of people directly exposed could range from 8 percent to 18 percent of what was then a population of seventeen million. These figures do not take into account the manual spraying of the perimeters of military bases, the spraying done from naval vessels, the spraying done from helicopters or by the RVN, or the contamination from discarded drums, emergency dumps, or again, from the displacement of chemicals after such spraying.

12. Birnbaum, "Health and Environmental Effects of Dioxins."

13. It was in 1935 that Du Pont coined its slogan "Better things for better living . . . through chemistry."

14. Arthur Galston, personal communication, 2007, and classroom presentation for a class on bioethics at Yale University, New Haven, 2007.

15. In 1949, at a Monsanto plant; in 1954, at Diamond Alkali; in 1964, at Dow:

Appeal to the Second Circuit Court, 27–30, available at www.ffrd.org/lawsuit/court
.htm (accessed 16 November 2012).

16. For an understanding of the relationship between Agent Orange and the environmental movement, see Zierler, *The Invention of Ecocide.*

17. Initial steps in the United States included several research trips to Viet Nam by American scientists. The zoologists Gordon Orians of the University of Washington and E. W. Pfeiffer of the University of Montana dug into their own pockets to make a two-week field trip in 1969. In 1970, commissioned by the AAAS, the biologist Matthew Meselson of Harvard led a team of researchers to collect data in as full-scale a field study as wartime conditions would allow. A study commissioned by the National Academy of Sciences, also begun in 1970 at the request of Congress and the Secretary of Defense, concluded in 1974 that "no evidence substantiating the occurrence of herbicide-induced defects was obtained," but added, significantly, "However, the potentially most definitive aspect of this examination has not yet been completed."

In Việt Nam, the internationally respected liver specialist Ton That Tung was one of the first scientists to draw world attention to the effects of Agent Orange at a meeting at the Quai d'Orsay in Paris in 1971. Attention was drawn to an increase in spontaneous abortions, molar pregnancies, and unusual births in the south through the work of Nguyen Thị Ngọc Phuong of the Tu Du Maternity Hospital in Ho Chi Minh City, working at times with Nguyen Can and Cung Dình Trung. A large genealogical study on the family histories of people thought to be affected by Agent Orange was overseen by Hoang Dinh Cau, longtime head of the 10–80 Committee. An epidemiological study comparing occurrences of birth defects in the children of northern soldiers who fought in sprayed areas in the south compared with their fellow soldiers from the same village who were stationed in the north was conducted by Le Cao Dại, who worked with Ton That Tung in the 1970s and with Hoang Dinh Cau and the 10–80 Committee in the 1980s and 1990s, and then served as head of the Viet Nam Red Cross's Agent Orange Victims Fund from its inception in 1998 until close to the time of his death in 2002.

Starting in the late 1970s, veterans' claims that Agent Orange was the cause of their illnesses spurred research in the United States—research that was often quite controversial, accompanied by charges of incompetence, obfuscation, withholding of evidence, and sometimes falsification of data. An aborted attempt by the VA, followed by studies by the Centers for Disease Control and the U.S. Air Force Ranch Hand Study, are places to start research that might seek to untangle—or, at least, illuminate—the interworkings of science and politics.

Several international scientific conferences on Agent Orange, also fraught with controversy, contributed to the development of scientific knowledge (e.g., Long Term Effects on Man and Nature of Herbicides and Defoliants Used in War, Ho Chi Minh City, 1983, and Herbicides in War: The Long-Term Effects on Man and Nature, Hanoi, 1993). In 2002, the first scientific conference jointly sponsored by the U.S. and Vietnamese governments, attended by scientists from roughly twenty countries, was held in Hanoi. Out of that conference came the two countries' first tentative steps toward working together on remediation projects. These steps, while at times still fraught with layers of misunderstandings, difficulties, and momentary dead ends, are ongoing.

In 2002, Wayne Dwernychuk of the Hatfield Group Consultants in Canada published the results of studies begun with Vietnamese partners in the late 1990s on residual dioxin in the soil around former air bases and other heavily contaminated areas, and the elevated levels of dioxin found in the blood, mother's milk, and fatty tissues of people and animals who lived on that land. In 2003, Jeanne Stellman and associates published a study that painstakingly mapped spray routes and compared them to census figures, furthering understanding of human exposure to the spray: see Stellman et al., "The Extent and Patterns of Usage of Agent Orange and Other Herbicides in Vietnam."

18. For the most current list, see the website of the Institutes of Medicine at http://www.iom.edu.

19. See the work of the Hatfield Group, Vancouver, Canada (www.hatfieldgroup .com), and of Arnold Schecter et al., "Recent Dioxin Contamination from Agent Orange in Residents of a Southern Vietnam City."

20. Erickson et al., *Vietnam Veterans' Risks for Fathering Children with Birth Defects*; Young and Reggiani, *Agent Orange and Its Associated Dioxin*, 304.

21. See, for example, Bruner-Tran et al., "Developmental Exposure of Mice to TCDD Is Associated with Adverse Pregnancy Outcomes in Adulthood."

22. Webster and Commoner, "Overview."

23. The countries are the United States, Viet Nam, South Korea, New Zealand, and Australia.

24. Interview with a family in Dong Nai, 2001.

25. Interview with a father in Thai Binh, 2000.

26. For contemporary accounts, see Buckingham, *Operation Ranch Hand*; Cecil, *Herbicidal Warfare*; Neilands et al., *Harvest of Death*; Westing, *Herbicides in War*; Young and Reggiani, *Agent Orange and Its Associated Dioxin*. For a current retrospective, see Zierler, *The Invention of Ecocide*.

27. Buckingham, *Operation Ranch Hand*, 155; Cecil, *Herbicidal Warfare*, 155.

28. Buckingham, *Operation Ranch Hand*, iii; Cecil, *Herbicidal Warfare*, 179. It was not the use of herbicides and defoliants, however, that first caused public alarm over the use of chemicals in Viet Nam. The use of various nauseating and asphyxiating gases, including apparently limited trials of the potentially lethal arsenic-containing DM (see Neilands et al., *Harvest of Death*, 30–32, 47), drew a strong outcry at home and abroad in early 1965, before the most intensive use of herbicides and defoliants began. While President Johnson's press secretary called the materials used "standard type riot control" agents, a foreign doctor in Viet Nam chronicled the casualties and fatalities he treated as a result of those gases (see Neilands et al.,

Harvest of Death, 102–13), and the *New York Times* editorialized, "Ordinary people everywhere . . . have a strong psychological revulsion, if not horror, at the idea of any kind of poisonous gas . . ." (quoted in Lewy, *America in Vietnam*, 102–13).

29. Lewy, *America in Vietnam*, 257–58. For a reference to Kennedy's desire to experiment with the counterinsurgency potential of the chemicals, see Cecil, *Herbicidal Warfare*, 155. Le Cao Dai speaks of the use of herbicides as a matter of U.S. initiative with the assistance of South Vietnam's Ngo Dinh Diem: Le Cao Dai, *Agent Orange in the Vietnam War*, 12. Guenter Lewy says the American Military Assistance Advisory Group brought the proposal for herbicide use to Washington from the South Vietnamese, and William Buckingham writes that Diem asked the United States to conduct the spraying: Lewy, *America in Vietnam*, 257; Buckingham, *Operation Ranch Hand*, iii.

30. U.S. Department of the Air Force, cited in Lewy, *America in Vietnam*, 259.

31. Ibid., 260.

32. Neilands et al., *Harvest of Death*, 118.

33. See Zierler, *The Invention of Ecocide*, for discussion of the political processes in the Nixon and Ford years that led to this decision, as well as for earlier decisions of the Kennedy and Johnson years.

34. Uhl and Ensign, GI *Guinea Pigs*.

35. U.S. Department of State, "Joint Statement between the Socialist Republic of Vietnam and the United States of America," press release, 16 November 2006, available at http://2001-2009.state.gov/p/eap/rls/prs/76322.htm (accessed 21 November 2012).

36. Ben Stocking, "U.S. to Help Clean Agent Orange Hotspot," Associated Press Worldstream, 9 February 2007.

37. Susan Hammond, War Legacies Project, personal communication, 2010.

38. See the website at http://www.aspeninstitute.org/policy-work/agent-orange /overview.

39. Much has been written about the ghosts of Viet Nam that haunt U.S. engagement in Iraq and Afghanistan. Perhaps it is not too much to extend the metaphor to our search there for chemical weapons of mass destruction — chemicals that turned out to be figments of our imagination, or, perhaps, to take metaphoric flight for a moment, of what Freud called "the return of the repressed."

40. See the website at http://www.aspeninstitute.org/policy-work/agent-orange /overview (accessed 21 November 2012).

41. See the website at http://www.time.com/time/magazine/article/0,9171,1595 236,00.html (accessed 21 November 2012).

42. For a detailed look at this landmark case, see Schuck, *Agent Orange on Trial*.

43. Gerson Smoger, presentation at The Ecological and Health Effects of the Vietnam War, Yale University, New Haven, 13–15 September 2002.

44. Tammy Leitner, "Military: Investigation into South Korea Agent Orange Is Over," CBS 5, Phoenix, 27 January 2012.

45. The original list had changed over time due to splits and mergers.

46. Class Action Complaint, January 2004.

47. The appeal to the Second Circuit Court and other court documents related to the VAVA lawsuit are available online at www.ffrd.org/lawsuit/court.htm.

48. See the website at www.vn-agentorange.org/paris_2009_tribunal_execsummary .html.

49. To give but a few examples: the coastal mangroves protected farmland from being inundated by seawater. After the war, this land could not be planted until it was desalinated. In other places, the soil itself was rendered too hard to plant and sometimes choked with tough *imperata* grasses.

50. International Federation of the Red Cross and Red Crescent, "Agent Orange: A Challenge Faced by the Red Cross and Red Crescent in Vietnam," working paper, 13 November 1999, in possession of author.

51. Merle Ratner, Agent Orange Relief and Responsibility Campaign, personal communication, 21 March 2010.

52. Fred Wilcox has made some of those letters available in *Scorched Earth*.

53. Susan Hammond, War Legacies Project, personal communication, 3 February 2012.

54. Ibid.

55. Hammond, personal communication, 2010.

56. Martin, *Vietnamese Victims of Agent Orange and U.S.–Vietnam Relations*.

57. International Federation of the Red Cross and Red Crescent, "Agent Orange," 9.

58. For further discussion, see, e.g., Gammeltoft et al., "Late-Term Abortion for Fetal Anomaly." The dissertation of Takeshi Uesugi will provide another introduction to these issues: "Delayed Reactions."

59. This is a double-edged sword. While the pictures call to the consciences of viewers, they can also serve to pathologize and objectify the people they depict. For discussion, see Kleinman and Kleinman, "The Appeal of Experience," and for an attempt to find a balance between averting the eyes and voyeurism, see Sontag, *Regarding the Pain of Others*.

60. See the work of Phung Tuu Boi, "From Research to Remediation," as a place to start. Although logic and story testify to the costs, attempts to quantify the economic effects of Agent Orange are fraught with questions about how to define the effects of Agent Orange, about how to separate those effects from the effects of other aspects of warfare and postwar malnutrition, about sampling and sample size, as well as about time frame and many other methodological questions—many of the same questions that attend studies in the physical and medical sciences. In one recent attempt to approach Agent Orange through economics, a socioeconomic impact assessment compared thirty affected and thirty unaffected households in Quang Trị Province. Researchers found that the affected families had 37 percent less income and 12 percent greater medical expenses than unaffected households.

When asked their priorities for spending any increased income, 96 percent of the affected families said they would use more money for health care. The researchers pointed out that the focus of the study on loss of income and increased medical costs did not account for social damage, such as diminished prospects of marriage, employment opportunities, and community involvement: Palmer, "The Legacy of Agent Orange."

When the consequences of Agent Orange are seen through the framework of economics, the debates over human health appear as only one corner of a larger picture that includes the destruction of the productive capacity of households, villages and vast ecological regions, and the absorption of resources for reconstruction. And Agent Orange itself is but one corner of the destructive power that left Viet Nam pocked with fifteen million to twenty-nine million bomb craters, along with thousands of destroyed villages, bridges, schools, hospitals, factories, hydraulic works, power stations, dikes, lake embankments, churches, and pagodas.

61. See Doray and Doray, "Conventional War and Chemical Warfare in A Luoi from a Psychological Angle"; Le and Johansson, "Impact of Chemical Warfare with Agent Orange on Women's Reproductive Lives in Vietnam"; Maitre, "The Painful Highlands."

CHAPTER 10

Refuge to Refuse

Seeking Balance

in the Vietnamese

Environmental

Charles Waugh   Imagination

Đời người khác nữa là hoa, sớm còn tối mất, nở ra lại tàn

[Human life is like a flower, here and open in the morning, closed and gone by night].

—Vietnamese proverb

The correspondence between human life and the natural world expressed in this proverb is not uncommon in traditional Vietnamese literature. Folk wisdom, whether expressed as a proverb, a sung poem, or a story, frequently arises from observations about nature or uses natural phenomena to explain human concerns. "Chim có tổ, người có tông" (Birds have nests, people have ancestors), goes one saying, and another puts it similarly: "con người có tổ có tông, như cây có cội, như song có nguồn" (people have ancestors, like trees have roots, like rivers have springs).[1] Likening the spirits of one's ancestors to the roots of trees or a river's fountainhead points toward a belief in a larger cosmic whole in which all natural things have a balancing spiritual counterpart, where human spirits can inhabit natural spaces, intermingling freely with the spirits of mountains, trees, and streams and, conversely, the spirits of those natural phenomena can have an influence on the human plane.[2] Thus, these sayings suggest not that Vietnamese traditionally saw themselves as one with nature, or more eco-centric than anthropocentric, but, rather, that they viewed themselves as one part of a balanced larger whole and that the same system of life that ordered the natural world was the one that ordered their own.

This sense of balance between the human and natural world expressed in this traditional literature was in many ways a defining feature of the traditional Vietnamese environmental imagination. It managed to last through the twentieth century's many years of war, when it was frequently drawn on by politicians and writers as a source of strength or as a refuge from the horrors of war. But as industrialization and modernization gathered momentum in the second half of the twentieth century, and intensified rapidly in the years after the *đổi mới* renovation in 1986, that balance was disrupted, and the Vietnamese environmental imagination has taken note. The world it describes is much like the real one, where toxic pollution and an unhealthy obsession with wealth are making Viet Nam and the Vietnamese environmentally, socially, psychologically, and spiritually ill at ease, if not downright sick. The optimistic view of the situation suggests Viet Nam's traditional balance needs to be regained; the pessimistic, that it can only be pined for nostalgically once it has been lost.

The traditional Vietnamese folk sayings presented earlier and many others like them rely on a deep sense of correspondence between the human and natural worlds. Viet Nam's folk poetry, *ca dao*, is also marked by this correspondence. For example, in "Love Lament," recorded by John Balaban, the speaker sings:

> Stepping into the field, sadness fills my deep heart.
> Bundling rice sheaves, tears dart in two streaks.
> Who made me miss the ferry's leaving?
> Who made this shallow creek that parts both sides?[3]

The poem's paddy setting reflects a traditional agrarian life that requires tending, despite the speaker's sadness. Harvesting rice, bundling the sheaves, and taking the grains to market provide the poem with a context that is imbued with a deep sense of the rural environment. But the speaker's questions about having missed the ferry and the creek dividing the two banks suggest that the speaker sees that rural environment as having been ordered by the same rules of life that have separated the speaker from his loved one. The same force responsible for the immediate, local geography is also responsible for whatever has caused the sadness between the speaker and his beloved, whether a change of season or of mind, a death, or any other separation.

This kind of correspondence between the natural world and how humans understand themselves can also be found in many of Viet Nam's most popular folk tales, where people regularly turn into plants, animals, or minerals, or vice versa. On the one hand, such transformations might suggest a leveling between the human and natural world. Both the woman who becomes a mountain staring out to sea for the husband she has lost and the Da Trang crab, a former human who lost a magic pearl that allowed him to speak with animals and who now ceaselessly digs through the sand to search for it, suggest that the natural world is just a blink away from human perception, that if humans are in the right mood or inclination, they may well end up experiencing the world in another form. A story like "The Snake Princess," however, retains a privileged position for humans. "'All animals, including snakes, can take the form of human beings if they know how to improve themselves. But human beings cannot take the form of animals,' [the snake princess] said, 'because they are the finest living things created by the gods. The gods want to keep them that way.' 'I am glad of that,' Do Sinh said. 'I do not care to be an animal.'"[4]

Despite introducing this hierarchy, however, this story also develops the idea that humans and animals share many qualities—both humans and snakes can be poisonous, for example, albeit in different ways—and can live in harmony with each other if they choose. (Do Sinh eventually marries a snake princess who has taken human form.) Perhaps this harmony is best expressed by the folk tale "Mister Thirty," in which a tiger takes care of an old woman after killing the only child she had to look after her. The tiger's care makes karmic sense in the world of the story and demonstrates the kind of balanced attitude Vietnamese traditionally held toward their environment. On the one hand, nature—especially the wild nature of the jungle—can be deadly. On the other, it can sustain human life. All it takes to bring the woman into Mister Thirty's care is for her to explain the balance itself: the old take care of the young so the young may later take care of the old; the tiger took something from her, so he had to give something in return. She sets aside her fear, and the tiger feels shame. They learn to live in harmony together, supporting each other with admiration and respect.[5]

These tales and the complicated human relationships with nature they contain remind us that the Vietnamese did not imagine nature as it is often conceived in the West. As Michael DiGregorio, Terry Rambo, and

Masayuki Yanigisawa have suggested, the Vietnamese did not tradition-ally view nature as something separate, a wilderness to be preserved: "for-ests were feared as places filled with ferocious animals and evil spirits. Such places should be avoided or, whenever possible, cleared and trans-formed into cultivated landscapes. The nature that was valued was a do-mesticated nature, a landscape filled with paddy fields, bamboo groves, canals, ponds, and villages, an ordered and largely humanized nature."[6] In other words, it is the human interaction with nature—the humanizing of it, so to speak—that puts it into balance.

But what makes this human-nature correspondence possible in Viet-namese folk literature is the belief that beneath the everyday surface level of life lies a reciprocal world where all things may be endowed with spirits. As Shaun Malarney has described, the "Vietnamese landscape was infused with an array of spirits who guarded or controlled the land. Humans lived on and owned their villages and fields, but success in human affairs re-quired ritual interaction with the guardian spirits of land, called most simply 'land spirits' (*tho cong* or *tho dia*)."[7] Any sort of land or water might be occupied by a former human spirit, or certain natural features might have spirits of their own, independent of human origin. With a spiritual belief such as this, a story in which the mountains and the sea have spirits that can take human form and compete for the privilege of marrying the king's daughter becomes possible. With such a belief, a fairy tale, a par-able, or a fable can not only deliver an ethical lesson or geographical ex-planation but also wind together everything on earth into the same cosmic sphere. Both the Buddhist belief in reincarnation and Viet Nam's more widespread tradition of ancestor worship reinforce such a view of humans, spirits, and nature in the Vietnamese environmental imagination.

In *Understanding Vietnam*, Neil Jamieson explains Vietnamese spiri-tual beliefs as they pertain to ancestor worship this way: "Within [Viet-namese] families the living, the dead, and those not yet born were joined in an intimate relationship of mutual dependence. . . . Ancestors remained active participants in family life, sharing in joy and sorrow, admonish-ing wickedness, chiding deviation from propriety. They worked from the nether world to contribute to the well-being of the family, watching over and assisting their descendants. . . . Ancestors could assist, advise, and sometimes punish their descendants, always for the good of the family."[8] Here, too, there is balance. As the saying goes, "Sống gởi thác về" (Life is a temporary stay, death is the return home).[9] The life one lives on earth is just one part of the larger realm of existence, one side to the eternal coin. Because both the living and dead are present in all places at all times, one need only reach out to the other side to draw on their support or imagine how the ancestors might judge a particular act to know the right thing to do. And, as Heonik Kwon reminds us, these "placed" ancestral spirits themselves are balanced by "unplaced" or wandering spirits, which means that less benevolent situations may also arise in which, instead of being relied on for assistance, a ghost may need to be placated before a human can be successful on a given piece of land.[10]

Jamieson's larger argument about twentieth-century Vietnamese culture relies on an ever shifting balance between yin and yang tendencies working within traditional Vietnamese values and institutions. Although he does not directly apply this system of dichotomies to Vietnamese attitudes toward the environment, his explanation of how these two tensions work through the notion of "harmony" are particularly apt. The yang mode of harmony is *lý*—doing things the one right way, as understood through the "notion of natural order that included the physical, social, and natural worlds."[11] I will return to this notion later. The yin mode of harmony is *điều*:

> *Dieu* always refers to interaction and dictates a willingness to adapt or modify one's position or actions to fit a concrete situation, to 'get in tune,' so to speak, to moderate one's stance in the interest of social harmony. *Ly* implies an absolute standard or frame of reference, while relativism is the essence of *dieu*. *Dieu* as a value means 'reasonable' in the sense of being moderate, of not being excessive. People who do not know moderation—who are too greedy or too rigid or too assertive— bring about their own downfall.[12]

This sense of moderation is certainly the one expressed in folk tales such as "The Snake Princess" and "Mister Thirty." Although Do Sinh kills some snakes that he thinks are poisonous, he protects others from being tormented by children. This balance is what makes him worthy of the Snake Princess's attention and is what leads to his deeper understanding and appreciation for the similarities between humans and other animals—and, thus, to his living a long and happy life. Mister Thirty's killing of the old woman's son is balanced by his taking care of the woman in her old age. The stories demonstrate quite clearly a sense of balance and the happiness or contentment that comes from it.

During the American War in Viet Nam, this sense of balance with the natural world served North Vietnam well. "We have a proverb," says General Vo Nguyen Giap in *After the Fire*, a documentary about the environmental consequences of the war. "The forests protect our soldiers but encircle our enemy."[13] Like Mister Thirty, the Vietnamese environment during the war could be deadly, but so, too, could it be put to good use. It only had to be approached with some respect and care, and without fear. This is the sense Ho Chi Minh attempted to foster through the campaign to plant trees at Tet. Each year, he sent out his Tet greetings to the country, often being photographed planting a tree or having a poster released depicting Uncle Ho watering or planting a tree, with a caption such as, "Vì lợi ích mười năm phải trồng cây" (For an advantage in ten years, one must plant a tree). Certainly, the wartime use of jungle foliage to mask supply routes, caves and tunnels to hide troops, hospitals, and command centers—and even the use of traditional materials such as bamboo to make weapons such as punji sticks and booby traps—all demonstrate a comfortable reliance on the environment. Even though Uncle Ho's message might be interpreted to suggest the trees would exist solely to serve human needs, it also suggests a kind of foresight and patience, as well as the sense that humans would have to provide some effort to sustain the natural world that in turn would sustain themselves.

The Vietnamese literature of the American War reinforces this notion. For example, the situation itself in Le Minh Khue's short story "The Distant Stars" makes this point: the protagonist who repairs the road after it has been bombed by the Americans hides within the earth until the danger has passed. But it's more than that. She describes the cave she lives in like an oasis. Even when it is scorching hot and dry outside, the cave remains cool and damp inside. Similarly, the forest she imagines fighting in is so deep, so protective, that it also becomes a kind of cave, closing off the sky and all the harm that may come from it. So at home is she in this wild place that when she recalls Hanoi, it is the ancient trees surrounding her house that stand out most in the description: "my house was ancient and deep within an alleyway where many green trees grew. Those trees were so old that creeping mistletoe now covered them."[14] In "A Day on the Road," another female warrior protagonist who has gone south and whose life experience seems close to Khue's dreams of the trees of her Hanoi home dismisses Saigon as a city without trees whose stores sell only cheap plastic goods, the whole city seeming "to float in midair, without clinging to anything solid."[15] From this, we can gather that Khue's narrator sees the absolute necessity of the natural world, both in the practical sense of needing cover from the American bombs but also in the sense that the natural world is what grounds human existence and makes it enjoyable. There can be no authentic one without the other.

Although in grimmer tones, Bao Ninh also captures the Vietnamese correspondence with nature in *The Sorrow of War*. In his Jungle of Screaming Souls, ghosts "were still loose, wandering in every corner and bush in the jungle, drifting along the stream, refusing to depart for the Other World."[16] The stream moans, an echo of the spirit world, and the parched lands writhe in pain, the landscape itself so laden with human spirits that "one imagines the souls of the dead flying away in such numbers they make a fog bank along the river."[17] The novel's protagonist, Kien, cannot escape the inextricably bound matrix of memory, landscape, and human spirits that the war created, and it is partially the pressure from this matrix that holds him immobile in his melancholia. Throughout the novel, humans and nature intertwine figuratively in similes that have blood "spraying from their backs, flowing like red mud," but also literally, as when soldiers had been "blasted into such small pieces that their remains had long since been liquidized into mud."[18] Whether it is Ninh's dark or Khue's lighter spirit-land correspondence, in this literature the connection itself cannot be dismissed or avoided. It is a given that human spirits are bound with the land.

At the same time, Le Minh Khue's environmental imagination includes the sense that the nature Vietnamese can best relate to is one that has received human intervention. While hiding in a cave from American bombs, the protagonist of "The Distant Stars" dreamily imagines a near future in which the Americans have finally been defeated, the trail whose craters she constantly fills will be paved over, electricity will be run into the forests, and timber mills will run day and night.[19] But Khue's work also foresees the type of behavior that ultimately comes to tilt the Vietnamese environmental imagination out of balance: "everything had changed. People were racing all over the place in a great commotion of selling and buying. It was as if a fever had infected the city."[20] DiGregorio, Rambo, and Yanagisawa describe this tipping of the scale in the late twentieth century: "Efforts to promote rapid industrialization and modernization did not begin with renovation policies in 1986 and the massive environmental problems associated with development did not begin with the arrival of foreign direct investment in the mid-1990s. Unlike other countries in Southeast Asia, Viet Nam entered this period of industrialization and modernization with a large catalog of unresolved environmental problems. . . . Over the past ten years [1993–2003], however, as the pace of change has increased, environmental issues have taken on a new force."[21] So while embracing the market economy has made many people in Viet Nam rich, it has also been accompanied by many negative aspects of global consumerism that have had severe consequences for the Vietnamese relationship with the environment—consequences that contemporary Vietnamese literature has not failed to note. Here, the correspondence between humans and the environment seems less powerful, less compelling as a social or cultural force, with the expediency of economic development taking precedence over everything else. Where before there had been a deep cultural grounding in the environment, now there is only alienation, discomfort, pollution, and the sense that life itself has fallen out of balance.

For one point of comparison, we can examine Uncle Ho's tree-planting campaign alongside that of President Nguyen Van Triet's, launched at Tet in 2008. The two quotes from Triet presented in the news suggested that the new campaign would make Viet Nam "greener, cleaner, and more beautiful," and that "we're trying to make forestry an important industry." While "greener, cleaner, and more beautiful" is presented at the head of the article, its status as a merely hollow echoing of Hanoi's "Xanh—Sạch—Đẹp" (Green, Clean, Beautiful) campaign is confirmed by the lack of development in the article for any need for those three qualities. What the article delves into, however, is the role of planting trees in the nation's continued economic development. It is because the planting will "contribute to the country's socio-economic development, security and defense" that it is worth doing.[22] Similarly, at the Tet tree planting in 2009, Triet added that planting trees was a good way to remember Uncle Ho, as well as to meet the nation's economic, social, and security needs. He repeated the previous years' comments by saying that planting trees would make the nation more "Xanh—Sạch—Đẹp," but this time he added that it would make the nation richer, as well.[23] Thus, even well-established mottoes such as "Xanh—Sạch—Đẹp" are no longer enough. Green, Clean, Beautiful just does not supply the cachet that "rich" instantly provides.

This sense of economic expediency over environmental concerns can be found just about everywhere in contemporary Vietnamese society.

For example, one of the most challenging and high-profile environmental problems Viet Nam faces is the remediation of the sites still heavily contaminated by the dioxin from the chemical defoliants used during the American war and the treatment and rehabilitation of the people who suffer illnesses from exposure to them. Ask any typical Vietnamese people what they think of the chemical companies who made the defoliants (which the Vietnamese routinely call *chất độc da cam*, or orange poison), and they will probably tell you that they are war criminals with a moral obligation to help their victims. Yet at the same time, Dow and Monsanto are doing a booming business in Viet Nam, selling weed killers, genetically modified herbicide-resistant crops, and other agricultural and household chemicals. Monsanto alone employs some forty people in the country and regularly visits the agriculture colleges to recruit new employees and to extol the virtues of genetically modified foods, all without the slightest hint of protest or even discussion.[24] So while there is generally recognizable opprobrium for these companies' role in the wartime defoliation, even that outrage is not enough to prevent them from continuing to do business in Viet Nam today.[25]

It might be argued that Viet Nam's environmental regulations do show concern for the environment. Yet because there is so little enforcement of those laws, the reality is that once again economic expediency takes precedence. For example, recent articles in Vietnamese newspapers, touting such headlines as "Capital's Rivers Carry Vast Amounts of Toxic Chemicals" and "Mekong Delta Water Pollution Worsens," often explain the nation's pollution problem in nearly agentless ways: "pollution in the Nhue River was caused by toxic waste water discharged from eight industrial areas, 358 craft villages and 266 enterprises and health centres."[26] No mention is made of who specifically caused the pollution; of regulating the industries, craft villages, enterprises or health centers; or of holding them to the regulations that already exist. Perhaps the situation is best captured in an article like this one, "Capital Moves to Solve Ammonia Pollution in Water," in which not a single culprit is named for having caused the city's water to be contaminated at eighteen times the limit at two of its treatment plants. Instead the emphasis is on the solution to the problem, which involves increasing the output of clean water from other treatment plants and bringing water from the Da River to the affected areas by contracting with "a private company for the first time, Viwaco . . . a subsidiary corporation of the Viet Nam Construction & Import Export Corp (Vinaconex). Viwaco is investing 267.3 billion Vietnamese dong (US$15.1 million) to build the water supply network for southwest Ha Noi."[27] Here environmental problems and economic expediency go hand in hand, and the solution is not to stop the environmental degradation that is causing so much ammonia to be in the water. It is simply to allow big business to do its thing, creating problems with one hand and making money from solving them with the other.

Hanoi's ammonia-in-the-water problem is not an isolated incident. Studies have shown pervasive contamination of virtually every waterway in Viet Nam, and air pollution in the largest cities regularly registers at up to eight times the World Health Organization's recommendations. Garbage is everywhere, making it seem that the list of pollution problems with the Vietnamese environment goes on and on, literally every place one looks. Yet Viet Nam's environmental problems do not end there.

Viet Nam's biodiversity is one of the greatest in the world, with several species found nowhere else. Between August 2007 and March 2009, TRAFFIC, the wildlife trade monitoring network, reported eighty-nine major trafficking stories in Viet Nam, including the confiscation of—or parts of—elephants, tigers, bears, and many other endangered and threatened species.[28] Many restaurants in Hanoi routinely offer endangered species such as pangolins, and even more commonly found are rice wine concoctions that contain bear bile, cobra, or other wildlife items that supposedly enhance virility. TRAFFIC reports that 50 percent of the population in Hanoi has tried wildlife products, that 45 percent of the population uses such products at least three times per year, and that the most common consumers of wildlife products are businessmen and government officials who regard the products as exotic and their ability to afford the high price as a display of status.[29]

Given this massive, multipronged attack on the Vietnamese environment, and with what Jamieson writes about *lý* in mind, it is easy to see how some Vietnamese since *đổi mới* may have conceived of the one right way of doing business as competing in the most aggressive way possible. Such Spencerian logic would suggest that capitalists would take every advantage possible and, at the same time, that they would prominently display whatever marks of status they could acquire. On the ground, that means if no one else is paying the expense of treating wastewater from their factories, and the authorities are not enforcing the laws, it would be foolish for any one company to take on the added expense. Better still, if some companies do pay for treating wastewater, and the authorities are not enforcing the laws, the situation arises where not treating wastewater becomes an advantage. Similarly, if some success has already been achieved, it has to be visibly demonstrated to others through the consumption and use of expensive things: driving a Mercedes sedan, building a house in the country, or eating a platter of virility-enhancing king cobra, pangolin, or crocodile.

Mediating capitalist *lý* with environmental *điều* might indeed make a return to a cosmologically healthy and whole world possible again. But as for contemporary Viet Nam, the overwhelming presence of consumerism — of producing and consuming things at whatever cost — suggests the type of "too greedy or too rigid or too assertive," off-balance lifestyle that can only end in serious detrimental consequences for both the environment and the people of Viet Nam.[30] Not surprisingly, these consequences can be seen not only in countless everyday examples, but also in the literary representations that continue to express and shape the Vietnamese environmental imagination.

For example, in the short story "There Was a Man Lying on the Roof," Phan Trieu Hai presents a Vietnamese urban setting so out of balance that the characters have lost their connection to the environment entirely, leaving the narrator alienated, discontented, and clinging nostalgically to an idealized past. The narrator and his wife live with his parents in a new house whose roof has been pitched at 23.5 degrees, to match the axial tilt of the earth. Despite the "agreeable harmony" the pitch of the roof inspires in all who see it, the house itself could not be more disagreeable. It is so permeated by the chemical smells of its building materials and paint that no one can stand to be in it "for more than a half a day at a time."[31] His wife tries to ameliorate the house's alien feeling by investing a significant share of their meager savings in potted plants, but they die immediately because they have been planted in the soil with no roots. Otherwise, his wife seems to spend all her time pointlessly organizing and reorganizing their money from one pile of bills into another, yelling at the cat, or burning their dinner. The narrator works as a picture-frame deliveryman — a job moving hollow things with little opportunity for advancement or the possibility of participating in the company's success — contending each day with the burning-hot asphalt of the streets and the asphyxiating pollution from traffic.

Like the plants with no roots, Hai's narrator is cut off entirely from his own history, from his own sense of culture and contentment. So he goes to the roof to escape, to stargaze and to feel the wind on his chest. He wishes only "for peace and quiet after a long day with the smoke and noise from automobiles and the ruckus and laughter of the crowds." But then his wife insists that after he sees the Hale-Bopp comet he may no longer go to the roof in the evening. After dreaming of "a silvery land where there were no factories, no houses, no living beings, nor trees," he wakes one night on the roof and believes he has seen the comet. He calls his family out to see it, and while he says he "saw Hale-Bopp growing brighter and brighter every moment, more and more splendid," his family "stayed there for a moment, staring in the sky [until his] father declared, 'Now, let's come in. Can't see a god-damned thing.'" His father's pronouncement breaks the spell. When the narrator looks up again after his family goes into the house, "searching one cloud cluster after another, looking for [the comet] in vain," he finds "nothing but clouds and clouds in the sky. And soon it would be dawn. . . . [The next day, he] would not be able to climb up to the roof anymore. Under the roof, [he] wouldn't know what to do to pass the day."[32]

Given the situation (according to the story, the comet would only appear in the early evening, and this scene takes place in the middle of the night; also, there is the larger reality of a contemporary Vietnamese urban night sky in which the light pollution would combine with the haze from the air pollution to make stars, let alone a comet, virtually impossible to see), we can only read the narrator's seeing the comet as a fantasy. The awful conditions of his life, whose public causes include two of Viet Nam's most urgent environmental problems—namely, pollution caused by factories and by traffic—and whose private causes include household chemical saturation and a spouse obsessed with money and buying things of which she can make very little sense, can only be escaped by being on the roof, and he can only escape the idea of not being able to go to the roof by imagining to have actually seen the comet. As he is sucked down into an unavoidable, toxic, consumerist life, his last pleasant connection to the environment will be taken from him, and all that will remain is an equally artificial memory of that connection. Perhaps this is why the narrator remarks that "nothing is closer to human beings than memories,"[33] since for him the richest, most balanced part of his life is now this interior, nostalgic part of himself that can imagine itself still connected to the environment.

It is not just Vietnamese writers who express this kind of alienation from the environment. Many Vietnamese American writers arguably can be said to have shared much of the same traditional folk stories and cultural upbringing as their Vietnamese counterparts, and their initiation into the American environment, which suffers from many of the same processes of toxification and consumerism, has also been problematic. In fact, in terms of life experience, one might argue that the Vietnamese who came to the United States after the war underwent an even more hurried introduction to industrialization and modernization than their counterparts in late-twentieth-century Viet Nam, leaving Vietnamese American writers just as—if not more—flummoxed by their new relationship to their environment.

Viet Dinh was born in Dalat and now lives in Delaware. His story "Rabbit in the Moon" tells of a young Vietnamese American man in Washington, DC, who is caught in a love triangle with a Japanese American woman named Hiroko and a white American man named David. It relies heavily on traditional Vietnamese folk tales, referencing them directly in telling the story of the boy in the moon and indirectly through adapting the story of Tan and Lang, the two brothers, who along with Tan's wife, Xuan Phu, are transformed into the traditional symbols of familial fidelity—areca, betel, and limestone. The narrator stakes out the problem of translating traditional Vietnamese beliefs into his new American environment and lifestyle when he tries to apply belief in the need to repay all karmic debts immediately when someone dies at Tet to Hiroko's grandmother suddenly passing. Hiroko replies, "'That stuff about the spirits ... makes a lot of sense ... [i]f it weren't for the fact that you're talking about a Vietnamese legend, my grandmother was Japanese, and this isn't even the Chinese New Year—it's the American one. . . . Besides ... [w]hen her spirit crosses the international date line, she'll lose her powers. . . . [I]t's still New Year's Day in Japan. She does lose her powers, doesn't she?'"[34]

Like the karmic debt the narrator accumulates over the course of the story, a strike by the city's sanitation workers causes garbage to pile up ominously. It lurks under the snow along the streets, reminding the narrator of severed bodies, and a pile of it falls on David, sending him to the emergency room and making the narrator imagine "jagged tin can lids, used syringes, [and] broken glass."[35] The danger the garbage represents—ill-health, damage, ruin—is the danger that the narrator returns to at the end of the story. He is aware he has only this one present moment to treasure and that, without question, a time will come when the beauty or happiness of that moment will fall apart. There is a balance to the view that producing something inevitably will produce waste, that something good eventually will turn bad or lose its charm, but the fact that the garbage piles and piles and piles suggests a world out of balance, a world of extremes where the price of decadence and self-indulgence is the ever increasing nearness of waste, suffering, ugliness, disease, and death. The narrator's over-consumption (eating $200 worth of sushi by himself, spending spirit money on seven pairs of "boxer-brief" underwear, having two lovers at the same time) flaunts the sensibilities of the spirits who aim to keep the world in balance, and he winds up with a lot of anxiety, a broken nose, and a raging case of crabs. The story's logic suggests that such over-consumption at the level of society cannot last, and that if something is not done, their living spaces will eventually become uninhabitable.

This need for a more natural, less consumer-oriented lifestyle is underscored by the story's resolution, in which the three main characters leave the city with the hope of "purification," driving out where "trees rose up like sentinels on either side of the road."[36] In the middle of the night, they swim in a reservoir, where they regard the absence of garbage as a kind of miracle, the cold water bracing them, cleansing them, so that the "stars—spirits—[could look] down, happy for the first time. Their job was done. They had gone home. It was a new world."[37] The more "natural" landscape (it is, after all, still a reservoir in a public park) is the kind of place that represents humans in harmony with nature. It is a green space, a watershed, a place where the glow of the city subsides so that they can finally see the stars in the sky. It is a place that represents human restraint, where the needs for clean water and the kind of green, open space that allows for free thinking and reconnecting with the spiritual have taken precedence over the quotidian and commercial.

While such restorations may still be available to individuals in both the United States and Viet Nam, it remains to be seen whether either country will moderate its capitalist *lý* with environmental *điều*. Setting aside the question for the United States, there are some signs that a rebalancing is in the works for Viet Nam. In the spring of 2009, the year of the buffalo,[38] news stories began to circulate with some frequency featuring titles such as "Development, Environmental Protection Must Find Balance,"[39] suggesting that the belief that they are not currently in balance is widespread, and that a correction is needed now. In March 2009, a host of scientists and academics joined together to stage a high-profile protest against the government's plans to open a massive bauxite mining operation in the central highlands, and in April, none other than Prime Minister Nguyen Tan Dung himself stepped in to halt the process and order an additional review of the project, citing concerns about (of course) the economy but also the environmental impact. General Vo Nguyen Giap had already joined the criticism of the project in January 2009, citing environmental concerns, as well as concerns about Chinese involvement.[40] A second environmental refiguring came to pass during the fall of 2008 and early 2009, when citizen groups joined with members of the international community in Hanoi to successfully petition to stop the development of a luxury hotel in Lenin Park, citing the ever increasing need for green space in the nation's capital.

With so many Vietnamese environmental laws looking for so long like so much lip service, it is hard to tell at this point whether these recent events and news items really are signs that mainstream Vietnamese attitudes are swinging back into the balance that its environmental imagination suggests is necessary. Perhaps another Vietnamese proverb has become useful again, this time with a greater sense of an ultimatum: "Còn trời còn nước còn non, còn trăng, còn gió hãy còn thú vui" (If we still have the sky, rivers, mountains, the moon, and the wind, we still have happiness).[41] With its cities' air choked by industrial pollution and traffic exhaust, its rivers near death from garbage and toxics, and its mountains under threat of illegal logging and strip mining, Viet Nam faces a critical choice. If a balance cannot be found, the Vietnamese may find it more and more difficult to find pleasure in this world, and one has to imagine that their ancestors will be rightfully incensed.

Notes

The epigraph is from Huynh, *Selected Vietnamese Proverbs*, 85. The Vietnamese text is by Huynh; the translation is mine.

1. Ibid., 43. The second translation is mine.

2. Cuc, "Vietnam."

3. Anonymous, "Love Lament," in Balaban, *Ca Dao Vietnam*, 27. Recordings are available at http://www.johnbalaban.com/ca-dao.html (accessed 25 March 2009).

4. "The Snake Princess," in Terada, *Under the Starfruit Tree*, 14–15.

5. "Mister Thirty" and "Da Trang Crab," in ibid., 18–21, 37–41.

6. DiGregorio et al., "Clean, Green, and Beautiful," 187.

7. Malarney, *Culture, Ritual, and Revolution in Vietnam*, 42.

8. Jamieson, *Understanding Vietnam*, 24.

9. Huynh, *Selected Vietnamese Proverbs*, 85.

10. Here, too, the concept of balance arises. As Heonik Kwon has argued, ghosts and ancestors are "relational"; one cannot exist without the other: Kwon, *Ghosts of War in Vietnam*, 7.

11. Jamieson, *Understanding Vietnam*, 21.

12. Ibid., 21.

13. General Nguyen Vo Giap, quoted in *Vietnam: After the Fire*, dir. J. Edward Milner, video recording, Cinema Guild, 1988. A colleague at Việt Nam National University has said that the saying can be attributed to Ho Chi Minh, but I have not been able to find a written source.

14. Khue, "The Distant Stars," 6.

15. Khue, "A Day on the Road," 40.

16. Ninh, *The Sorrow of War*, 6.

17. Ibid., 4, 120.

18. Ibid., 5, 25.

19. Khue, "The Distant Stars," 4.

20. Khue, "A Day on the Road," 41.

21. DiGregorio et al., "Clean, Green, and Beautiful," 171–72.

22. "Nation Plants Trees to Honour Uncle Ho," *Viet Nam News*, 13 February 2008, http://vietnamnews.vnagency.com.vn/showarticle.php? num=03POL130208 (accessed 2 April 2009).

23. "Chủ tịch nước Nguyễn Minh Triết phát động tết trồng cây," *Tuoi Tre Online*, 2 February 2009, http://www.tuoitre.com.vn/Tianyon/Index.aspx?ArticleID=2997 69&ChannelID=3 (accessed 13 April 2009).

24. University of Agriculture and Forestry, "Công ty Monsanto giao lưu tuyển dụng tại trường ĐH NL TPHCM," available online at http://nls.hcmuaf.edu.vn /contents.php?ids=1612&ur=nls (accessed 3 April 2009). "Biotechnology and Monsanto," *Bao Kinh Te Viet Nam*, 10 December 2008, available online at https://www .ven.vn/economic-social/biotechnology-and-monsanto (accessed 2 April 2009).

25. While an outright ban of those chemical companies doing business in Việt Nam might bring serious repercussions from the WTO—of which Việt Nam is now a member—trying the companies in a Vietnamese court would not risk sanctions and could provide a framework for holding the companies accountable, much like the 1999–2006 case in South Korea. And yet this option has not been taken.

26. "Capitol's Rivers Carry Vast Amounts of Toxic Chemicals," *Viet Nam News*, 26 March 2009, available online at http://vietnamnews.vnagency.com.vn/show article.php? num=06SOC260309 (accessed 2 April 2009).

27. "Capital Moves to Solve Ammonia Water Pollution," VietNamNet, 28 March 2009, available online at http://english.vietnamnet.vn/social/2009/03/838948 (accessed 2 April 2009).

28. TRAFFIC, search for articles on Vietnam, 14 April 2009, available online at http://www.traffic.org/display/Search?searchQuery=vietnam&moduleId=1805190 (accessed 2 April 2009).

29. TRAFFIC, *A Matter of Attitude*, 28.

30. Jamieson, *Understanding Vietnam*, 21.

31. Hai, "There Was a Man Lying on the Roof," 401–2.

32. Ibid., 409–10.

33. Ibid., 402.

34. Dinh, "Rabbit in the Moon," 79–80.

35. Ibid., 86.

36. Ibid., 101.

37. Ibid.

38. What could be a better symbol of human-environment balance than the buffalo? For a traditional Buddhist story that demonstrates how the ox helps humans find balance, see "Great Joy," in Conover, *Kindness*, 111–13.

39. "Development, Environmental Protection Must Find Balance," *Viet Nam News*, 11 March 2009. See also "Bàn cách cứu sông Tô Lịch," *Nong Nghiep*, 7 May 2009, available online at http://nongnghiep.vn/nongnghiepvn/vi-VN/61/158/48/48/48/32374/Default.aspx (accessed 9 May 2009); "Phát hiện 2 xưởng mạ gây ô nhiễm sông Nhuệ," *An ninh Thu Do*, 9 May 2009, available online at http://www.anninhthudo.vn/Tianyon/Index.aspx?ArticleID =48022&ChannelID=80 (accessed 9 May 2009). These are just a few articles that turn up on searches of news websites for "cân môi trường" (environmental balance).

40. "P[rime] M[inister] Orders Review of Bauxite Mining," *Thanh Nien News* (Vietnam), available online at http://www.thanhniennews.com /politics/?catid=1& newsid=48423 (accessed 2 May 2009); "Giap, Vietnamese War Hero Fires Salvo over Mining Plan," Agence-France Presse, available online at http://www.google .com/hostednews/afp/article/ALeqM5hLP_W5udM211fT26FEep07c4ANDQ (accessed 9 May 2009).

41. Huynh, *Selected Vietnamese Proverbs*, 80; my translation.

CHAPTER 11

Missing in Action in the

H. Bruce Franklin   Twenty-First Century

Today, the United States of America has two national flags. One is the colorful red, white, and blue banner created during the American Revolution, with stars that represent, in the words of the 1777 Continental Congress, "a new constellation." The other is the black-and-white POW/MIA flag, America's emblem of the Vietnam War.

The POW/MIA flag is the only one besides the Star-Spangled Banner that has ever flown over the White House, where it has fluttered yearly since 1982. As visitors from around the world stream through the Rotunda of the U.S. Capitol, they pass a giant POW/MIA flag, the only flag that has ever been displayed amid the epic paintings and heroic statues, given this position of honor in 1987 by the Congress and the President of the United States. The POW/MIA flag flies over every U.S. Post Office, thanks to a law passed by Congress and signed by the president in 1997. During the 1980s and 1990s, the legislatures and governors of each of the fifty states issued laws mandating the display of this flag over public facilities such as state offices, municipal buildings, toll plazas, and police headquarters. The POW/MIA flag also hangs over the trading floor of the New York Stock Exchange and waves at countless corporate headquarters, shopping malls, union halls, and small businesses. It is sewn into the right sleeve of the official Ku Klux Klan white robe and adorns millions of bumper stickers, buttons, home windows, motorcycle jackets, watches, postcards, coffee mugs, T-shirts, and Christmas tree ornaments.

The flag symbolizes our nation's veneration of its central image: a handsome American prisoner of war, his silhouetted head slightly bowed to reveal behind him the ominous shape of a looming guard tower. A strand of barbed wire cuts across just below his firm chin. Underneath runs the motto: "YOU ARE NOT FORGOTTEN."

This colorless banner implies that the Vietnam War may never end. It demonstrates to the world both the official U.S. government position since 1973 and a profoundly influential national belief: Viet Nam may still secretly hold American prisoners of war. This was the official reason why every twentieth-century postwar administration—those of presidents Richard Nixon, Gerald Ford, Jimmy Carter, Ronald Reagan, George Bush, and Bill Clinton—reneged on the pledge in the 1973 Paris Peace Agreement that the United States would help rebuild Viet Nam and then waged relentless economic and political warfare against that nation.[1] Even when President Clinton announced in 1995 that Washington was finally establishing diplomatic relations with Viet Nam, he claimed that the primary motive was to further "progress on the issue of Americans who were missing in action or held as prisoners of war."[2]

To comprehend the meaning of all this, one must first recognize that there is no rational basis or evidence for the belief that Americans were kept captive in Viet Nam after the war. Indeed, it runs *counter* to reason, common sense, and overwhelming evidence.

None of the armed forces has listed a single prisoner of war (POW) or even a single person missing in action (MIA) since 1994 (when the only person still listed as a prisoner, for "symbolic" reasons, was reclassified as deceased at the request of his family). There are, it is true, 1,739 Americans listed as "unaccounted for" from the war in Viet Nam, Laos, and Cambodia, but not one of these is classified as a prisoner, a possible prisoner, or even missing. Most of the "unaccounted for" were *never* listed as POW or even as MIA, because well over half were originally *known* to have been killed in action in circumstances that prevented the recovery of their bodies. Their official designation has always been "KIA/BNR" (Killed in Action/Body Not Recovered). Crews of airplanes that exploded in flight or crashed within sight of their aircraft carrier, soldiers whose deaths were witnessed by others unable to retrieve their bodies, or men blown apart so completely that there were no retrievable body parts—all these are listed in the total of "unaccounted for." All that is missing is their *remains*. The KIA/BNR category was never included with the missing in action during the Vietnam War; it was lumped together with the POW/MIA category only after the Paris Peace Agreement was signed in 1973.

The confusion thus created was quite deliberate. But this miasma was relatively mild compared with that generated by the bizarre POW/MIA concoction itself. Arguably the cagiest stroke of the Nixon presidency was the slash, forever linking "POW" and "MIA." In all previous wars, there was one category — "Prisoners of War" — consisting of those known or believed to be prisoners. There was an entirely separate and distinct category of those "Missing in Action." The Pentagon internally maintained these as two separate categories throughout the war and its aftermath. But for public consumption, the Nixon administration publicly jumbled the two categories together into a hodgepodge called POW/MIA, thus making it seem that *every missing person might be a prisoner*. Because this possibility cannot be logically disproved, the POW/MIA invention perfectly fulfilled its original purpose: to create an issue that could never be resolved.

It also created an almost impenetrable fog of confusion that clouds the issue right up through the present. Although prisoners of war were previously not considered either missing or unaccounted for, once the MIAs became defined as possible POWs, then all the POW/MIAs could be dumped into the category "Unaccounted-For," which then became synonymous in the popular mind with POW/MIA. So when it is reported that there are still almost 1,800 "unaccounted for" from the Vietnam War, people assume that any or all of them might still be languishing in Vietnamese prisons. "MIA" and "POW" and "unaccounted for" have even become interchangeable terms, as manifested by a question I'm frequently asked, usually in an incredulous tone: "Don't you believe there are MIAs?" — or, even more revealing, "Don't you believe in MIAs?"

IN ALL MAJOR WARS, many combatants die without being identified or having their bodies recovered. There are more than 8,100 unaccounted for from the Korean War and 78,791 still unaccounted for from the Second World War. So the total of 1,742 unaccounted for in the Indochina war is astonishingly small, especially since 81 percent of the missing were airmen mainly lost over the ocean or in the mountains or tropical rain forest, many in planes that exploded at supersonic speeds. In fact, the proportion of unaccounted-for Americans to the total killed in action is far smaller for the Indochina War than for any previous war in the nation's history, even though this was its longest war and ended with the battlefields in the possession of the enemy. For the Second World War, after which the United States was free to explore every battlefield, those still unaccounted for represent 21.8 percent of the total killed. For the Korean War, the figure is 24 percent. In contrast, the unaccounted for from the Indochina War constitute only 3.1 percent of those killed. To get another perspective on these numbers, consider the fact that on the other side there are between 200,000 and 300,000 Vietnamese missing in action.

During the war, the Pentagon listed as a POW anyone reported as *possibly* being a prisoner anywhere in Viet Nam, Laos, Cambodia, or China at any time from 1963 to 1973, whether or not there was credible evidence of capture and even if there was evidence of subsequent death. After the Peace Agreement in 1973, all but fifty-six men on the Pentagon's internal lists were either released or reported to have died in captivity. In the following years, intensive analysis resolved each of these remaining cases. Except for one who had defected, all had died. The one defector, Robert Garwood, is the only captured person who survived the war and was not returned to the United States during Operation Homecoming in 1973.

Despite many investigations by congressional committees, federal agencies, and private organizations, there has yet to be a shred of verifiable or even credible evidence that any U.S. POWs were withheld by Viet Nam. Debriefing of all the returning POWs, ongoing aerial and satellite reconnaissance, covert raids, as well as interrogations of thousands of Vietnamese refugees and defectors, including high-ranking military and intelligence officials, all point to one conclusion: except for Garwood, there were no surviving POWs. Even offers of huge rewards—still amounting to millions of dollars—have produced nothing but waves of phony pictures, fake dog tags, and other bogus "evidence."

Then there is the question of motive. Why in the world would Viet Nam keep U.S. prisoners for years and decades after the war?

To torture them, of course, a perfectly plausible motive, given the inscrutable cruelty of Asians—as depicted in a century and a half of Yellow Peril propaganda in American culture, including countless Hollywood images. Besides, these Asians are communists, so add three-fourths of a century of Red Menace propaganda, and no further explanation is needed.

One ostensibly more rational motive is offered by POW/MIA evangelists: the prisoners are being used as "hostages" or "bargaining chips." But what good are hostages to a nation that denies holding any? How can you bargain with a chip that you swear does not exist?

A belief that runs counter to reason, common sense, and all evidence but that is widely and deeply held by a society is a myth—in the fullest and most rigorous sense. A myth is a story of ostensibly historic events or beings crucial to the worldview and self-image of a people, a story that appears as essential truth to its believers, no matter how bizarre it may seem from outside that society or when subjected to rational analysis. Indeed, myths must defy commonplace plausibility and transcend everyday logic. Myths are often central to cultures, and may be their most distinctive features, which is why many anthropologists and archaeologists find them so essential to understanding a society.

To comprehend the POW/MIA myth, we need to trace its history. For the first fifteen years of U.S. covert and overt combat in Viet Nam—that is, from 1954 to 1969—there was not even a POW/MIA concept. Its seeds were sown in 1968, the year of the Tet Offensive and its aftermath, including President Lyndon B. Johnson's withdrawal from the election campaign, the assassinations of Martin Luther King Jr. and Robert Kennedy, the tidal wave of urban rebellions, the opening of peace negotiations in Paris, and the nomination of Richard Nixon as the Republican peace candidate. Remember that in his acceptance speech Nixon declared, "As we look at America, we see cities enveloped in smoke and flame," and then vowed that "if the war is not ended when the people choose in November," "I pledge to you tonight that the first priority foreign policy objective of our next Administration will be to bring an honorable end to the war in Vietnam."[3]

Nixon had no intention of ending the Vietnam War without preserving a U.S. client government in Saigon. But how many Americans in 1968 could have predicted that he would be able to continue the war year after bloody year until 1973? Perhaps even fewer than those who remembered that back in 1954, as vice president, he had been the first administration official to advocate sending American troops to fight in Viet Nam because, as he put it, "The Vietnamese lack the ability to conduct a war by themselves or govern themselves."[4]

Nixon, however, had several formidable problems. Negotiations had already opened in Paris. The Tet Offensive had convinced most Americans and even much of his own Defense Department that the war was unwinnable. The antiwar movement was growing ever more powerful, domestically and within the armed forces. There was certainly no enthusiasm for the war. What could he do?

What he needed was something to wreck the negotiations, shift the apparent goal of the war, counter the antiwar movement, and generate some zeal for continued combat. Soon after his inauguration, Nixon and an enterprising businessman named H. Ross Perot solved his problem by concocting a brand new issue: demanding a "full accounting" for Americans missing in action and the release of American prisoners of war as a *precondition* of any peace accord.[5] This was truly a brilliant, albeit demonic, strategy.

This issue created, for the first time, sizable emotional support for the war. It deadlocked the Paris negotiations for four years. It counteracted the antiwar movement. It even provided a basis for continuing economic and political warfare against Viet Nam for decades after the United States had conceded defeat.

The POW/MIA issue also neutralized another White House and Pentagon problem that had been building throughout 1968: American revulsion at the torture and murder of the prisoners of U.S. and Saigon forces.

The fate of Saigon's prisoners had in fact been one of the root causes of the insurgency against the Diem government, whose infamous Law 10/59 (promulgated in 1959) branded those who had fought for independence against France "Communists, traitors, and agents of Russia and China" and decreed the "sentence of death" for any person actively resisting Diem's rule. The ensuing wholesale arrest, torture, and execution of hundreds of thousands of people, featuring portable guillotines and displays of victims' heads and intestines on stakes, helped lead in 1960 to the outbreak of organized armed struggle and the formation of the National Liberation Front (NLF).[6] As the war developed, anyone even suspected of loyalty to the "Viet Cong" was subject to torture and summary execution. Only in the last few years of the war were any captured combatants accorded a semblance of prisoner-of-war status.

Two books published in 1968 exposed the barbaric treatment of prisoners by U.S. and Saigon forces: *In the Name of America*, a documentary chronicle by twenty-nine prominent American clergymen of U.S. war crimes in Viet Nam, with several sections devoted to the torture, mutilation, and murder of prisoners; *Against the Crime of Silence*, the proceedings of the 1967 War Crimes Tribunal held in Denmark and Sweden with extensive testimony by American veterans about their own participation in the systematic torture and execution of prisoners by both U.S. and Saigon soldiers and officials.[7] At the same time, the issue exploded into the consciousness of tens of millions of Americans as they actually watched, in their own homes, the chief of the Saigon national police execute a manacled NLF prisoner.

Americans were soon to witness even worse pictures and accounts of U.S. and Saigon soldiers torturing and slaughtering prisoners, both combatants captured in battle and civilians rounded up in sweeps through hamlets and villages. As early as May 1968 came the first published descriptions of the My Lai massacre of March. The CIA's Phoenix program, designed to wipe out the insurgent infrastructure by imprisoning and assassinating tens of thousands of suspects, was launched in mid-1968; U.S. intelligence officers attached to Phoenix later testified that they never saw any of its prisoners survive interrogation.[8] Soldiers captured by U.S. forces were, in violation of the 1949 Geneva Convention Relative to the Treatment of Prisoners of War, turned over to the Saigon government, whose appalling prison camps were gradually being exposed to American readers and viewers, most dramatically in Tom Harkin's photographs of the notorious tiger cages of Con Son Island, where the few survivors were almost all permanently disfigured and severely crippled by torture.[9]

The Saigon government's tiger cages would soon be transfigured by American media magic into images of the prison conditions of captured Americans, thus reversing the direction of popular outrage. But neutralizing protest about what was being done to Vietnamese prisoners by Washington and Saigon was merely a bonus from turning American "POW/MIAs" into the main bone of contention with Hanoi.

The first goal was to deadlock the Paris peace talks. Accordingly, just five days after Nixon's inauguration, his representative at the talks introduced the POW/MIA issue. A month later, both the Department of Defense and Department of State began laying the groundwork for a massive campaign at home.

Domestically, the issue was a masterful stroke. After all, how else could any deeply emotional support for the war be generated? Certainly not by holding out the old, discredited promises of military victory. And who would be willing to fight and die for the notoriously corrupt generals ruling Saigon? But supporting our own prisoners of war and missing in action was something no loyal American would dare oppose. It also seemed easy to understand, requiring no knowledge of the history of Viet Nam and the war. One measure of the campaign's success was the sale of more than fifty million POW/MIA bumper stickers in the next four years.[10]

The Nixon administration's "go public" campaign, designed to "marshal public opinion" for "the prompt release of all American prisoners of war," was initiated on 1 March 1969 and officially launched on 19 May.[11] It was immediately and enthusiastically promoted by the media, which, in the relatively restrained language of the *New York Times* editorial staff, denounced "the Communist side" as "inhuman," asserted that "at least half of the 1,300 Americans missing in action in Vietnam are believed to be alive," and insisted that "the prisoner-of-war question is a humanitarian, not a political issue."[12]

Perot was put in charge of building mass support, and he was soon rewarded. Thanks to intervention by the White House, his Electronic Data Systems corporation got 90 percent of the computer work on Medicare claims, enabling Perot to become what one writer in 1971 dubbed "the first welfare billionaire."[13]

Perot was to buy "full-page ads in the nation's 100 largest newspapers" and run "United We Stand," a heart-wrenching program about POWs on TV stations in fifty-nine cities.[14] Meeting with Perot in the Oval Office, the president approved Perot's plan "to mobilize massive popular support" for the war, including "charter planes to transport to Paris approx. 100 wives and children of American POWs," where they would stage a Christmas vigil "with heavy press and television coverage" to embarrass Hanoi's delegation; appearances by Perot on numerous TV programs, including *Meet the Press*, the *Today* show, and *The Mike Douglas Show*; and a national conference to launch the National League of Families.[15]

On 6 November, Congress unanimously passed and President Nixon signed a bill declaring 9 November a National Day of Prayer for U.S. prisoners of war in Viet Nam. Right on schedule, Perot's United We Stand ran full-page advertisements featuring a picture of two small children praying, "Bring our Daddy home safe, sound and soon." Headlined "The Majority Speaks: Release the Prisoners," the ads demanded the immediate release of all U.S. POWs. On 13–14 November, the House Subcommittee on National Security Policy of the Committee on Foreign Affairs held hearings to denounce "the ruthlessness and cruelty of North Vietnam" and to provide a pep rally for a congressional resolution demanding the release of American POWs.[16] The resolution was passed unanimously by both the Senate and the House in December; it was immediately exploited by U.S. negotiators in Paris.[17] Perot soon was off to Vientiane with two chartered jets filled with Christmas presents for the POWs and, according to Alexander Butterfield's report to the president, "Reporters from *Time, Life, Newsweek*, AP, UPI, *Los Angeles Times, Reader's Digest, Look, New York Times, Washington Post, Dallas Morning News*, and some five–six other publications." As Butterfield explained, "We were able to give Ross a good bit of behind-the-scenes assistance."[18]

During the campaign's formative months in early 1969, officials from the Department of State and Department of Defense flew all over the country to build an organization of family members under the leadership of Sybil Stockdale, whose husband was the highest-ranking naval officer imprisoned in Viet Nam and who herself had been working closely with Naval Intelligence since May 1966.[19] By June, Stockdale had made herself the national coordinator of an organization she christened the National League of Families of American Prisoners in Southeast Asia.[20] With Henry Kissinger advising that our "propaganda offensive in the POW issue" required an ostensibly independent citizens' movement and stressing the need to make it appear that "there is no U.S. Government involvement with the ladies," the White House meticulously choreographed every step in building and using this organization.[21]

In the spring of 1970, Stockdale received a phone call from Republican Senator Robert Dole, who asked whether she could "deliver 1,000 family members" to a POW/MIA "extravaganza" he was planning for 1 May at Constitution Hall if he were to arrange government transportation for them. Dole pledged to orchestrate political support, putting Vice President Spiro Agnew and a bipartisan lineup of senators and representatives on the stage, and having Democratic Representative Clement Zablocki turn his Subcommittee on National Security Policy into a publicity forum just prior to the event.[22] Dole, Stockdale, and Perot collaborated in organizing the festivities, aided by a host of senators and representatives, including such prominent Democrats as Senate Majority Leader Mike Mansfield and Senator Edmund Muskie.[23] The Zablocki committee devoted days of hearings to doing publicity work for Senator Dole's 1 May POW/MIA rally, as exemplified by this exchange:

MR. ZABLOCKI: Just a final question, Senator Dole. What arrangements are being made for national television coverage, which could be used, then, worldwide?

SENATOR DOLE: We are contacting the networks, and there will be press conferences Friday with Mrs. Stockdale and Mr. Perot and others. I will be on the "Today Show" tomorrow with reference to this program. . . . We have talked to Peter Kenney at NBC, he is working on it; we have talked to Mr. Galbraith of CBS, and ABC has been most helpful, and generally they are coming around.[24]

The day after the rally, Stockdale presided in Washington over the constitutional convention that transformed her network into the National League of Families of American Prisoners and Missing in Southeast Asia. Its structure and bylaws had been defined three days earlier by Stockdale, a handful of wives chosen by her, and the attorney Charles Havens, with whom she had worked when he was in the Office of International Security Affairs. Within three weeks of its incorporation, the league received its tax-exempt status as a "non-partisan, humanitarian" organization from the IRS.[25]

From then through the rest of the century, the National League of Families would play changing but always crucial roles in the evolution of the POW/MIA issue. Almost all of its principal organizers and activists were wives or parents of career officers, not draftees, mainly because the vast majority of missing and captured men were flight officers. Sponsored in its early years by the White House, the Department of Defense, and the Republican National Committee, the league in the 1980s would become the official liaison between the Department of Defense and the American public on all POW/MIA matters.[26] The league designed the POW/MIA flag and gets much of its current income from selling it to the U.S. government, the fifty state governments that have mandated its display, and private organizations and citizens.

Meanwhile, Congress obediently placed in the Capitol Rotunda a POW exhibit designed and financed by Perot. On 4 June 1970, Speaker of the House John McCormack was the featured speaker during the televised ceremony inaugurating Perot's display, with figures of two POWs besieged by huge cockroaches and rats.[27] By the end of the year, this tableau was being set up in State Capitol buildings across the country; the *Steve Canyon* cartoon strip was featuring relatives of POW/MIAs in its daily sagas; the ABC television network had presented a "POW/MIA Special"; President Nixon had created a national Prisoner of War Day; the *Ladies' Home Journal* had published an article with a tear-out letter for readers to mail; and the U.S. Post Office, amid special fanfare by the president, had issued 135 million POW/MIA postage stamps.[28]

America's vision of the war was being transformed. The actual photographs and TV footage of massacred villagers, napalmed children, Vietnamese prisoners being tortured and murdered, wounded GIs screaming in agony, and body bags being loaded by the dozen for shipment back home were being replaced by simulated images of American POWs in the savage hands of Asian communists.

Second only to the POW/MIA flag in inculcating the POW/MIA myth is the POW/MIA bracelet. It was devised by the militant pro-war organization known as VIVA (Victory in Vietnam Association).

Applauded by the right-wing press for counterdemonstrating in 1965 against "peaceniks," VIVA soon got an important patron. By October 1966, Gloria Coppin, wife of Los Angeles industrialist Douglas Coppin, whose Hydro-Mill Corporation manufactured airplane parts for major military contractors, was providing a headquarters and contacts with wealthy and influential members of Southern California society. In March 1967, VIVA received a state charter from California as an educational institution, and less than two months later, the IRS granted it tax-exempt status as a "charitable and educational" organization.[29] VIVA was now able to hold the first of its lucrative annual Salute to the Armed Forces formal dinner dances, organized by its Ladies Auxiliary (made up of wives of wealthy business, military, and political leaders), which allowed the guests—including Barry Goldwater, Alexander Haig, H. Ross Perot, Bob Hope, Mayor Sam Yorty of Los Angeles, and Governor Ronald Reagan—to receive tax deductions for their contributions.[30] With brimming coffers, VIVA expanded rapidly and planned ever more ambitious campaigns to thwart the antiwar movement.

But meanwhile, the Tet Offensive, as well as ensuing offensives mounted by the insurgents throughout 1968 and 1969, had made talk of U.S. "victory" in Viet Nam ring hollow and become politically embarrassing. By the time the elections were held in November 1968, "peace," not "victory," had become the catchword, as the nation bet on Nixon's secret peace plan. So in 1969, VIVA ceased to be the Victory in Vietnam Association and became Voices in Vital America.

A few months later, members of VIVA and Robert Dornan, later a Republican representative from California but then a right-wing TV talk-show host in Los Angeles and a close friend of Gloria Coppin's, contrived the idea of selling bracelets engraved with the names of POWs and MIAs to promote and fund the POW/MIA campaign. In addition to Coppin, who was the chair of VIVA's board of directors from its founding until 1974, one of the prime movers in VIVA's bracelet manufacturing was Carol Bates, who was to take over the directorship of the National League of Families in 1976 and then, in 1984, become a principal coordinator of the POW/MIA issue for the Defense Intelligence Agency.[31] The prototype bracelets were produced just in time for the 1970 Salute to the Armed Forces Ball, where Governor Ronald Reagan was the keynote speaker, Bob Hope and Martha Raye were made co-chairs of the bracelet campaign, and H. Ross Perot was named Man of the Year.[32]

The bracelet idea quickly mushroomed into a propaganda coup and financial bonanza for the POW/MIA campaign, especially for VIVA, which was soon wholesaling bracelets to the National League of Families, Perot's United We Stand, and Junior Chambers of Commerce across the country. By mid-1972, VIVA was distributing more than ten thousand bracelets a day. Bracelets were prominently worn by such luminaries as President Nixon, General William Westmoreland, Billy Graham, George Wallace, Charlton Heston, Bill Cosby, Pat Boone, Cher and Sonny Bono, Fred Astaire, Johnny Cash, Steve Allen, Princess Grace of Monaco, and Bob Hope, who personally distributed more than a thousand. The bracelet also became a kind of fetish for sports stars such as Willie Shoemaker, Don Drysdale, Lee Trevino (who claimed it saved his golf game), and Jack Kramer (who swore it cured his tennis elbow).[33]

Before American combat in Viet Nam ended, perhaps ten million Americans were wearing POW/MIA bracelets.[34] The influence on the national imagination cannot be calculated. Each person who wore a bracelet vowed never to remove it until his or her POW/MIA was either found to be dead or returned home from Vietnamese prison. Millions of people thus developed profound emotional bonds with the man on their wrist. Countless American schoolchildren went through formative years linked to these amulets. How could they not continue to believe that their POW/MIAS were alive?

With growing popular and almost unanimous congressional support on the POW/MIA issue, the Nixon administration was able to stalemate the Paris talks for almost four years by demanding that Hanoi account for America's missing in action and negotiate the release of American prisoners separately from the question of U.S. withdrawal. Throughout 1969, the other side insisted that the release of prisoners of war could not be considered separately from a resolution of the war itself. Although this was the customary position of warring powers, it was denounced by the administration and the media as "unprecedented," "inhuman," and "barbaric." What the Vietnamese wanted to talk about was ending the war and the U.S. occupation of half their country. But the more Hanoi and the insurgents refused to negotiate separately about the POW issue, the more Washington made it the central issue of the negotiations. In the final negotiating session of the year, the head of the U.S. delegation "scarcely mentioned the question of peace, devoting his formal remarks to the prisoner problem."[35]

Nixon had in fact carried out a brilliant propaganda coup. At first, the Vietnamese simply denounced the POW/MIA issue as a "perfidious maneuver to camouflage the fact that the United States is pursuing the war ... and misleading public opinion, which demands that the United States end the war and withdraw its troops."[36] When they became more flexible and suggested that they would set a date for the release of all prisoners of war if the United States would set a date for withdrawal from their country, the administration accused them of "ransoming" the POWs and using them as "hostages" and "bargaining chips." The administration's line was echoed by the media. For example, the *Christian Science Monitor* ran a five-part series that labeled Hanoi's position "a cruel ploy" and concluded with this bizarre argument: "Never before, in any other war ... have prisoners been held as international hostages, ransomed to a political and military settlement of the war."[37] This dizzying inversion of history conveniently ignored the fact that the United States, like most nations, had never been involved in a war in which either side released all its prisoners prior to an agreement to end the war. But through the strange logic of the administration's negotiating position and its masterful public relations campaign, the American prisoners of war had indeed been successfully transformed—in the public mind—into "bargaining chips" and "hostages" held for "ransom." These metaphors not only would increasingly influence the debates about negotiations to end the war but would also eventually become central to the postwar POW/MIA myth.

How is it possible to comprehend this truly astonishing position, which seemed ready to trade countless American and Vietnamese lives for several hundred prisoners who would presumably be released anyhow at the conclusion of the war? By early 1971, President Nixon could explicitly declare that U.S. ground and air forces would remain in Viet Nam "as long as there is one American prisoner being held prisoner by North Vietnam." Since North Vietnam was making the release of the prisoners contingent on U.S. withdrawal, the logic of Nixon's position could be, as Tom Wicker put it, that "we may keep both troops and prisoners there forever."[38] If that seems absurd, what would follow if it could be made to appear that North Vietnam was concealing some of its prisoners? Then, since it could never be proved that some missing American was not "being held prisoner by North Vietnam," the war could literally go on forever.

Rationality, however, has never been a component of the POW/MIA issue. As Jonathan Schell observed, by 1972 "many people were persuaded that the United States was fighting in Vietnam in order to get its prisoners back," and the nation's main sympathy was no longer for "the men fighting and dying on the front," who "went virtually unnoticed as attention was focused on the prisoners of war," "the objects of a virtual cult": "Following the President's lead, people began to speak as though the North Vietnamese had kidnapped four hundred Americans and the United States had gone to war to retrieve them."[39]

Perhaps the most startling and penetrating judgment comes from Gloria Coppin, VIVA's longtime chair. Although still a fervent believer in the existence of live POWs, she has also come to a painful sense of how she and many others may have been manipulated. As she put it in an interview in 1990, "Nixon and Kissinger just used the POW issue to prolong the war. Sometimes I feel guilty because with all our efforts, we killed more men than we saved."[40]

The Nixon administration's four-year campaign to secure the release of American prisoners of war separate from U.S. withdrawal from Viet Nam was doomed, along with its other war goals, by the peace accord signed in Paris on 27 January 1973. The agreement called for the complete withdrawal of all U.S. forces from Viet Nam within sixty days and the return of all prisoners of war to be "carried out simultaneously with and completed not later than the same day" as the U.S. withdrawal.[41]

Hanoi had already delivered to Washington a complete list of its prisoners of war and those who had died in captivity. Within the stipulated two months, all the living prisoners on the list were repatriated. Both

Viet Nam and Laos returned or accounted for *more*, rather than *fewer*, than those listed by the Pentagon and State Department as probably captured in each country. The return of the prisoners was staged as Operation Homecoming, an event transformed by an awesome media blitz into a public relations coup for President Nixon, who boasted at his formal White House dinner party for the ex-POWs that he had achieved "the return of all of our prisoners of war" as part of his successful conclusion of the war in Viet Nam.[42]

Article 21 of the Paris Peace Agreement guaranteed that "the United States will contribute to healing the wounds of war and to postwar reconstruction of the Democratic Republic of Viet-Nam." On 1 February, Nixon wrote a secret letter to Prime Minister Pham Van Dong, pledging that this reconstruction aid to Hanoi would be at least $3.25 billion.[43] But when Henry Kissinger brought this document to Hanoi in early February, he simultaneously confronted the Hanoi government with "some 80 files of individuals who we had reason to believe had been captured," as he testified during the Senate hearings in September 1973 to confirm him as secretary of state. Because "we are extremely dissatisfied" with Hanoi's accounting for these MIAs, Kissinger concluded, "we cannot proceed in certain other areas such as economic aid."[44] In other words, Kissinger and Nixon were using the MIA issue to renege on Nixon's secret pledge, whose very existence was denied by the White House until 1976.

Why did Kissinger's list contain eighty names? The *highest* number of such "discrepancy" cases (unaccounted-for men deemed by the Pentagon as likely to have been captured or whose fate would be known by the Vietnamese) then publicly claimed or secretly listed by the government was fifty-six. The truth finally came in 1992 when Roger Shields, head of Pentagon POW/MIA affairs in 1973, acknowledged that Washington had deliberately included on Kissinger's list a number of cases that the Vietnamese could not possibly account for.[45] Thus, the Nixon administration created an issue that could never be resolved.

Having no intention of honoring the U.S. pledge of aid, Nixon made *accounting* for the MIAs the issue. But accounting is a meaningless issue unless there is some belief in the possibility of live POWs. Hence, each postwar administration tried to exaggerate this possibility of live POWs. But no administration could afford to claim there actually were POWs, because then it would be expected to rescue them. True believers, however, knew that reconnaissance, espionage, and the debriefing of defectors would have to reveal POWs to U.S. intelligence. Hence, by the late 1970s, the POW myth was beginning to incorporate belief in a government conspiracy precisely the opposite of the real one. While the government was pretending that there might be POWs, the POW/MIA myth saw the government pretending there might not be POWs.

Not all the machinations of the Pentagon, political opportunists, scam artists, the media, and presidents can create a true myth unless that myth resonates with deep psycho-cultural needs of a society. There are some fairly obvious needs being met by the images of American POWs tortured year after year by sadistic Asian communists. We, not the Vietnamese, become the victims as well as the good guys. The American fighting man becomes a hero betrayed by his government and the antiwar movement, especially by unmanly people such as the bureaucrats in control of the government, "peaceniks," cowards, and those who would rather make love than war. This stab-in-the-back theme, with its loud echoes of the myth of national betrayal central to the rise of Nazism, is one way of convincing ourselves that *we* didn't really lose the war. It also suggests that American manhood itself is threatened and must be rescued if we are to restore America's military might and determination. So it is no surprise that the POW/MIA myth has been functioning as a potent agent of militarism.

Yet the POW/MIA myth expresses even deeper psycho-cultural cravings. Sometimes it's hard to see what is most peculiar about something in one's own culture because the culture is, after all, also inside one's own head. So I remained only dimly conscious of another level of meaning of the POW/MIA myth until I had a startling encounter in 1991 while I was a visiting professor at Meiji University in Tokyo. Several Japanese scholars of American Studies expressed their keen interest in the POW/MIA myth. They said that on some levels they thought they understood the myth, that from their study of the POW movies and other cultural artifacts they saw that the prisoner of war was functioning in American society as an icon of militarism. "But," one said, "that's what we find so puzzling. When militarism was dominant in Japan, the last person who would have been used as an icon of militarism was the POW. What did he do that was heroic? He didn't fight to the death. He surrendered." I was flabbergasted. Here I had been studying the POW/MIA myth for years and had missed its most essential and revealing aspect. Only then did I realize that this is a myth of imprisonment, a myth that draws deep emotional power by displacing onto Viet Nam the imprisonment, helplessness, and alienation felt by many Americans in an epoch when alien economic, technological, and bureaucratic forces control much of their lives.

Because the postwar POWs are imaginary beings, elaborating the POW/MIA myth and implanting it deep in America's collective imagination has been the job of art forms that specialize in imaginary beings: novels, comic books, TV soaps, videogames, and, of course, movies. Although the story of American prisoners abandoned in Southeast Asia could not become a major American myth until the dream factory geared up its assembly line for mass production of the essential images, Hollywood was actually involved in creating bits of the history that its POW rescue movies would soon fantasize.

The character central to the POW/MIA story as mythologized in the 1980s was retired Special Forces Colonel "Bo" Gritz, who organized raids into Laos to rescue POWs he imagined as captives of Asian communists. Gritz claimed that he had to accept this mission because the only two other men capable of such intense "action" were unavailable: "both Teddy Roosevelt and John Wayne are dead."[46]

But other men of action were at least available to help: Captain James T. Kirk of the *Starship Enterprise*, Dirty Harry, and a Hollywood star who had just moved into the White House. William Shatner put up $10,000 and received movie rights to the Gritz story. Clint Eastwood contributed $30,000 and was assigned a crucial role in the adventure.[47] And Ronald Reagan's administration was secretly arranging funding and logistics.[48]

By 1980, the POW myth envisioned a conspiracy high in the government to deny the existence of American prisoners. The villains were government bureaucrats, devious CIA operatives, and liberal politicians, personified by President Jimmy Carter. With the inauguration of Reagan in early 1981, the myth developed a new twist: the good president walled off by a cabal of scheming bureaucrats and liberals now known collectively as the "gatekeepers." There could be no doubt about the president's sincerity. After all, Reagan had been active with POW issues ever since he had actually been a POW of Asian communists during the Korean War—as the star of the 1954 movie *Prisoner of War*.

There was one man in America who could get past the all-powerful gatekeepers and bring the truth to the good president: Clint Eastwood. Gritz's plan hinged on two tête-à-têtes between Eastwood and Reagan. On the night of 27 November 1982, after receiving confirmation that Gritz's team had crossed the Mekong River into Laos, Eastwood was to fly from his ranch in Shasta, California, to a prearranged meeting at Reagan's Santa Barbara ranch to inform the president about the raid. When the raiders had actually released live American POWs, they would relay the message to Eastwood, who would then once again fly to see his old friend Reagan, who would then have to do what he wanted to do all along: send U.S. aircraft and military forces to rescue the POWs.[49] When the raiders returned from Laos to Thailand on 3 December, they found this message from a team member in California:

> CLINT AND I MET WITH PRESIDENT ON 27TH. PRESIDENT SAID: QUOTE, IF YOU BRING OUT ONE U.S. POW, I WILL START WORLD WAR III TO GET THE REST OUT. UNQUOTE.[50]

Gritz's raids, however, did not turn out like a Hollywood production. The American heroes did not ambush and wipe out hordes of Asian communists. In fact, almost as soon as they arrived in Laos they were ambushed, routed, and forced to flee back to Thailand.[51] The raiders of course encountered no POWs. Yet three days before the news of Gritz's first raid burst upon the public and while he was conducting an unsuccessful second raid, President Reagan, who had been kept closely informed, publicly declared that from now on "the government bureaucracy" would have to understand that the POW/MIA issue had become "the highest national priority."[52]

Reagan had been preparing for this since early 1981, when his administration had sent Congressmen Billy Hendon and John LeBoutillier to Laos, partly to prepare for the raids that Gritz was organizing.[53] LeBoutillier, working closely with White House liaisons and Ann Mills Griffiths, head of the National League of Families, set up Skyhook II, an organization that raised large sums of money, ostensibly to free POWs. Griffiths set up covert bank accounts in Bangkok to receive the funds. Carol Bates (wartime coordinator of VIVA's bracelet campaign) and Griffiths, operating with the White House's help, then moved Skyhook II funds through the Bangkok accounts to mercenary forces in Laos known as the "Lao resistance."[54] This byzantine, illegal funding of covert operations outdid Iran-Contra, for it included a self-sustaining mechanism. The "Lao resistance" produced a stream of phony evidence of live POWs for LeBoutillier to use in his Skyhook II propaganda to raise more funds for the Lao resistance, which was then able to supply still more phony evidence of live

POWs to raise still more funds and so on.[55] Reagan would soon make Griffiths coequal with the State and Defense Department representatives in his POW/MIA Interagency Group, and in 1984 he placed Bates in a key position in his expanded POW/MIA section of the Defense Intelligence Agency.

The first POW rescue movie, *Uncommon Valor*, began shooting amid the media hoopla about Gritz's raids. Starring Gene Hackman as a thinly veiled counterpart of Gritz, the film made it to the screen for the Christmas season of 1983. Reviewers, who at first dismissed it as a "grind actioner" and "bore" with "comic-strip-level heroism," were soon trying to comprehend the startling audience response to what turned out to be the "biggest movie surprise" of the 1983–84 season. The best explanation seemed to come from "an ordinary moviegoer who said with satisfaction of the bloody ending in which dozens of the enemy are mowed down by the Americans, 'We get to win the Vietnam War.'"[56]

Uncommon Valor presents a tableau of a nation run by bureaucrats, politicians, and shadowy secret agents in business suits who revile and betray its true warrior heroes. Hackman is a retired colonel whose efforts to rescue his MIA son are continually menaced by "the politicians" and omnipresent government agents equipped with high-tech spy mikes and phone taps. The idealism, virility, martial powers, and heroism of men who dedicate their lives to rescuing their abandoned comrades, sons, and fathers are presented as the alternative to a weak, decadent America subjugated by materialism, hedonism, and feminism. This perspective is a familiar element in the culture of fascism and Nazism.[57]

Hackman re-establishes patriarchal order by recruiting a team composed of Vietnam veterans who have all been victimized by an American society that castrates military and manly virtue. Their rescue mission also rescues them from the corrupting and degrading bonds of civilian life. The most revealing salvations are for two team members liberated from women.[58]

An expert on conducting ambushes has been kept from his true identity by a wife who now convinces him to hide from Hackman, whom she tries to block physically as she shrieks, "It's taken me ten years to get that goddamn war out of his head." Shoving her aside, Hackman rends these enfeebling domestic fetters, shouting, "What did you send your wife out here for? Don't you have the guts to come out here and talk to me yourself?"

A helicopter pilot has become an even more miserable prisoner of peace, permanently shut in from the world behind sunglasses and headset, and married to a blond floozy whom we see about to traipse out to happy hour at a local club. Embodying the fusion of American women with hedonism and materialism, she finally asks Hackman, "If he did go, how much would he be paid?"

Hackman himself is called to his mission by the memory of his son as a young boy coming to his parents' bedroom for help. While his wife lies oblivious in sleep, he reaches out to clutch his son's hand, a bond that becomes the pivotal symbol of the movie. His sleeping wife (who never speaks a word in the film) personifies women's irrelevance to the bonds between warriors and between fathers and sons.[59] Hackman explicitly articulates the central message: "There's no bond as strong as that shared by men who have faced death in battle."

The bonding among the men is first consummated in their training camp, a world without women where they regain their killing skills. The pleasures of this buddy-buddy society are ritualized as the men dance with each other, some holding their assault rifles at upright angles from the groin as they bump bottoms. Thus primed, these rugged heroes are ready to slaughter hordes of puny little Asians, rescue their enslaved comrades, give the Vietnam War a noble ending, and redeem America.

The following year came *Missing in Action*, with Chuck Norris as retired Special Forces Colonel James Braddock, a fantasized version of retired Special Forces Colonel James "Bo" Gritz. Here the myth took more potent shape, with Norris as lone superhero—incarnate in a fetishized male body—replacing Hackman's buddy-buddy team of manly warriors and graphically dramatizing how much more erotically exciting it is to make war, not love. There is no secret about the meaning and tremendous popular allure of *Missing in Action*, which were expressed in full-page ads showing Norris, headband half-restraining his savage locks, sleeves rolled up to reveal bulging biceps, and a huge machine gun seeming to rise from his crotch, which is blackened by its great shadow. Below ran the message: "THE WAR'S NOT OVER UNTIL THE LAST MAN COMES HOME!"[60]

Because the power of these movies flows from some of the deepest elements of American culture, they were able to transform the POW/MIA *issue* into a true *myth*. After all, one foundation of American culture is the mythic frontier, with its central images of white captives tortured by cruel nonwhite savages until they can be rescued by the first great American hero, the lone frontiersman who abandons civilized society to merge with the wilderness. The movies that transmuted what had been a fringe right-wing political issue of the mid-1970s into a central national myth did so precisely by using these primal cultural materials.[61] Hollywood moved us from seeing American POWs in Viet Nam as quintessential symbols of betrayed American manhood in *The Deer Hunter* (1978) through the formative POW rescue movies *Uncommon Valor* (1983) and *Missing in Action* (1984) to the apotheosis of the myth in *Rambo: First Blood Part II* (1985). *The Deer Hunter* explicitly calls attention to its use of the mythic frontier and frontiersman, fleshed out in the early nation-state by James Fennimore Cooper's *Deerslayer*. But it is *Rambo* that uses the old mythic elements to turn Sylvester Stallone, as muscled as the giant he-men in Nazi propaganda posters, into the true American superhero of our epoch.

At the beginning of the movie, Rambo himself is a prisoner in America. Thoroughly alienated from civil society by his experience in the Vietnamese wilderness—what GIs called "Injun country"—he is the only one who can rescue the tortured white captives from their savage captors. Rambo can do this by merging with the wilderness even more completely than the Vietnamese can. Why? Because he, like the mythic frontiersman, has coalesced with the Indian and the wilderness. Another character tells us that Rambo is of "German Indian descent," "a hell of a combination." Rambo—his long, dark hair restrained by a headband, a necklace dangling above his bare muscled chest, armed with a huge caricature of a bowie knife and a bow that shoots exploding arrows—conceals himself behind trees and waterfalls and literally rises out of the mud and water to ambush the savages in their own primitive land.

Rambo's vast power—over his enemies and his audiences—derive also from other American mythic heroes. America's most popular author, Edgar Rice Burroughs, created two of Rambo's forebears: a veteran of a defeated army who uses his expertise in martial arts to fight for good causes in alien lands against seemingly insurmountable odds (John Carter) and a bare-chested muscular he-man who merges completely with the tropical jungle to carry out spectacular deeds of heroism (Tarzan). Rambo also incorporates one of America's most distinctive cultural products: the comic-book hero who may seem to be an ordinary human being but really possesses superhuman powers that allow him to fight, like Superman, for "truth, justice, and the American way" and to personify national fantasies, like Captain America. No wonder Rambo can stand invulnerable against the thousands of bullets fired at him, many at point-blank range, by America's enemies.

Like the mythic frontiersman, Rambo confronts his antithesis not in the Indian but in feminized, devious, emasculating civil society as embodied by Murdock, the arch-bureaucrat who represents the Washington administration and those who manipulate the computerized technology used to control the lives of everyday men. The climax comes when Rambo, after rescuing the POWs, hurls himself on top of the prostrate Murdock and forces this fake man to whimper and moan in terror of our hero's gigantic phallic knife.

Thus, *Rambo* projects a fantasy in which the audience gets to violate the enemies of everyday life, the boss and his computerized control over work life, the bureaucrats and politicians who conspire to emasculate America's virility and betray the American dream. American men find their surrogates both in the POWs who embody humiliated, betrayed, enslaved American manhood and in the warrior hero who can rescue them when he escapes the imprisonment of post-Vietnam America.[62]

Six weeks after the opening of *Rambo*, President Reagan projected himself in its star role—while hyping the film with a presidential plug—as he declared (ostensibly as a microphone test before his national address on the release of U.S. hostages in Beirut), "Boy, I saw *Rambo* last night. Now I know what to do the next time this happens."[63] Two weeks later, members of Congress "signaled a new tough-minded attitude" on foreign relations by invoking the image of Rambo a dozen times in debating a foreign aid bill.[64] Rambo's political repercussions ricocheted around the world. For example, President Saddam Hussein of Iraq in 1990 defiantly responded to the U.S. threat of war with his own bluster in the guise of cultural criticism, "The Americans are still influenced by Rambo movies, but this is not a Rambo movie."[65]

As *Rambo* packed theaters with audiences who howled with pleasure and wildly cheered every slaying of a Vietnamese or Russian by its invulnerable hero, the nation was flooded with Rambo "action dolls," watches, walkie-talkies, water guns, bubble gum, pinball machines, sportswear for all ages, TV cartoons, and even "Rambo-Grams," messages delivered by head-banded musclemen sporting bandoleers across their bare chests. A *Rambo* TV cartoon serial, designed by Family Home Entertainment "for ages 5–12," transformed Rambo into "liberty's champion," a superman engaged in global struggles against evil. And for "adult" audiences, there were pornographic video spinoffs such as *Ramb-Ohh!* (1986) and *Bimbo: Hot Blood Part I!* (1985) and *Bimbo 2: The Homecoming!* (1986).

The advent of *Rambo* helped make the MIA religion not only a prominent feature of American culture but also a lucrative market. Rescuing POWs from the evil Vietnamese communists now became almost a rite of passage for Hollywood heroes, as the formula degenerated through *P.O.W.: The Escape*, the 1986 Israeli production starring David Carradine, to *Operation Nam*, a 1987 Italian production starring John Wayne's son Ethan Wayne, which might be called the first spaghetti rescue movie. In 1987 the first issue of *Vietnam Journal* appeared; *Vietnam Journal* is a comic book that prominently displayed on every cover the POW/MIA logo next to a lead about an MIA feature. In 1985, Jack Buchanan published *M.I.A. Hunter*, a mass-market POW rescue novel featuring Mark Stone, a former Green Beret who "has only one activity that gives meaning to his life—finding America's forgotten fighting men, the P.O.W.'s the government has conveniently labeled M.I.A.'s, and bringing them back from their hell on earth."[66] By 1991, Buchanan had published fourteen more volumes in what had become the immensely popular M.I.A. Hunter series, each promising more blood than the last, including *M.I.A. Hunter: Cambodian Hellhole* (1985), *M.I.A. Hunter: Hanoi Deathgrip* (1985), *M.I.A. Hunter: Mountain Massacre* (1985), *M.I.A. Hunter: Exodus from Hell* (1986), *M.I.A. Hunter: Blood Storm* (1986), *M.I.A. Hunter: Saigon Slaughter* (1987), and *Back to Nam* (1990).

The cultural products that disseminate the MIA mythology and give it potent forms in the popular imagination have tended increasingly to project a vast government cover-up and conspiracy. *Vietnam Journal*, for example, ran a three-part series in 1990 titled, "Is the U.S. Hiding the Truth about Missing Soldiers?" (issues 11–13). The answer, of course, was yes. In the 1989 TV movie *The Forgotten*, starring Keith Carradine and Stacy Keach, high-level government officials actually conspire to torture and assassinate POWs held by Viet Nam until 1987 so they would not reveal that these officials had colluded with North Vietnam to sabotage a POW rescue mission. Jack Buchanan's M.I.A. Hunter constantly battles against "Washington" and its sinister operatives; in *Cambodian Hellhole*, he can pursue his quest only "after demolishing a C.I.A. hit team sent to arrest him." So by the end of the 1980s, the POW/MIA myth had emerged from American popular culture in the shape of an ominous Frankenstein's monster beginning to haunt its ingenious creators in Washington.

The monster became a more serious problem as corporations from Europe and Asia began to stake out major investments in Viet Nam, barred to U.S. corporations by the U.S. embargo. Pressure was building for the normalization of relations.

On 9 April 1991—one month after declaring, "By God, we've kicked the Vietnam syndrome once and for all!"—President George H. W. Bush handed Viet Nam what he called a "Road Map" toward normalizing relations within two years—contingent on Viet Nam's making what Washington deemed satisfactory progress in resolving "all remaining POW/MIA cases."[67] Instantly, the smoldering POW/MIA issue was fanned into a firestorm.

In May, Senator Jesse Helms, in the name of all Republicans on the Senate Foreign Relations Committee, released a one-hundred-page pseudo-history alleging that thousands of U.S. POWs had been abandoned in Indochina and that some were still alive, betrayed by a vast Washington conspiracy. Although at no time during the war did the Pentagon or White House believe there could be more than a few hundred U.S. POWs, Helms's treatise claimed that Hanoi had held "5000" U.S. POWs.[68] Where did Helms get the figure five thousand? From a *New York Times* story published in 1973. However, the figure five thousand in that story referred not to U.S. POWs but to the number of prisoners Hanoi was demanding from Saigon.[69] The report's principal author was later exposed as having falsified much of its "evidence" about abandoned POWs.[70] Nevertheless, well over 100,000 copies of Helms's volume continued to be mailed out by the Senate Foreign Relations Committee.

SENATOR BOB SMITH, who helped engineer the Helms document, next tried to set up a Senate committee to ballyhoo its thesis. But Smith's efforts seemed doomed because the Senate was due to recess on 2 August 1991.

Suddenly, on 17 July, one of the most spectacular media coups in U.S. history began, orchestrated largely by Smith and his associates. A photograph purportedly showing three U.S. POWs from the Vietnam War still held captive in Indochina exploded as the lead story on the TV and radio networks. Newspapers across the country front-paged the picture of the trio under banner headlines. The "prisoners" were identified as three pilots shot down over Viet Nam and Laos between 1966 and 1970. Within a week, photographs ostensibly showing two more POWs in Indochina—

identified as Daniel Borah Jr. and Donald Carr—hit the media. According to a poll by the *Wall Street Journal* and NBC News, 69 percent of the American people now believed that U.S. POWs were being held in Indochina, and 52 percent were convinced that the government was derelict in not getting them back.[71] A headline in the *Wall Street Journal* on 2 August read "Bring on Rambo." The same day, a stampeded Senate unanimously passed Smith's resolution to create a Senate Select Committee on POW/MIA Affairs—along with a resolution to fly the POW/MIA flag over federal buildings.

The photos that launched the Senate committee later proved as bogus as all other "evidence" of postwar POWs. "Daniel Borah" turned out to be a Lao highlander who had happily posed because he never had his photograph taken before.[72] "Donald Carr" was a German bird smuggler photographed at a rare bird sanctuary in Bangkok.[73] The picture of the three alleged POWs was a doctored version of a 1923 photograph reproduced in a Soviet magazine in 1989; the three men were actually holding a poster extolling collective farming (mustaches had been added and a prominent picture of Stalin had been subtracted).[74]

All the photographs were the handiwork of notorious scam artists. Each was used to blitz the media and the public—and thus help create the Senate Select Committee. Senator Smith displayed the "Daniel Borah" pictures on the *Today* show.[75] The picture of the threesome had been released by Captain Red McDaniel, head of the right-wing American Defense Institute, who has been promising the faithful since 1986 that as soon as they contributed enough money, he would produce live POWs. McDaniel got it from Jack Bailey, head of a crooked POW/MIA fundraising operation known as Operation Rescue. Bailey, who had conspired to fake the "Donald Carr" photos, assaulted two ABC reporters on camera when they confronted him in the rare bird sanctuary where the pictures had been shot.[76]

Bob Smith was made the vice chairman of the Senate committee. The chairman was John Kerry, who may have been unaware of how the POW/MIA issue had been used back in 1971, when he joined hundreds of other antiwar Vietnam veterans to throw their medals at the Capitol Building. Panic-stricken by these actions and the growing antiwar movement among POW/MIA wives, Nixon's aide H. R. Haldeman had then ordered the White House staff "to be doubly sure we are keeping the POW wives in line."[77]

Ironically, Kerry now accepted the spurious history of the POW/MIA issue promulgated by those bent on continuing the conflict, including the preposterous notion that the government during the war and ever since had been minimizing and perhaps concealing the possibility of prisoners being kept after the United States withdrew. The committee refused to permit testimony about how the POW/MIA issue was created and used by the government to legitimize hostilities against Viet Nam from 1969 on. The only witnesses allowed to testify were either government apologists or POW/MIA movement militants.[78] Although the Senate Select Committee found not a shred of credible evidence of postwar POWs, its final report asserted that the POW/MIA issue should continue to have the "highest national priority."[79] But this conclusion did not satisfy the POW/MIA zealots, who claimed that the POWs still languishing in Viet Nam had been betrayed by Kerry and committee member John McCain. In the twenty-first century, the political futures of both Kerry and McCain would suffer from this alleged betrayal.

Two months after the Senate Select Committee issued its voluminous report, a poll by the *Wall Street Journal* disclosed that two-thirds of Americans believed that U.S. POWs "are still being held in Southeast Asia."[80] The poll did not measure how many of the other third believed Brzezinski's fable of hundreds of American officers being massacred in "cold blood." Though conveniently disposing of the belief in live POWs—which eventually would be biologically impossible anyhow—this scenario has become a fantasy that may allow the POW/MIA myth to endure indefinitely.

While the Select Committee had the media spotlighting the POW/MIA issue in 1992, President Bush was fighting for his political life. The very man who had boasted about healing America's Vietnam wounds was now trying to win re-election by reopening them, turning what Bill Clinton had or had not done during the Vietnam War into the Republicans' main campaign issue. Meanwhile, Ross Perot was campaigning as the wartime champion of the POWs and a Rambo-like hero who would rescue the dozens allegedly still alive in Indochina as well as the nation itself.

UNLIKE BUSH AND CLINTON, Perot had no national party apparatus. What he used as a remarkably effective substitute was a ready-made national infrastructure, a network of activists motivated by religious fervor and coordinated by grassroots organizations: the POW/MIA movement. Perot chose former POW James Stockdale as his running mate and former POW Orson Swindle as his campaign manager. At his typical rally, Perot sat with former POWs and family members on a stage bedecked with POW flags. POW activists and organizations were central to the petition campaigns that got Perot on the ballot in every state.[81]

Portraying himself as the lone outsider from Texas ready to ride into Washington to save us from its sleazy bureaucrats and politicians who had betrayed the POWs and the American people, Perot cut deeply into President Bush's constituency. Without Perot's candidacy, Bush probably would have beaten Bill Clinton in a one-on-one race. If so, then the POW/MIA issue was central to the election's outcome.

In the closing days of the presidential campaign, George Bush claimed he was on the verge of ending hostilities by forcing Viet Nam into resolving the POW/MIA issue. He now presented himself as the man who was about to lead the nation to "begin writing the last chapter of the Vietnam War."[82]

President Bush was responding to two events. One was Viet Nam's all-out efforts to resolve the POW/MIA issue, including actions utterly unprecedented between hostile states, such as opening their military archives to U.S. inspection, conducting joint searches throughout their country, and allowing short-notice U.S. inspection of suspected prison sites. The other was the pressure from U.S. corporations anxious not to lose lucrative business opportunities to foreign competitors already swarming into Viet Nam.[83]

But neither corporate anxiety nor Vietnamese cooperation could overcome the potent forces wielding the POW/MIA issue, forces that still included its original engineer, Richard Nixon. On 30 December 1992, Nixon sent a judiciously leaked memo to the Senate Select Committee, insisting that "it would be a diplomatic travesty and human tragedy to go forward with normalization" until Hanoi "fully accounts for the MIAs." As the *Los Angeles Times* observed, "Nixon's written statement provides the strongest evidence so far that he and officials of his former Administration constitute a powerful and determined, though largely hidden, lobby against normalization."[84]

So instead of following his own Road Map, Bush merely allowed U.S. enterprises to begin negotiating for future business. This left a curious situation in the early months of the Clinton administration: U.S. corporate interests, which had supported and profited from the Vietnam War, furtively leaning on the former antiwar demonstrator to end the war. Even the *Wall Street Journal*, for decades one of the master builders of the POW/MIA myth, ran a major story headlined "President Clinton, Normalize Ties with Vietnam" and arguing that, "by any account, the Vietnamese have more than met" all the conditions of the Road Map, including the requested "help in resolving the fate of American MIAs."[85] The Clinton administration began tiptoeing toward normalization. "Bill Clinton may be on the verge of finally ending the Vietnam War," declared the 12 April *Wall Street Journal*, which went on to warn, however, of "an orchestrated campaign" to stop him.[86]

Right on cue, the same day's *New York Times* featured a sensational front-page story about a "top secret" document "discovered" in Moscow by "Harvard researcher" Stephen Morris and "authenticated by leading experts" (unnamed) as a Russian translation of an alleged 1972 report to Hanoi's Politburo. This "smoking gun" "proves" that Viet Nam withheld "hundreds" of U.S. POWs. For an "expert" opinion, the *Times* turned to Zbigniew Brzezinski, who in 1978 had persuaded Jimmy Carter not to normalize relations with Viet Nam. Since, as Brzezinski knew, there has never been any credible evidence of postwar U.S. POWs in Viet Nam, he offered an explanation that was sooner or later destined to become part of the POW/MIA mythology: "'The Vietnamese took hundreds of American officers out and shot them in cold blood.'"[87]

In a replay of the phony photos of 1991, the "smoking gun" now exploded as the lead story on every TV network, including PBS, whose balanced coverage showcased a *MacNeil/Lehrer NewsHour* panel on 13 April consisting of three disinterested "experts"—Brzezinski, Kissinger, and Morris himself. Brzezinski's massacre scenario was repeated in newspaper editorials across the country. Headlines blared "North Vietnam Kept 700 POWs after War: 'Smoking Gun' File Exposes '20 Years of Duplicity'"; "POWs: The Awful Truth?" and "We Can't Set Up Ties with Killers of Our POWs."[88]

Not one of the "facts" about POWs in this spurious document conforms to the historical record.[89] Yet this clumsy hoax helped maintain the trade embargo for almost a year. And when President Clinton finally did call off the embargo in 1994, he claimed that he was doing so to get more "answers" about the MIAs, because "any decisions about our relationships with Vietnam should be guided by one factor and one factor only—gaining the fullest possible accounting for our prisoners of war and our missing in action."[90] Then in 1995, fifty years after the beginning of U.S. hostilities against the Democratic Republic of Viet Nam, Washington at long last established diplomatic relations with this first nation to break free from colonialism after the Second World War. To do so, President Clinton had to deftly undercut the POW/MIA lobby by naming as the first U.S. Ambassador Douglas (Pete) Peterson, a former Air Force fighter pilot who had spent six and a half years as a POW in Hanoi.

Four years later, the U.S. Embassy sponsored a breakthrough conference in Hanoi, which brought together American Studies scholars from Viet Nam and the United States. At a reception for the conference at the ambassador's residence, I asked Peterson his opinion of the POW/MIA issue. He called it a "hoax" and went on to expound on all the damage it had caused. Peterson thus expressed the virtually unanimous view of the 591 actual POWs released at the conclusion of the war, who were well aware that there were no hidden or secret prisoners. One of these actual former POWs is Senator John McCain.

The POW/MIA myth may not be as politically potent today as it was in 1992, when it helped prevent George H. W. Bush from being reelected and thus allowed Bill Clinton to begin his eight years in the White House. But it was deployed as a political weapon, with perhaps game-changing effects, in each of the first three presidential elections of the twenty-first century. In each one, the weapon's potency derived from the now almost unchallenged belief that there were—and might even still be—American POWs left in Viet Nam. And in each case, the candidate targeted by the weapon lost.

In 2000, Senator John McCain, running as America's late-twentieth-century iconic hero—the Vietnam POW—overwhelmed his four Republican opponents in the New Hampshire primary, crushing the runner-up, George W. Bush, by nineteen points. But in the next primary, in South Carolina, McCain's "Straight Talk Express" was violently derailed by a series of explosive charges. The most damaging charge was that, as a member of the Senate Select Committee on POW/MIA Affairs, he had viciously betrayed those hundreds or thousands of his fellow POWs left behind in Viet Nam. The main ingredients for this charge came from a 1992 article by Ted Sampley, "John McCain: The Manchurian Candidate," which argued that McCain had been brainwashed by the Vietnamese and might very well be acting as their secret agent.[91] McCain's campaign never recovered from the electoral defeat or the shattered image inflicted in South Carolina.

In 2004, the defeat of Senator John Kerry by incumbent President George W. Bush has been widely attributed to the heavily bankrolled "swift boating" by the organization Swift Vets and POWs for Truth, an assault that torpedoed Kerry's status as a heroic Vietnam veteran.[92] But more than three months before the Swift Vets first went public in a 4 May press conference, the campaign to use the POW/MIA issue to destroy Kerry's Vietnam credentials was launched by Sydney Schanberg, one of the most fanatical of the POW/MIA cultists. Using long discredited "evidence" that Viet Nam held "many" American POWs after the war to be used "as future bargaining chips," Schanberg's article "When John Kerry's Courage Went M.I.A" appeared on 24 February in the *Village Voice* and was soon widely disseminated in various forms. Schanberg claimed that as chair of the Senate Select Committee, Kerry had deliberately "covered up voluminous evidence" of "perhaps hundreds" of these left-behind POWs.

In 2008, Schanberg recycled his anti-Kerry article, along with other articles that he had been reissuing for decades, as "McCain and the POW Cover-up," an especially vitriolic assault on John McCain, who was then in what seemed to be a tight presidential race with Barack Obama. As he had done in earlier articles, Schanberg drew heavily on Sampley's "The Manchurian Candidate." There was nothing surprising or even new in Schanberg's piece. But what some people found startling—indeed, shocking—was where it was published: in the *Nation*, one of America's leading liberal journals and historically a major opponent of both the Vietnam War and the postwar revanchist campaigns against Viet Nam.[93]

Even more appalling, liberal and progressive media responded by deliriously ballyhooing Schanberg's POW/MIA fantasy. Democratic-Underground.com ran excerpts from and links to the *Nation*'s article, along with ads for POW/MIA flags, pins, and bracelets. *Daily Kos, Huffington Post*, Alternet.org, and many others reprinted the piece, some adorning it with large images of the POW/MIA flag. *Democracy Now!*, the nationally syndicated progressive radio and TV show, ran a long, adulatory interview with Schanberg on 23 October and provided a link on its website to a longer version of his article published online by the Nation Institute.[94] Scattered protests from some historians, antiwar activists, and Vietnam Veterans Against the War were drowned out by denunciations—from right, left, and center—of McCain as a betrayer of all those POWs abandoned in Viet Nam. The true history of the phony POW/MIA issue has evidently now been buried under a myth so sacred, and so central to our nation's cultural memory, that to question it amounts to heresy.

In the decades since the Vietnam War, joint U.S.-Vietnamese search teams have combed the country for possible remains. The remains of scores of men whose names were engraved on POW/MIA bracelets have been positively identified. Swarms of U.S. tourists, businesspeople, and returning veterans have visited all parts of Viet Nam. Hanoi has actually opened its secret records of those captured to American researchers. Today we should know, with as much certainty as could ever be possible, that there are not now, and there never were, American prisoners held in Viet Nam after the war. So why are those hundreds of thousands of POW/MIA flags still flying in every part of America?

The short answer is that those flags seem to symbolize our culture's dominant view of America as victim—victim of the Vietnam War and victim of all the peoples we have bombed and invaded since 1975. As George H. W. Bush so revealingly put it in 1991, while celebrating the beginning of our endless wars in the Middle East and southwestern Asia, "By God, we've kicked the Vietnam syndrome once and for all!" In a nation still festooned in those black-and-white banners, the true history and crucial lessons of the Vietnam War are now missing in action.

Notes

Major portions of this chapter appeared in an earlier form in *Vietnam and Other American Fantasies*, copyright 2000 H. Bruce Franklin and published by the University of Massachusetts Press; reprinted by permission of the University of Massachusetts Press.

1. See Martini, *Invisible Enemies*.
2. "Clinton on Vietnam's Legacy," *New York Times*, 12 July 1995.
3. Nixon, *Nixon Speaks Out*, 235.
4. Richard M. Nixon, speech to the Overseas Press Club, March 29, 1954, in Gettleman et al., *Vietnam and America*, 52.
5. Memorandum from Peter Flanigan, 30 June 1969, Nixon Presidential Materials Project, White House Special Files, National Archives and Records Administration (hereafter, NARA), Haldeman box 133, Perot folder. For a more extensive account with additional documentation, see Franklin, *M.I.A.*, 50–56, 188–92.
6. Law 10/59, together with other documents on the formation of the NLF, is reprinted in Gettleman et al., *Vietnam and America*, 156–91. The NLF estimated that

prior to its formation, the Diem government had killed 90,000 and imprisoned 800,000, including 600,000 crippled by torture: Nguyen, *South Vietnam*, 12.

7. Baron et al., *In the Name of America*; Duffett, *Against the Crimes of Silence*.

8. Gettleman et al., *Vietnam and America*, 410–11; Hersh, *My Lai 4*; Zinn, *A People's History of the United States*, 469–70.

9. Article 12 of the Geneva Convention stipulates: "Prisoners of war may only be transferred by the Detaining Power to a Power which is a party to the Convention and after the Detaining Power has satisfied itself of the willingness and ability of such transferee Power to apply the Convention." South Vietnam was not a party to the convention. For a description of South Vietnam's Con Son prison island, see Don Luce, "Behind Vietnam's Prison Walls," *Christian Century*, 19 February 1969, 261–64. Luce, who speaks Vietnamese, later led Representatives Augustus Hawkins and William Anderson through the secret access to the tiger cages, which were photographed for *Life* by Tom Harkin. The chief American adviser to the South Vietnamese prison system, Frank "Red" Walton (former police commander of the Watts district of Los Angeles), had first told the visiting congressional delegation that Con Son was like "a Boy Scout recreational camp." After they found the cages, Walton angrily told them, "You aren't supposed to go poking your nose into doors that aren't your business": "The Tiger Cages of Con Son," *Life*, 17 July 1970, 27–29.

10. "Final Report of the House Select Committee on Missing Persons in Southeast Asia," 94th Cong., 2d sess., 13 December 1976, 136.

11. Ibid., 106, 135; "Laird Appeals to Enemy to Release U.S. Captives," *New York Times*, 20 May 1969; Clarke, *The Missing Man*, 32.

12. "Inhuman Stance on Prisoners" (editorial), *New York Times*, 29 May 1969.

13. Memorandum from Arthur Burns, 9 April 1969, and memorandum from Peter Flanigan, 30 June 1969, both in NARA, Haldeman box 133, Perot folder; Robert Fitch, "H. Ross Perot: America's First Welfare Billionaire," *Ramparts*, November 1971, 42–51.

14. "Projects Proposed by Ross Perot," memorandum from Alexander Butterfield to H. R. Haldeman, John Ehrlichman, Henry Kissinger, and Bryce Harlow, 24 October 1969, NARA, Haldeman box 133, Perot folder.

15. NARA, Haldeman box 55, John Brown folder.

16. "American Prisoners of War in Vietnam: Hearings before the Subcommittee on National Security Policy and Scientific Developments of the Committee on Foreign Affairs, House of Representatives," 91st Cong., 1st sess., 13–14 November 1969, 2, 6.

17. "American Prisoners of War in Southeast Asia, 1970: Hearings before the Subcommittee on National Security Policy and Scientific Developments of the Committee on Foreign Affairs, House of Representatives," 91st Cong., 2d sess., 29 April, 1 May, 6 May 1970, 2.

18. "Message from Perot," memorandum for the President from Alexander

Butterfield, NARA, President's Handwriting Files, box 4. Nixon has written a big double-underlined "Good!" on this.

19. "Wives Organizing to Find 1,332 GI's Missing in War," *New York Times*, 31 July 1969; Joseph Lelyveld, "'Dear Mr. President'—The POW Families," *New York Times Magazine*, 3 October 1971, 56; Stockdale and Stockdale, *In Love and War*, 133–46, 206–8, 210–13, 230–31, 306–7.

20. Stockdale and Stockdale, *In Love and War*, 310–11; testimony of Sybil Stockdale, "American Prisoners of War in Southeast Asia, 1970," 61.

21. "POW Policy in Vietnam," memorandum for the president from Henry A. Kissinger, 2 October 1969, NARA, President's Office Files, Series A: Documents Annotated by the President, box 3. The first major media event using the wives was a methodically planned meeting to be held on 12 December between the president and a carefully selected delegation led by Sybil Stockdale. "Dick Capen and his people have worked hard to put together the package," Alexander Butterfield wrote to Colonel Hughes, a fellow White House staff member, on 4 December, but "a final decision has been made that there will be no fathers among those invited so wives and mothers must be substituted for the 2 sets of parents," the "demographic spread" must be widened, and "there must be at least 1 and preferably 2 more enlisted men represented, without exceeding a total of 23 ladies": memorandum from Butterfield to Colonel Hughes, 4 December 1969, NARA, Haldeman box 55, Hughes folder. Lyn Nofziger asked Butterfield for "a brief bit on each POW wife we might be able to make use of . . . on the Hill": Lyn Nofziger to Alexander Butterfield, 4 December 1969, NARA, Butterfield box 8. Butterfield asked Hughes to forward the president's preplanned answers to possible questions from the press "so that I can complete the required scenario": Butterfield to Hughes, 8 December 1969, NARA, Haldeman box 55, Hughes folder.

22. Stockdale and Stockdale, *In Love and War*, 373.

23. "American Prisoners of War in Southeast Asia, 1970," 20.

24. Ibid., 27.

25. Stockdale and Stockdale, *In Love and War*, 375–76; Clarke, *The Missing Man*, 32; Powers, "The National League of Families and the Development of Family Services," 5.

26. See Clarke, *The Missing Man*, 34–35, on early government connections with the league. Representative Les Aspin introduced into the *Congressional Record* of 22 January and 31 January 1972 letters proving that the Republican National Committee was actually managing the fundraising campaign of the National League and that Senator Robert Dole, of the Republican National Committee, had placed "advisers" in the league's structure who coordinated its activities and public statements with his own.

27. "American Prisoners of War in Southeast Asia, 1970," 66–79; "Exhibit to Stir Opinion on POW's Open in Capitol," *New York Times*, 5 June 1970.

28. Jon M. Van Dyke, "Nixon and the Prisoners of War," *New York Review of Books*, 7 January 1971, 35; Richard A. Falk, "Pawns in Power Politics," reprinted in "American Prisoners of War in Southeast Asia, 1971: Hearings before the Subcommittee on National Security Policy and Scientific Developments of the Committee on Foreign Affairs, House of Representatives," 92d Cong., 1st sess., 23–25, 30–31 March, 1, 6, 20 April 1971, 474; Kraak, *Family Efforts on Behalf of United States Prisoners of War and Missing in Action in Southeast Asia*, 16, 18.

29. Russell Kirk, "Students for Victory," *National Review*, 31 May 1966, 535; Koenigsamen, "Mobilization of a Conscience Constituency," 36, 38.

30. Koenigsamen, "Mobilization of a Conscience Constituency," 37, 77–78.

31. Clarke, *The Missing Man*, 40; Koenigsamen, "Mobilization of a Conscience Constituency," 65, 72; telephone interview with Mike Sasek, Defense Intelligence Agency, 9 October 1990.

32. Koenigsamen, "Mobilization of a Conscience Constituency," 44–46; "Reminder of Vietnam Stays on Hand," *Los Angeles Times*, 13 February 1989; telephone interview with Gloria Coppin, 23 September 1990. Coppin reports that at the ball, Perot refused to help finance the bracelets and even refused her plea for a loan to initiate production.

33. Koenigsamen, "Mobilization of a Conscience Constituency," 44–50, 78; "Unit for POW's Has New Project," *New York Times*, 26 February 1973. Other VIVA publicity products included matchbooks, bumper stickers, "missing man" stationery, Christmas cards, T-shirts, and sweatshirts; many of these were wholesaled to other political organizations.

34. Koenigsamen, "Mobilization of a Conscience Constituency," 55; "Unit for POW's Has New Project"; "Reminder of Vietnam Stays on Hand."

35. "U.S. Gives Enemy List of Missing," *New York Times*, 31 December 1969.

36. Ibid.

37. "Vietnam Unique: POWs Languish as Political Pawns," *Christian Science Monitor*, 12 December 1970; the series had begun on November 27.

38. *Public Papers of the Presidents of the United States: Richard Nixon*, 1971, 541; Tom Wicker, "Illogic in Vietnam," *New York Times*, 25 May 1971.

39. Jonathan Schell, "The Time of Illusion IV: For the Re-election of the President," *New Yorker*, 23 June 1975, 76, reprinted in Schell, *The Time of Illusion*, 231.

40. Telephone interview with Gloria Coppin, 23 September 1990.

41. "Agreement on Ending the War and Restoring Peace in Viet-Nam," in Gettleman et al., *Vietnam and America*, 474–75.

42. Richard Nixon, "Remarks at a Reception for Returned Prisoners of War, May 24, 1973," in *Public Papers of the Presidents of the United States: Richard Nixon, 1973* (Washington, DC: GPO, 1975), 558.

43. Nixon's secret letter is reprinted in Franklin, *M.I.A.*, 204–7.

44. "Confirmation Hearings of Dr. Henry Kissinger as Secretary of State, September 7, 10, 11, and 14, 1973," as reprinted in "Americans Missing in Southeast

Asia: Hearings before the House Select Committee on Missing Persons in Southeast Asia," pt. 5, 17, 25 June, 21 July, 21 September 1975, 175.

45. "Long Shadow of the MIA's Still Stalks a Pentagon Official," *New York Times*, 20 September 1992.

46. Quoted in Patterson and Tippin, *The Heroes Who Fell from Grace*, 102. Patterson, who was Gritz's second in command during the first raid, published an account in *Soldier of Fortune* magazine while Gritz was still in Southeast Asia, leading to a break between the two who had fought together in the Special Forces in Viet Nam. Getting to the truth about Bo Gritz's adventures is a formidable task, especially since each of the three participants who have written extensively about them— Gritz, Patterson, and Scott Barnes—accuses the other two of being inveterate liars.

47. "Daring Search for POWs Told," *Los Angeles Times*, 31 January 1983; "'Star-Studded' Raid Fails to Free POWs," *Star-Ledger*, 1 February 1983; "Private Raid on Laos Reported," *New York Times*, 1 February 1983; Patterson and Tippin, *The Heroes Who Fell from Grace*, 52. Most of the stories about the Gritz raids were broken by the *Los Angeles Times*, which received a series of oral and written messages from him in January and February 1983.

48. Report of the Select Committee on POW/MIA Affairs, 302.

49. "Daring Search for POWs Told"; Patterson and Tippin, *The Heroes Who Fell from Grace*, 50, 70, 92–107.

50. Patterson and Tippin, *The Heroes Who Fell from Grace*, 146. A less theatrical version is reported in "Eastwood Told Reagan of Planned POW Raid," *Los Angeles Times*, 25 February 1983.

51. Patterson and Tippin, *The Heroes Who Fell from Grace*, 128–29, 147, 176; Barnes with Libb, *Bohica*, 34.

52. "Remarks at a Meeting of the National League of Families of American Prisoners and Missing in Southeast Asia, January 28, 1983," *Public Papers of the Presidents of the United States: Ronald Reagan, 1983* (Washington, 1984), 131.

53. Report of the Select Committee on POW/MIA Affairs, 155.

54. Ibid., 305–10, 334–35.

55. Ibid., 221, 276–80.

56. Richard Freedman, review of *Uncommon Valor*, *Star-Ledger* (Newark, N.J.), 16 December 1983; Aljean Harmetz, "Two Holiday Movies Turn into Surprise Successes," *New York Times*, 13 February 1984.

57. For an incisive analysis of the proto-fascist content of the POW rescue films and other movies, see Hoberman, "The Fascist Guns in the West," 53–61, which also appeared in a revised form in *American Film* in March 1986.

58. My analysis of the role of gender in the POW rescue movies owes a considerable debt to Jeffords, *The Remasculinization of America*.

59. Ibid., 148.

60. For an excellent analysis of the creation of Norris's persona in the *Missing in Action* films, see Williams, "*Missing in Action*," 129–44. For an exceptionally insight-

ful overview of the psychosocial significance of the "POW-MIA/Avenger subgenre," tracing its cinematic history back to Norris's 1978 film *Good Guys Wear Black*, see Kern, "MIAs, Myth, and Macho Magic." A detailed explication of *Missing in Action* is given in Franklin, *M.I.A.*, 146–50.

61. Any exploration of the role of the frontier myth in American culture owes much to Slotkin, *Regeneration through Violence*, together with Slotkin, *The Fatal Environment*. Hellman, *American Myth and the Legacy of Vietnam*, cogently relates the frontier myth to the imagined role of the Green Berets in Viet Nam. My analysis is also indebted to Studler and Desser, "Never Having to Say You're Sorry." Other important writings on the cultural implications and effects of *Rambo* include Kunz, "First Blood Redrawn"; Waller, "*Rambo*."

62. For a more thorough explication of *Rambo*, see Franklin, *M.I.A.*, 150–59.

63. "Reagan Cites 'Rambo' as Next-Time Example," *Star-Ledger*, 1 July 1985; "Reagan Gets Idea from 'Rambo' for Next Time," *Los Angeles Times*, 1 July 1985.

64. "'Machismo' on Capitol Hill," *New York Times*, 14 July 1985.

65. "Iraq Spurns 'U.S.-Imposed' Council Solution; Saddam Vows Fight for Kuwait," *Star-Ledger*, 1 December 1990.

66. Buchanan, *M.I.A. Hunter*, jacket copy.

67. "'Road Map' to Renew Ties with Hanoi Could Lead to Some Trade by Year End," *Wall Street Journal*, 15 April 1991; "Concerned Citizen Newsletter," *National League of Families of American Prisoners and Missing in Southeast Asia*, 31 May 1991.

68. U.S. Senate Committee on Foreign Relations Republican Staff, "An Examination of U.S. Policy toward POW/MIAs," interim report, 23 May 1991, 5–8.

69. Ibid., November 1991, 5–8.

70. *Hearings before the Select Committee on POW/MIA Affairs*, Part I of II, 5, 6, 7, and 15 November 1991, 443–47.

71. Poll reported in "Minor Memos," *Wall Street Journal*, 2 August 1991.

72. Telephone interview with Commander Gregg Hartung, Public Affairs Office, U.S. Department of Defense, 23 September 1991. Since then, the Lao highlander has been extensively interviewed and photographed.

73. Interview with James Bamford, the investigative reporter who led the ABC team that exposed the fraud, 28 February 1992. Bamford played for me the extensive videos showing the bird sanctuary, the bird smuggler, and the unmasking of the scam.

74. U.S. Department of Defense press conference, 2 July 1992; "U.S. Is Sure Photo of Missing Is Fake," *New York Times*, 19 July 1992.

75. "Baker Presses Vietnam on MIAs, Cambodia," *St. Louis Post-Dispatch*, 25 July 1991; UPI story datelined Olney, Ill., story tag "mia-borah," 22 July 1991; *Report of the Select Committee on POW/MIA Affairs*, 319.

76. *Peter Jennings's World News*, ABC, 11–12 February 1992.

77. Memorandum from H. R. Haldeman to General Hughes, April 26, 1971, and

"POW/MIA Wives," Memorandum from General James D. Hughes to Haldeman, April 29, 1971, Haldeman Box 77, General Hughes folder.

78. My efforts to testify, which persisted from February through December 1992, were officially rebuffed not only by the staff and in letters from Senator Kerry but also by Senator Kerry and Senator Grassley when I appeared with each of them on national television.

79. Report of the Select Committee on POW/MIA Affairs, 164.

80. *Wall Street Journal*, 23 April 1993.

81. David Jackson, "MIAs' Kin Want Perot as President," *Dallas Morning News*, 19 May 1992; telephone interview with David Jackson, 18 May 1992; telephone interview with John LeBoutillier, 12 June 1992; "It's Businessman Perot and Not War Hero Bush Who Attracts a Following among U.S. Veterans," *Wall Street Journal*, 2 July 1992.

82. "Bush Sees Gain in Vietnam Ties," *Los Angeles Times*, 24 October 1992.

83. "Corporations Ask Bush to Lift Vietnam Ban," *New York Times*, 9 May 1992; "Vietnam: The Big Buildup Begins," *Washington Post*, 9 December 1992.

84. "Nixon Opposing U.S.-Vietnam Normalization Policy: He Could Influence Any Move by Bush Administration to End Trade Embargo," *Los Angeles Times*, 9 January 1993.

85. "President Clinton, Normalize Ties with Vietnam," *Wall Street Journal*, 8 March 1993.

86. "Clinton Prepares to Relax Policy on Vietnam as U.S. Business Urges Access to New Market," *Wall Street Journal*, 12 April 1993.

87. "U.S. to Press Hanoi to Explain '72 POW Report," *New York Times*, 13 April 1993.

88. "North Vietnam Kept 700 POWs after War," *Washington Times*, 12 April 1991; "'Smoking Gun' File Exposes 'Twenty Years of Duplicity,'" *USA Today*, 12 April 1991; "POWs: The Awful Truth?" *Washington Post*, 15 April 1991; "We Can't Set Up Ties with Killers of Our POWs," *Jersey Journal*, 18 April 1991.

89. References are to a photocopy of the English-language text sent by fax from the Moscow bureau of the *New York Times* to the Foreign Desk, with a cover letter referring to it as a "Sept 15, 1972 Vietnamese Top Secret report, recently discovered in Soviet Communist Party archives—confirming that Vietnam was holding on to far more US POWs than it had publicly admitted." I am grateful to the *New York Times* reporter Steven A. Holmes for this copy. For detailed exposés of this spurious document, see Nayan Chanda, "Research and Destroy," *Far Eastern Economic Review*, 6 May 1993, 20; H. Bruce Franklin, "M.I.A.sma," *Nation*, 10 May 1993, 616.

90. "In Clinton's Words: 'Fullest Possible Accounting' of MIA's," *New York Times*, 4 February 1994.

91. Ted Sampley, "John McCain: The Manchurian Candidate," *U.S. Veteran Dispatch*, December 1992.

92. For an exploration of the Swift Vets campaign and its media links, see Franklin, "'Vietnam' in the New American Century."

93. The article appeared in mid-September, in the issue dated 6 October. The *Nation* had evident amnesia about articles it had printed years earlier that had exposed and debunked the very "evidence" cited by Schanberg.

94. John Funk, "Sydney Schanberg: McCain and the POW Cover-up," Democratic Underground, 19 September 2008, www.democraticunderground.com/discuss /duboard.php?az=view_all&address=103x385452 (accessed 21 September 2008); U.S. Army Paratrooper, "Addressing McCain on Veterans Issues," *Daily Kos*, 28 September 2008, http://dailykos.com/story/2008/9/28/24017/1623/180/613073 (accessed 30 September 2008); Peter Dreier, "McCain No Friend to Vets," *Huffington Post*, 28 September 2008, http://huffingtonpost.com/peter-dreier/mccain-no -friend-to-vets_b_129847.html (accessed 30 September 2008); Sydney H. Schanberg and the Nation Institute, "John McCain Has a Bizarre History of Hiding Evidence about His Fellow POWs," Alternet.org, 21 September 2008, http://alternet.org /election08/99721?page=entire (accessed 26 September 2008); Amy Goodman and Juan González, "Report: McCain Suppressed Info on Fellow Vietnam POWs Left Behind," *Democracy Now!*, 23 October 2008, http://democracynow.org/2008/10/23 /report_mccain_suppressed_info_on_fellow (accessed 25 October 2008).

Abbas, Ackbar, and John Nguyet Erni, eds. *Internationalizing Cultural Studies: An Anthology*. New York: Blackwell, 2005.

Ahn Jung-hyo. *White Badge: A Novel of Korea*. New York: Soho, 1989.

Allen, Michael. *Until the Last Man Comes Home: POWS, MIAS, and the Unending Vietnam War*. Chapel Hill: University of North Carolina Press, 2009.

Anderson, Benedict. *Imagined Communities: Reflections on the Origins and Spread of Nationalism*. London: Verso, 1991.

Appiah, Kwame Anthony. *Cosmopolitanism: Ethics in a World of Strangers*. New York: W. W. Norton, 2006.

Archibugi, Daniele, ed. *Debating Cosmopolitics*. London: Verso, 2003.

Armes, Roy. *Third World Film Making and the West*. Berkeley: University of California Press, 1987.

Balaban, John, ed. *Ca Dao Vietnam: Vietnamese Folk Poetry*. Port Townsend, WA: Copper Canyon, 2003.

Barnes, Scott, with Melva Libb. *Bohica*. Canton, OH: Bohica, 1987.

Barnett, Louise. *Atrocity and American Military Justice in Southeast Asia*. New York: Routledge, 2010.

Baron, Melvyn, Dodge Ely, and Seymour Melman. *In the Name of America: A Study Commissioned and Published by Clergy and Laymen Concerned about Vietnam*. New York: E. P. Dutton, 1968.

Basch, Linda, Nina Glick Schiller, and Cristina Szanton Blanc. *Nations Unbound: Transnational Projects, Postcolonial Predicaments, and Deterritorialized Nation-States*. Amsterdam: Gordon and Breach, 1994.

Beattie, Keith. *The Scar That Binds: American Culture and the Vietnam War.* New York: New York University Press, 1998.

Berlant, Lauren, ed. *Compassion: The Culture and Politics of an Emotion.* New York: Routledge, 2004.

Bilton, Michael, and Kevin Sim. *Four Hours in My Lai.* New York: Penguin, 1992.

Birnbaum, Linda S. "Health and Environmental Effects of Dioxins." Paper presented at the Yale Vietnam Conference 2002: The Ecological and Health Effects of the Vietnam War, New Haven, 13–15 September 2002.

Borneman, John, *Subversions of International Order: Studies in the Political Anthropology of Culture.* Albany: State University of New York Press, 1998.

Borstelmann, Thomas. *The 1970s: A New Global History from Civil Rights to Economic Inequality.* Princeton, NJ: Princeton University Press, 2011.

Bradley, Mark Philip. *Imagining Vietnam and America: The Making of Postcolonial Vietnam, 1919–1950.* Chapel Hill: University of North Carolina Press, 2000.

———. *Vietnam at War.* New York: Oxford University Press, 2009.

Bradley, Mark Philip, and Marilyn B. Young, eds. *Making Sense of the Vietnam Wars: Local, National, and Transnational Perspectives.* New York: Oxford University Press, 2008.

Brennan, Timothy. *At Home in the World: Cosmopolitanism Now.* Cambridge, MA: Harvard University Press, 1997.

Bruner-Tran, K. L., S. Gladson, T. Nayyar, and K. G. Osteen. "Developmental Exposure of Mice to TCDD Is Associated with Adverse Pregnancy Outcomes in Adulthood." Abstract. UCSF-CHE Summit on Environmental Challenges to Reproductive Health and Fertility, San Francisco, January 2007.

Brush, Peter. "Recounting the Casualties at Khe Sanh." *Vietnam* 20, no. 1 (2007): 28–37.

Buchanan, Jack. *M.I.A. Hunter.* New York: Jove, 1985.

Buckingham, William A. *Operation Ranch Hand: The Air Force and Herbicides in Southeast Asia, 1961–1971.* Washington, DC: Office of Air Force History, 1982.

Burchett, Wilfred. *Grasshoppers and Elephants: Why Viet Nam Fell.* New York: Urizen, 1977.

Capps, Walter. *The Unfinished War: Vietnam and the American Conscience,* 2d ed. Boston: Beacon, 1990.

———, ed. *The Vietnam Reader.* New York: Routledge, 1991.

Carroll, Peter N. *It Seemed Like Nothing Happened: The Tragedy and Promise of America in the 1970s.* New York: Holt, Rinehart, and Winston, 1982.

Carson, Clayborne, and Kris Shepard, eds. *A Call to Conscience: The Landmark Speeches of Dr. Martin Luther King, Jr.* New York: Warner, 2001.

Carter, James M. *Inventing Vietnam: The United States and State Building, 1954–1968.* Cambridge: Cambridge University Press, 2008.

Carter, Jimmy. *A Government as Good as Its People.* New York: Simon and Schuster, 1977.

Catton, Philip. *Diem's Final Failure: Prelude to America's War in Vietnam.* Lawrence: University Press of Kansas, 2002.

Cecil, Paul Frederick. *Herbicidal Warfare: The Ranch Hand Project in Vietnam.* New York: Praeger, 1986.

Chapman, Jessica. "Staging Democracy: South Vietnam's 1955 Referendum to Depose Bao Dai." *Diplomatic History* 30, no. 4 (September 2006): 671–703.

Cheah, Pheng, and Bruce Robbins, eds. *Cosmopolitics: Thinking and Feeling beyond the Nation.* Minneapolis: University of Minnesota Press, 1998.

Clarke, Douglas L. *The Missing Man: Politics and the MIA.* Washington, DC: National Defense University, 1979.

Clifford, James. *Routes: Travel and Translation in the Late Twentieth Century.* Cambridge, MA: Harvard University Press, 1997.

Connerton, Paul. *How Societies Remember.* Cambridge: Cambridge University Press, 1989.

Conover, Sarah. *Kindness: A Treasury of Buddhist Wisdom for Children and Parents.* Spokane: Eastern Washington University Press, 2001.

Cowie, Jefferson. *Stayin' Alive: The 1970s and the Last Days of the Working Class.* New York: New Press, 2012.

Cumings, Bruce. *The Origins of the Korean War: Liberation and the Emergence of Separate Regimes, 1945–47.* Princeton, NJ: Princeton University Press, 1981.

———. *Parallax Visions: Making Sense of American–East Asian Relations at the End of the Century.* Durham, NC: Duke University Press, 1999.

Dang Thuy Tram. *Last Night I Dreamed of Peace: The Diary of Dang Thuy Tram,* trans. Andrew X. Pham. New York: Harmony, 2007.

Daum, Andreas W., Lloyd C. Gardner, and Wilfried Mausbach, eds. *America, the Vietnam War, and the World: Comparative and International Perspectives.* New York: Cambridge University Press, 2003.

Davis, Christina L. "Do WTO Rules Create a Level Playing Field? Lessons from the Experience of Peru and Vietnam." *Negotiating Trade: Developing Countries in the WTO and NAFTA,* ed. John Odell, 219–56. Cambridge: Cambridge University Press, 2006.

Derrida, Jacques. *On Cosmopolitanism and Forgiveness.* New York: Routledge, 2002.

Devine, Jeremy M. *Vietnam at 24 Frames a Second.* Austin: University of Texas Press, 1999.

DiGregorio, Michael, A. Terry Rambo, and Masayuki Yanagisawa. "Clean, Green, and Beautiful: Environment and Development under the Renovation Economy." *Postwar Vietnam: Dynamics of a Transforming Society,* ed. Hy V. Luong, 171–99. Lanham, MD: Rowman and Littlefield, 2003.

Dinh, Viet. "Rabbit in the Moon." *Michigan Quarterly Review* 44, no. 1 (2005): 79–105.

Donnelly, Jack. *Universal Human Rights in Theory and Practice.* Ithaca, NY: Cornell University Press, 2003.

Doray, Bernard, and Concepcion de la Garza Doray. "Conventional War and Chemical

Warfare in A Luoi from a Psychological Angle." *Victims of Agent Orange/Dioxin in Vietnam: The Expectations*, Proceedings of International Conference. Hanoi: Research Centre for Gender, Family, and Environment in Development, 2006.

Douzinas, Costas. *Human Rights and Empire: The Political Philosophy of Cosmopolitanism*. New York: Routledge-Cavendish, 2007.

Dudley, William, and David Bender, eds. *The Vietnam War: Opposing Viewpoints*. San Diego: Greenhaven, 1990.

Duffett, John, ed. *Against the Crime of Silence: Proceedings of the International War Crimes Tribunal, Stockholm-Copenhagen*. New York: Simon and Schuster, 1968.

Duiker, William J. *Vietnam: Revolution in Transition*. Boulder, CO: Westview, 1995.

———. *Vietnam since the Fall of Saigon*. Athens: Center for International Studies, Ohio University, 1989.

Dwernychuk, L. Wayne, Hoang Dinh Cau, Christopher T. Hatfield, Thomas G. Boivin, Tran Manh Hung, Phung Tri Dung, and Nguyen Dinh Thai. "Dioxin Reservoirs in Southern Viet Nam—A Legacy of Agent Orange." *Chemosphere* 47 (2002): 117–37.

Edelman, Lee. *No Future: Queer Theory and the Death Drive*. Durham, NC: Duke University Press, 2004.

Edmundson, Mark. "In the New Vietnam." *Raritan* 28, no. 2 (2008): 154–63.

Ehrhart, W. D. *In the Shadow of Vietnam*. Jefferson, NC: McFarland, 1977.

Elliott, David W. P. "Official History, Revisionist History, and Wild History." *Making Sense of the Vietnam Wars: Local, National, and Transnational Perspectives*, ed. Mark Philip Bradley and Marilyn B. Young, 277–304. New York: Oxford University Press, 2008.

———. *The Vietnamese War: Revolution and Social Change in the Mekong Delta, 1930–1975*. New York: M. E. Sharpe, 2003.

Engelmann, Larry. *Tears before the Rain: An Oral History of the Fall of South Vietnam*. New York: Oxford University Press, 1990.

Erickson, J. David, et al. *Vietnam Veterans' Risks for Fathering Children with Birth Defects*. Atlanta: Center for Environmental Health, U.S. Department of Health and Human Services, 1984.

Erni, John Nguyet, and Siew Keng Chua, eds. *Asian Media Studies: Politics of Subjectivities*. Oxford: Blackwell, 2005.

Fforde, Adam. "Rethinking the Political Economy of Conservative Transition: The Case of Vietnam." *Journal of Communist Studies and Transition Politics* 26, no. 1 (March 2010): 126–46.

Figley, Charles R., and Seymour Leventman. *Strangers at Home*. New York: Routledge, 1990.

Fox, Diane Niblack. "Fire, Spirit, Love, Story." *Journal of Vietnamese Studies* 3, no. 2 (2008): 218–21.

Franklin, H. Bruce. *M.I.A., or, Mythmaking in America*. New Brunswick, NJ: Rutgers University Press, 1993.

————. *Vietnam and Other American Fantasies*. Amherst: University of Massachusetts Press, 2000.

————. "'Vietnam' in the New American Century." *The United States and the Legacy of the Vietnam War*, ed. John Roper, 33–50. London: Palgrave Macmillan, 2007.

Gaiduk, Ilya V. *The Soviet Union and the Vietnam War*. Chicago: I. R. Dee, 1996.

Galston, Arthur W. "Science and Social Responsibility: A Case History." *Annals of the New York Academy of Sciences* 196 (7 June 1972): 223–35.

Gammeltoft, Tine, Minh Hang Tran, Thi Hiep Nguyen, and Thi Thuy Hanh Nguyen. "Late-Term Abortion for Fetal Anomaly: Vietnamese Women's Experiences." *Reproductive Health Matters* 16 (2008): 46–56.

Gendreau, Francis, Nolwen Henaff, and Jean-Yves Martin. "Les Consequences demographiques et economiques des epandages d'agent orange." Paper presented at Conference Internationale sur les Effets des Epandages de Defoliants au Viet-Nam (1961–1971), Paris, 2005.

Gerzon, Mark. *A Choice of Heroes: The Changing of American Manhood*. Boston: Houghton-Mifflin, 1982.

Gettleman, Marvin, Jane Franklin, Marilyn B. Young, and H. Bruce Franklin, eds. *Vietnam and America: A Documented History*. New York: Grove, 1995.

Gibson, James William. *Warrior Dreams: Violence and Manhood in Post-Vietnam America*. New York: Hill and Wang, 1994.

Gillis, John R., ed. *Commemorations: The Politics of National Identity*. Princeton, NJ: Princeton University Press, 1994.

Gilroy, Paul. *Postcolonial Melancholia*. New York: Columbia University Press, 2006.

Greene, Bob, ed. *Homecoming: When the Soldiers Returned from Vietnam*. New York: Putnam, 1989.

Greiner, Bernd. *War without Fronts: The USA in Vietnam*. New Haven, CT: Yale University Press, 2009.

Gresser, Charis, and Sophia Tickell. *Mugged: Poverty in Your Coffee Cup*. Oxford: Oxfam International, 2002.

Gustafsson, Mai Lan. *War and Shadows: The Haunting of Vietnam*. Ithaca, NY: Cornell University Press, 2009.

Hagopian, Patrick. *The Vietnam War in American Memory: Veterans, Memorials, and the Politics of Healing*. Amherst: University of Massachusetts Press, 2009.

Halbwachs, Maurice. *On Collective Memory* (1952), trans. Lewis A. Coser. Chicago: University of Chicago Press, 1992.

Harnly, Caroline D. *Agent Orange and Vietnam: An Annotated Bibliography*. Metuchen, NJ: Scarecrow, 1988.

Harriman, Averell. *America and Russia in a Changing World*. New York: Doubleday, 1971.

Hassler, Alfred. "They Call It a 'Third Solution.'" *Moral Argument and the War in Vietnam*, ed. Paul Menzel, 201–12. Nashville: Aurora, 1971.

Hellman, John. *American Myth and the Legacy of Vietnam*. New York: Columbia University Press, 1986.

Herring, George C. *America's Longest War: The United States and Vietnam, 1950–1975*. 4th ed. Boston: McGraw-Hill, 2002.

Hersh, Seymour. *My Lai 4*. New York: Random House, 1970.

Hertz, Robert. "The Pre-eminence of the Right Hand: A Study in Religious Polarity" (1909). *Right and Left: Essays on Dual Symbolic Classification*, ed. R. Needham, 89–113. Chicago: University of Chicago Press, 1960.

Hirschman, Charles, Samuel Preston, and Vu Manh Loi. "Vietnamese Casualties during the American War: A New Estimate." *Population and Development Review* 21, no. 4 (December 1995): 783–812.

Hirshfeld, Alan. *Parallax: The Race to Measure the Cosmos*. New York: W. H. Freeman, 2001.

Hixson, Walter. *The Myth of American Diplomacy: National Identity and U.S. Foreign Policy*. New Haven, CT: Yale University Press, 2008.

Hoberman, J. "The Fascist Guns in the West: Hollywood's 'Rambo' Coalition." *Radical America* 19, no. 6 (1985): 53–61.

Hollinger, David. *Postethnic America: Beyond Multiculturalism*. New York: Basic, 1995.

Howley, Kerry. "Catfish Terror." *Reason* 37, no. 7 (December 2005): 15.

Hunt, David. *Vietnam's Southern Revolution: From Peasant Insurrection to Total War*. Amherst: University of Massachusetts Press, 2008.

Hunter, Allen, ed. *Rethinking the Cold War*. Philadelphia: Temple University Press, 1998.

Huynh, Dình Te. *Selected Vietnamese Proverbs: Tục Ngữ Việt Nam Chọn Lọc*. Oakland, CA: Center for International Communication, 1990.

Institute of Medicine. *Veterans and Agent Orange: Update 1998*. Washington, DC: National Academy Press, 1999.

Ishay, Micheline R. *The History of Human Rights: From Ancient Times to the Globalization Era*. Berkeley: University of California Press, 1994.

Iwabuchi, Koichi, Stephen Muecke, and Mandy Thomas, eds. *Rogue Flows: Trans-Asian Cultural Traffic*. Hong Kong: Hong Kong University Press, 2004.

Jacobs, Seth. *America's Miracle Man in Vietnam: Ngo Dinh Diem, Religion, Race, and U.S. Intervention in Southeast Asia, 1950–1957*. Durham, NC: Duke University Press, 2004.

Jamieson, Neil. *Understanding Vietnam*. Berkeley: University of California Press, 1993.

Jeffords, Susan. *The Remasculinization of America: Gender and the Vietnam War*. Bloomington: Indiana University Press, 1989.

Kaiko, Takeshi. *Into a Black Sun: Vietnam, 1964–1965*. New York: Kodansha International, 1983.

Kaldor, Mary. *Global Civil Society: An Answer to War*. Cambridge: Polity Press, 2003.

Kaledin, Eugenia. *Daily Life in the United States, 1940–1959*. Westport, CT: Greenwood, 2000.

Kalman, Laura. *Right Star Rising: A New Politics, 1974–1980.* New York: W.W. Norton, 2010.

Kant, Immanuel. *To Perpetual Peace: A Philosophical Sketch*, trans. Ted Humphrey. Indianapolis: Hackett, 2003.

Kaplan, Amy, and Donald Pease, eds. *Cultures of United States Imperialism.* Durham, NC: Duke University Press, 1993.

Kaplan, Caren. *Questions of Travel: Postmodern Discourses of Displacement.* Durham, NC: Duke University Press, 1996.

Karnow, Stanley. *Vietnam: A History.* New York: Penguin, 1983.

Keen, Suzanne. *Empathy and the Novel.* Oxford: Oxford University Press, 2007.

Kern, Louis J. "MIAs, Myth, and Macho Magic: Post-apocalyptic Cinematic Visions of Vietnam." *Search and Clear: Critical Responses to Selected Literature and Films of the Vietnam War*, ed. William J. Searle, 37–54. Bowling Green, OH: Bowling Green State University Popular Press, 1988.

Kiernan, Ben. *Blood and Soil: A World History of Genocide and Extermination from Sparta to Darfur.* New Haven, CT: Yale University Press, 2007.

Kim Seong-nae. "Mourning Korean Modernity in the Memory of the Cheju April Third Incident." *Inter-Asia Cultural Studies Reader*, ed. Kuan-Hsing Chen and Chua Beng Huat, 191–206. London: Routledge, 2007.

Kingston, Maxine Hong. *China Men.* New York: Vintage, 1989.

———. *The Fifth Book of Peace.* New York: Knopf, 2003.

———. *The Woman Warrior.* New York: Knopf, 1976.

Kleinman, Arthur, and Joan Kleinman. "The Appeal of Experience, The Dismay of Images: Cultural Appropriations of Suffering in Our Times." *Social Suffering*, ed. Arthur Kleinman, Veena Das, and Margaret M. Lock, 1–23. Berkeley: University of California Press, 1997.

Koenigsamen, Janet L. "Mobilization of a Conscience Constituency: VIVA and the POW/MIA Movement." PhD diss., Kent State University, 1987.

Kolko, Gabriel. "China and Vietnam on the Road to the Market." *Journal of Contemporary Asia* 31, no. 4 (2001): 431–40.

———. *Vietnam: Anatomy of a Peace.* London: Routledge, 1997.

Kraak, Charles F. *Family Efforts on Behalf of United States Prisoners of War and Missing in Action in Southeast Asia.* Carlisle Barracks, PA: Army War College, 1975.

Kunz, Don. "First Blood Redrawn." *Vietnam Generation* 1 (Winter 1989): 94–111.

Kuzmarov, Jeremy. *The Myth of the Addicted Army: Vietnam and the Modern War on Drugs.* Amherst: University of Massachusetts Press, 2009.

Kuznick, Peter J., and James Gilbert, eds. *Rethinking Cold War Culture.* Washington, DC: Smithsonian Institution Press, 2001.

Kwon, Heonik. *After the Massacre: Commemoration and Consolation in Ha My and My Lai.* Berkeley: University of California Press, 2006.

———. *Ghosts of War in Vietnam.* New York: Cambridge University Press, 2008.

Laderman, Scott. "'The Other Side of the War': Memory and Meaning at the War

Remnants Museum of Vietnam." *Decentering America*, ed. Jessica C. E. Gienow-Hecht. New York: Berghahn, 2007.

———. *Tours of Vietnam: War, Travel Guides, and Memory*. Durham, NC: Duke University Press, 2009.

Lake, Anthony, ed. *The Vietnam Legacy: The War, American Society, and the Future of American Foreign Policy*. New York: New York University Press, 1976.

Lam, Mariam B. "Circulating War Memories: The Diary of Đặng Thùy Trâm." *Journal of Vietnamese Studies* 3, no. 2 (June 2008): 172–79.

———. "Circumventing Channels: Indie Filmmaking in Post-Socialist Viet Nam and Beyond." *Glimpses of Freedom: Independent Cinema in Southeast Asia*, ed. May Ingawanij and Benjamin McKay, 87–106. Ithaca, NY: Cornell University Press, 2012.

———. *Not Coming to Terms: Viet Nam, Post-trauma, and Cultural Politics*. Durham, NC: Duke University Press, forthcoming.

Lambek, Michael. "The Past Imperfect: Remembering as Moral Practice." *Tense Past: Cultural Essays in Trauma and Memory*, ed. Paul Antze and Michael Lambek, 235–54. London: Routledge, 1996.

Lawrence, Mark Atwood. *Assuming the Burden: Europe and the American Commitment to War in Vietnam*. Berkeley: University of California Press, 2005.

Le Cao Dai. *Agent Orange in the Vietnam War: History and Consequences*. Hanoi: Vietnam Red Cross Society, 2000.

Lembcke, Jerry. *The Spitting Image: Myth, Memory, and the Legacy of Vietnam*. New York: New York University Press, 2000.

Le Minh Khue. "A Day on the Road." *The Stars, the Earth, the River*, ed. Wayne Carlin, trans. Bac Hoai Tran and Dana Sachs, 37–54. Willimantic, CT: Curbstone, 1997.

———. "The Distant Stars." *The Stars, the Earth, the River*, ed. Wayne Carlin, trans. Bac Hoai Tran and Dana Sachs, 1–20. Willimantic, CT: Curbstone, 1997.

Lepore, Jill. *The Name of War: King Philip's War and the Origins of American Identity*. New York: Vintage, 1998.

Le Thi Nham Tuyet, and Annika Johansson. "Impact of Chemical Warfare with Agent Orange on Women's Reproductive Lives in Vietnam—A Pilot Study." *Victims of Agent Orange/Dioxin in Vietnam: The Expectations*, Proceedings of International Conference. Hanoi: Research Centre for Gender, Family, and the Environment, 2006.

Le Trong Cuc. "Vietnam: Traditional Cultural Concepts of Human Relations with the Natural Environment." *Asian Geographer* 18, nos. 1–2 (1999): 67–69.

Levy, Emmanuel. *Cinema of Outsiders: The Rise of Independent Film*. New York: New York University Press, 1999.

Lewy, Guenter. *America in Vietnam*. New York: Oxford University Press, 1978.

Logan, William, and Keir Reeves, eds. *Places of Pain and Shame: Dealing with "Difficult Heritage."* London: Routledge, 2009.

Logevall, Fredrik. *Choosing War: The Lost Chance for Peace and the Escalation of the War in Vietnam*. Berkeley: University of California Press, 1999.

Lowenthal, David. "Preface." *The Art of Forgetting*, ed. Adrian Forty and Susanne Küchler, vi–xiii. New York: Berg, 1999.

Luce, Don, and John Sommer. *Vietnam: The Unheard Voices*. Ithaca, NY: Cornell University Press, 1969.

Luong, Hy Van. "Economic Reform and the Intensification of Rituals in Two North Vietnamese Villages, 1980–90." *The Challenge of Reform in Indochina*, ed. Börje Ljunggren. Cambridge, MA: Harvard Institute for International Development, 1993.

———. *Revolution in the Village: Tradition and Transformation in North Vietnam, 1925–1988*. Honolulu: University of Hawai'i Press, 1992.

MacPherson, Myra. *Long Time Passing: Vietnam and the Haunted Generation*. New York: New American Library, 1984.

Maitre, Jacques. "The Painful Highlands." *Victims of Agent Orange/Dioxin in Vietnam: The Expectations*, Proceedings of International Conference. Hanoi: Research Centre for Gender, Family, and Environment in Development, 2006.

Malarney, Shaun K. *Culture, Ritual, and Revolution in Vietnam*. Surrey: Routledge-Curzon, 2002.

———. "'The Fatherland Remembers Your Sacrifice': Commemorating War Dead in North Vietnam." *The Country of Memory: Remaking the Past in Late Socialist Vietnam*, ed. Hue-Tam Ho Tai, 46–76. Berkeley: University of California Press, 2001.

———. "Return to the Past? The Dynamics of Contemporary Religious and Ritual Transformation." *Postwar Vietnam: Dynamics of a Transforming Society*, ed. Hy Van Luong, 225–56. New York: Rowman and Littlefield, 2003.

Mann, Michael. *The Dark Side of Democracy: Explaining Ethnic Cleansing*. New York: Cambridge University Press, 2005.

Mariscal, George, ed. *Aztlán and Viet Nam: Chicano and Chicana Experiences of the War*. Berkeley: University of California Press, 1999.

Martin, Michael F. *Vietnamese Victims of Agent Orange and U.S.-Vietnam Relations*. Washington, DC: Congressional Research Service, 2009.

Martini, Edwin A. *Agent Orange: History, Science, and the Politics of Uncertainty*. Amherst: University of Massachusetts Press, 2012.

———. *Invisible Enemies: The American War on Vietnam, 1975–2000*. Amherst: University of Massachusetts Press, 2007.

Masur, Matt. "Exhibiting Signs of Resistance: South Vietnam's Struggle for Legitimacy, 1954–1960." *Diplomatic History* 33, no. 2 (April 2009): 293–313.

McMahon, Robert. "Contested Memory: The Vietnam War and American Society, 1975–2001." *Diplomatic History* 26, no. 2 (spring 2002): 159–84.

McNamara, Robert. *In Retrospect: The Tragedy and Lessons of Vietnam*. New York: Vintage, 1995.

Merritt, Greg. *Celluloid Mavericks: A History of American Independent Film*. New York: De Capo Press, 2000.

Mieczkowski, Yanek. *Gerald Ford and the Challenges of the 1970s*. Lexington: University Press of Kentucky, 2005.

Miller, Arthur. "Political Issues and Trust in Government: 1964–1970." *American Political Science Review* 68, no. 3 (September 1974): 951–72.

Miller, Edward. "Vision, Power, and Agency: The Ascent of Ngo Dinh Diem, 1945–54." *Journal of Southeast Asian Studies* 35, no. 3 (October 2004): 433–58.

Miller, Edward, and Tuong Vu. "The Vietnam War as a Vietnamese War: Agency and Society in the Study of the Second Indochina War." *Journal of Vietnamese Studies* 4, no. 3 (fall 2009): 1–19.

Miller, Toby, Nitin Govil, John McMurria, Richard Maxwell, and Ting Wang, eds. *Global Hollywood 2*. London: British Film Institute, 2005.

Morris, David B. "About Suffering: Voice, Genre, and Moral Community." *Social Suffering*, ed. Arthur Kleinman, Veena Das, and Margaret Lock, 25–47. Berkeley: University of California Press, 1997.

Mosse, George. *Fallen Soldiers: Reshaping the Memory of the World Wars*. Oxford: Oxford University Press, 1990.

Moyn, Samuel. *The Last Utopia: Human Rights in History*. Cambridge, MA: Harvard University Press, 2010.

Neilands, J. B., G. H. Orians, E. W. Pfeiffer, Alje Vennema, and Arthur H. Westing. *Harvest of Death: Chemical Warfare in Vietnam and Cambodia*. New York: Free Press, 1972.

Nelson, Deborah. *The War behind Me: Vietnam Veterans Confront the Truth about U.S. War Crimes*. New York: Basic, 2008.

Ngo Vinh Long. "The Socialization of South Vietnam." *The Third Indochina War: Conflict between China, Vietnam, and Cambodia, 1972–1979*, ed. Odd Arne Westad and Sophie Quinn-Judge, 127–51. New York: Routledge, 2006.

Nguyen, Lien-Hang T. "Cold War Contradictions: Toward an International History of the Second Indochina War, 1969–1973." *Making Sense of the Vietnam Wars: Local, National, and Transnational Perspectives*, ed. Mark Philip Bradley and Marilyn B. Young, 219–49. New York: Oxford University Press, 2008.

———. *Hanoi's War: An International History of the War for Peace in Vietnam*. Chapel Hill: University of North Carolina Press, 2012.

Nguyen, Viet Thanh. "Speak of the Dead, Speak of Viet Nam: The Ethics and Aesthetics of Minority Discourse." *New Centennial Review* 6, no. 2 (2007): 7–37.

Nguyen Khac Vien, ed. *South Viet Nam: From the N.F.L. to the Provisional Revolutionary Government*. Hanoi: Vietnamese Studies, 1970.

Nguyen-vo, Thu-huong. *The Ironies of Freedom: Sex, Culture, and Neoliberal Governance in Vietnam*. Seattle: University of Washington Press, 2008.

Nietzsche, Friedrich. *On the Advantage and Disadvantage of History for Life* (1873), trans. Peter Preuss. Indianapolis: Hackett, 1980.

Ninh, Bao. *The Sorrow of War*. New York: Riverhead, 1996.

Nixon, Richard M. *Nixon Speaks Out: Major Speeches and Statements by Richard Nixon in the Presidential Campaign of 1968*. New York: Nixon–Agnew Campaign Committee, 1968.

Norindr, Panivong. "Vietnam: Chronicles of Old and New." *Contemporary Asian Cinema: Popular Culture in a Global Frame*, ed. Anne Tereska Ciecko, 45–57. New York: Berg, 2006.

Nussbaum, Martha, ed. *For Love of Country?* Boston: Beacon, 1996.

———. "Patriotism and Cosmopolitanism." *For Love of Country?*, ed. Martha Nussbaum, 3–17. Boston: Beacon, 1996.

Oliver, Kendrick. *The My Lai Massacre in American History and Memory*. Manchester, UK: Manchester University Press, 2007.

Ondaatje, Michael. *The English Patient*. New York: Knopf, 1993.

Palmer, Michael G. "The Legacy of Agent Orange: A Socio-economic Impact Assessment from Central Vietnam." *Victims of Agent Orange/Dioxin in Vietnam: The Expectations*, Proceedings of International Conference. Hanoi: Research Centre for Gender, Family, and Environment in Development, 2006.

Patterson, Charles J., and G. Lee Tippin. *The Heroes Who Fell from Grace: The True Story of Operation Lazarus, the Attempt to Free American POWs from Laos in 1982*. Canton, OH: Daring, 1985.

Pelley, Patricia M. *Postcolonial Vietnam: New Histories of a National Past*. Durham, NC: Duke University Press, 2002.

Phan Trieu Hai. "There Was a Man Lying on the Roof." *Love after War: Contemporary Fiction from Viet Nam*, ed. Wayne Karlin and Ho Anh Thai, 400–11. Willimantic, CT: Curbstone, 2003.

Phung Tuu Boi. "From Research to Remediation." Paper presented at the annual meeting of the Association for Asian Studies, Boston, 2007.

Polner, Murray. *No Victory Parades: The Return of Vietnam Veterans*. New York: Holt, Rinehart and Winston, 1971.

Pomonti, Jean-Claude. *La rage d'être vietnamien*. Paris: Le Seuil, 1972.

Porter, Gareth. *A Peace Denied: The United States, Vietnam, and the Paris Agreement*. Bloomington: Indiana University Press, 1975.

Power, Samantha. *"A Problem from Hell": America and the Age of Genocide*. New York: Harper Perennial, 2007.

Powers, Iris R. "The National League of Families and the Development of Family Services." *Family Separation and Reunion: Families of Prisoners of War and Servicemen Missing in Action*, ed. Hamilton I. McCubbin, Barbara B. Dahl, Philip J. Metres Jr., Edna J. Hunter, and John A. Plag, 1–10. Washington, DC: U.S. Government Printing Office, 1974.

Prados, John. *Vietnam: The History of an Unwinnable War, 1945–1975*. Lawrence: University Press of Kansas, 2009.

Pratt, John Clark, ed. *Vietnam Voices: Perspectives on the War Years, 1941–1982*. New York: Penguin, 1984.

Preston, Andrew. *The War Council: McGeorge Bundy, the NSC, and Vietnam*. Cambridge, MA: Harvard University Press, 2006.

Quinn-Judge, Sophie. "From the *Quiet American* to the Paris Peace Conference: The Search for a Third Force in Vietnam." *Vietnam and the West: New Approaches*, ed. Wynn Wilcox, 155–74. Ithaca: Cornell University Press, 2010.

———. "Through a Glass Darkly: Reading the History of the Vietnamese Communist Party, 1945–1975." *Making Sense of the Vietnam Wars: Local, National, and Transnational Perspectives*, ed. Mark Philip Bradley and Marilyn B. Young, 111–34. New York: Oxford University Press.

Rabel, Roberto. *New Zealand and the Vietnam War: Politics and Diplomacy*. Auckland: Auckland University Press, 2005.

Randolph, Stephen. *Powerful and Brutal Weapons: Nixon, Kissinger, and the Easter Offensive*. Cambridge, MA: Harvard University Press, 2007.

Renan, Ernest. "What Is a Nation?" *Nation and Narration*, ed. Homi K. Bhabba, 8–22. New York: Routledge, 1990.

Report of the Select Committee on POW/MIA Affairs, United States Senate. Washington, DC: U.S. Government Printing Office, 1993.

Rodgers, Daniel. *The Age of Fracture*. Cambridge, MA: Harvard University Press, 2011.

Rotter, Andrew J. *The Path to Vietnam: The Origins of the American Commitment to Southeast Asia*. Ithaca, NY: Cornell University Press, 1987.

Rowlands, Michael. "Remembering to Forget: Sublimation as Sacrifice in War Memorials." *The Art of Forgetting*, ed. Adrian Forty and Susanne Küchler, 129–45. Oxford: Berg, 1999.

Sallah, Michael, and Mitch Weiss. *Tiger Force: A True Story of Men and War*. Boston: Little, Brown, 2006.

Santerre, Charles R. "Catfish Inspection: Consumer Protection or Protectionism?" *Food Technology* 65, no. 5 (May 2011): 164.

Sato, Gayle. "Reconfiguring the 'American Pacific': Narrative Reenactments of Viet Nam in Maxine Hong Kingston's *The Fifth Book of Peace*." *Japanese Journal of American Studies* 16 (2005): 111–33.

Scarry, Elaine. *The Body in Pain: The Making and Unmaking of the World*. New York: Oxford University Press, 1985.

———. "The Difficulty of Imagining Other People." *For Love of Country?*, ed. Martha Nussbaum, 98–110. Boston: Beacon, 1996.

Schecter, Arnold, ed. *Dioxins and Health*. New York: Plenum Press, 1994.

Schecter, Arnold, Le Cao Dai, Olaf Papke, Joelle Prange, John D. Constable, Muneaki Matsuda, Vu Duc Thao, and Amanda Piskac. "Recent Dioxin Contamination from Agent Orange in Residents of a Southern Vietnam City." *Journal of Occupational and Environmental Medicine* 43, no. 5 (May 2001): 435–43.

Schecter, Arnold, Marian Pavuk, Rainer Malish, and John Jake Ryan. "Are Vietnamese

Food Exports Contaminated with Dioxin from Agent Orange?" *Journal of Toxicology and Environmental Health: Part A* 66, no. 15 (2003): 1391–404.

Schell, Jonathan. *The Time of Illusion.* New York: Knopf, 1976.

Schlecker, Markus, and Kirsten W. Endres. "Psychic Experience, Truth, and Visuality in Post-war Vietnam." *Social Analysis* 55, no. 1 (spring 2011): 1–22.

Schuck, Peter H. *Agent Orange on Trial: Mass Toxic Disasters in the Courts.* Cambridge, MA: Harvard University Press, 1986.

Schulman, Bruce, and Julian Zelizer, eds. *Rightward Bound: Making America Conservative in the 1970s.* Cambridge, MA: Harvard University Press, 2008.

Schulzinger, Robert. *A Time for Peace: The Legacy of the Vietnam War.* New York: Oxford University Press, 2006.

Schwenkel, Christina. *The American War in Contemporary Vietnam: Transnational Remembrance and Representation.* Bloomington: Indiana University Press, 2009.

———. "From John McCain to Abu Ghraib: Tortured Bodies and Historical Unaccountability of U.S. Empire in Vietnam." *American Anthropologist* 111, no. 1 (March 2009): 30–42.

———. "Recombinant History: Transnational Practices of Memory and Knowledge Production in Contemporary Vietnam." *Cultural Anthropology* 21, no. 1 (2006): 3–30.

Scruggs, Jan, and Joel L. Swerdlow. *To Heal a Nation: The Vietnam Veterans Memorial* (1985). New York: Harper Collins, 1992.

Severo, Richard, and Lewis Milford. *The Wages of War: When America's Soldiers Came Home—From Valley Forge to Vietnam.* New York: Simon and Schuster, 1989.

Shafer, Michael D. *The Legacy: The Vietnam War in the American Imagination.* Boston: Beacon, 1990.

Shaw, Rosalind. *Memories of the Slave Trade: Ritual and Historical Imagination in Sierra Leone.* Chicago: University of Chicago Press, 2002.

———. *Rethinking Truth and Reconciliation Commissions: Lessons from Sierra Leone.* Special Report 130. Washington, DC: United States Institute of Peace, 2005.

Slotkin, Richard. *The Fatal Environment: The Myth of the Frontier in the Age of Industrialization, 1800–1890.* New York: Atheneum, 1985.

———. *Regeneration through Violence: The Mythology of the American Frontier, 1600–1860.* Middletown, CT: Wesleyan University Press, 1973.

Song, Min. *Strange Future: Pessimism and the 1992 Los Angeles Riots.* Durham, NC: Duke University Press, 2005.

Sontag, Susan. *Regarding the Pain of Others.* New York: Farrar, Straus, and Giroux, 2003.

Spivak, Gayatri. "Cultural Talks in the Hot Peace: Revisiting the 'Global Village.'" *Cosmopolitics: Thinking and Feeling beyond the Nation,* ed. Pheng Cheah and Bruce Robbins, 329–48. Minneapolis: University of Minnesota Press, 1998.

Srikanth, Rijani. *The World Next Door: South Asian American Literature and the Idea of America.* Philadelphia: Temple University Press, 2004.

Statler, Kathryn. *Replacing France: Alliance Politics and the American Commitment to Vietnam, 1953–1961.* Lexington: University Press of Kentucky, 2007.

Stellman, Jeanne Mager, Steven D. Stellman, Richard Christian, Tracy Weber, and Carrie Tomasallo. "The Extent and Patterns of Usage of Agent Orange and Other Herbicides in Vietnam." *Nature* 422 (17 April 2003): 681–87.

Stern, Lewis M. *The Vietnamese Communist Party's Agenda for Reform: A Study of the Eighth National Party Congress.* Jefferson, NC: McFarland, 1998.

Stockdale, Jim, and Sybil Stockdale. *In Love and War.* New York: Harper and Row, 1984.

Stokes, Melvyn, and Richard Maltby, eds. *Hollywood Abroad: Audiences and Cultural Exchange.* London: British Film Institute, 2005.

Stroud, Kandy. *How Jimmy Won: The Victory Campaign from Plains to the White House.* New York: William Morrow, 1977.

Studler, Gaylyn, and David Desser. "Never Having to Say You're Sorry: *Rambo*'s Rewriting of the Vietnam War." *Film Quarterly* 42 (fall 1988): 9–16.

Suttmeier, Bruce. "Seeing Past Destruction: Trauma and History in Kaikō Takeshi." *Positions: East Asia Cultures Critique* 15, no. 3 (2008): 457–86.

Tai, Hue-Tam Ho, ed. *In the Country of Memory: Remaking the Past in Late Socialist Vietnam.* Berkeley: University of California Press, 2001.

Tan, Viet. *Viec ho* [The work of family ancestor worship]. Hanoi: Nha xuat ban van hoa dan toc, 2000.

Taylor, Philip. *Goddess on the Rise: Pilgrimage and Popular Religion in Vietnam.* Honolulu: University of Hawai'i Press, 2005.

Terada, Alice M. *Under the Starfruit Tree: Folktales from Vietnam.* Honolulu: University of Hawai'i Press, 1989.

Terry, Wallace. *Bloods: An Oral History of the Vietnam War by Black Veterans.* New York: Ballantine, 1984.

TRAFFIC. *A Matter of Attitude: The Consumption of Wild Animal Products in Ha Noi, Viet Nam.* Hanoi: TRAFFIC Southeast Asia, Greater Mekong Programme, 2007.

Trullinger, James W. *Village at War: An Account of Conflict in Vietnam.* Palo Alto, CA: Stanford University Press, 1994.

Turse, Nick. *Kill Anything That Moves: The Real American War in Vietnam.* New York: Metropolitan Books/Henry Holt and Co., 2013.

Uesugi, Takeshi. "Delayed Reactions: 'Conjuring' Agent Orange in Twenty-First Century Viet Nam." PhD diss., McGill University, 2012.

Uhl, Michael, and Tod Ensign. *GI Guinea Pigs.* New York: Playboy, 1980.

Vertovec, Steven, and Robin Cohen, eds. *Conceiving Cosmopolitanism: Theory, Context, and Practice.* Oxford: Oxford University Press, 2002.

Vo, Chuong-Dai. "Memories That Bind: Dang Thuy Tram's Diaries as Agent of Reconciliation." *Journal of Vietnamese Studies* 3, no. 2 (2008): 196–207.

Vo Quy. "The Wounds of War: Vietnam Struggles to Erase the Scars of 30 Violent Years." *Ceres* 24 (March–April 1992): 13–16.

Vuong Tri Nhan. "*The Diary of Dang Thuy Tram* and the Postwar Vietnamese Mentality." *Journal of Vietnamese Studies* 3, no. 2 (2008): 180–95.

Waller, Gregory A. "*Rambo*: Getting to Win This Time." *From Hanoi to Hollywood*, ed. Linda Dittmar and Gene Michaud, 113–28. New Brunswick, NJ: Rutgers University Press, 1990.

Webster, Thomas, and Barry Commoner. "Overview: The Dioxin Debate." *Dioxins and Health*, ed. Arnold Schecter, 1–50. New York: Plenum, 1994.

Wecter, Dixon. *When Johnny Comes Marching Home*. Cambridge, MA: Houghton-Mifflin, 1944.

Werbner, Richard, ed. *Memory and the Postcolony*. London: Zed, 1998.

Westad, Odd Arne. *The Global Cold War: Third World Interventions and the Making of Our Times*. Cambridge: Cambridge University Press, 2007.

Westad, Odd Arne, and Sophie Quinn-Judge, eds. *The Third Indochina War: Conflict between China, Vietnam, and Cambodia, 1972–1979*. New York: Routledge, 2006.

Westing, Arthur. *Herbicides in War: The Long-Term Ecological and Human Consequences*. Philadelphia: Taylor and Francis, 1984.

Wilcox, Fred. *Scorched Earth: Legacies of Chemical Warfare in Viet Nam*. New York: Seven Stories Press, 2011.

Williams, Raymond. *Marxism and Literature*. Oxford: Oxford University Press, 1977.

Williams, Tony. "*Missing in Action*: The Vietnam Construction of the Movie Star." *From Hanoi to Hollywood*, ed. Linda Dittmar and Gene Michaud, 129–44. New Brunswick, NJ: Rutgers University Press, 1990.

Wilson, Dean. "Colonial Viet Nam on Film: 1896 to 1926." PhD diss., City University of New York, 2007.

Wilson, Jim. *The Sons of Bardstown: Twenty-Five Years of Vietnam in an American Town*. New York: Crown, 1994.

Wilson, Richard A. *The Politics of Truth and Reconciliation in South Africa: Legitimizing the Post-apartheid State*. New York: Cambridge University Press, 2001.

Winter, Jay, and Jean-Louis Robert. *Capital Cities at War: Paris, London, Berlin, 1914–1919*. New York: Cambridge University Press, 1997.

Winter, Jay, and Emmanuel Sivan, eds. *War and Remembrance in the Twentieth Century*. New York: Cambridge University Press, 1999.

Wong, Sau-ling C. *Reading Asian American Literature*. Princeton, NJ: Princeton University Press, 1993.

World Bank. *East Asia and Pacific Economic Update*, vol. 1. Washington, DC: World Bank, 2011.

Young, Alvin L., and G. M. Reggiani. *Agent Orange and Its Associated Dioxin: Assessment of a Controversy*. New York: Elsevier, 1988.

Young, Marilyn B. "Epilogue: 'The Vietnam War in American Memory.'" *Vietnam and America: A Documented History*, ed. Marvin Gettleman, Jane Franklin, Marilyn B. Young, and H. Bruce Franklin, 515–22. New York: Grove, 1995.

———. *The Vietnam Wars, 1945–1990*. New York: Harper Perennial, 1990.

Yui, Daizaburo. "Perception Gaps between Asia and the United States of America: Lessons from 12/7 and 9/11." *Crossed Memories: Perspectives on 9/11 and American Power*, ed. Laura Hein and Daizaburo Yui, 54–79. Tokyo: Center for Pacific and American Studies, University of Tokyo, 2003.

Zaretsky, Natasha. *No Direction Home: The American Family and the Fear of National Decline, 1968–1980*. Chapel Hill: University of North Carolina Press, 2007.

Zhai, Qiang. *China and the Vietnam Wars, 1950–1975*. Chapel Hill: University of North Carolina Press, 2000.

Zhang, Xudong. *Postsocialism and Cultural Politics: China in the Last Decade of the Twentieth Century*. Durham, NC: Duke University Press, 2008.

Zierler, David. *The Invention of Ecocide: Agent Orange, Vietnam, and the Scientists Who Changed the Way We Think about the Environment*. Athens: University of Georgia Press, 2011.

Zinn, Howard. *A People's History of the United States*. New York: Harper Colophon, 1980.

———. *The Twentieth Century: A People's History*. New York: Harper and Row, 1984.

ALEXANDER BLOOM is a professor of history and American Studies at Wheaton College in Massachusetts and a former Fulbright senior lecturer in American intellectual and cultural history at the Universita di Roma Tre. He is the author of *Prodigal Sons: The New York Intellectuals and Their World* (1986) and the editor of *Long Time Gone: Sixties America Then and Now* (2001) and, with Wini Breines, of *"Takin' It to the Streets": A Sixties Reader* (third edition, 2011).

DIANE NIBLACK FOX teaches anthropology and Vietnamese Studies at the College of the Holy Cross. She lived and worked in Viet Nam in 1991–2001 and is writing a book based on narratives recounted by people there dealing with postwar birth anomalies.

H. BRUCE FRANKLIN, a former navigator and intelligence officer in the Strategic Air Command, is the John Cotton Dana Professor of English and American Studies at Rutgers University, Newark. He is the author or editor of nineteen books on American culture and history, including *Vietnam and Other American Fantasies* (2000) and *War Stars: The Superweapon in the American Imagination* (revised edition, 2008).

WALTER L. HIXSON is a Distinguished Professor of History at the University of Akron. He is the author of several books and articles on U.S. foreign policy, including *The Myth of American Diplomacy: National Identity and U.S. Foreign Policy* (2008).

HEONIK KWON is an anthropologist and professorial senior research fellow in social science at Trinity College, University of Cambridge. His recent works focus on the social history of the Vietnam War, comparative history of the Cold War, and contemporary history of the Korean War.

SCOTT LADERMAN is an associate professor of history at the University of Minnesota, Duluth. He is the author of *Tours of Vietnam: War, Travel Guides, and Memory* (Duke, 2009).

MARIAM B. LAM is an associate professor of comparative literature, media, and cultural studies and the director of Southeast Asian Studies at the University of California, Riverside. She is the founding co-editor of the *Journal of Vietnamese Studies* and is completing several projects on postcolonial Indochinese film, Southeast Asian transnational and diasporic culture, and post–Cold War cultural redevelopment.

NGO VINH LONG is a professor of Asian Studies at the University of Maine, where he has taught courses on China, Japan, South Asia, Southeast Asia, and Viet Nam since 1985. His specialties include social and economic development in Asia and U.S. relations with Asian countries.

EDWIN A. MARTINI is an associate dean in the College of Arts and Sciences and an associate professor of history at Western Michigan University. He is the author of *Invisible Enemies: The American War on Vietnam, 1975–2000* (2007) and *Agent Orange: History, Science, and the Politics of Uncertainty* (2012).

VIET THANH NGUYEN is an associate professor of English and American Studies and Ethnicity at the University of Southern California. He is the author of *Race and Resistance: Literature and Politics in Asian America* (2002). The Radcliffe Institute for Advanced Study and the American Council of Learned Societies have supported the research from which his essay is drawn, a book on the ways that the Vietnam War has been remembered by different countries.

CHRISTINA SCHWENKEL is an associate professor of anthropology at the University of California, Riverside. She is the author of *The American War in Contemporary Vietnam: Transnational Remembrance and Representation* (2009).

CHARLES WAUGH is an associate professor of English at Utah State University, where he teaches courses in fiction writing, American Studies, and contemporary Vietnamese and American literature. He is the coeditor and cotranslator (with Nguyen Lien) of *Family of Fallen Leaves: Stories of Agent Orange by Vietnamese Writers* (2010).

Page references in italics indicate illustrations. A page reference followed by t *indicates a table. As much as possible, the diacritical marks used by the authors have been retained. When terms have appeared both with and without diacritical marks, the term has been indexed without diacritics. Diacritics have been ignored in alphabetization. U.S. government entities can be found under* United States government.

Carter, Jimmy (*continued*)
  political warfare against Viet Nam by,
  260; intervention in Afghanistan by,
  52; and the *Mayagüez* incident, 74;
  presidential campaign and election of,
  75–77; on public discontent with government, 75; role in government conspiracy about POWs, 275, 286; on the
  Vietnam War, 52, 143
Casualties of War, 49
Catch-22, 49–50
Catfish Farmers of America, 194
Catfish Institute, 188, 206n62
catfish wars, 183–206; ads about Vietnamese vs. American catfish, 188,
  190–91, 203n18, 206n62; Agent
  Orange's role in, 9, 187–88, 203n17;
  antidumping petition, 185, 194–98,
  201, 204n34; catfish exports' growth,
  186, 198–99; catfish prices, 187, 195–96,
  202–3n14; catfish quality, Vietnamese
  vs. American, 183, 193–94, 201–2nn1–2,
  204n33; and classification/meaning of
  "catfish," 185, 191–92, 194–95, 199–200,
  204n35; FDA regulation of catfish, 188–
  89, 192–93, 196, 199, 204n31, 204–5n38;
  fluoroquinolones in catfish, 184; and
  free trade vs. protectionism, 9, 13, 185,
  193–95, 197–201, 204n32; labeling/mar-
  keting catfish, 189, 191–96, 199, 203n21,
  204n35, 204–5n38, 206n62; off-flavor
  of catfish, 189, 203n23; overview of,
  9, 200–201; USDA regulation of catfish, 199–200; U.S. tariffs on, 197–99;
  and U.S.–Viet Nam trade agreement,
  186–87, 192–93, 196–97, 200–201; Vietnamese catfish banned by southern
  U.S. states, 183–85; and Viet Nam's
  capitalist transformation, 185–86 (see
  also *doi moi*); Viet Nam's status as a
  non-market economy, 197–98, 205n49;
  xenophobia's role in, 185, 188, *191*, 200
Catholic opposition to Thieu, 36–37
Cato Institute, 204n32

CBS *Evening News*, 25
Cecil, Paul Frederick, 218
Centers for Disease Control, 237n17
Centre for Assistance and Development
  of Movie Talents, 164–65
CGV, 173–74
Chambers, Dennis, 60
Châu Quang Phước, 163
Cha Ye-ryeon, 175
chemicals, infatuation vs. caution with,
  215–16, 236n13
chemical warfare, 218, 220, 238–39n28,
  239n39. See also Agent Orange
Cheong Seura: *Hardship Brings Dollars*,
  171–72
Chiến thắng Tây Bắc (North West Vic-
  tory), 160
Children of Viet Nam (Da Nang), 232
China Beach, 49
China Men (Kingston), 135–36
Chinese aid to DRV, 32
Chinh Luan, 31
Christian Century, 79
Christian Science Monitor, 271
Chuyện của Pao (Pao's Story), 174–75
CIA, 37, 265
Cinema Department (Ministry of Culture
  and Information), 161
cinema development and transnational
  politics, 155–82; censorship, 161, 175,
  178; Cinema Department (Ministry of
  Culture and Information), 161; cultural
  citizenship's role in, 168; distributors,
  173–74; domestic vs. diasporic films,
  161–62; economic embargo, effects of
  lifting, 161; Fafilm, 161; film criticism's
  new directions, 158, 166–79; film festivals, 162–63, 170–71; Film Studies
  Program (University of Social Sciences
  and Humanities), 163, 180n12; Ford
  Foundation's role in, 163–65, 180n12;
  and the globalization of culture, 157;
  Hà Nội Cinémathèque archive, 165,
  180n15; history of Vietnamese cinema,

Eagleburger, Lawrence, 74
East Meets West, 233
Eastwood, Clint, 275–76
Ehrhart, W. D., 60
Elliott, David W. P., 45, 55n1
Ellsberg, Daniel, 59
Enfants de la Dioxine, Les (Dioxin's Children), 231
English Patient, The (Ondaatje), 145–46
environmentalism in Vietnamese culture, 242–58; air and water pollution, 250–51, 253, 256; bauxite-mine protest, 256; biodiversity, 251; buffalo as symbol of, 255, 258n38; vs. consumerism, 252–55; culpability for pollution, 250, 257n25; economic development's role in, 248–49; Hanoi hotel project opposed, 256; human and natural world in balance, 242–48, 253–54, 257n10; industrialization/modernization's role in, 243, 248–49, 254; overview of, 10–11; poetry, 243; proverbs and folk stories, 242–44, 246, 253, 255; remediation of dioxin-contaminated sites, 250; spiritual beliefs, 245–46, 255; tree planting/use, 247, 249; Vietnamese regulations, 250; virility-enhancing wildlife products, 11; water treatment plants, 250–52; yin and yang, 246, 251–52, 255. *See also* Agent Orange
Envoy Media Partners, 173
EPA (Environmental Protection Agency), 215–16, 221–22

Fafilm, 161
Fairbank, John K., 67
Far Eastern Economic Review, 24, 43n67, 187, 202–3n14
Farm Security and Rural Investment Act (2002), 193
Faulkner, William, 59
FDA regulation of catfish, 188–89, 192–93, 196, 199, 204n31, 204–5n38
Federation of American Scientists, 219–20

Feldman, Robert, 233
Ferraris, Carl J., Jr., 192
FFRD (Fund for Reconciliation and Development), 230–31
Film History (Bordwell), 164
Film Studies Program (University of Social Sciences and Humanities), 163, 180n12
First World War, national experience of, 91
FitzGerald, Frances, 28
Five Forbids policy, 32
Fog of War, The (E. Morris), 154n47
Food, Conservation, and Energy Act (2008), 199
Ford, Gerald, 36–38, 58, 70–74, 260
Ford Foundation, 163–65, 180n12, 222–23
Forever the Moment (Lim Soon-rye), 170
forgetting, nation's creation via, 12–14
Forgotten, The, 281
Forster, E. M.: *A Passage to India*, 146
Fox, Diane Niblack, 9–10, 13. *See also* Agent Orange
Franco-Vietnamese Friendship Association, 231
Franklin, H. Bruce, 11–12. *See also* POW/MIAs
Frater, Patrick, 174
free trade vs. protectionism, 9, 13, 185, 193–95, 197–201, 204n32
French colonialism, 85–86
French Resistance, 93
Freud, Sigmund, 239n39
Friel, John, 200
friendship forests, 104
Friendship Village, 228, 233
From Hollywood to Hanoi (Thi Thanh Nga), 161
Fulbright, J. William, 67
Full Metal Jacket, 49
Fulvi, Giovanna, 176
Fund for Reconciliation and Development (FFRD), 230–31

107; state memorial vs. private ritual practice, 110, *111*; symbolic interaction with the Other at, 105; tombstones in, 109, 129n11

Hong Anh, 175

Ho Ngoc Nhuan, 23–24

Hope, Bob, 269–70

Hubbard, Carroll, 73

Hue (Thua Thien Province), 30

Huffington Post, 288

Hussein, Saddam, 53, 280

Hutchinson, Tim, 189, 191, 194–95, 204n31, 204n35, 204–5n38

Huyền thoại bất tử (*The Legend Is Alive*; Lưu Hùynh), 178

Hùynh, Lưu: *Áo luạ Hà Đong*, 162, 166; *Huyền thoại bất tử* (*The Legend Is Alive*), 178; *Passage of Life*, 162

Hydro-Mill Corporation, 269

IFRC (International Federation of Red Cross and Red Crescent Societies), 229, 233

IM Pictures, 175

India–Pakistan partition, 181n19

L'Indochine (Wargnier), 161, 182n40

Institute of Cinematographic Art and Conservation, 161

International Agency for Research on Cancer, 216

International Association of Democratic Lawyers, 226

International Dioxin Conference (International Symposium on Halogenated Persistent Organic Pollutants), 214

International Federation of Red Cross and Red Crescent Societies (IFRC), 229, 233

International Monetary Fund, 53, 142, 198

International People's Tribunal of Conscience in Support of the Vietnamese Victims of Agent Orange, 226

International Symposium on Haloge-nated Persistent Organic Pollutants (International Dioxin Conference), 214

International Trade Commission (ITC), 195, 201

In the Name of America, 264

Into a Black Sun (Takeshi Kaiko), 138–41

Iran-Contra scandal, 52

Iraq, 52–53, 132, 151, 239n39

Iraq war (2003–2011), 11

Isaacson, Walter: "The Last Battle of Vietnam," 223

ITC (International Trade Commission), 195, 201

Jackson, Michael: *The Politics of Storytelling*, 234–35

James, David, 163

Jameson, Frederic, 157

Jamieson, Neil: *Understanding Vietnam*, 245–46, 251

Japanese surrender (1945), 86

Jayne, William, 65

Jeong, Ji-yeong: *White Badge*, 169–70

Jeonju International Film Festival (2008), 170

Jo An, 175

"John McCain: The Manchurian Candidate" (Sampley), 287

Johnson, Lyndon B., 44–45, 60, 66, 219–20, 263

Joint General Staff (RVN), 33

Journal of Vietnamese Studies, 3

Junior Chambers of Commerce, 270

Kaiko, Takeshi: *Into a Black Sun*, 138–41

Kaledin, Eugenia, 86

Kant, Immanuel, 141

Karnow, Stanley, 50, 120, 131n31

Keach, Stacy, 281

Keen, Suzanne, 152nn5–6, 154n47

Keitel, Harvey, 162

Kennedy, Edward, 26–27

Kennedy, John F., 218–19

Kennedy, Robert, 263

live POWs, 276–77; photos of alleged POWs, 282–83, 294nn72–73; as a political weapon, 287–88; postage stamps for, 269; and prisoners tortured by U.S./Saigon forces, 264–65, 289–90n6; rescue movies, 48–49, 277–81; rescue novels and comic books, 281; Senate Select Committee on, 283–85, 287, 295n78; United We Stand program for, 266–67, 270, 290–91n18; and U.S. corporate interests, 285–86; U.S. reconstruction aid tied to return of, 273; Vietnamese cooperation on the issue, 285, 289; Vietnamese MIAs, locating remains of, 113–15; Viet Nam's return of POWs, 47–48, 272–73; "You are not forgotten" motto, 260. *See also under* Nixon, Richard M.

P.O.W.: The Escape, 281

Preston, Andrew, 44

PRG (Provisional Revolutionary Government): counterattacks against ARVN, 36–37; destruction of, 5; establishment of, 17; on a government of national concord, 31–32; highlands provinces attacked by (1975), 38; Paris Accords signed by, 16–17; U.S. policy on, 18

Prisoner of War Day, 269

Program to Improve the Life of Anticommunist Refugees, 29

protectionism. *See* free trade vs. protectionism

Provisional Revolutionary Government. *See* PRG

PSDF (Popular Self-Defense Forces), 20–21, 40n10

Quang Nam Da Nang Fund, 231

Quang Nam Province, 29

Quang Nam Red Cross, 232

Quảng Trị citadel battle (1972), 118, 130n24

Quang Tri Province, 29, 118–19

Quiet American, The (Mankiewicz), 160

"Rabbit in the Moon" (Dinh), 254–55

race and cosmopolitanism, 135–38, 153n18

racism, Eurocentric, 145–46

Rambo, Terry, 244–45, 248–49

Rambo films, 48–49, 279–81

Ranch Hand Study (U.S. Air Force), 237n17

Rand Corporation, 219

Raye, Martha, 270

Reagan, Ronald: Central American right-wing regimes promoted by, 52; and Eastwood, 275–76; economic/political warfare against Viet Nam by, 260; intervention in Afghanistan by, 52; on *Rambo,* 280; role in POW rescue attempts, 275–77; Vietnam Veterans Memorial opposed by, 50–51; on the Vietnam War, 48; VIVA supported by, 269–70

reconciliation in memoryscapes, 103–31; ambivalence about, 127–28; via commemoration, 104, 126–29; via comment books and memorial dedications, 124, 126, 131n38; community of trauma, emergence of, 121; DMZ's role in, 7–8, 117–19, 130nn20–21, 130nn27–28; via forgetfulness, 115, 127–28, 131n48; global capitalism's effects on postwar remembrance, 128; and graves as homes for the dead, 113; Khe Sanh/Ta Con base, 7–8, 12, 105, 117, 120–24, 122, 130n29, 131nn31–33 (*see also* Highway 9–Khe Sanh Victory Museum); via locating/reburying remains of MIAs, 113–15, 130n17; meaning of memoryscapes, 103; meaning of reconciliation, 128; overview of, 7–8, 103–5, 127; remembrance/benefits to RVN war dead and their families, 128–29; via ritual offerings, 126; via the spirit world, 104–5, 111–13, 114–15, 126; and topographies of memory, 7–8, 103, 118, 127; via truth commissions, 131n48. *See also* Ho Chi Minh City Martyrs' Cemetery

Agent Orange/Dioxin (VAVA), 225–26, 230, 232

Vietnam Association of Seafood Exporters and Producers (VASEP), 196

Vietnam: A Television History, 50

Việt Nam: At the Crossroads (Do), 161

Việt Nam Cinema Association, 159, 161

Vietnam Courier, 20

Vietnamese-American War, 2. *See also* Vietnam War

Vietnamese International Film Festival (ViFF), 163

Vietnamese Ministry of Culture, Sports, and Tourism, 170

Vietnamese society, postwar, 16–43; economic blockade's effects on, 34–36; hunger/starvation in the central provinces, 29–30, 34–35; Laos invasion, opposition to, 22–24; and the National Council of National Reconciliation and Concord, 17–19; overview of, 5; Paris Accords' effects on, 16–17, 24–26, 32; political organizations dissolved, 38–39; and rice storage, 35; Thieu's repression of, 5, 21, 24–28, 34–36; unemployment's effects on, 35; workers' demonstrations and hunger strikes, 35. *See also* refugees

Việt Nam Film Studios, 160

Vietnamization program, 20–22, 40nn9–10

Vietnam Journal, 281

Việt Nam on the Road to Victory, 160

Vietnam Report, 18–19

Vietnam Resource Center, 41n20

Vietnam syndrome, 58–83; and American arrogance and cultural ignorance, 67, 79; American cynicism and pessimism after the war, 69–70, 74, 77, 80; and American recovery from the war, 68; Americans' struggle with meaning of the war's end, 60, 77–78; analysts and media on the defeat,

65–66; George H. W. Bush on, 53; and Carter's presidential campaign and election of, 75–77; the country as broken, sense of, 65; and criticism of the war, 66–67; definition of, 59; and forgetting, 68; homecoming for veterans, 60–65; Korean War vs. Vietnam War, 62–63, 81n16; and the *Mayagüez* incident, 72–74; national impact of the war, 77–79; overview of, 6, 58–59, 80; parades lacking for veterans, 63; Reagan's attempt to bury, 48; Second World War vs. Vietnam War, 60–63; Senate committee hearings on the war, 67; U.S. foreign policy, and the American image, 71–72; and visibility of the war, 78–79

Vietnam Veterans Against the War, 288–89

Vietnam Veterans Memorial ("the Wall"; Washington Mall), 50–51, 61

Vietnam War: ceasefire proposed in, 21–22; chemicals used in (*see* Agent Orange); Cold War context of (*see* Cold War in Vietnamese communities); first-response aid to Vietnamese after, 227; heartland policy during, 37–38; Hollywood films about, 47–50, 147, 155 (*see also* cinema development and transnational politics); Korean soldiers in, 169; vs. Korean War, 62–63, 81n16; Laos invasion, 22–24; legacies of, 4–5 (*see also* Agent Orange); mop-up operations during, 21, 33; names for, 1–2, 85; narrations about, 3–5; nation-state analysis of, 3; post-1975 period, studies of, 4–5; president's war-making abilities during, 74; vs. Second World War, 60–63; South Korean soldiers' brutality during, 138; as a transnational war, 2; U.S. bombing during, 145; U.S. intervention in, 22–24, 52; U.S. withdrawal demanded,